EASY PIANO

Snowfall

ISBN 0-634-06217-4

7777 W. Bluemound Rd. P.O. Box 13819 Milwaukee, WI 53213

Visit Hal Leonard Online at
www.halleonard.com

BABY, IT'S COLD OUTSIDE

from the Motion Picture NEPTUNE'S DAUGHTER

By FRANK LOESSER

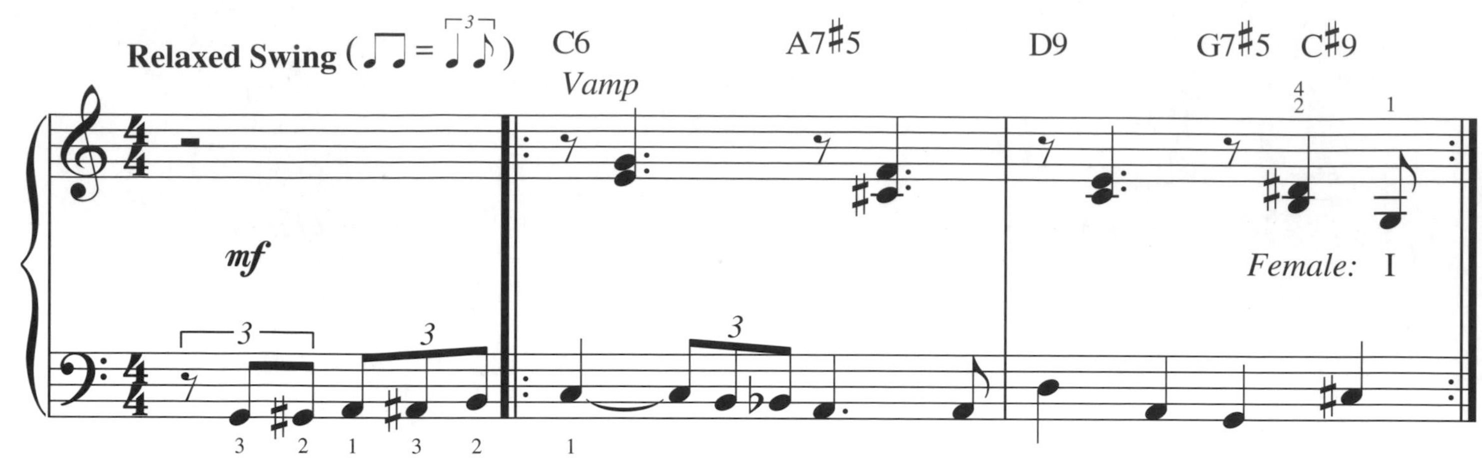

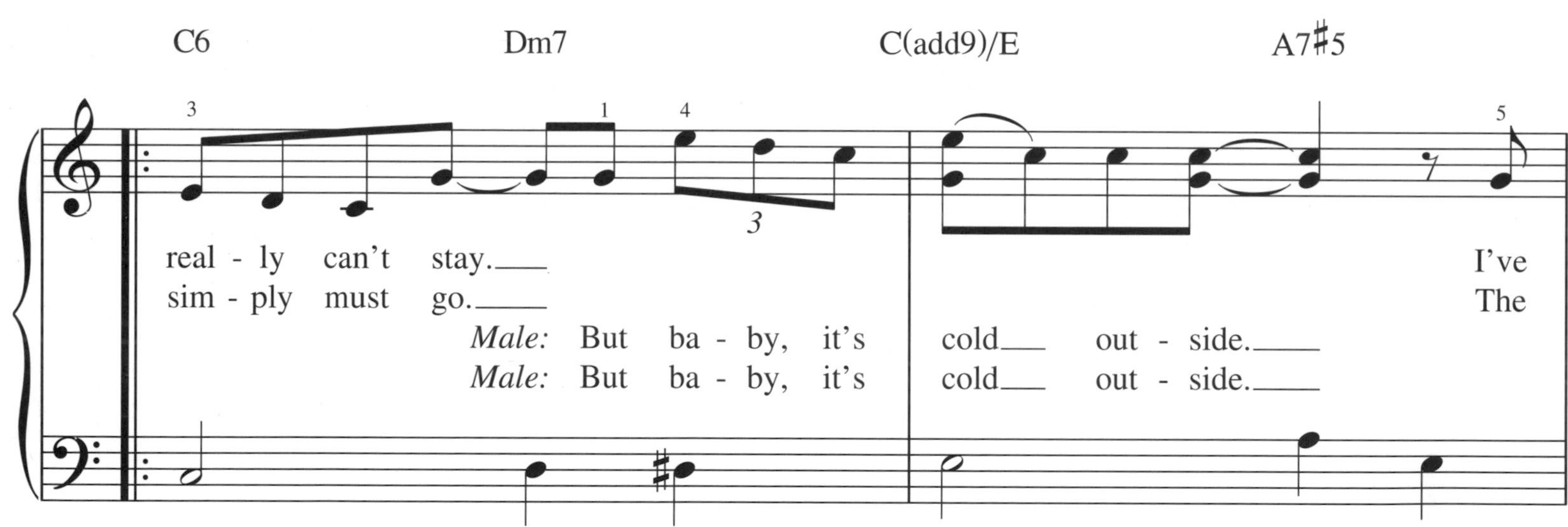

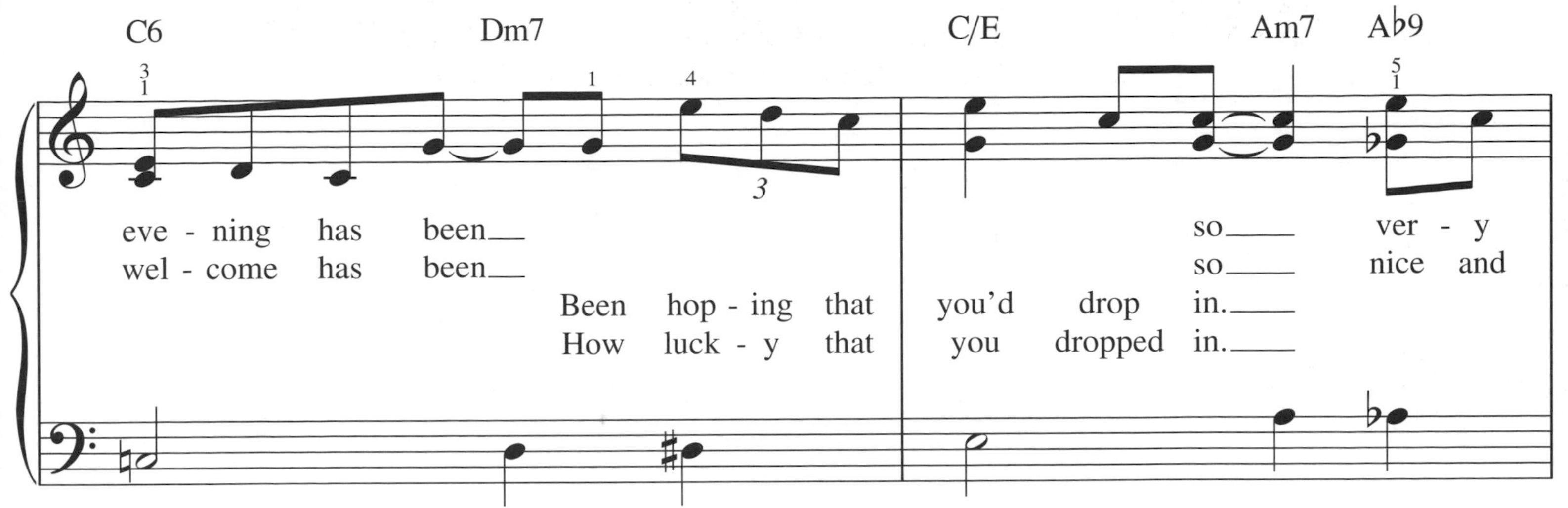
C6 Dm7 C/E Am7 A♭9
eve - ning has been so very - y
wel - come has been so nice and
Been hop - ing that you'd drop in.
How luck - y that you dropped in.

Gm9 C9♯11 Gm9 C13 F♯9
nice. My
warm. My
I'll hold your hands. They're just like ice.
Look out the win - dow at the storm.

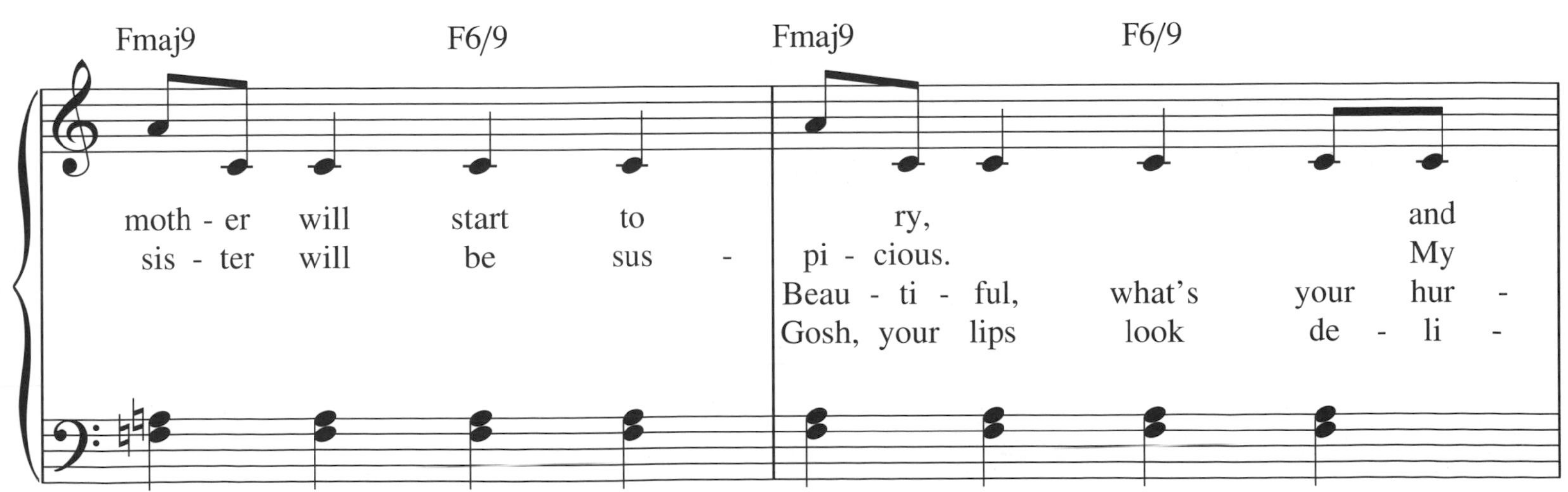
Fmaj9 F6/9 Fmaj9 F6/9
moth - er will start to ry, and
sis - ter will be sus - pi - cious. My
Beau - ti - ful, what's your hur -
Gosh, your lips look de - li -

Fm7/B♭ B♭9 Fm7/B♭ B♭7
Fa - ther will be pac - ing the floor. So
broth - er will be there at the door. My
ry? Lis - ten to the fi - re - place roar.
cious. Like waves up - on a trop - i - cal shore.
C9♯11 B♭13♯11 A7♯9 E♭9♯11
real - ly, ha! I'd bet - ter scur - ry! Well,
maid - en aunt's mind is vi - cious. Well,
Beau - ti - ful, please don't hur -
Gosh, your lips are de -
D13 D7♭13 Dm7/G G7
may - be just a half a drink more. My
may - be just a cig - a - rette more. I've
ry. Put some rec - ords on while I pour.
li - cious. Nev - er such a bliz - zard be - fore.
C6 Dm7 C(add9)/E A7♯9
neigh - bors might think. Say!
got to get home. (Spoken:) Say, darling,
Ba - by, it's bad out there!
Ba - by, you'd freeze out there.

Dm7 G9 Dm7 G7♯9
— What's in this drink? I
can you lend me your comb? You've
No cabs to be had out there.
It's up to your knees out there.
C6 Dm7 C(add9)/E Am7 A♭9
wish I knew how to break the
real - ly been grand, but don't you
Your eyes arc like star - light now
I thrill when you touch my hand.
Gm9 C9♯11 Gm9 C13 F♯9
spell. I
see. There's
I'll take your hat. Your hair looks swell.
How can you do this thing to me?
Fmaj9 E♭13
ought to say, "No, no, no, sir!" At
bound to be talk to - mor - row. At
Mind if I move in
Think of my life - long

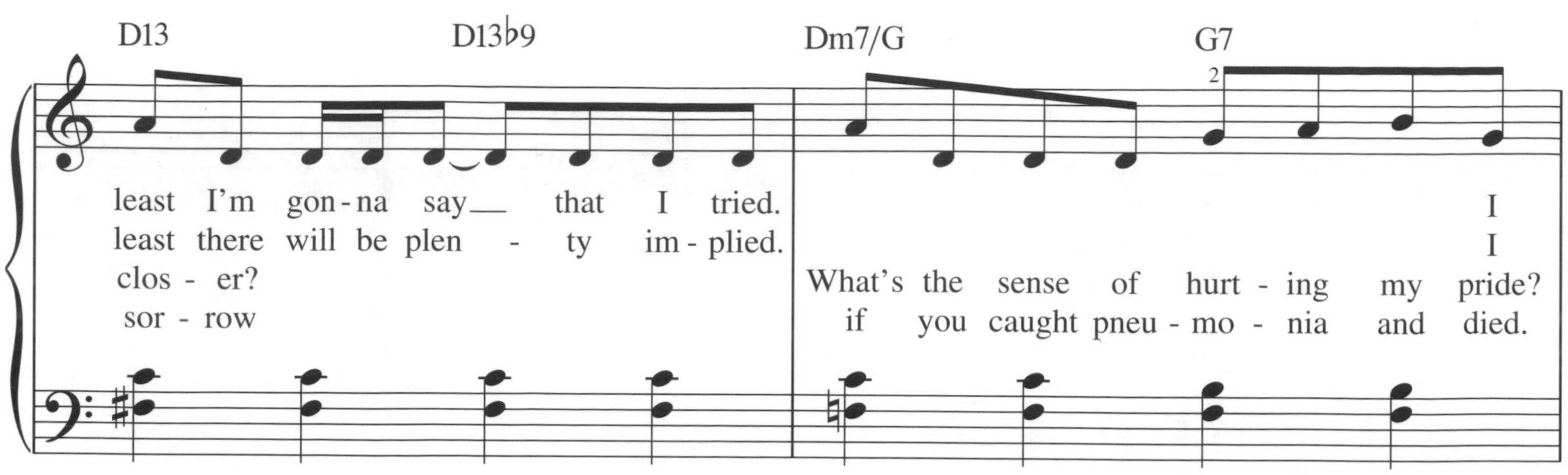
D13
D13♭9
Dm7/G
G7
least I'm gon-na say__ that I tried.
least there will be plen - ty im-plied.
clos - er?
sor - row
I
I
What's the sense of hurt - ing my pride?
if you caught pneu - mo - nia and died.

C6
B♭13♯11
A7
real - ly can't stay.
real - ly can't stay.
Oh ba - by, don't hold out.
Get o - ver that old doubt.
Both: Ah, but it's

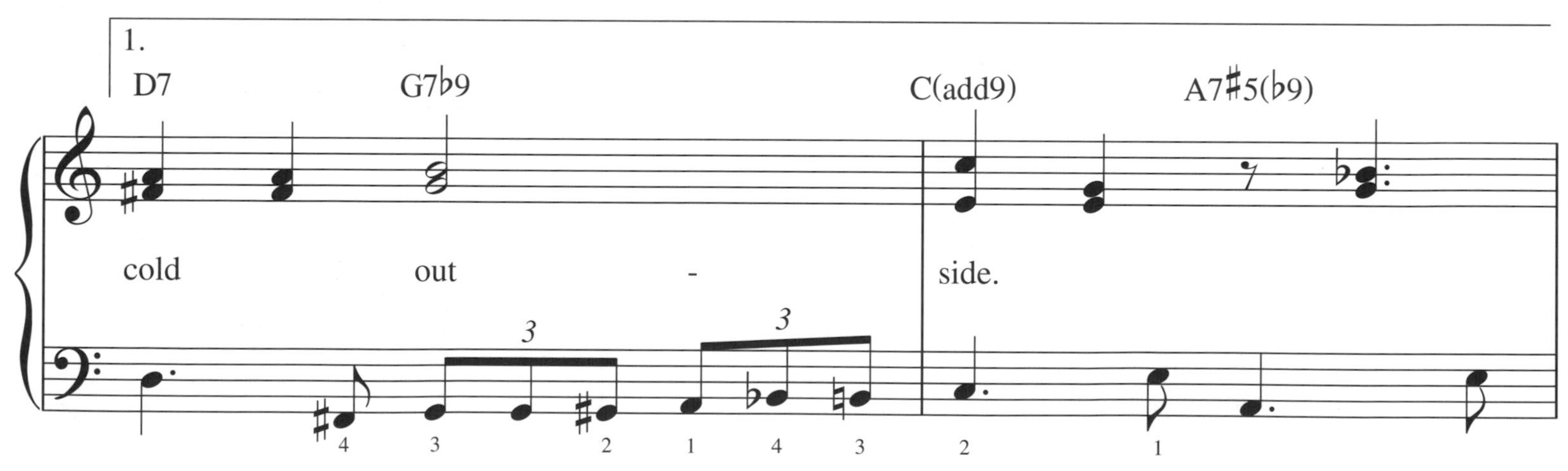
1.
D7
G7♭9
C(add9)
A7♯5(♭9)
cold out - side.

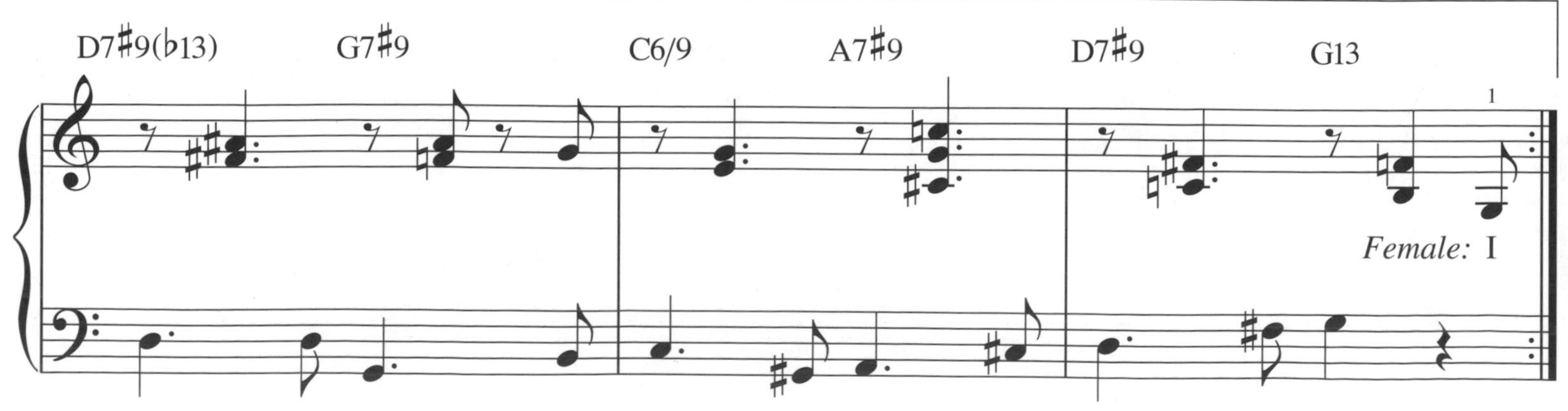
D7♯9(♭13)
G7♯9
C6/9
A7♯9
D7♯9
G13
Female: I

2.
D7
cold
Fm7
out
C9
E7♯9
Fmaj9
F♯7♯5(♭9)
side.
Dm7/G
G7
C13♯11

CHANUKAH

Words by SHELDON SECUNDA
Music by SHOLOM SECUNDA
Moderately
Dm A7 D7 G A7/E
mf
Ddim7 A7 Dm A7 D7
When the win - ter winds start blow - ing,
I re - call when I was young - er,
G A7/E D7 Gm Dm Gm
it's just na - ture's way of show - ing Cha - nu - kah will
how I used to yearn and hun - ger for this spe - cial
Dm B♭7 A A7
soon be here.
time of year,

Dm
Bb7
G#dim7
A7
and it's still so ver - y dear.

N.C.
Dm
A7b9
Cha - nu - kah,
Cha - nu - kah,
Cha - nu - kah,

Dm
A7b9
Dm
Cha - nu - kah, a hol - i -
Cha - nu - kah, a time for
Cha - nu - kah, each home is

Gm
Dm
Bb7
A
A7b5
D7
day that drives a - way all care.
giv - ing gifts to those we love.
filled with laugh - ter, song and cheer.

Gm
D7
Gm6
A7
Dm
To Coda
Cha - nu - kah,
Cha - nu - kah,
Fall - ing snow,
Cha - nu - kah,
Cha - nu - kah,
can - dles glow
Am
Bm7♭5
Dm
1. Gm
the sea - son
a time for
love by peo - ple
Dm/A
A7
Dm
A7
2. B♭dim7
ev - 'ry - where.
giv - ing thanks to
Dm/A
A7
Dm
God a - bove.
With pride re -

D
D7
Gm
call - ing might - y Ju - dah Mac - ca - bee
C
C7
and how he brave - ly fought to set his
F
B♭
peo - ple free. Men - or - ah can - dles burn -
E7
A
- ing through the nights. the beau - ty

Dm
C♯dim7
Gm6
A7
of the Feast of Lights.
N.C.
D.S. al Coda
CODA
Gm/D
Dm
proclaim that Cha -
nu - kah is
A7
Dm
here.
D6

CHRISTMAS BACK HOME

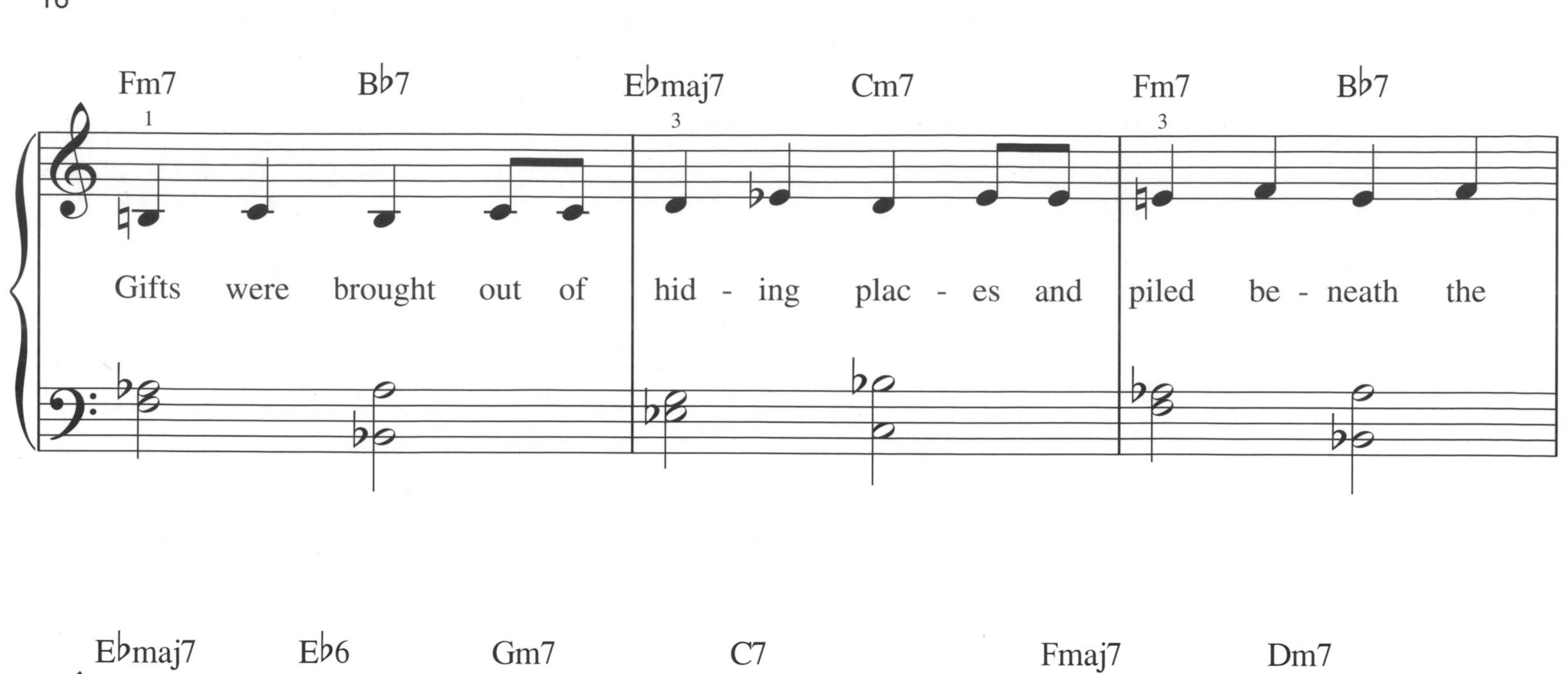
Fm7
Bb7
Ebmaj7
Cm7
Fm7
Bb7
Gifts were brought out of hid - ing plac - es and piled be - neath the

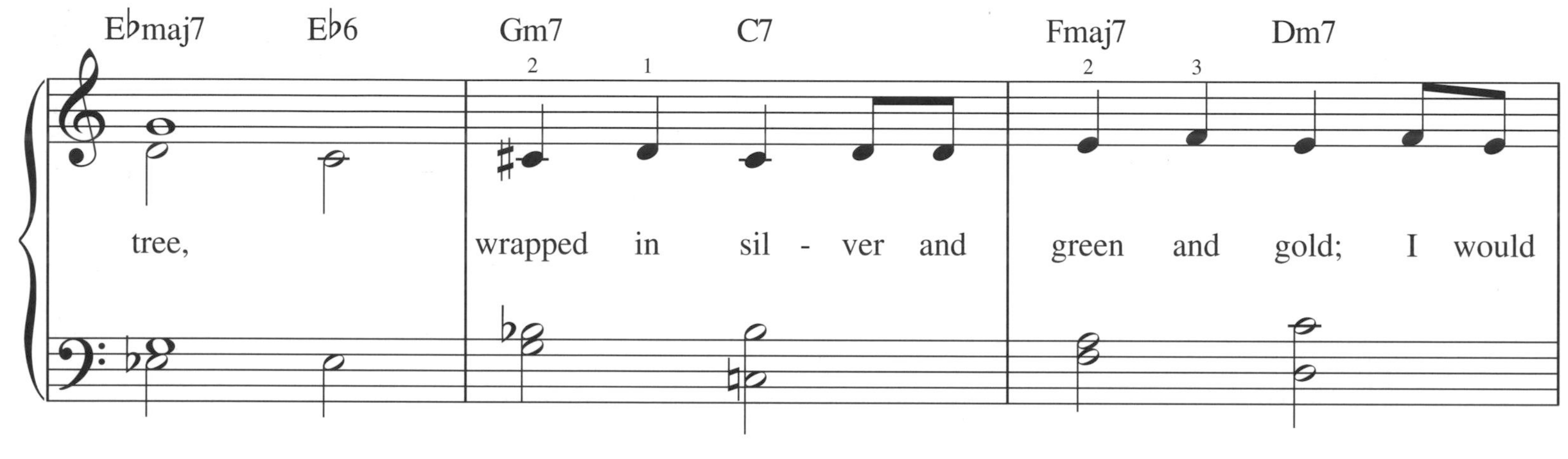
Ebmaj7
Eb6
Gm7
C7
Fmaj7
Dm7
tree, wrapped in sil - ver and green and gold; I would

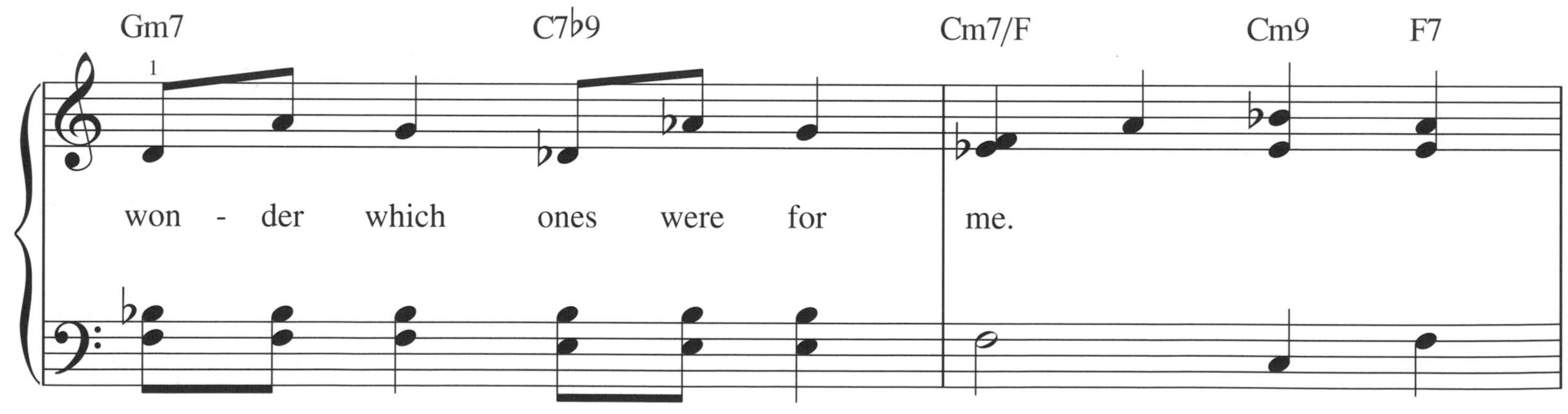
Gm7
C7b9
Cm7/F
Cm9
F7
won - der which ones were for me.

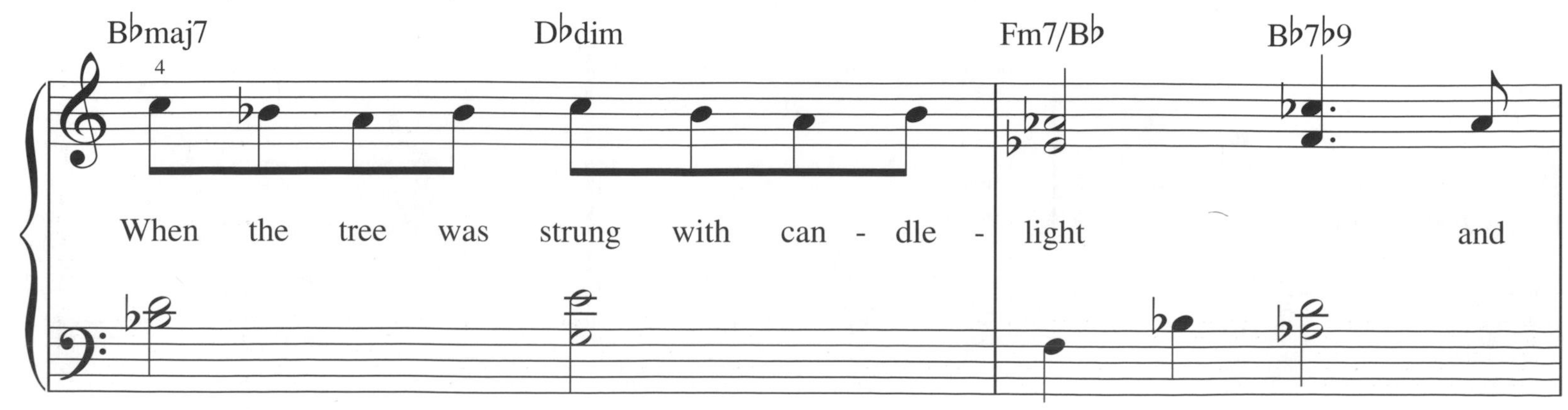
Bbmaj7
Dbdim
Fm7/Bb
Bb7b9
When the tree was strung with can - dle - light and

E♭m7
Cdim
D♭m7
G♭7
lov - ing smiles would make our fac - es bright, then
Fmaj7
Fdim
Em7
Am7
N.C.
we would sing a cho - rus of "Si - lent Night," when it was
D9
G9
Em7
Am7
Christ - mas back home, when it was
D7
G7♯5(♭9)
Cmaj9
Fmaj7
C
Christ - mas back home.

CHRISTMAS CHILD

Words and Music by
LOONIS McGLOHON

Dm7♭5
G7
1.,3.
Em7
F6
G7
2.,4.
C
bring us peace on earth.
show us where You are.
B♭/C
C13
F
Em
Christ - mas Child,
Christ - mas Child,
Gm7/D
B♭/C
C9
Fmaj7
F6
C/D
on this ho - ly night
all the world
G
Dm7
G7sus
G7
quiet - ly kneels in Your ra - diant light.

C(add2)
F(add2)
B♭(add2)
Christ - mas Child
sleep in peace.
An - gels watch a -

E♭(add2)
A♭
D♭(add2)
bove
till You wake and
touch our lives with

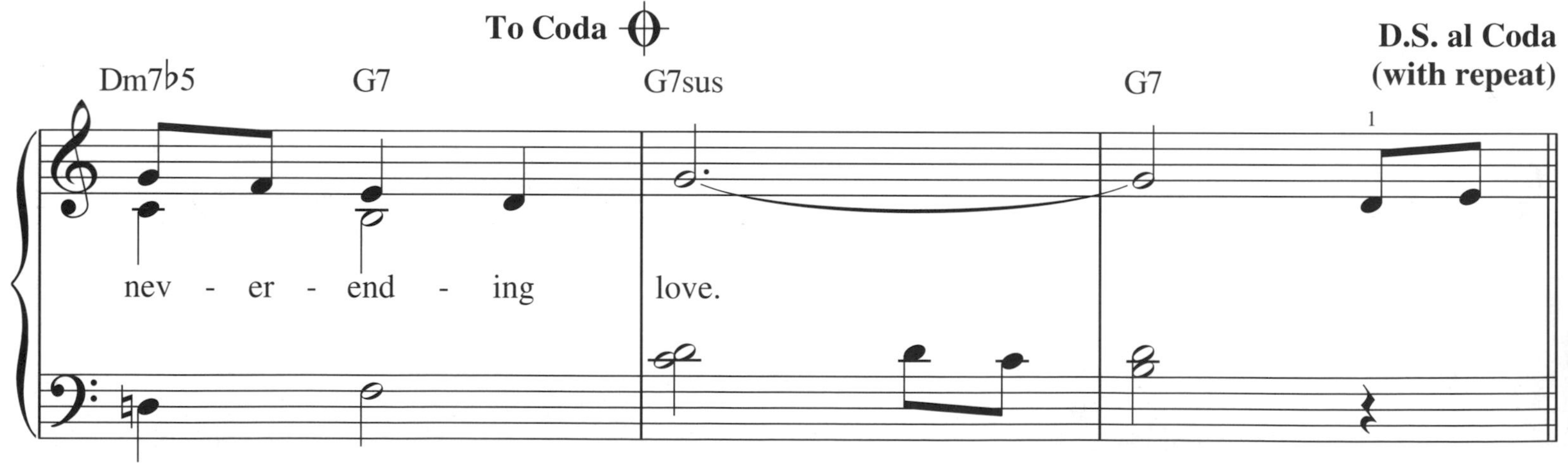
To Coda
D.S. al Coda (with repeat)
Dm7♭5
G7
G7sus
G7
nev - er - end - ing
love.

CODA
C/G
A♭(add2)
love.
Till You wake and

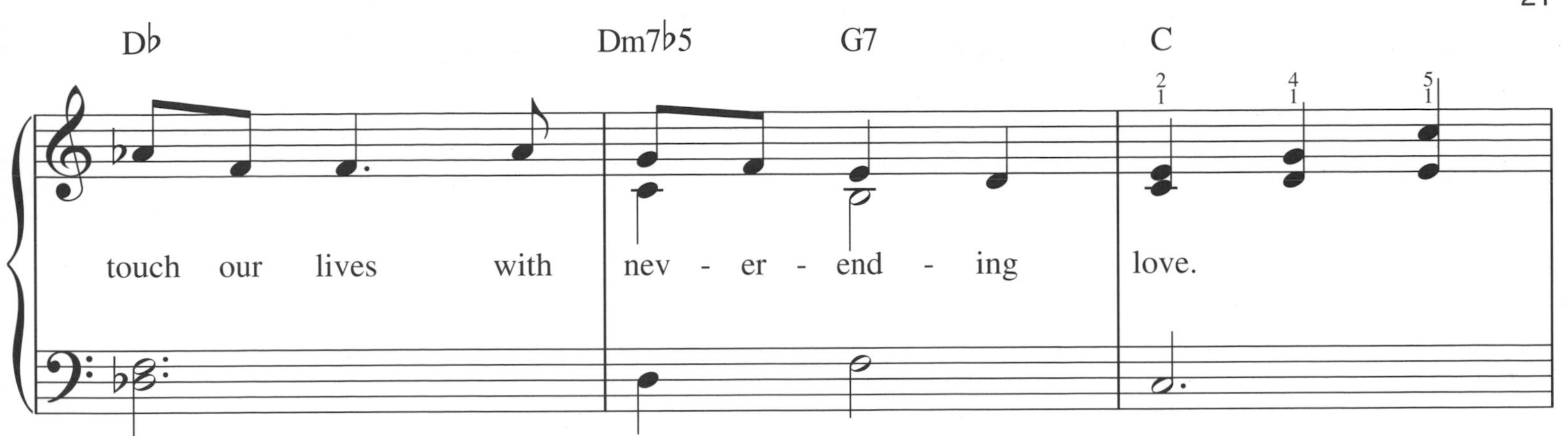
D♭
Dm7♭5
G7
C
touch our lives with nev - er - end - ing love.

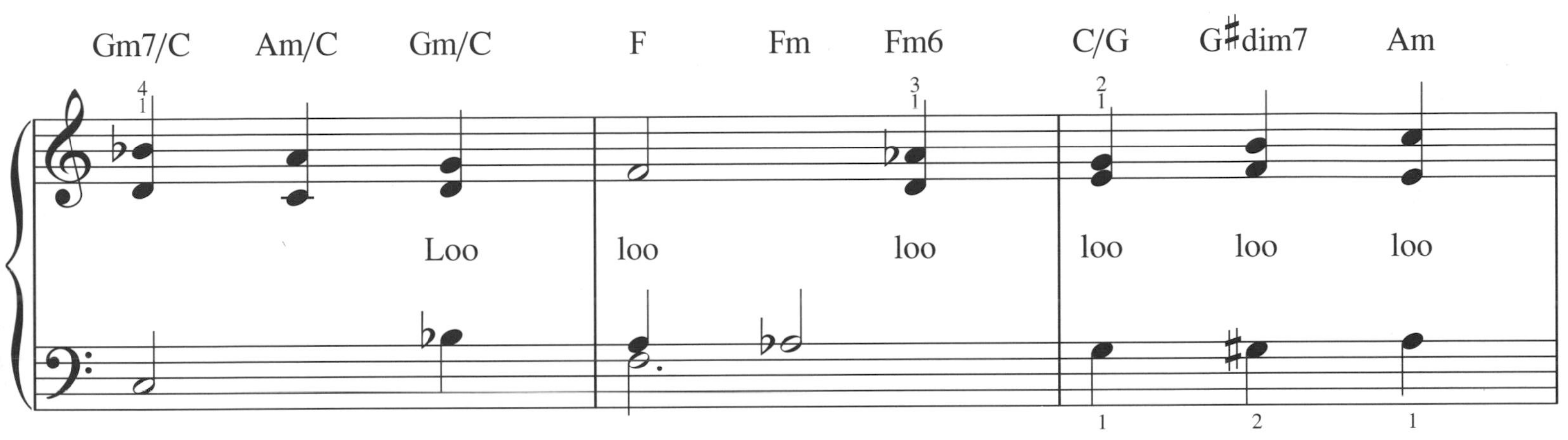
Gm7/C
Am/C
Gm/C
F
Fm
Fm6
C/G
G♯dim7
Am
Loo loo loo loo loo loo

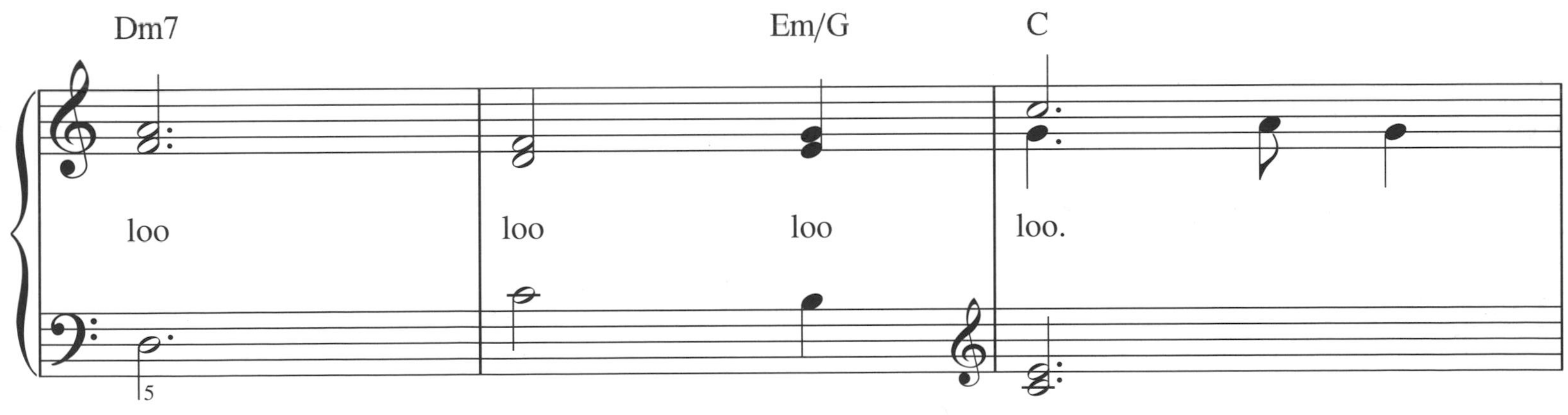
Dm7
Em/G
C
loo loo loo loo.

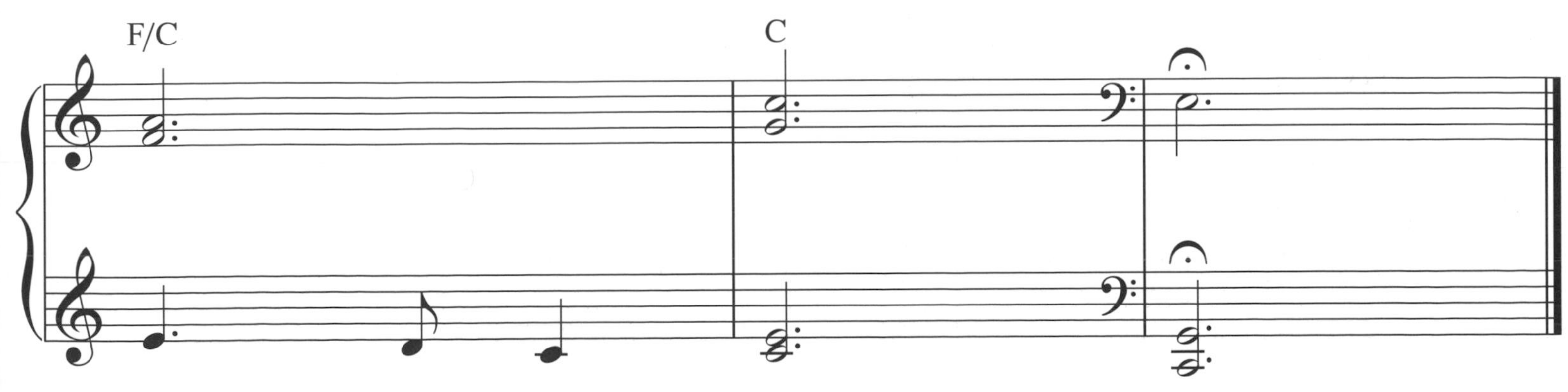
F/C
C

THE CHRISTMAS SHOES

Words and Music by LEONARD AHLSTROM
and EDDIE CARSWELL

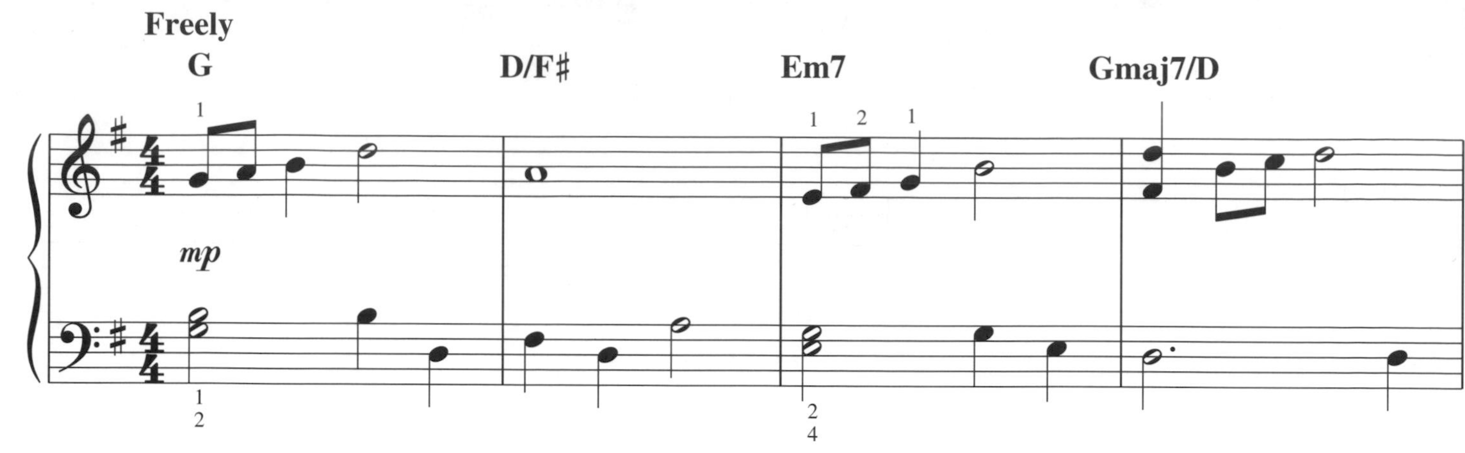

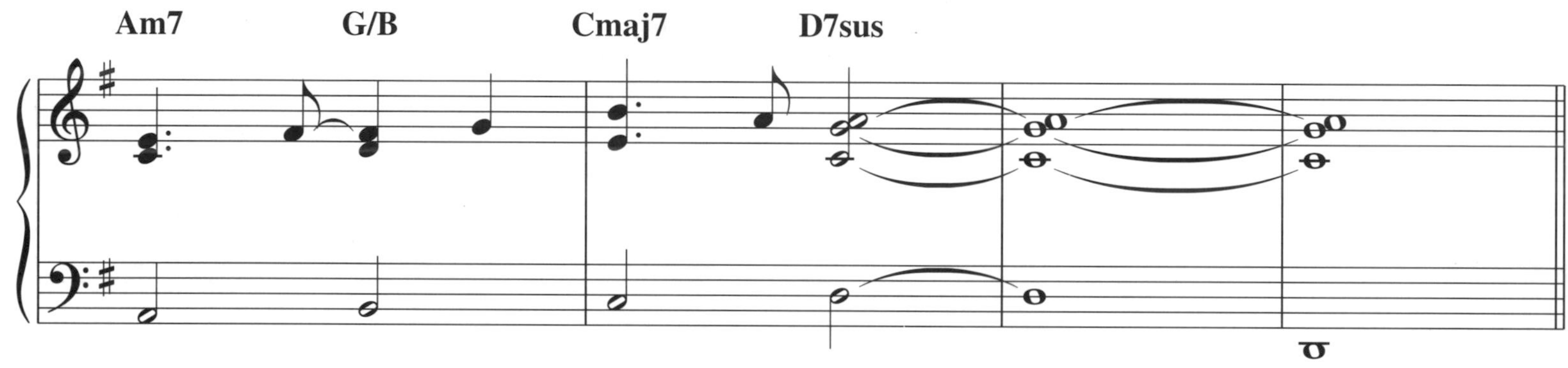

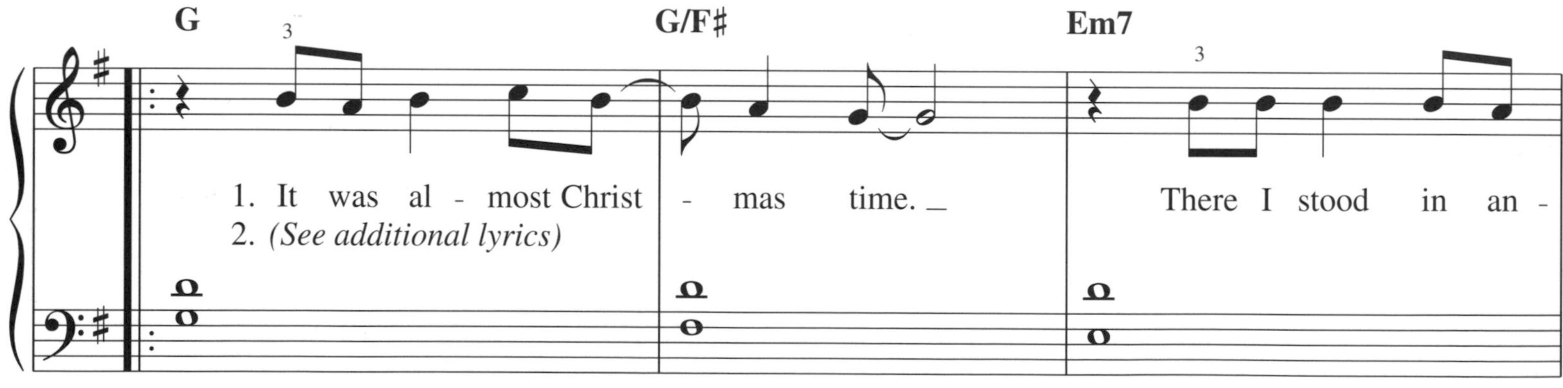

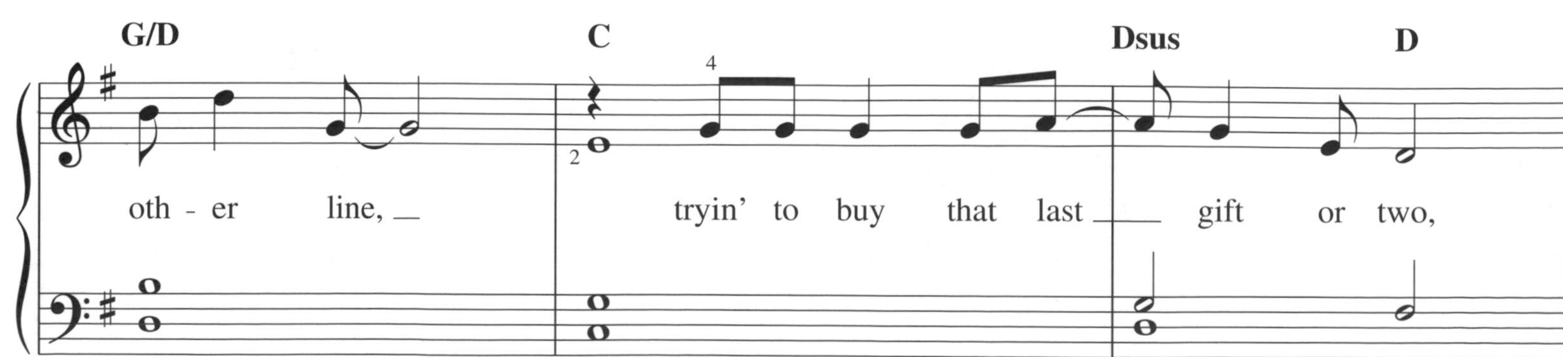

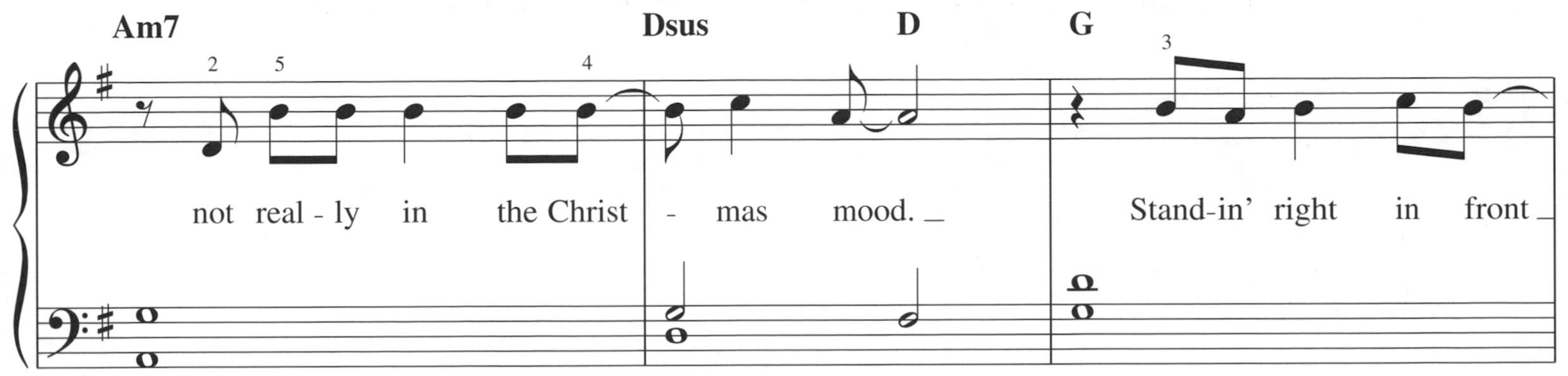
Am7
Dsus
D
G
not real - ly in the Christ - mas mood.
Stand-in' right in front

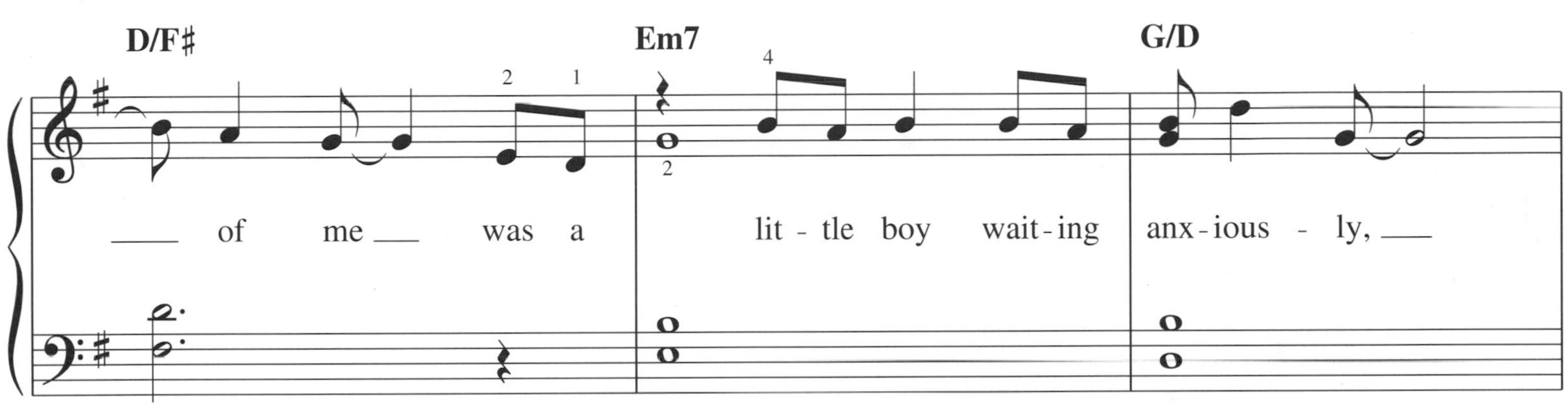
D/F♯
Em7
G/D
of me was a lit - tle boy wait-ing anx-ious - ly,

C
Dsus
D
Am7
pac - in' 'round like lit - tle boys do,
and in his hands he

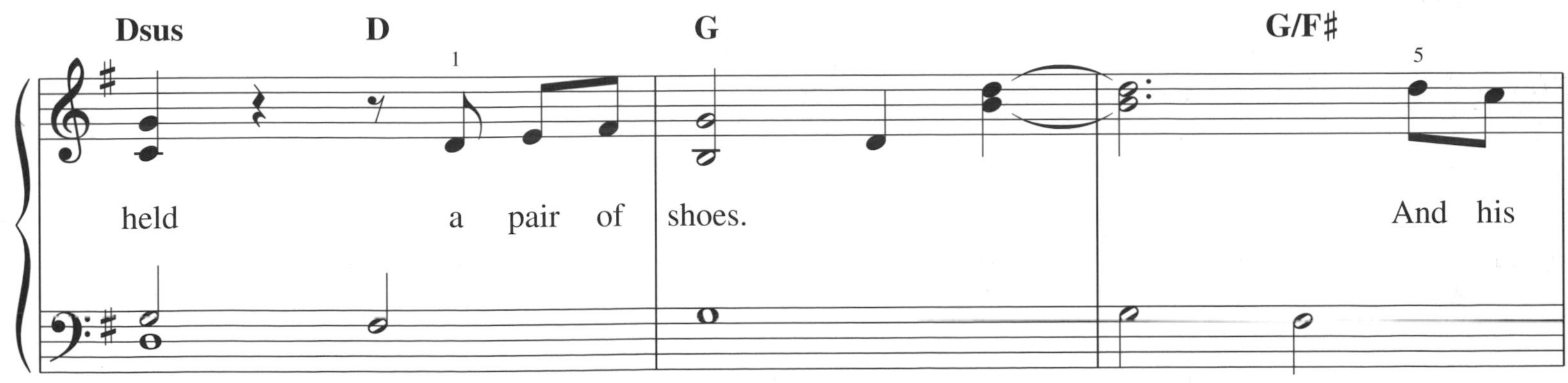
Dsus
D
G
G/F♯
held a pair of shoes.
And his

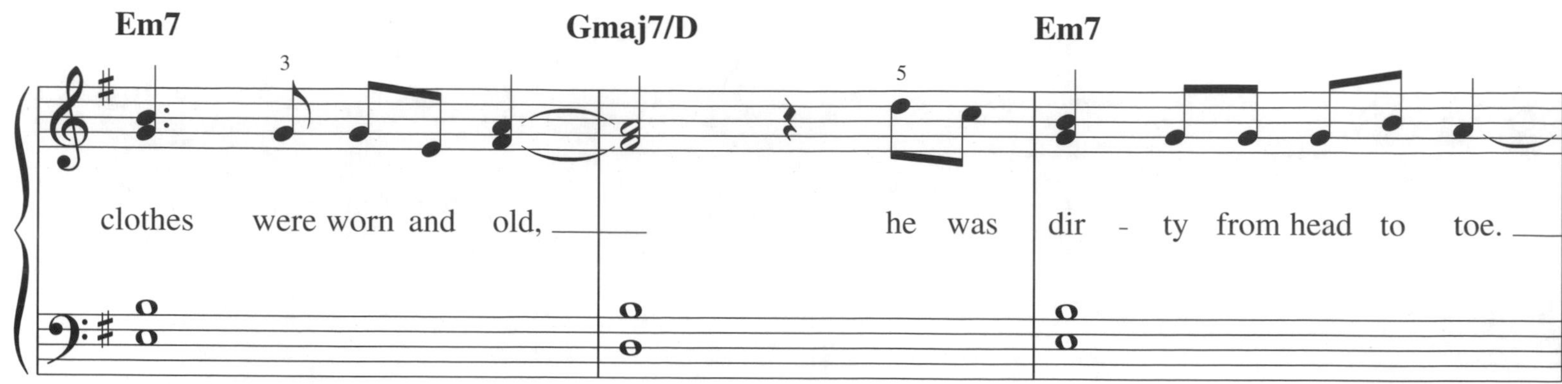
Em7
Gmaj7/D
Em7
clothes were worn and old, he was dir - ty from head to toe.

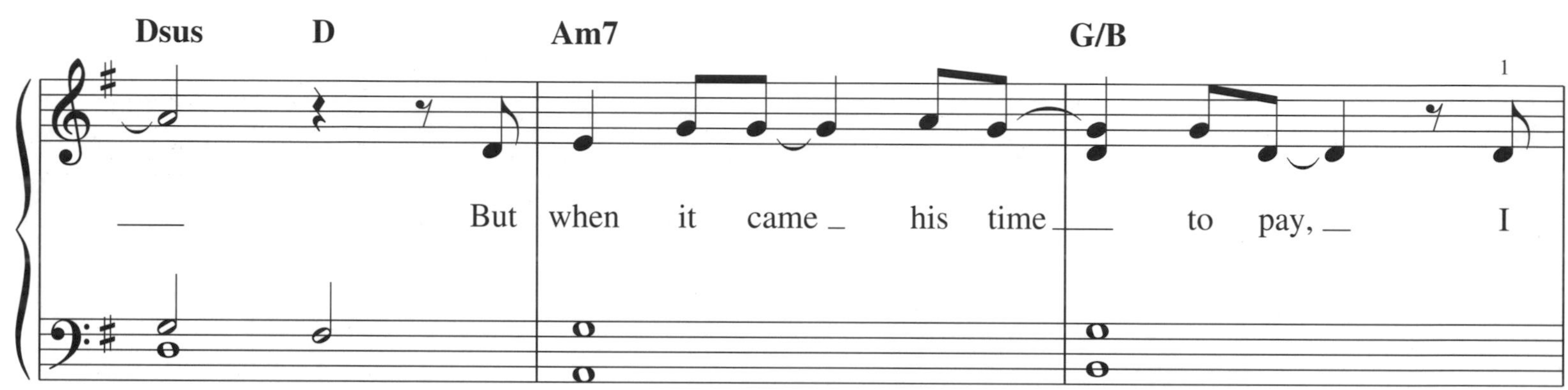
Dsus
D
Am7
G/B
But when it came his time to pay, I

G/C
Dsus
D
Chorus
could-n't be - lieve what I heard him say, "Sir, I wan - na

A
E
F♯m
E
buy these shoes for my ma - ma, please. It's

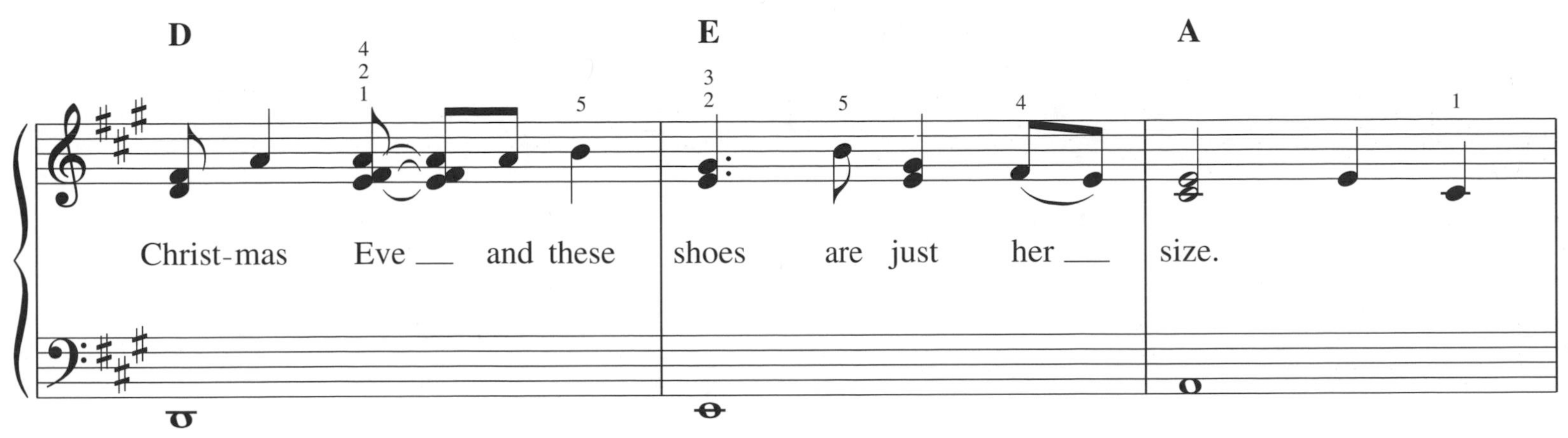
D
E
A
Christ-mas Eve and these shoes are just her size.

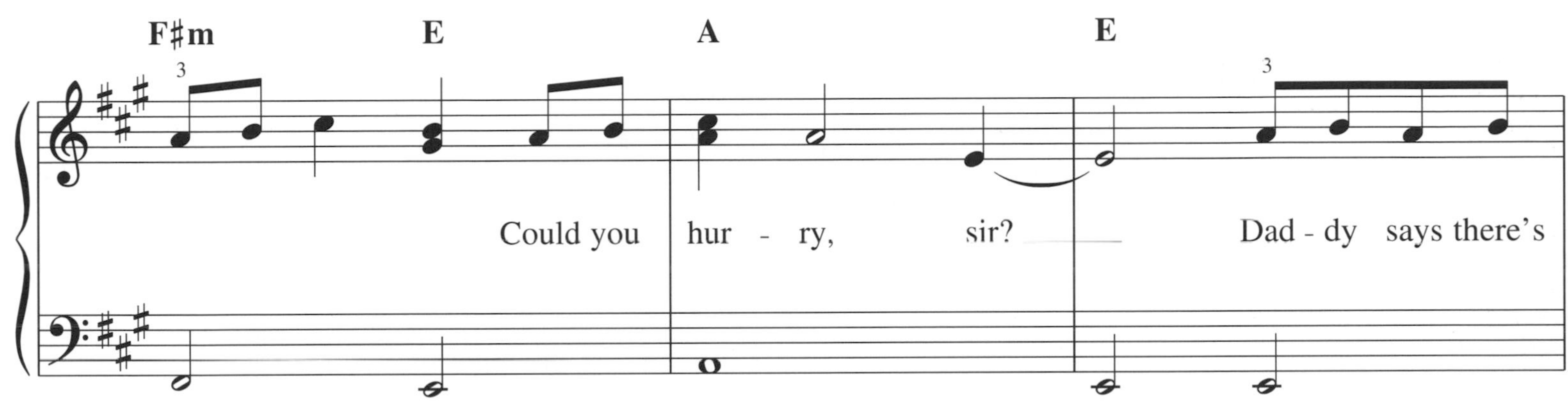
F♯m
E
A
E
Could you hur - ry, sir? Dad - dy says there's

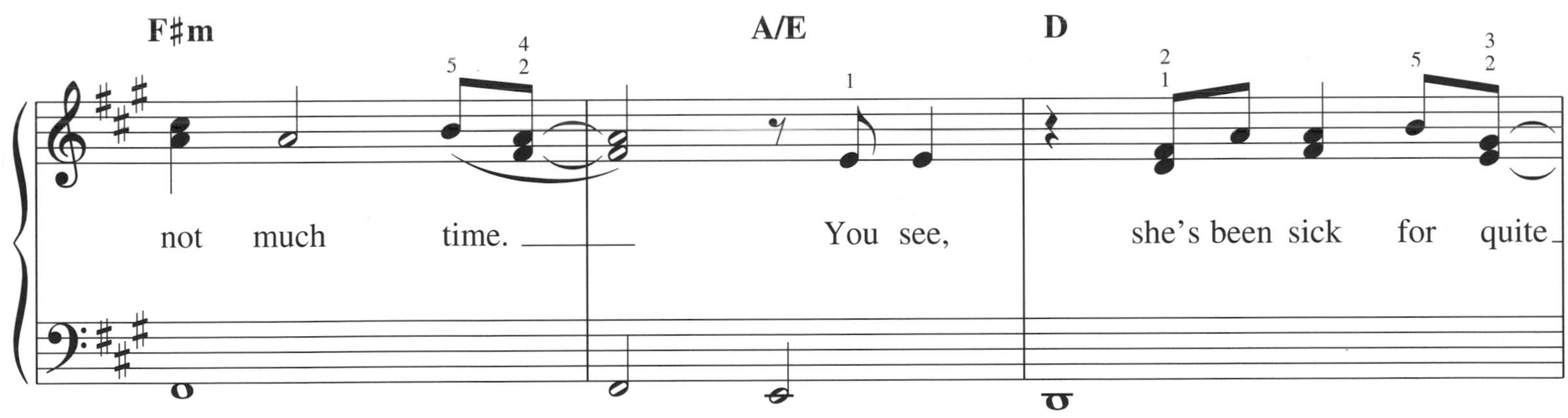
F♯m
A/E
D
not much time. You see, she's been sick for quite

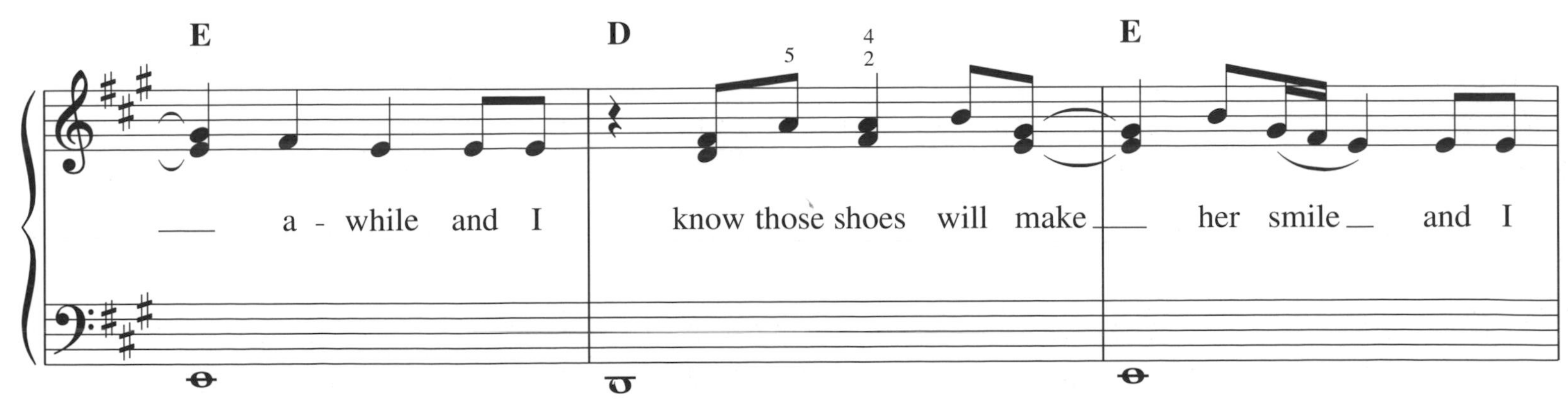
E
D
E
a - while and I know those shoes will make her smile and I

D
Esus
E
Bm7
A/C♯
5
5
5
2
want her to look beau - ti - ful ___ if Ma - ma ___ meets

To Coda
1.
D
E7
A
E/G♯
Je - sus to - night."

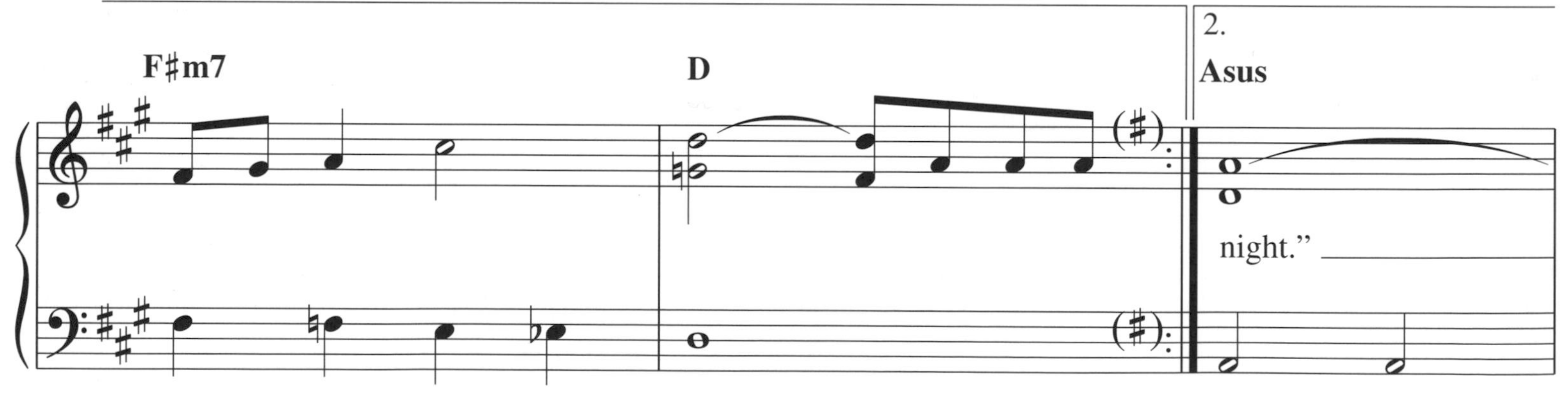
2.
F♯m7
D
Asus
(♯)
(♯)
night." ___

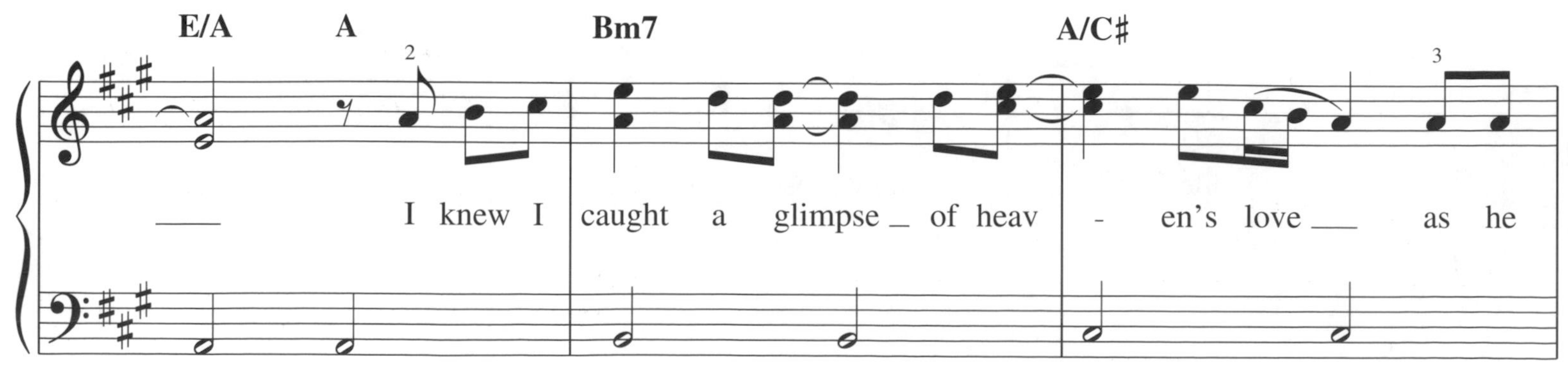
E/A
A
Bm7
A/C♯
2
3
___ I knew I caught a glimpse _ of heav - en's love ___ as he

E
F♯m7
G
thanked me and ran out.
I knew that God had sent that lit -

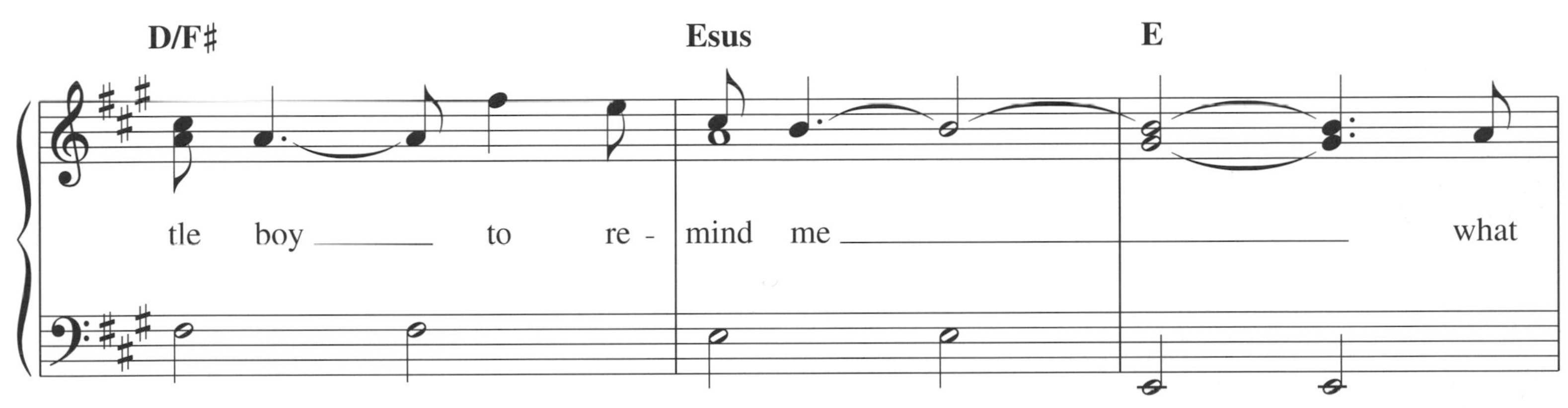
D/F♯
Esus
E
tle boy to re - mind me
what

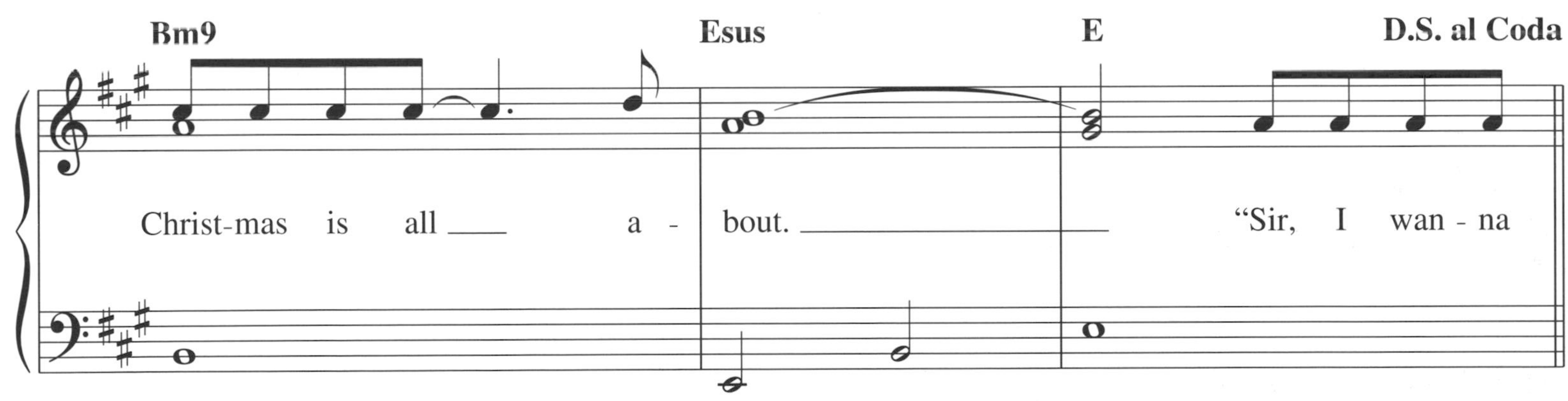
Bm9
Esus
E
D.S. al Coda
Christ-mas is all a - bout.
"Sir, I wan - na

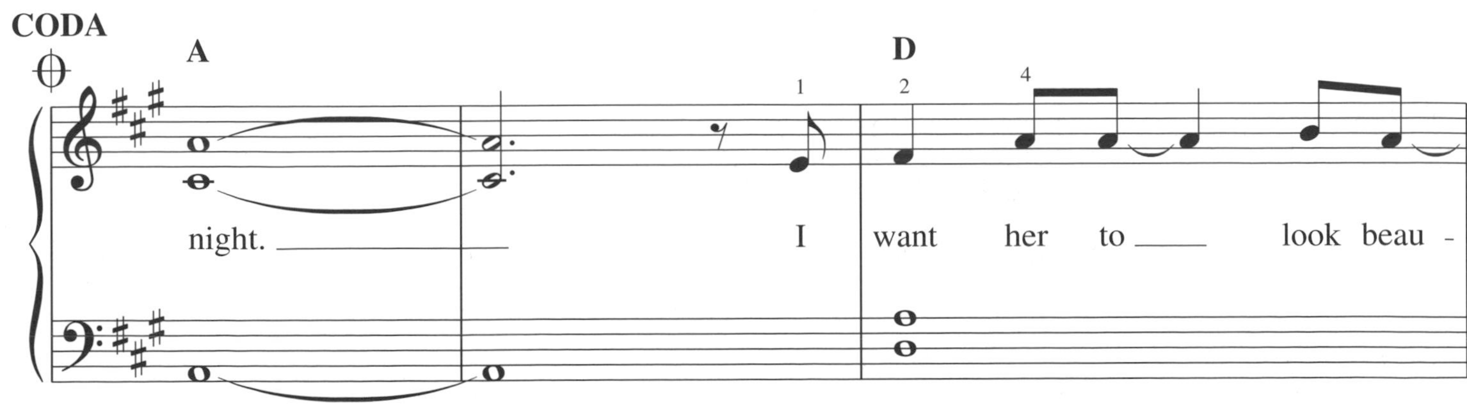
CODA
A
D
night.
I want her to look beau -

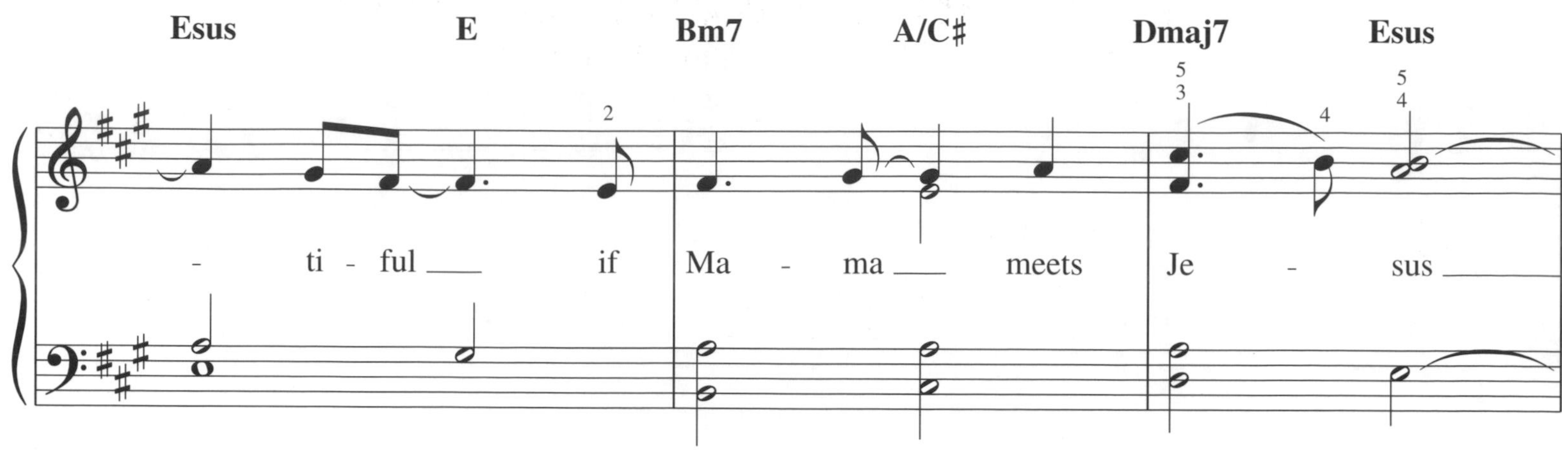

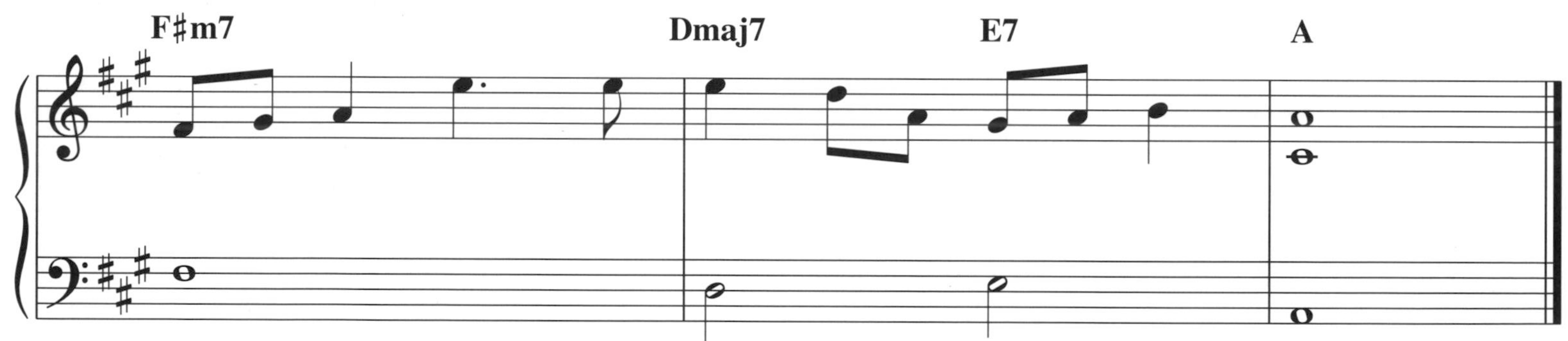

Additional Lyrics

2. They counted pennies for what seemed like years,
Then the cashier said, "Son, there's not enough here."
He searched his pockets frantic'lly,
Then he turned and he looked at me.
He said, "Mama made Christmas good at our house,
Though most years she just did without.
Tell me, sir, what am I gonna do?
Somehow I've gotta buy her these Christmas shoes."
So, I laid the money down,
I just had to help him out.
And I'll never forget the look on his face when he said,
"Mama's gonna look so great."
Chorus:

THE CHRISTMAS SONG
(Chestnuts Roasting on an Open Fire)

Music and Lyric by MEL TORME
and ROBERT WELLS

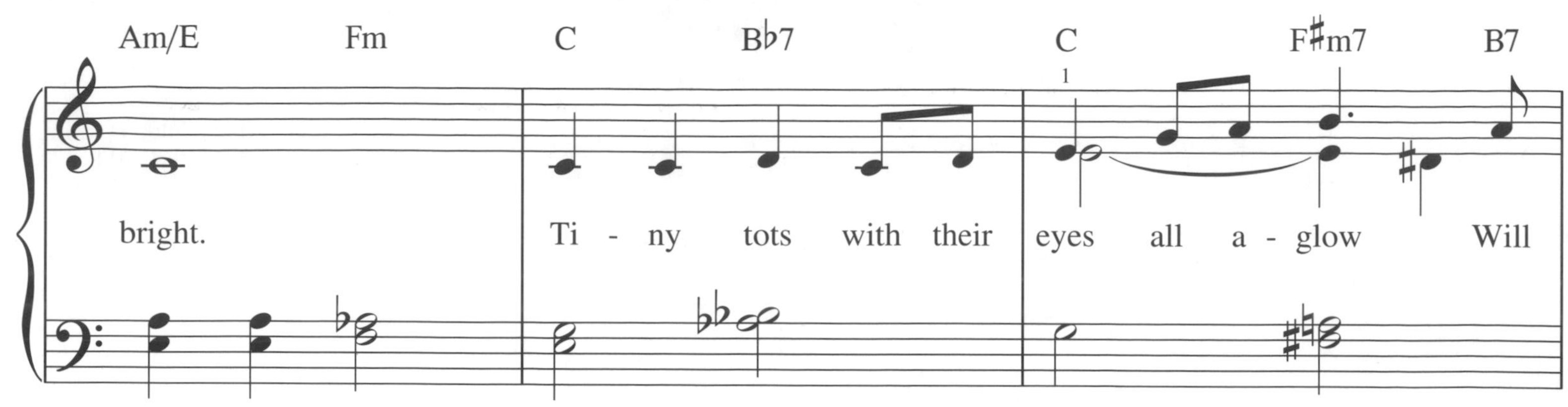
Am/E
Fm
C
B♭7
C
F♯m7
B7
bright.
Ti - ny tots with their
eyes all a - glow Will

Em7
A7
Dm7
G7
C
Gm7
C7
find it hard to sleep to -
night. They know that
San - ta's on his

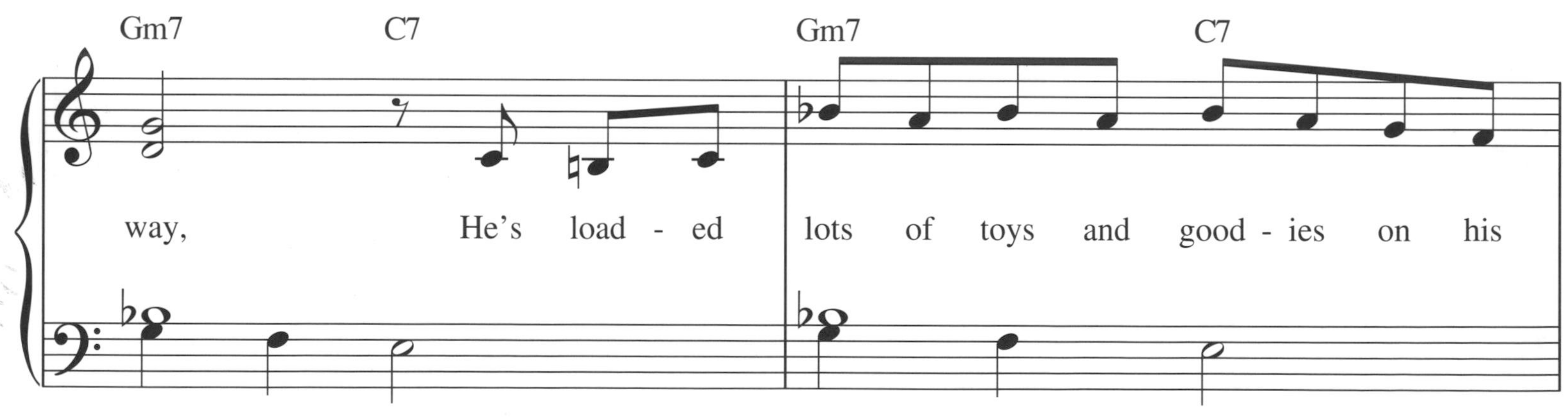
Gm7
C7
Gm7
C7
way, He's load - ed
lots of toys and good - ies on his

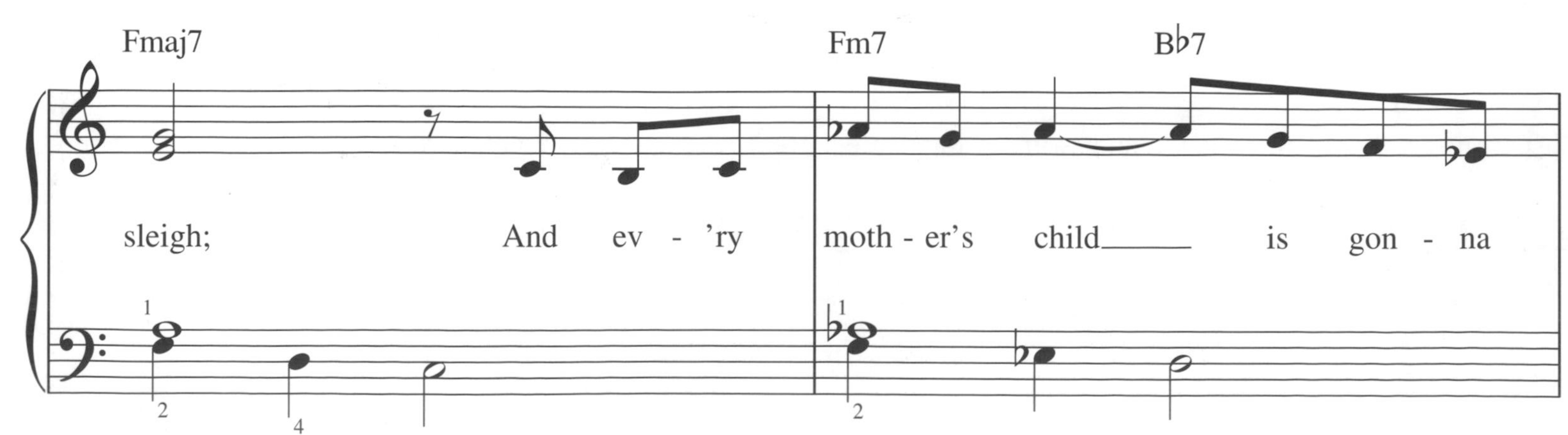
Fmaj7
Fm7
B♭7
sleigh; And ev - 'ry
moth - er's child is gon - na

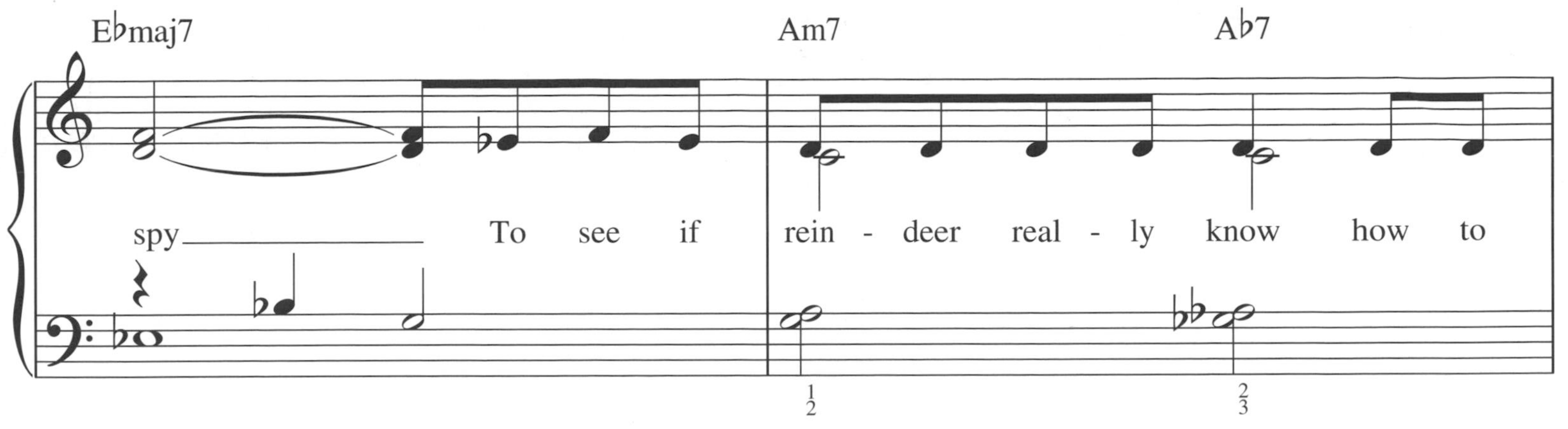
E♭maj7
Am7
A♭7
spy To see if rein - deer real - ly know how to

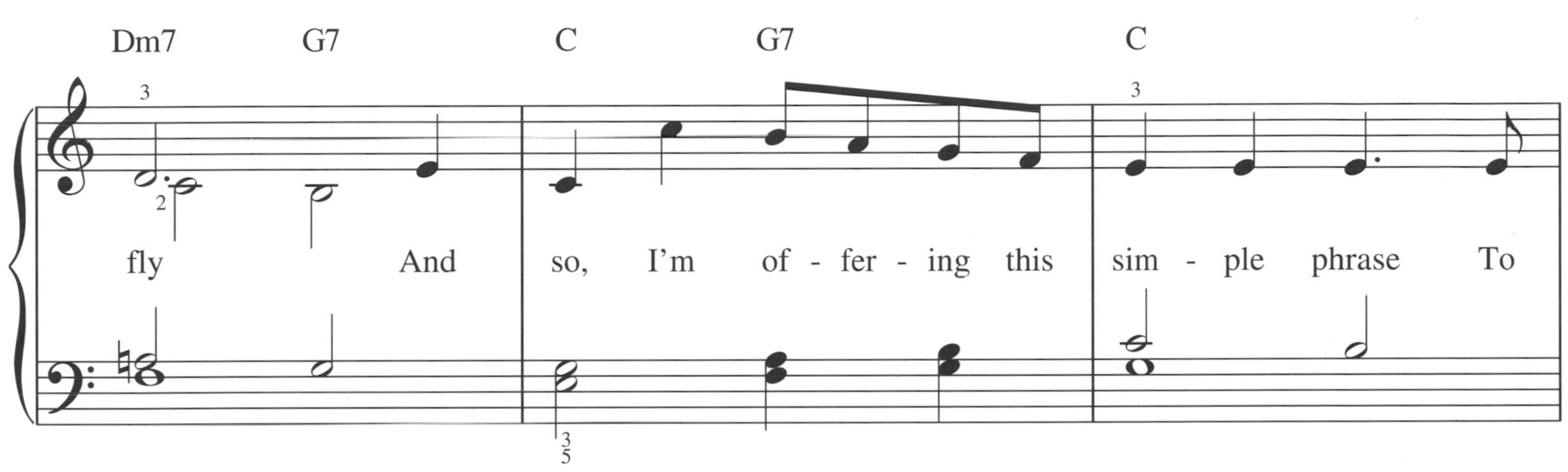
Dm7
G7
C
G7
C
fly And so, I'm of - fer - ing this sim - ple phrase To

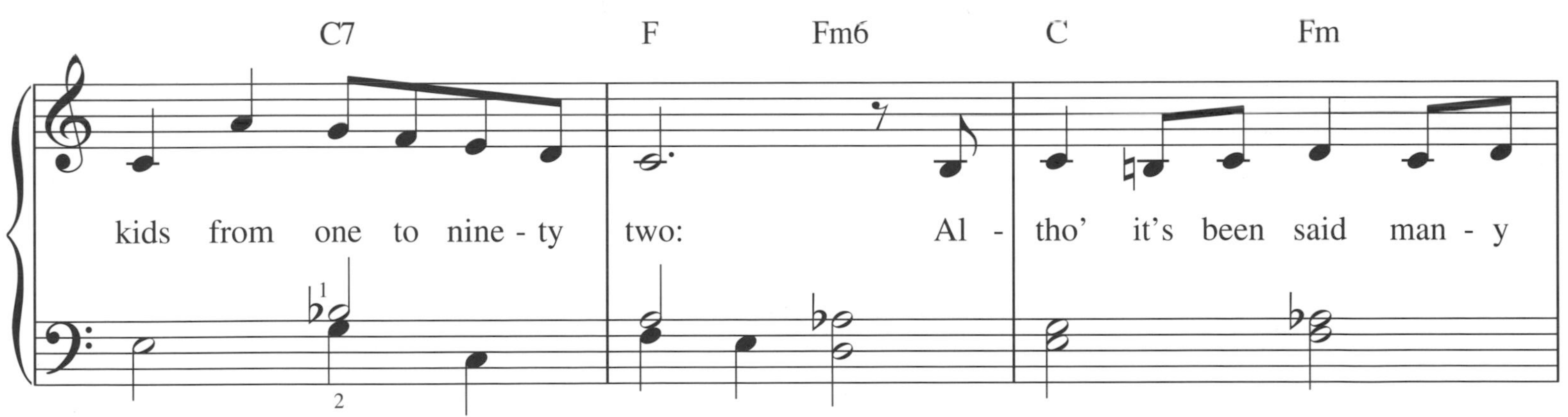
C7
F
Fm6
C
Fm
kids from one to nine - ty two: Al - tho' it's been said man - y

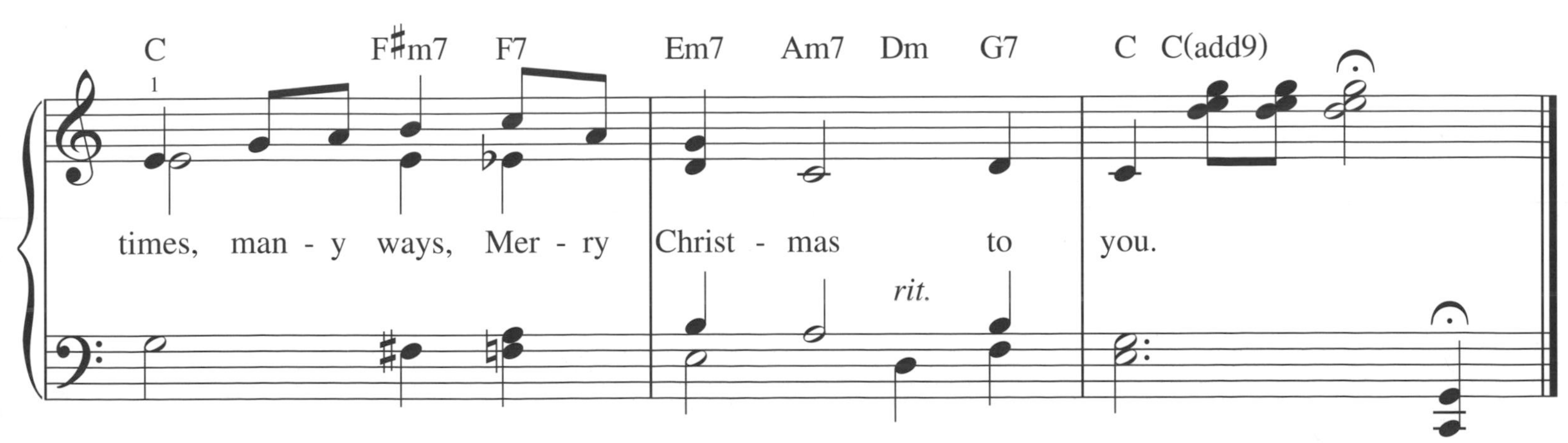
C
F♯m7
F7
Em7
Am7
Dm
G7
C
C(add9)
times, man - y ways, Mer - ry Christ - mas to you.
rit.

CHRISTMAS TIME IS HERE

from A CHARLIE BROWN CHRISTMAS

Words by LEE MENDELSON
Music by VINCE GUARALDI

1.
2.
Gm7
B♭/C
Fmaj9
Fmaj9
fa - v'rite time of year.
love and dreams to share.
D♭maj7
G♭13♯11
D♭maj7
Sleigh - bells in the air,
beau - ty ev - 'ry -
G♭13♯11
Am7
E♭9
D7
where.
Yule - tide by the fire - side and
Gm7
D♭9
C13
Fmaj9
joy - ful mem - 'ries there.
Christ - mas time is

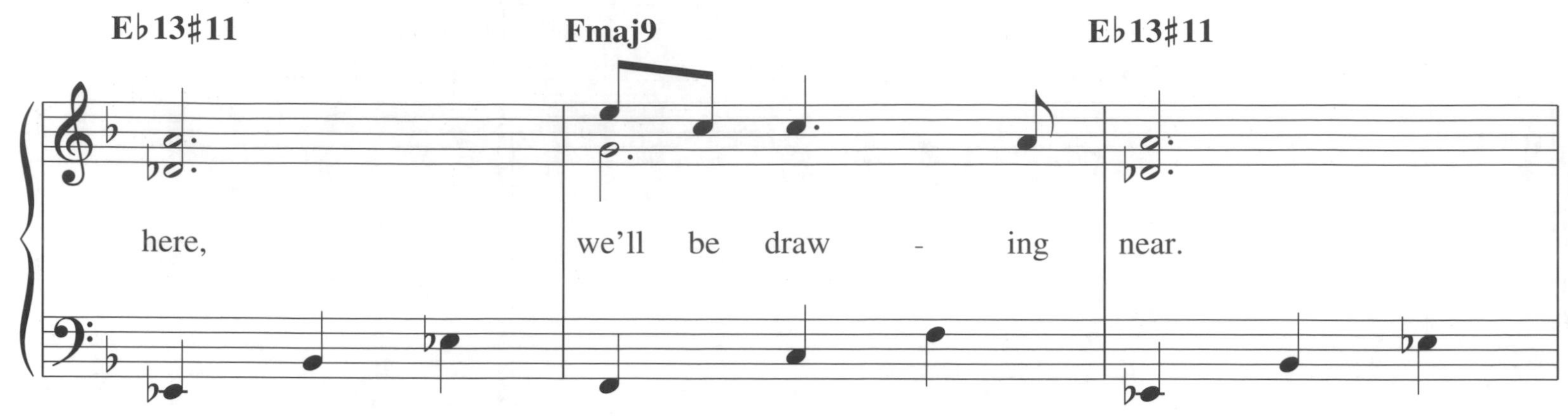
E♭13♯11
Fmaj9
E♭13♯11
here,
we'll be draw - ing
near.

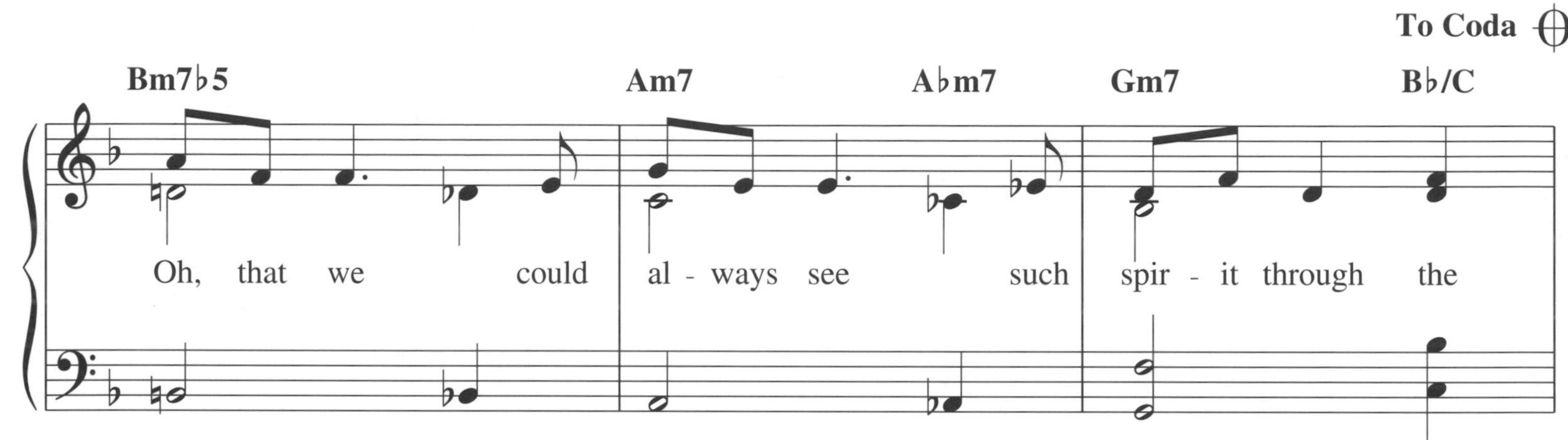
To Coda
Bm7♭5
Am7
A♭m7
Gm7
B♭/C
Oh, that we could
al - ways see such
spir - it through the

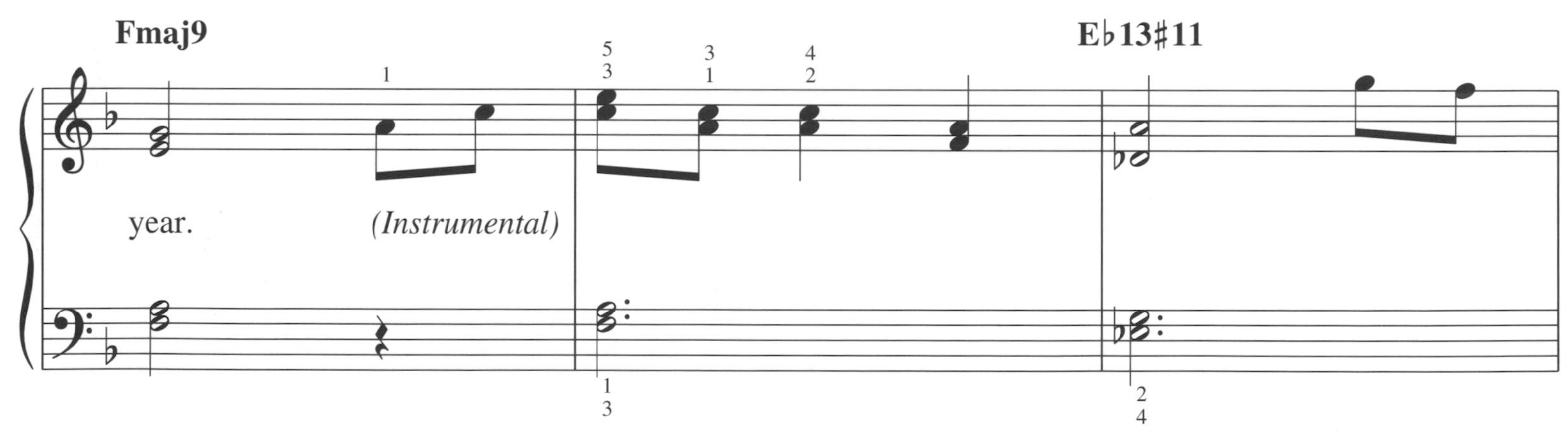
Fmaj9
E♭13♯11
year.
(Instrumental)

Fmaj9
E♭13♯11
Bm7♭5
B♭m7

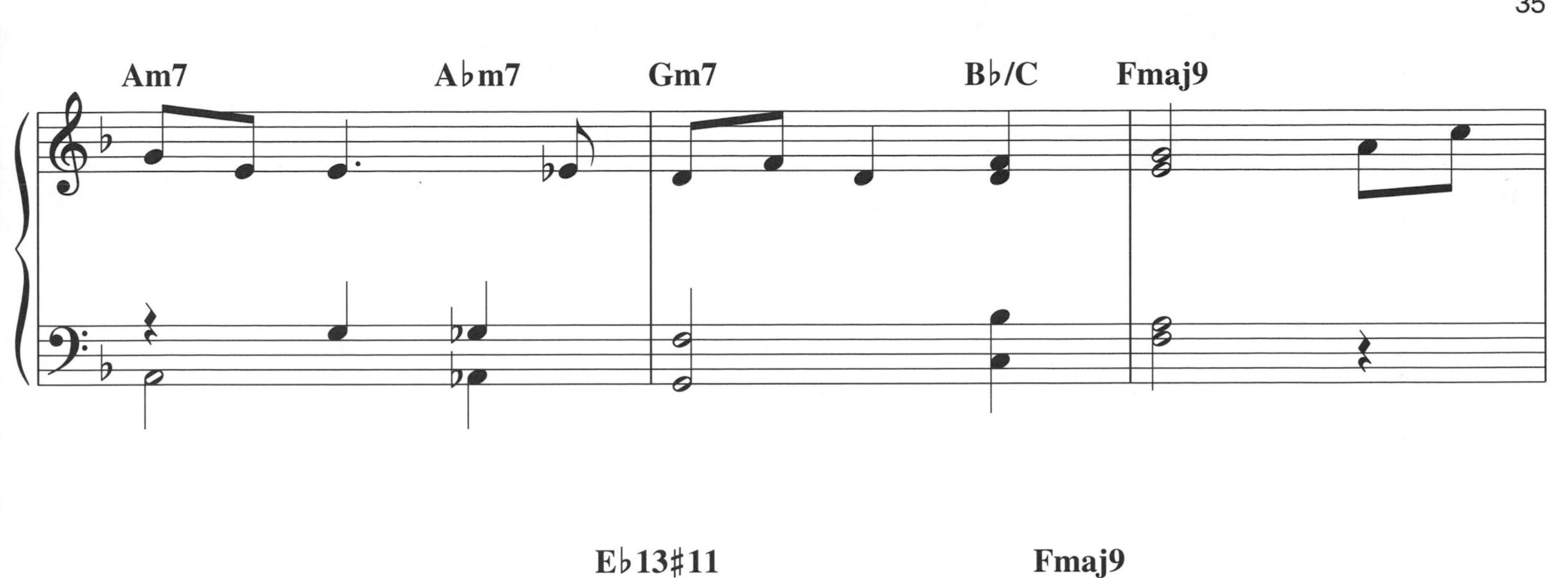
Am7
A♭m7
Gm7
B♭/C
Fmaj9

E♭13♯11
Fmaj9

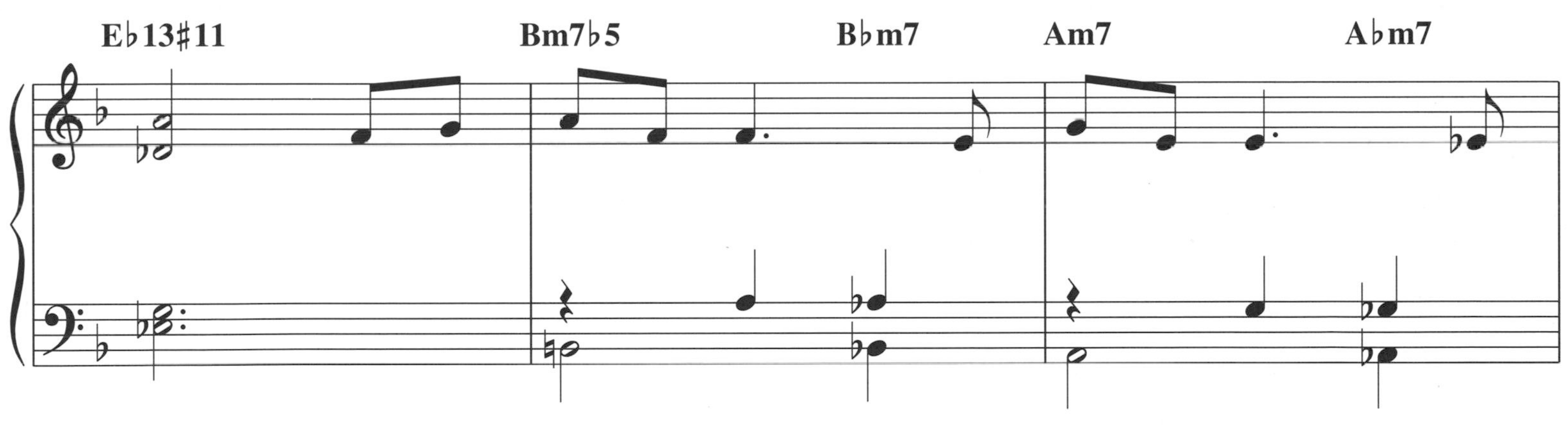
E♭13♯11
Bm7♭5
B♭m7
Am7
A♭m7

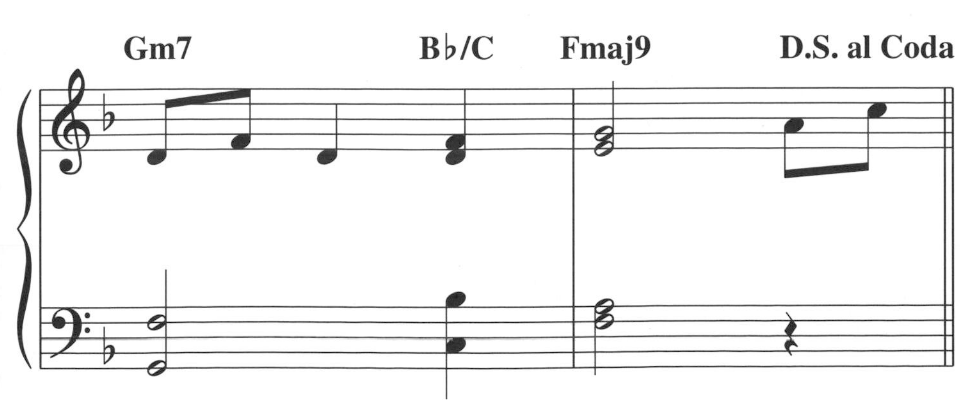
Gm7
B♭/C
Fmaj9
D.S. al Coda

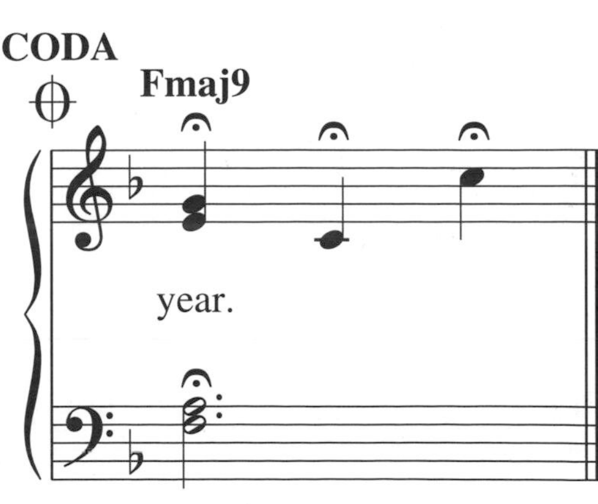
CODA
Fmaj9
year.

A CRADLE IN BETHLEHEM

Words and Music by AL BRYAN
and LAWRENCE STOCK

Dm
C♯dim/E
F6
D7/F♯
Gsus
G7
say "A - men." A

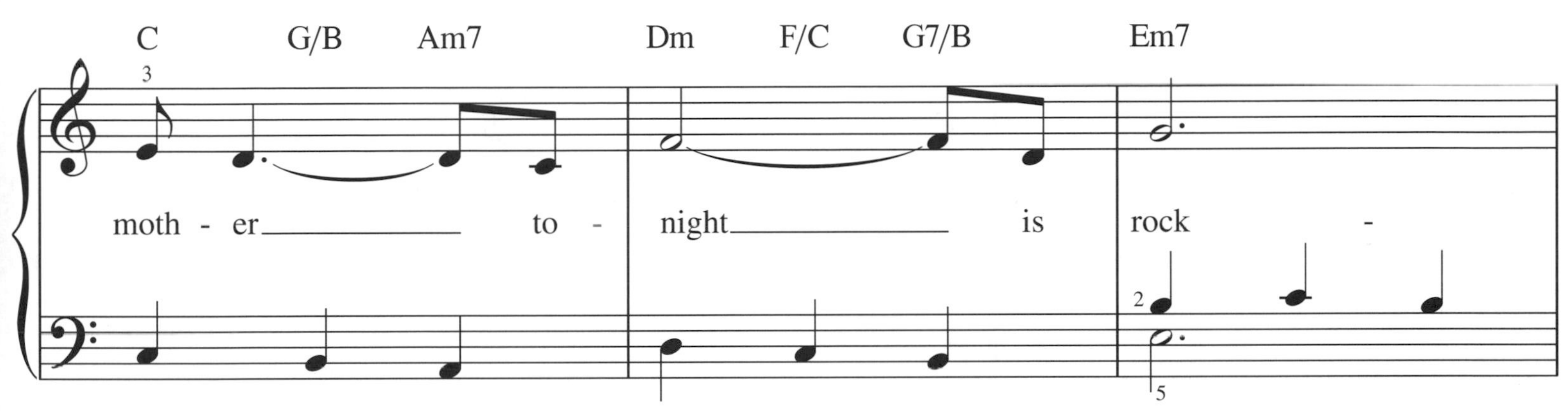
C
G/B
Am7
Dm
F/C
G7/B
Em7
moth - er to - night is rock -

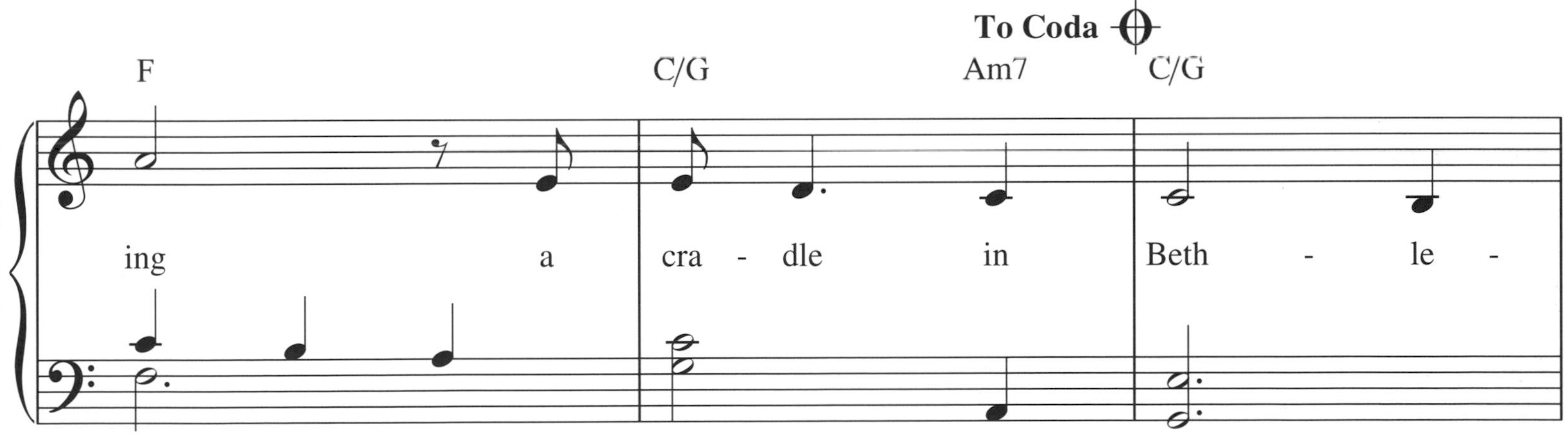
To Coda
F
C/G
Am7
C/G
ing a cra - dle in Beth - le -

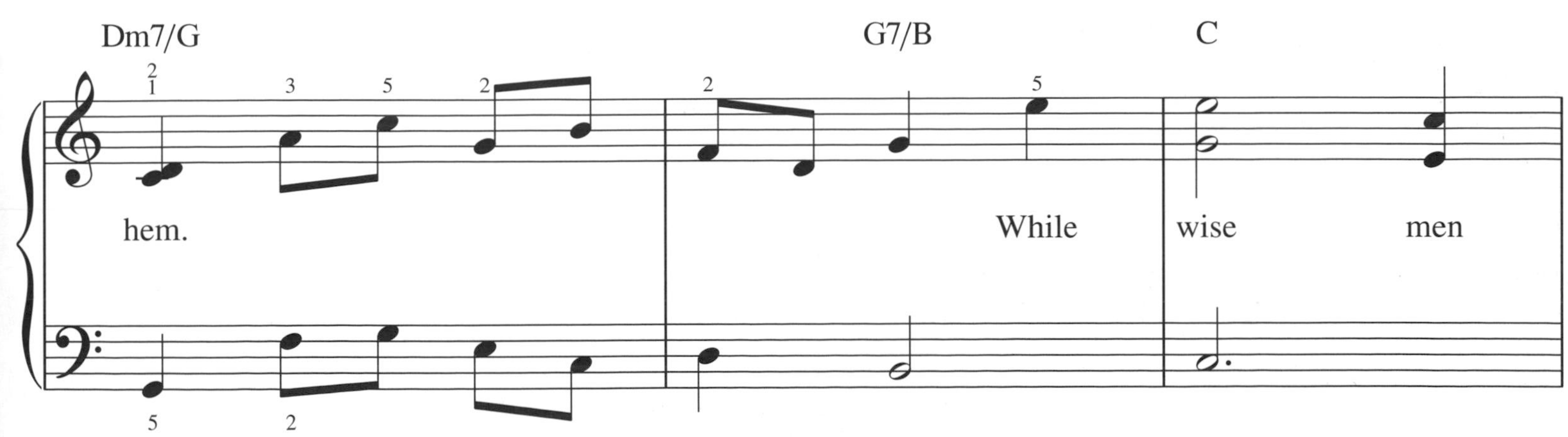
Dm7/G
G7/B
C
hem. While wise men

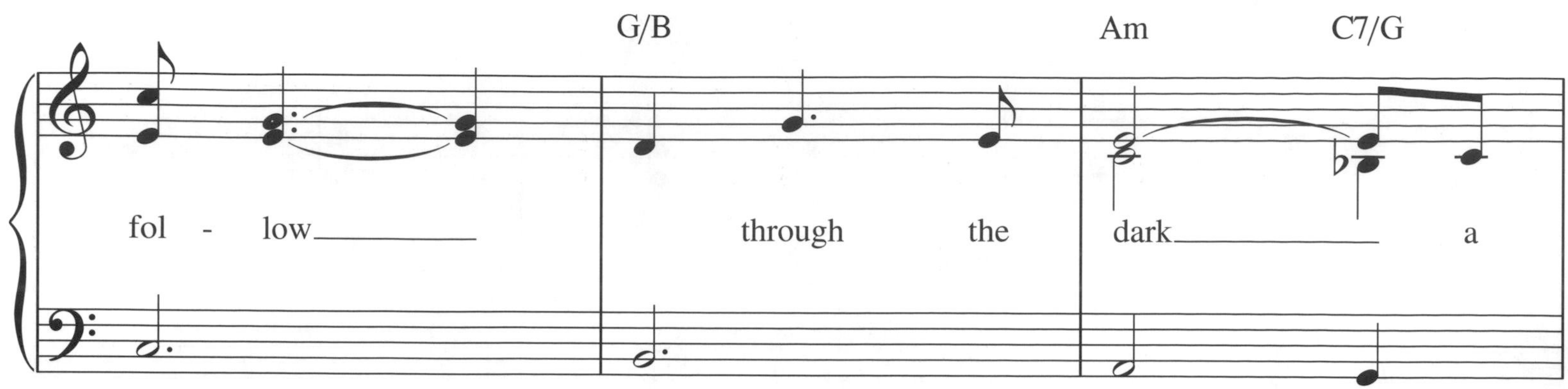
G/B
Am
C7/G
fol - low through the dark a

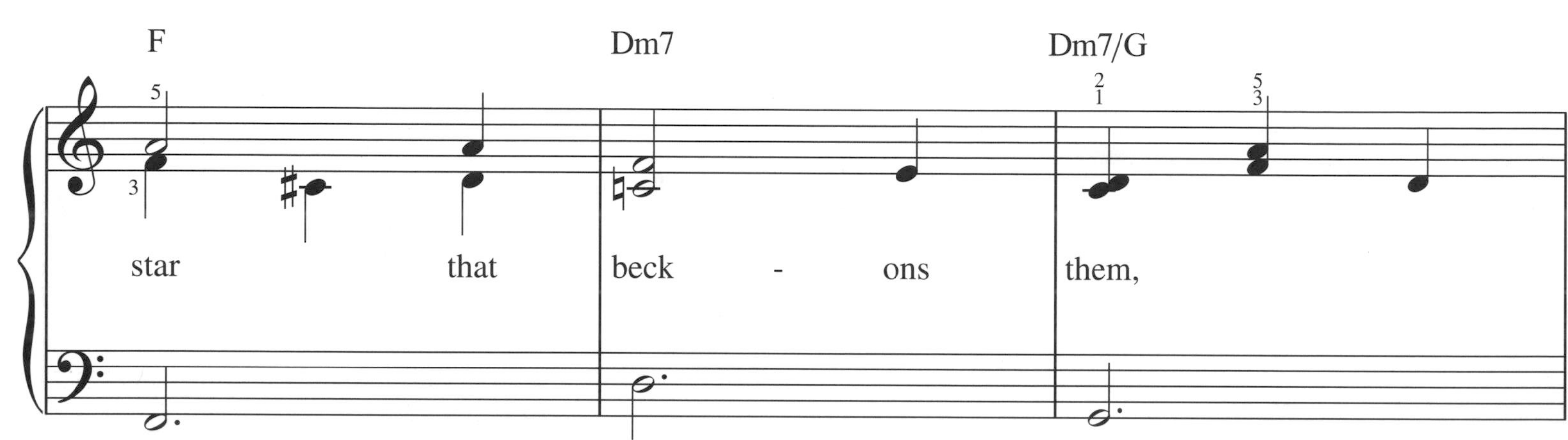
F
Dm7
Dm7/G
star that beck - ons them,

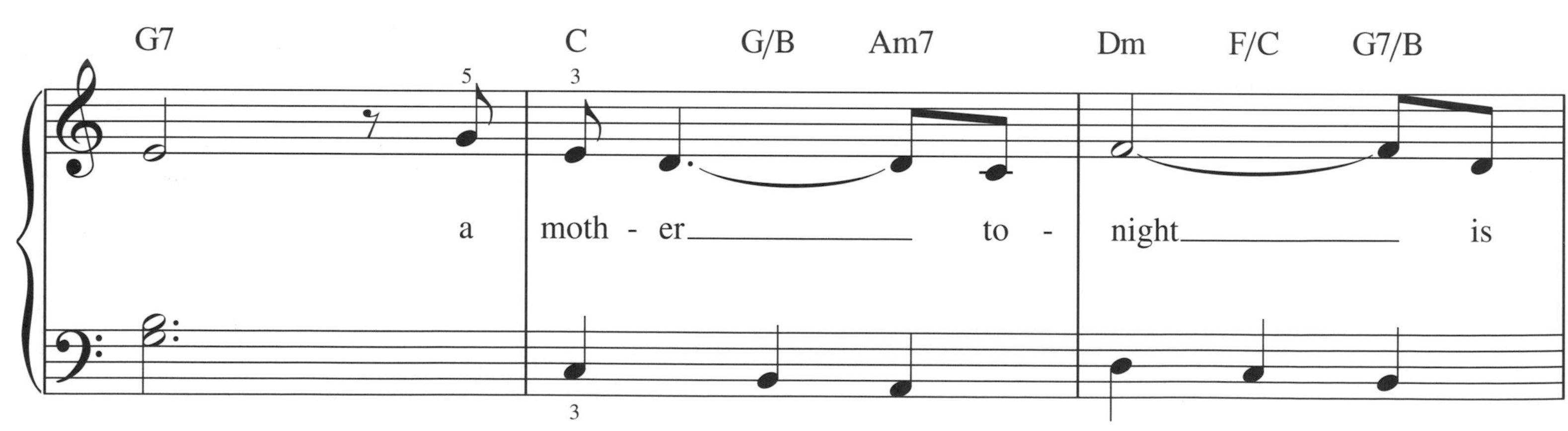
G7
C
G/B
Am7
Dm
F/C
G7/B
a moth - er to - night is

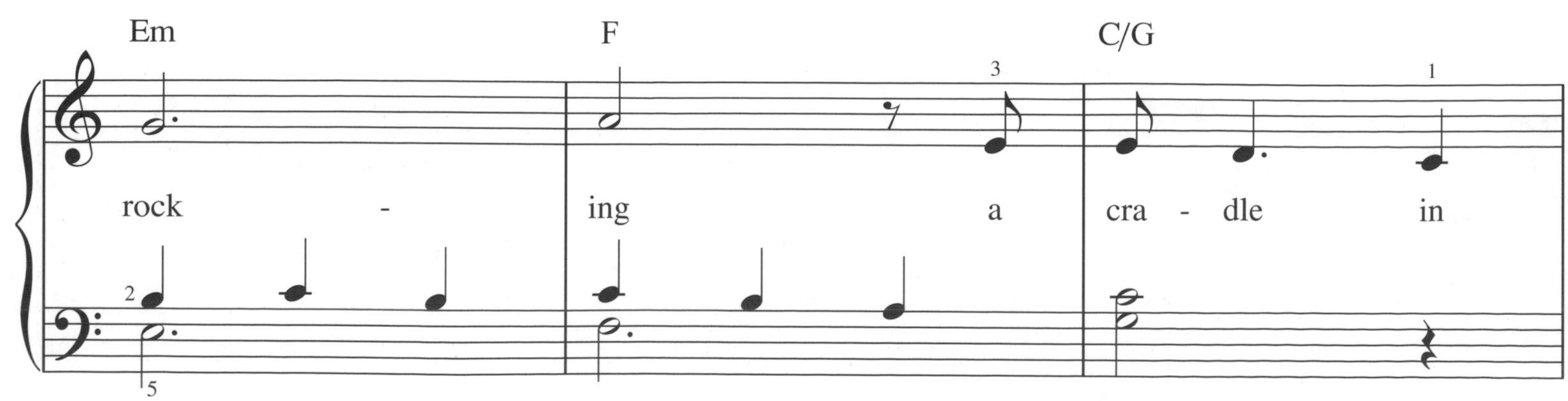
Em
F
C/G
rock - ing a cra - dle in

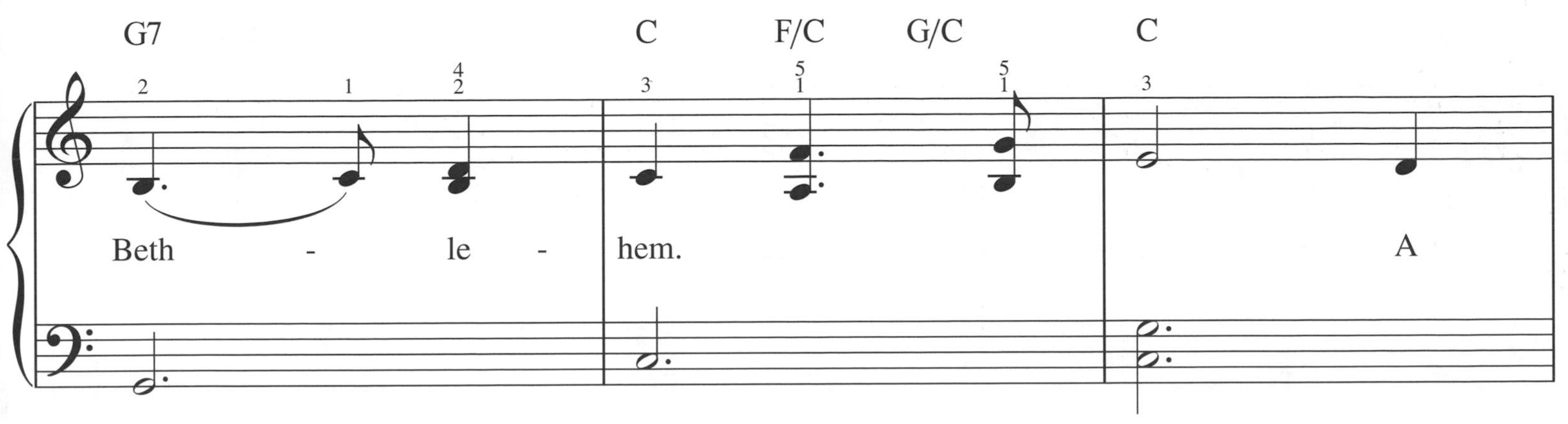
G7
C
F/C
G/C
C
Beth - le - hem.
A

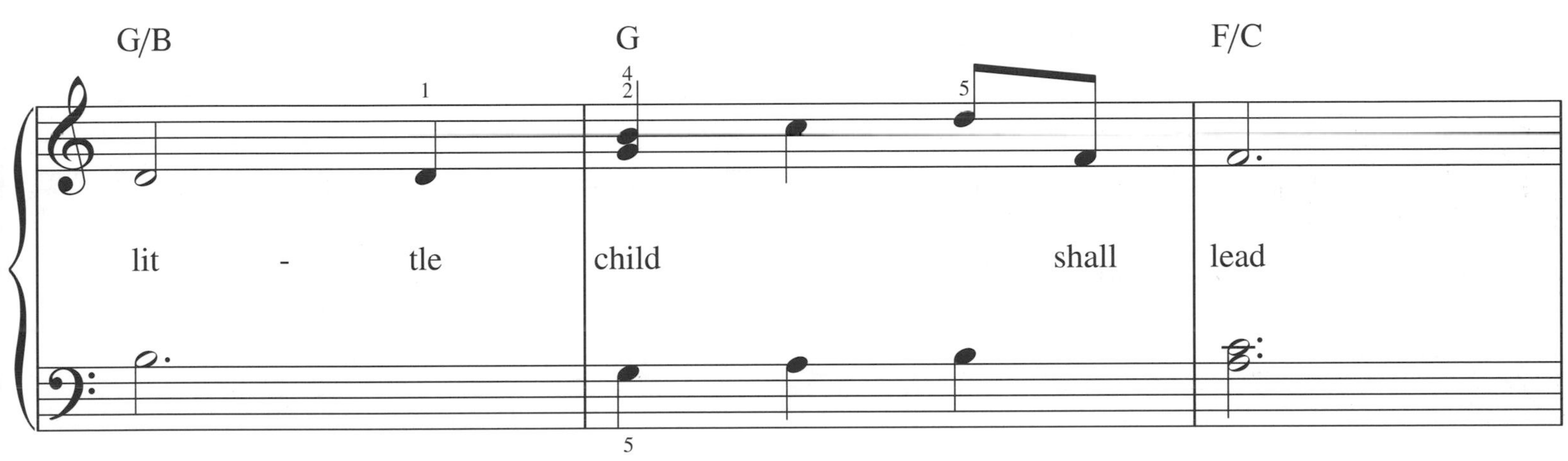
G/B
G
F/C
lit - tle child shall lead

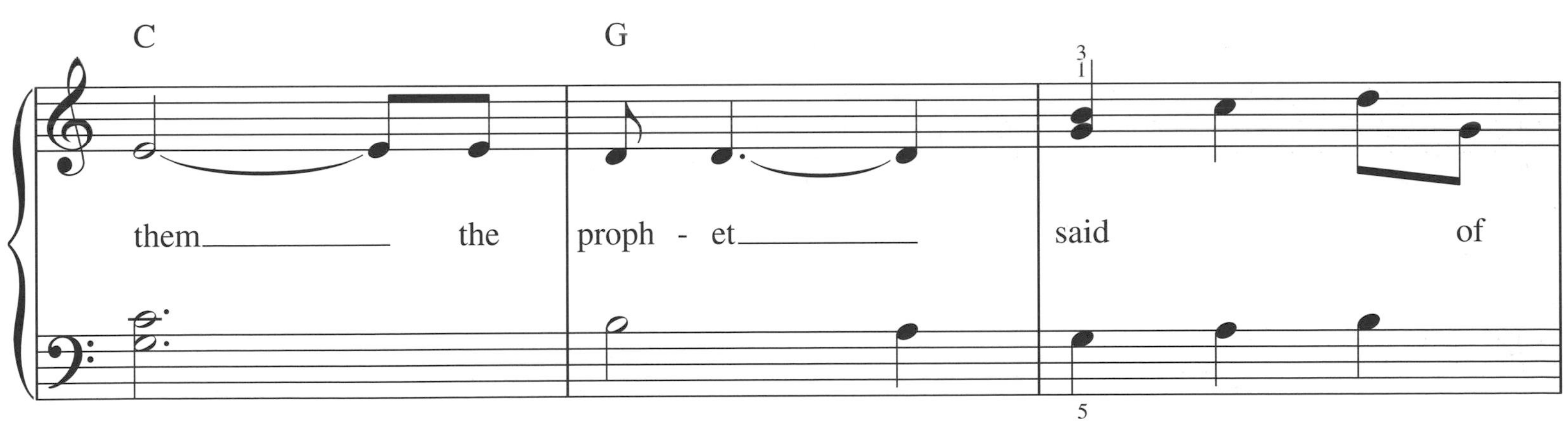
C
G
them the proph - et said of

C
Am6
old. In storm and

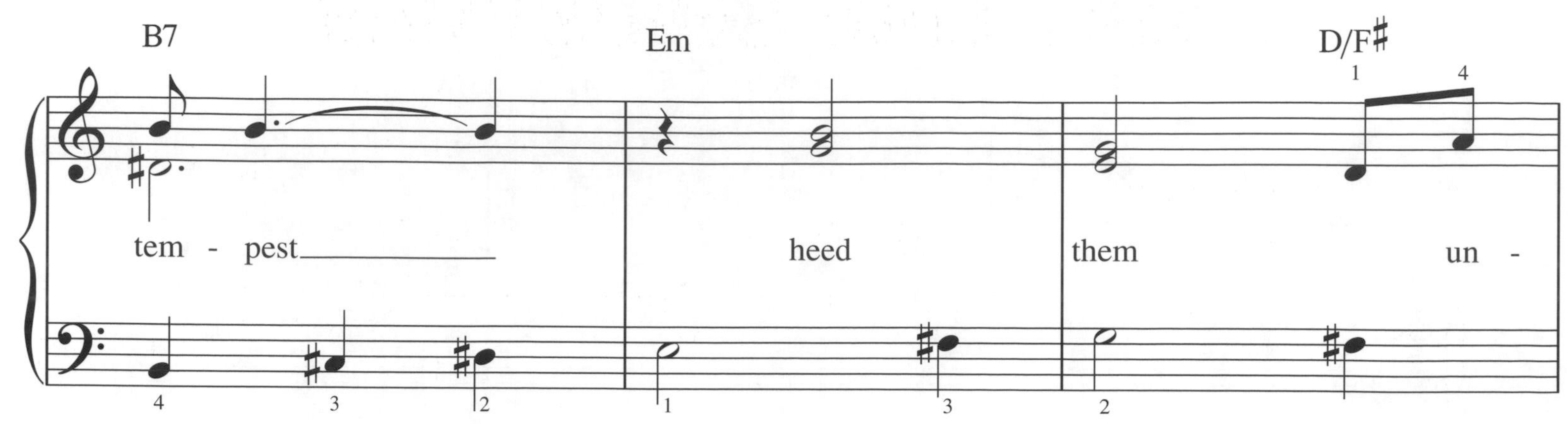
B7
Em
D/F♯
tem - pest
heed
them
un -

Em
Am
D7/F♯
Dm7/G
til
the
bell
is
tolled.

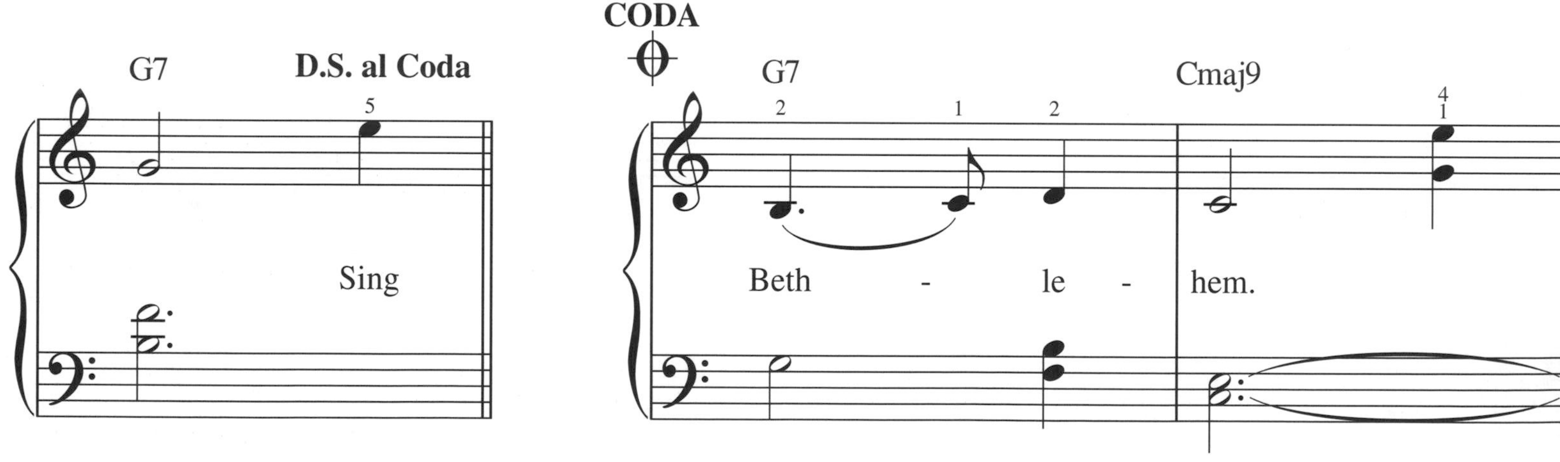
G7
D.S. al Coda
Sing
CODA
G7
Cmaj9
Beth - le - hem.

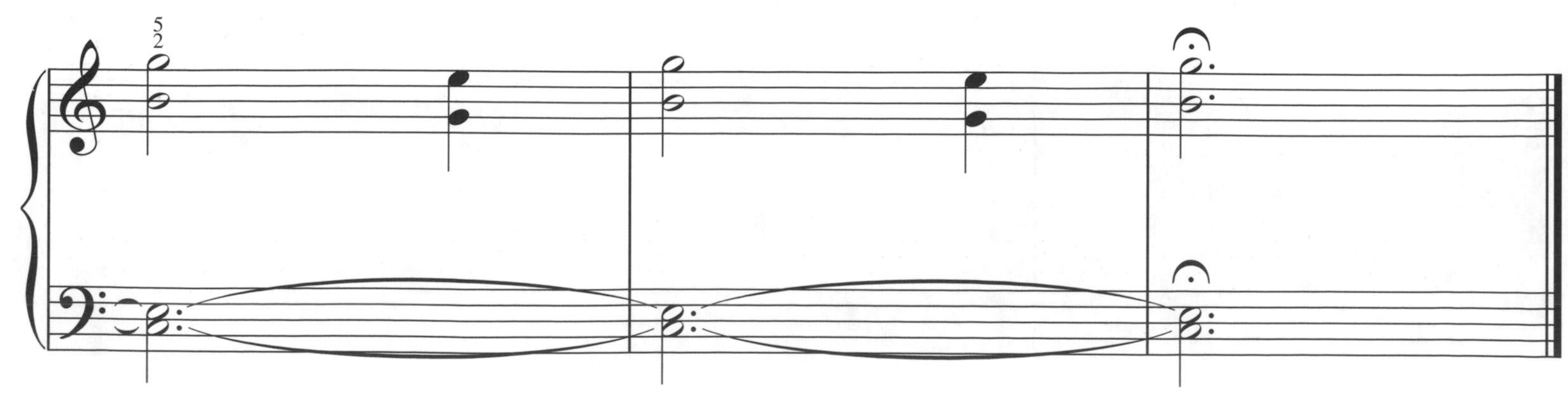

A DAY LIKE CHRISTMAS

Words and Music by LENORE ROSENBLATT
and MICHAEL S. BURNS

G(add2) Am7 D7 G(add2)
quar-rels be-tween us a - side and re - mem - ber the good in our
Am7 D7 Em Cm6/E♭ G/D A/C♯
lives. There's a love that em-brac - es the whole hu-man race in our
Cm C/D D G B7/D♯ Em
hearts on Christ - mas Eve. If ev - 'ry day could
Cmaj9 D7 G Em7 C(add2) D7
be a day like Christ - mas, if we

G B7/D♯ Em C B7/D♯
kept the Christ - mas spir - it all year
Em G/D
through, what a
C G/B Am7 Em
won - der - ful world this would be, filled with
To Coda
C G/B A7sus A7 C/D D G B7/D♯ Em
joy, hope and peace, if ev - 'ry day could

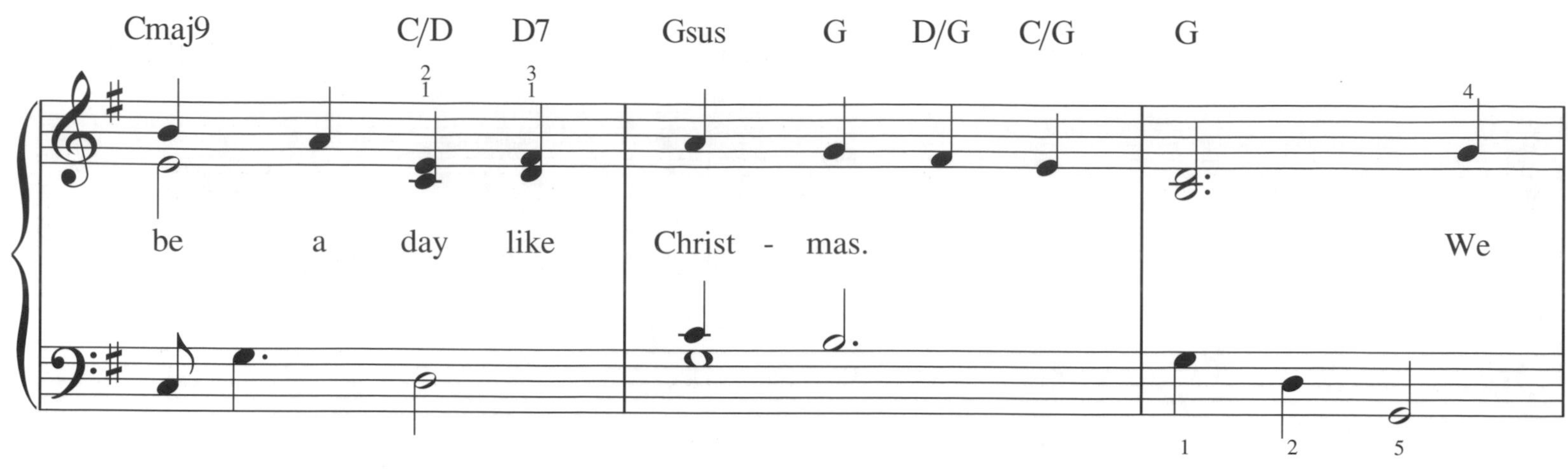
Cmaj9
C/D
D7
Gsus
G
D/G
C/G
G
be a day like Christ - mas. We

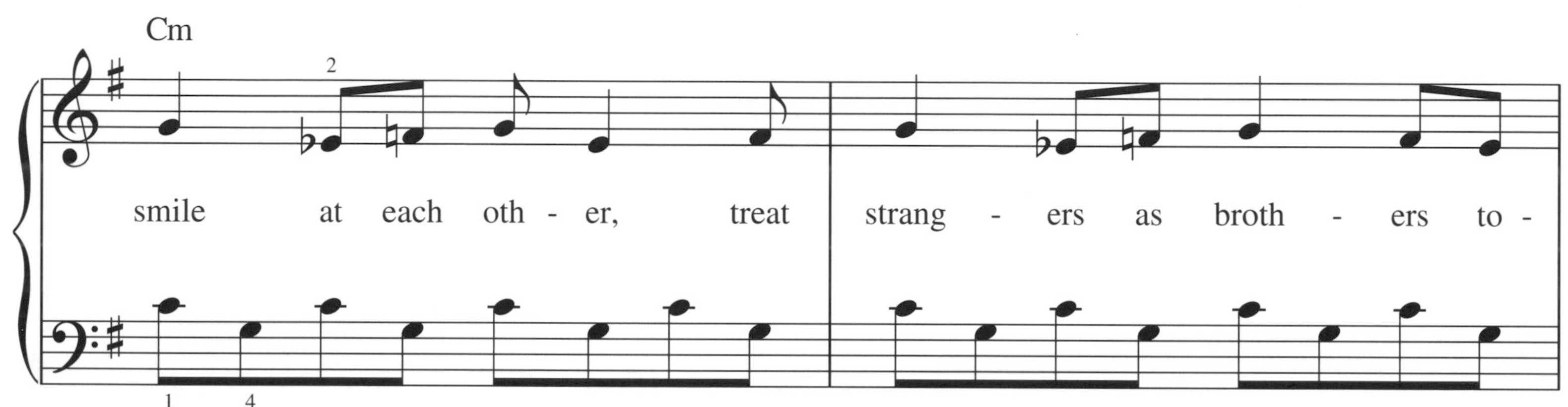
Cm
smile at each oth - er, treat strang - ers as broth - ers to -

G
Am7
B♭dim
G/B
day. There's a

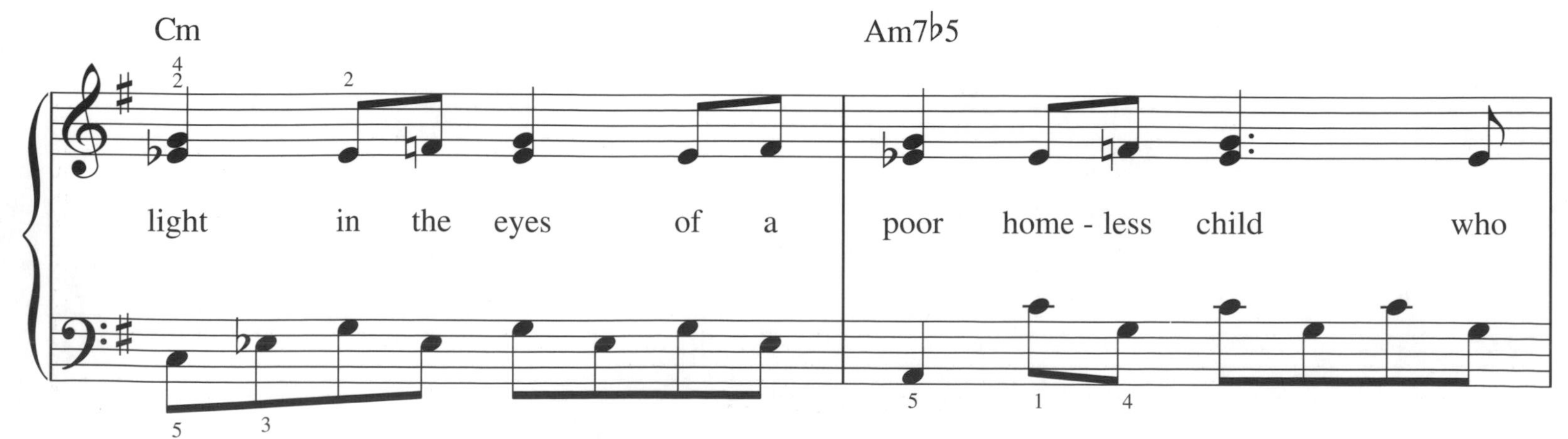
Cm
Am7♭5
light in the eyes of a poor home - less child who

G/D
B7/D♯
Em
C(add2)
D
D.S. al Coda
hugs the gift that San - ta gave. If
CODA
Cmaj9
C/D
B7/D♯
Em
Em(maj7)
Em7
be a day like Christ - mas
G/A
A7
G/D
B/D♯
Em
If ev - 'ry day could
Cmaj7
C/D
D7
Cm6/G
G
be a day like Christ - mas.

DO THEY KNOW IT'S CHRISTMAS?

Words and Music by M. URE
and B. GELDOF

F
Dm
G
Throw your arms a - round the world at Christ-mas - time.

C
F
G
But say a prayer, to pray for the

C
F
G
oth - er ones at Christ - mas - time. It's hard, but when you're

C
F
hav - ing fun there's a world out - side your win -

G
C
F
- dow, and it's a world of dread and fear where the

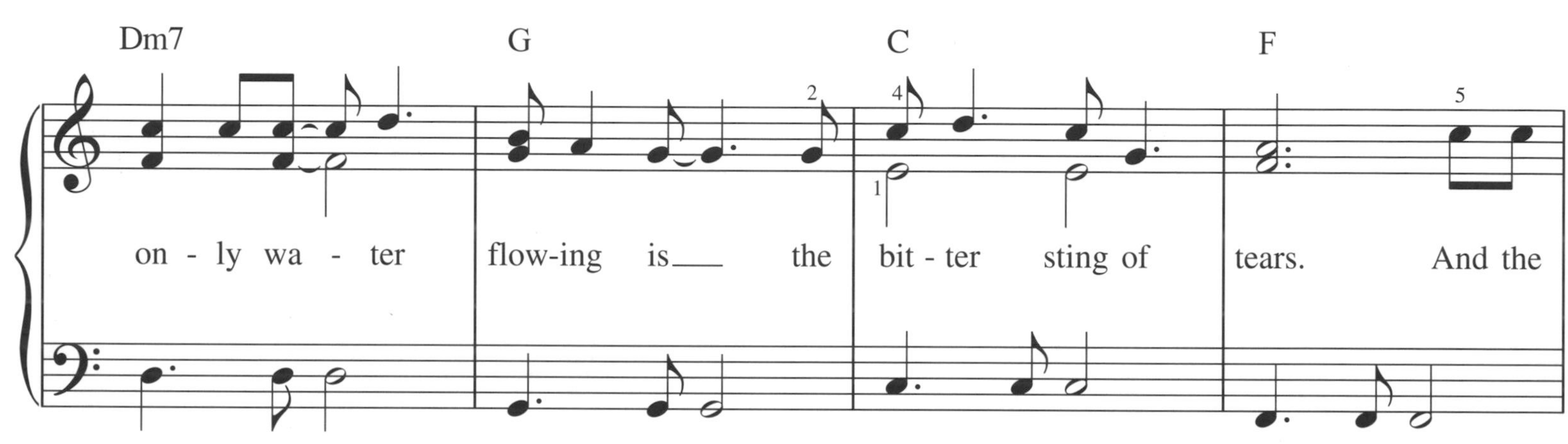
Dm7
G
C
F
on - ly wa - ter flow-ing is the bit - ter sting of tears. And the

Dm7
G
C
Christ-mas bells that ring there are the clang - ing chimes of doom.

F
Dm7
G
C
Well, to - night thank God it's them in - stead of you.

Csus
C
F
G
3
And there won't be snow in Af - ri - ca this Christ -

C
F
G
2
- mas - time.
The great - est gift they'll get this year is life.

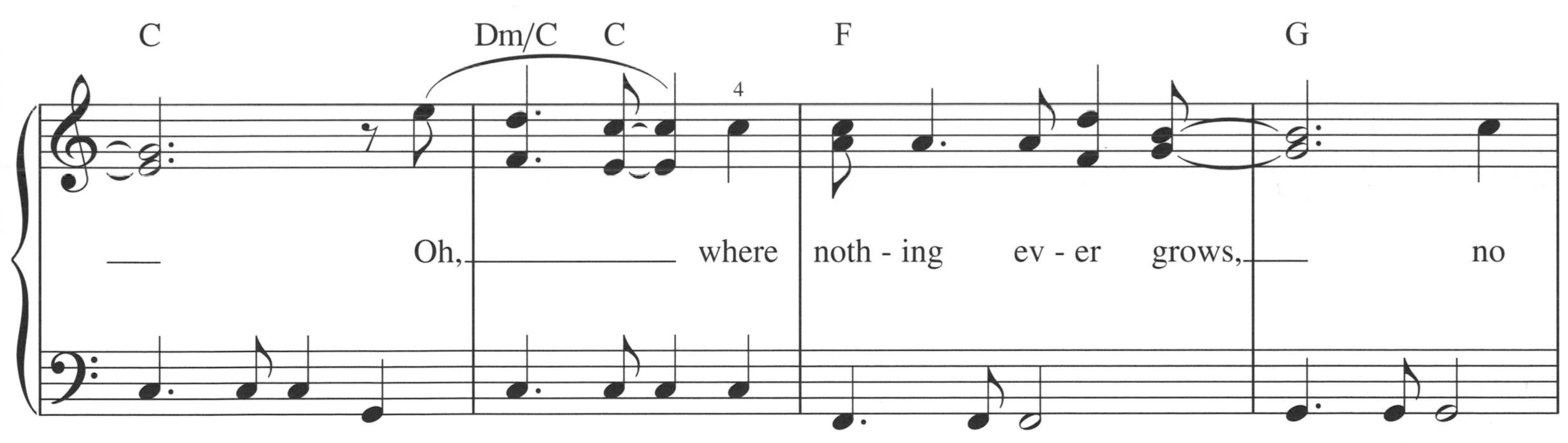
C
Dm/C
C
F
G
4
Oh, where noth - ing ev - er grows, no

C
F
Dm7
F/G
3
1
5
rain or riv - ers flow, do they know it's Christ - mas - time at

C
F
C
Am
G
2
5
3
all?
Here's to you, raise a
glass for ev - 'ry - one;

Am
G
F
F/G
here's to them un - der -
neath that burn - ing sun.
Do they know it's
Christ - mas - time at

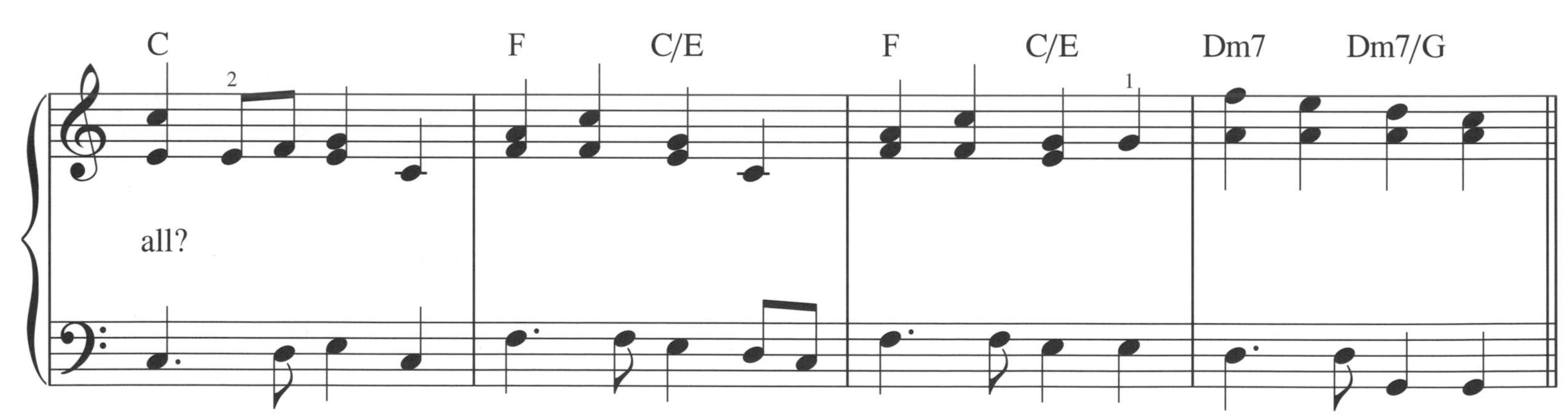
C
F
C/E
F
C/E
Dm7
Dm7/G
2
1
all?

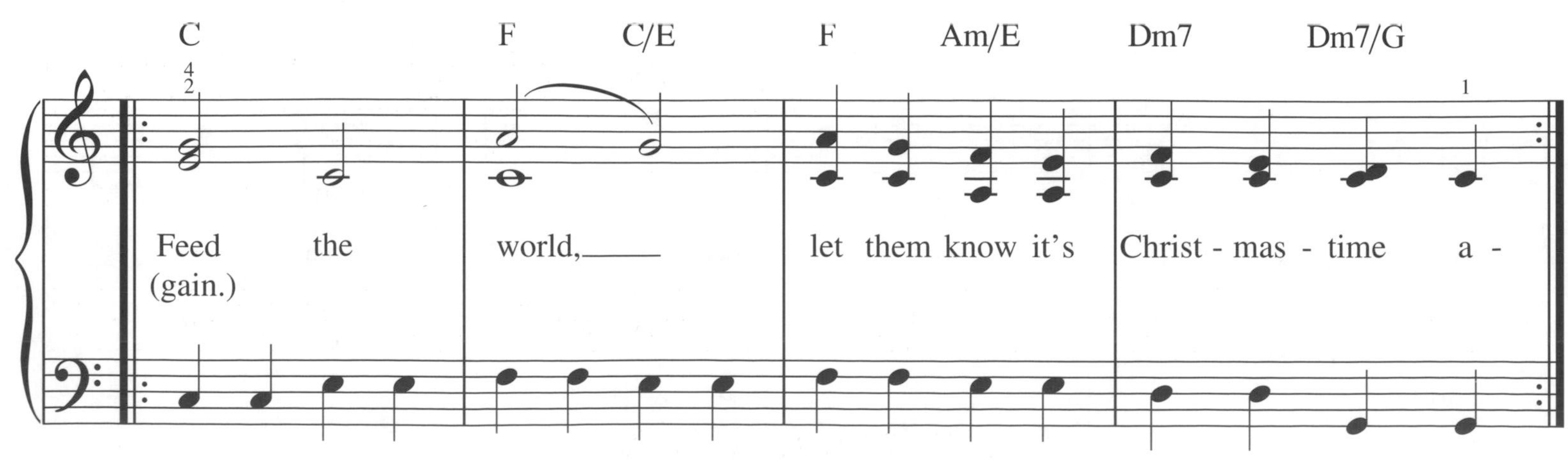
Repeat and Fade
C
F
C/E
F
Am/E
Dm7
Dm7/G
4
2
1
Feed the
(gain.)
world,
let them know it's
Christ - mas - time a -

EMMANUEL

Words and Music by
MICHAEL W. SMITH

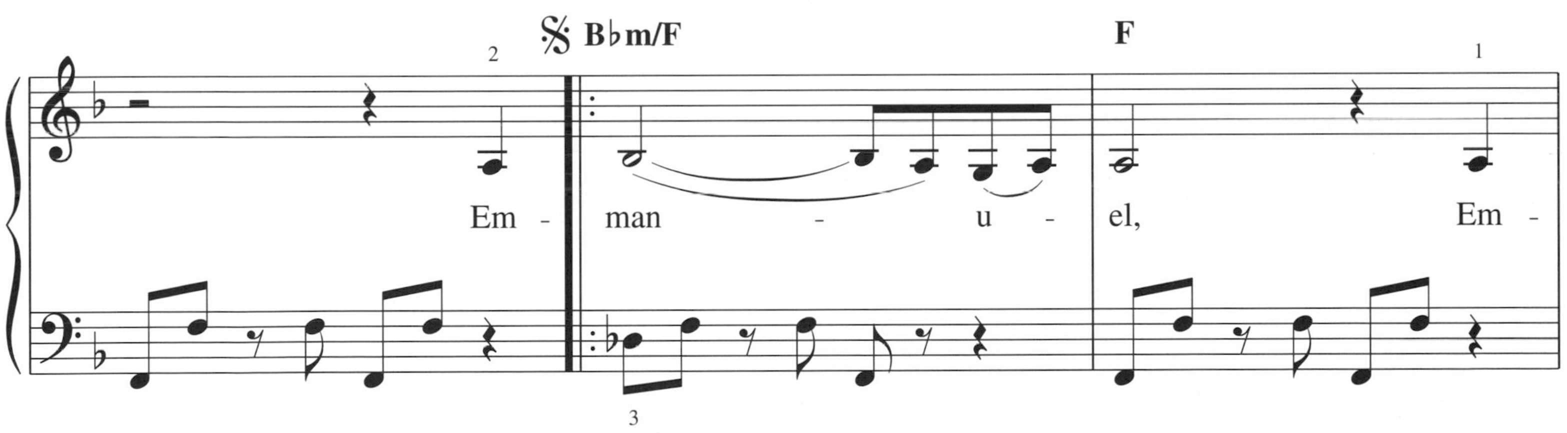

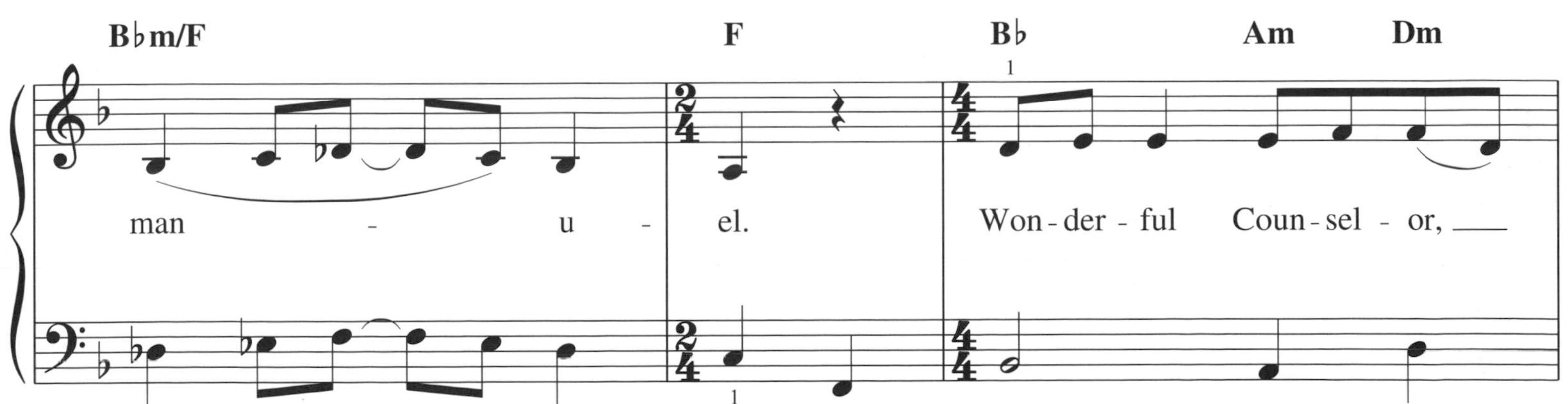

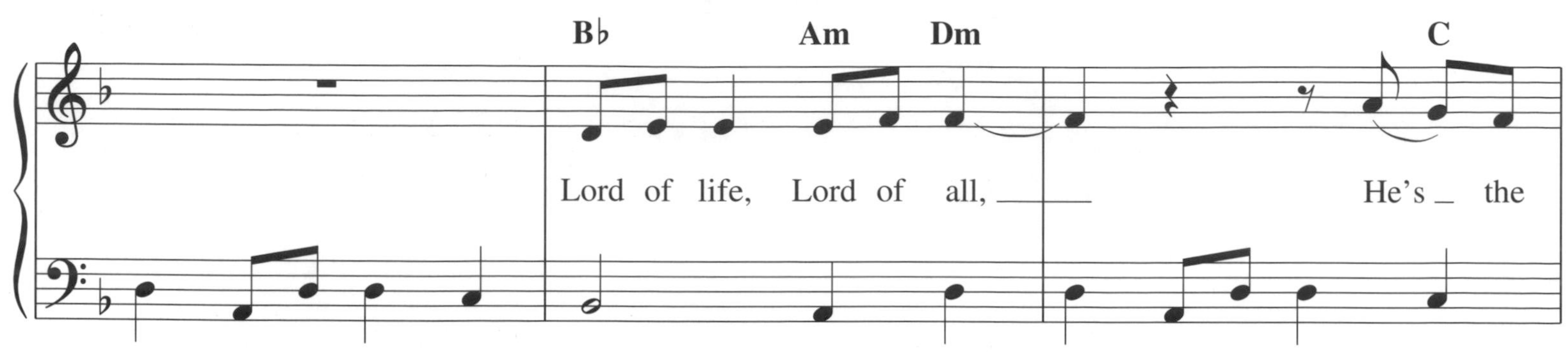
B♭
Am
Dm
C
Lord of life, Lord of all, He's the

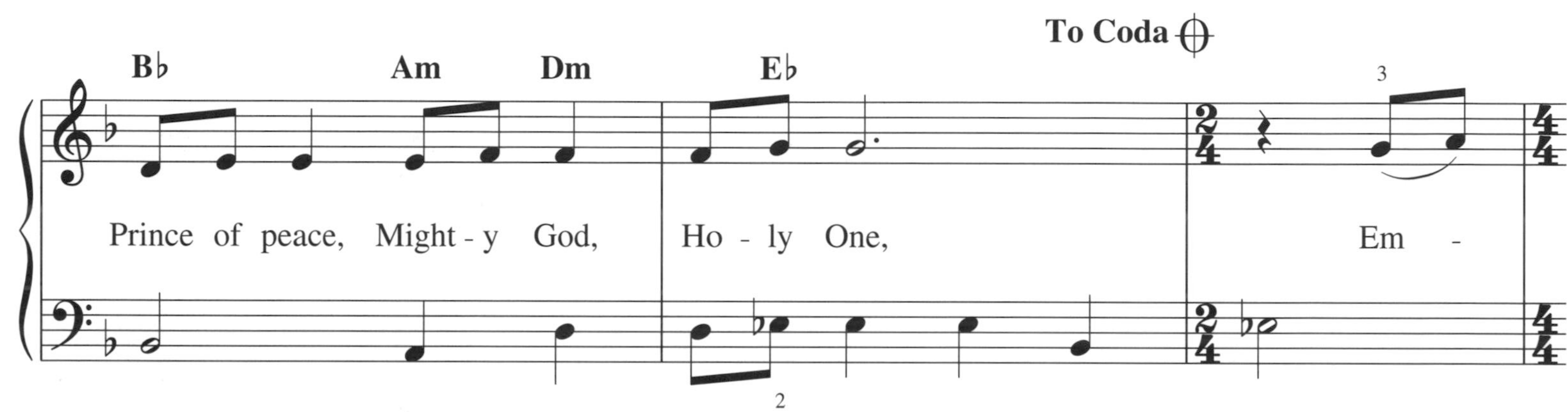
To Coda
B♭
Am
Dm
E♭
Prince of peace, Might - y God, Ho - ly One, Em -

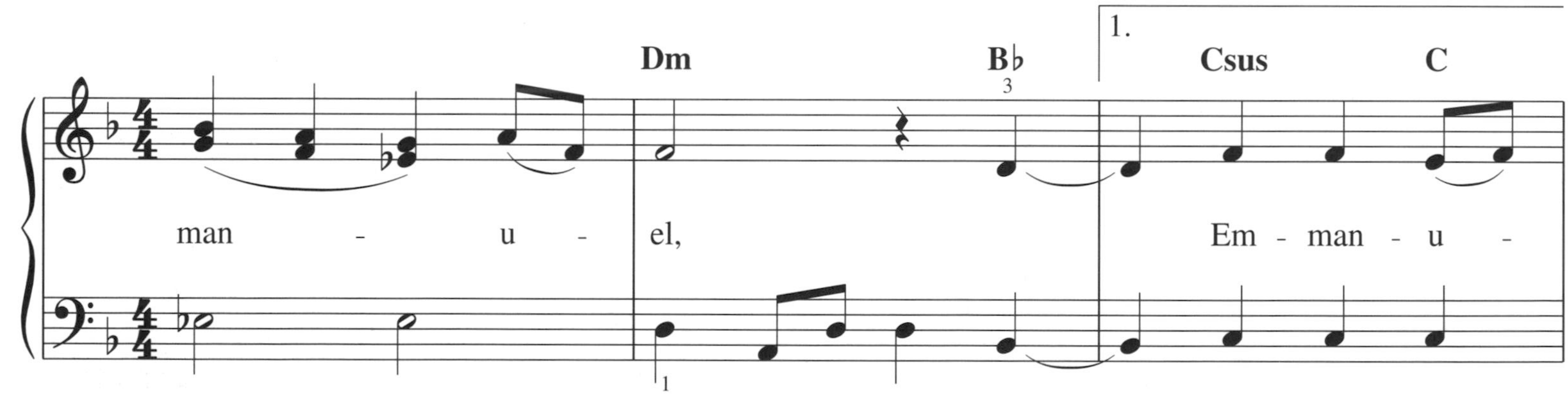
1.
Dm
B♭
Csus
C
man - u - el, Em - man - u -

2.
F
Csus
D♭
el. Em - Em - man - u - el.

D.S. al Coda
C7sus
B♭m
C7sus
C
F
Em -

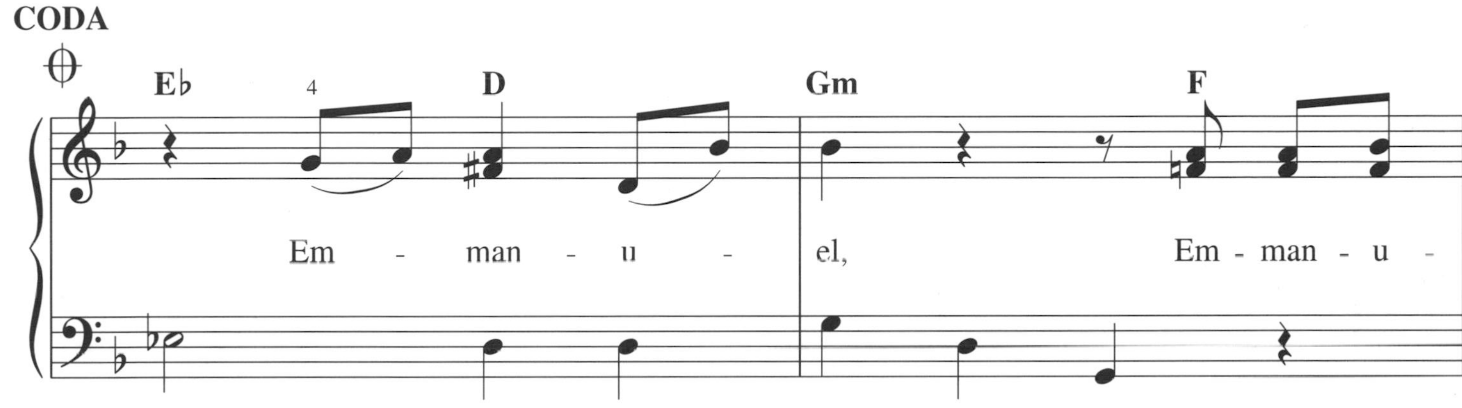
CODA
E♭
D
Gm
F
Em - man - u - el,
Em - man - u -

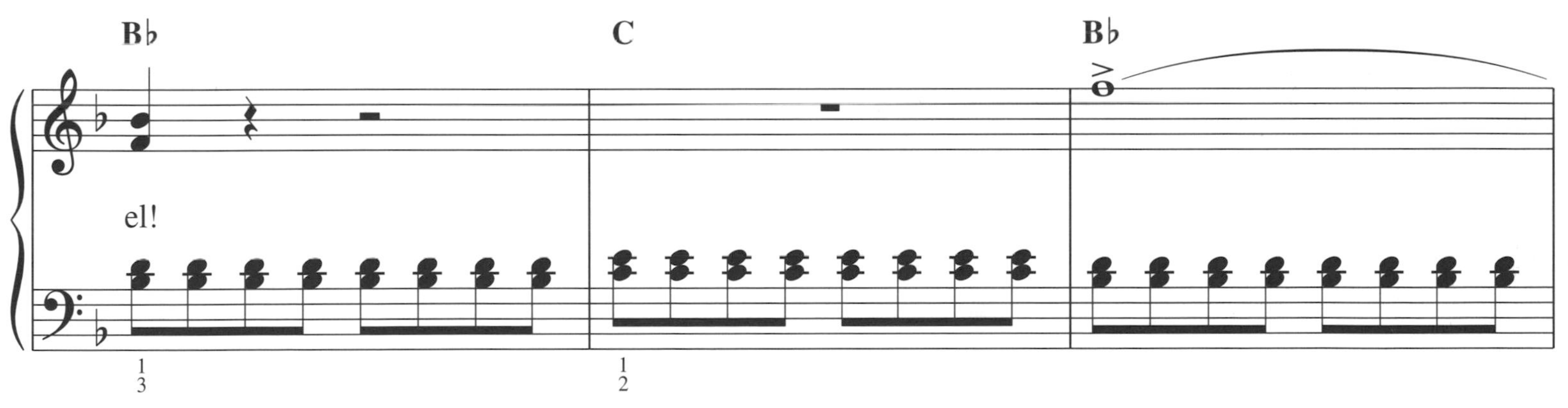
B♭
C
B♭
el!

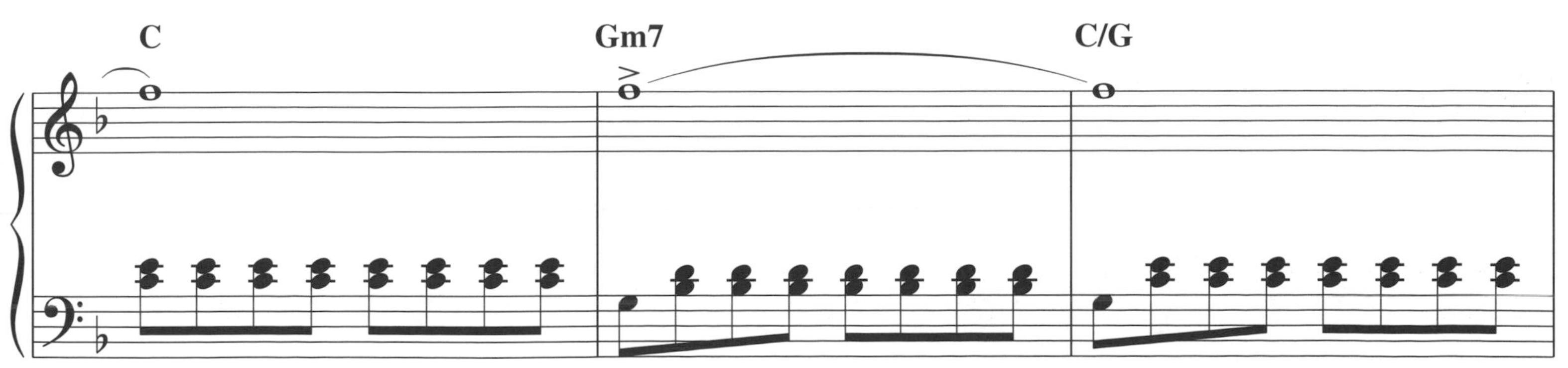
C
Gm7
C/G

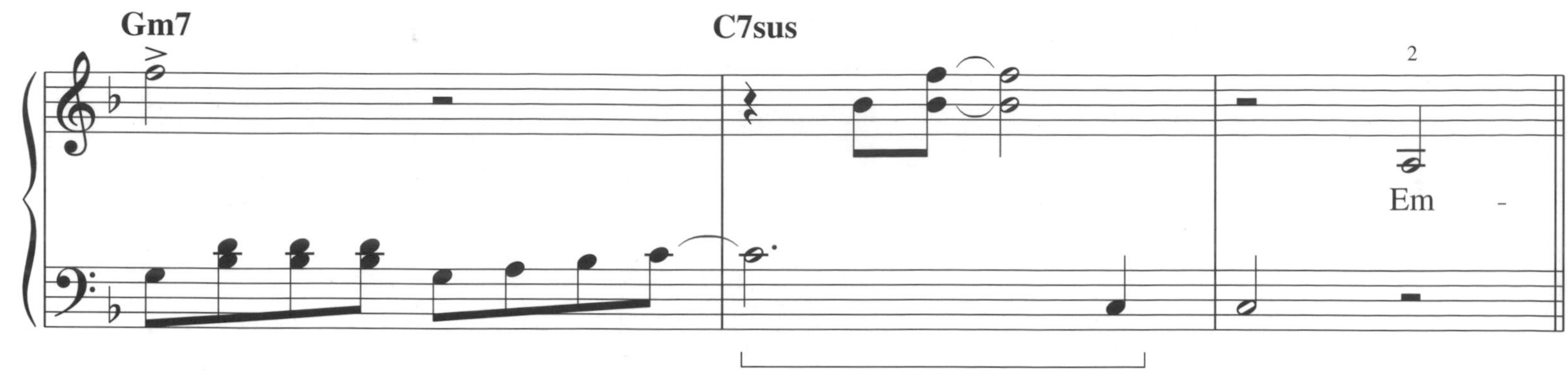
Gm7
C7sus
2
Em -

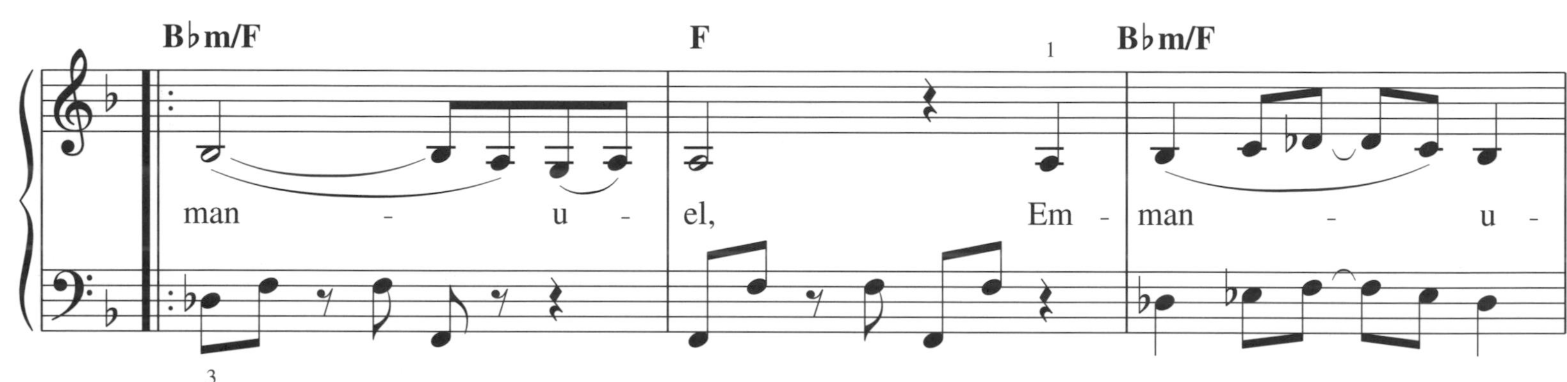
B♭m/F
F
1
B♭m/F
man - u - el, Em - man - u -
3

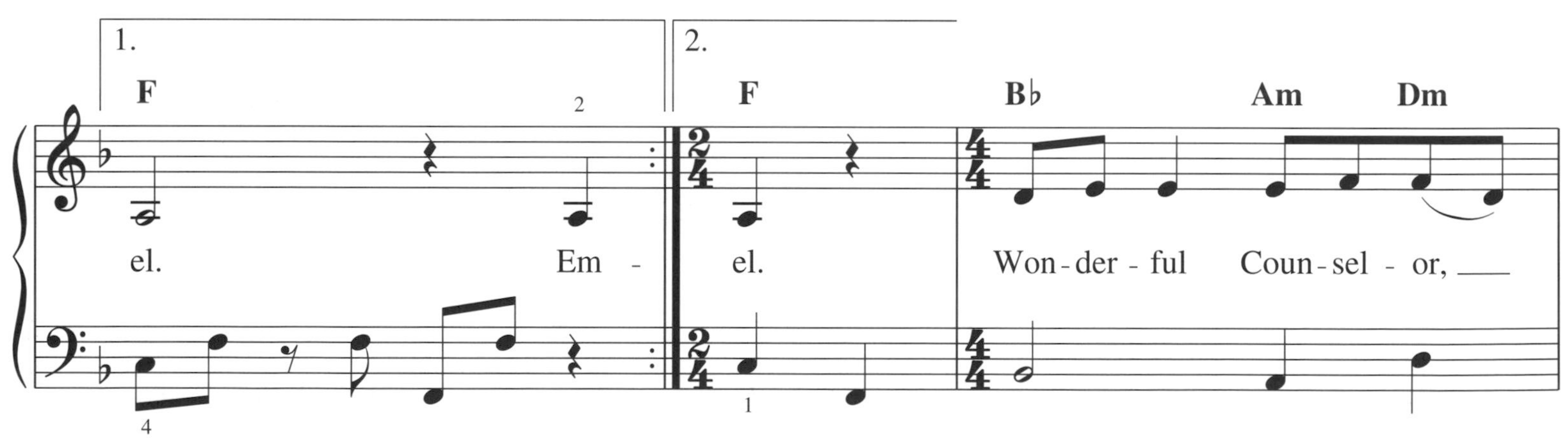
1.
2.
F
2
F
B♭
Am
Dm
el. Em - el.
Won - der - ful Coun - sel - or,
4
1

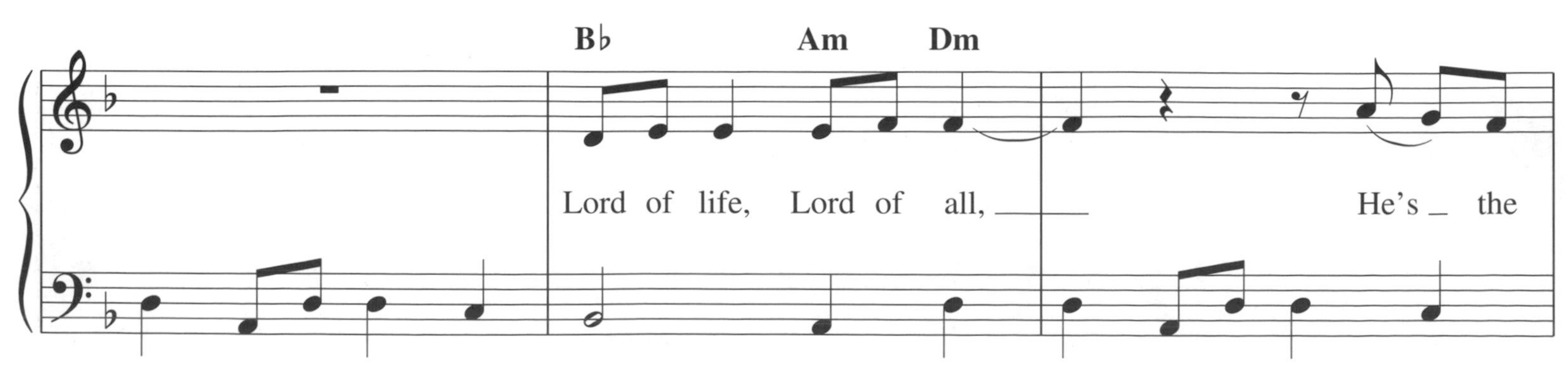
B♭
Am
Dm
Lord of life, Lord of all,
He's the

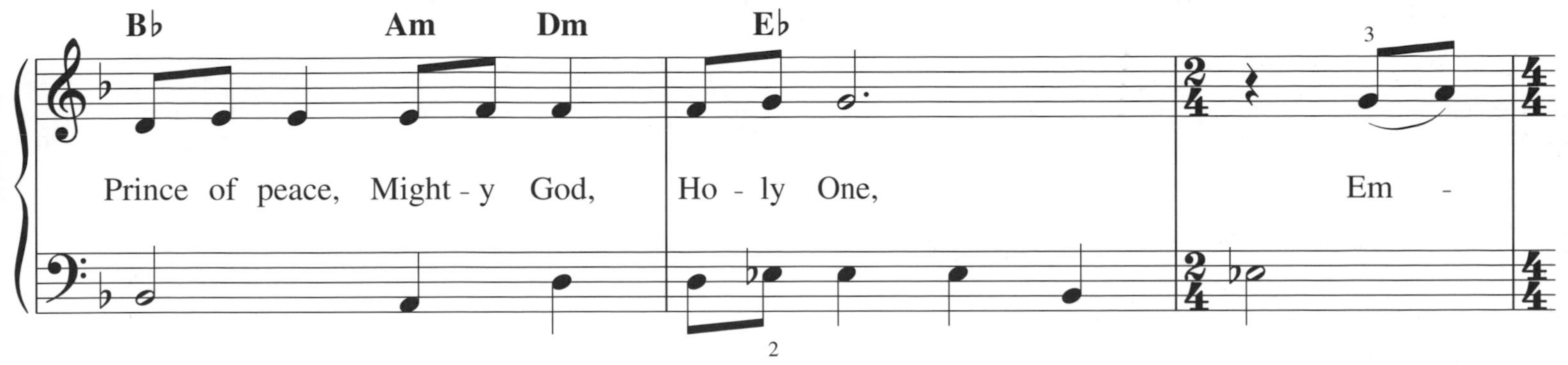
B♭
Am
Dm
E♭
Prince of peace, Might - y God, Ho - ly One, Em -

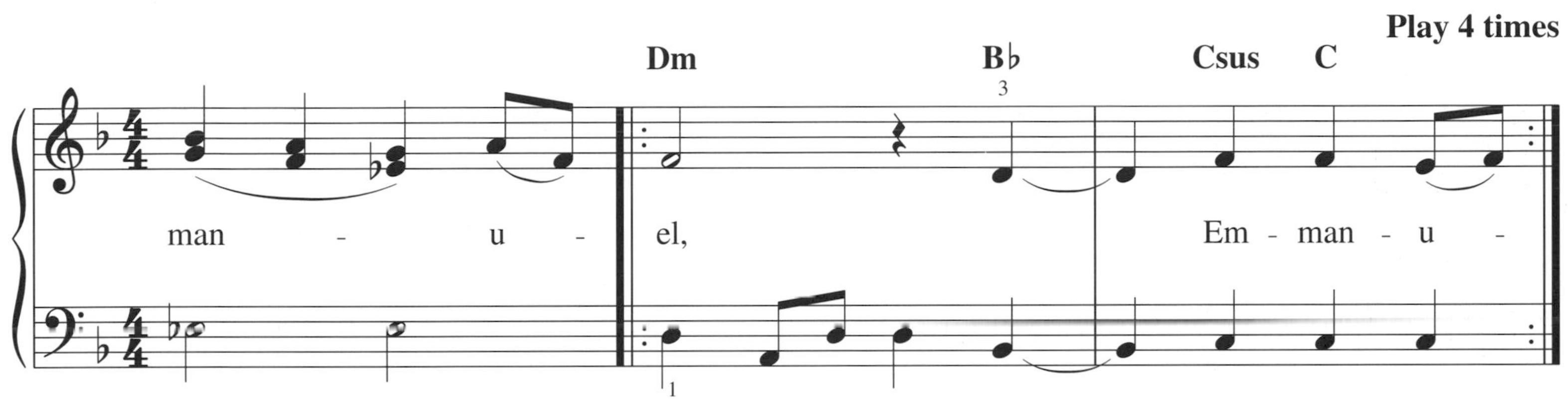
Play 4 times
Dm
B♭
Csus
C
man - u - el, Em - man - u -

B♭m/F
F
B♭m/F
el. Em - man - u -

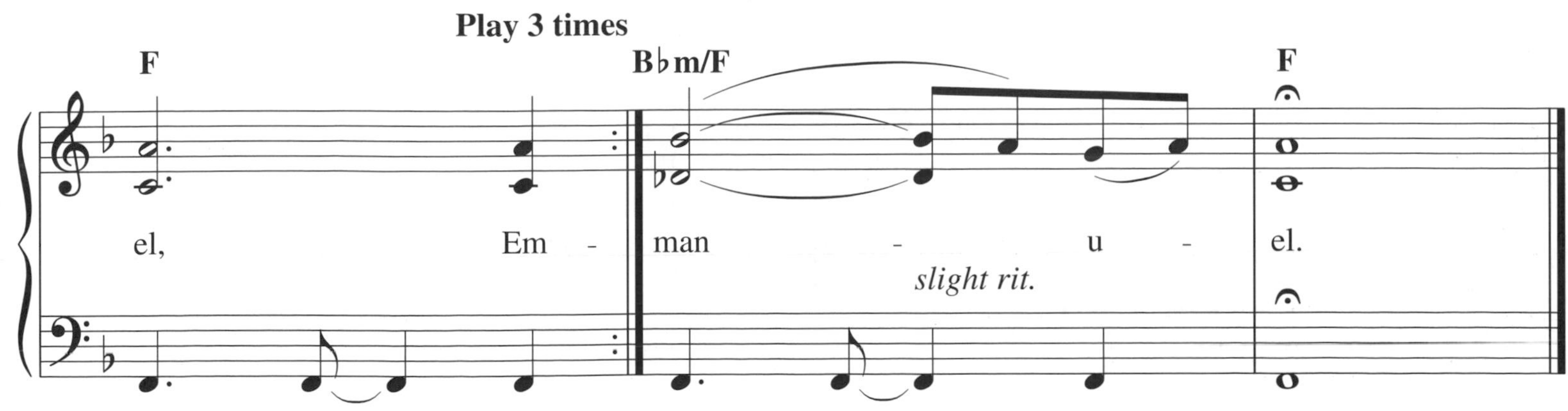
Play 3 times
F
B♭m/F
F
el, Em - man - u - el.
slight rit.

DO YOU HEAR WHAT I HEAR

Words and Music by NOEL REGNEY
and GLORIA SHAYNE

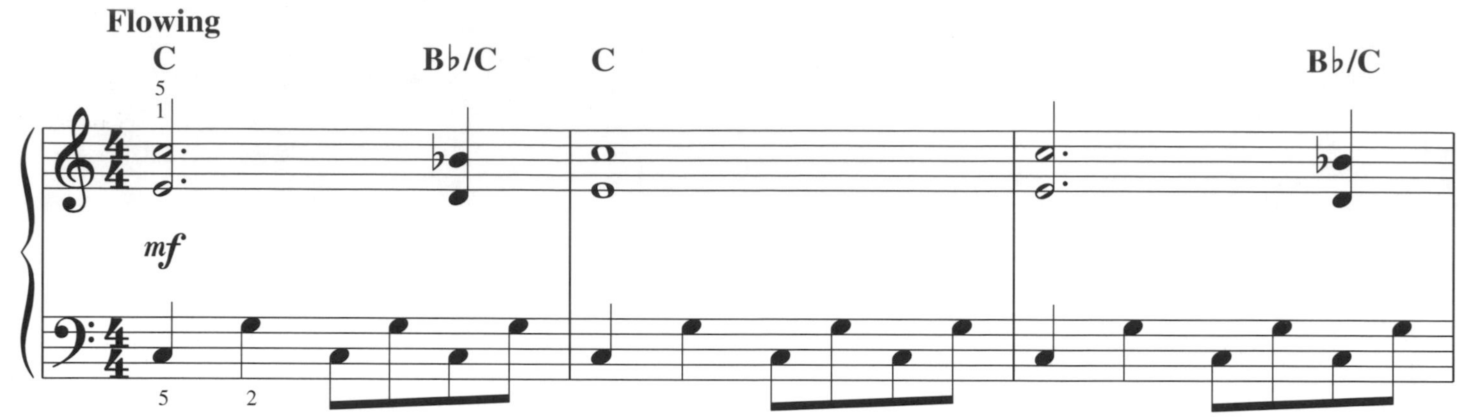

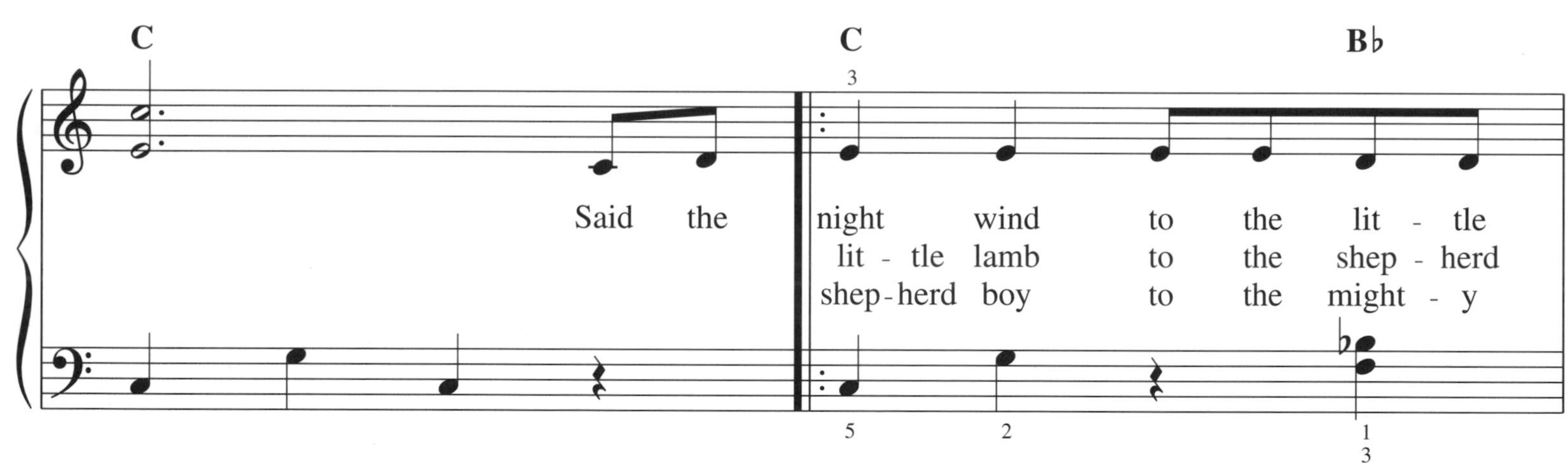

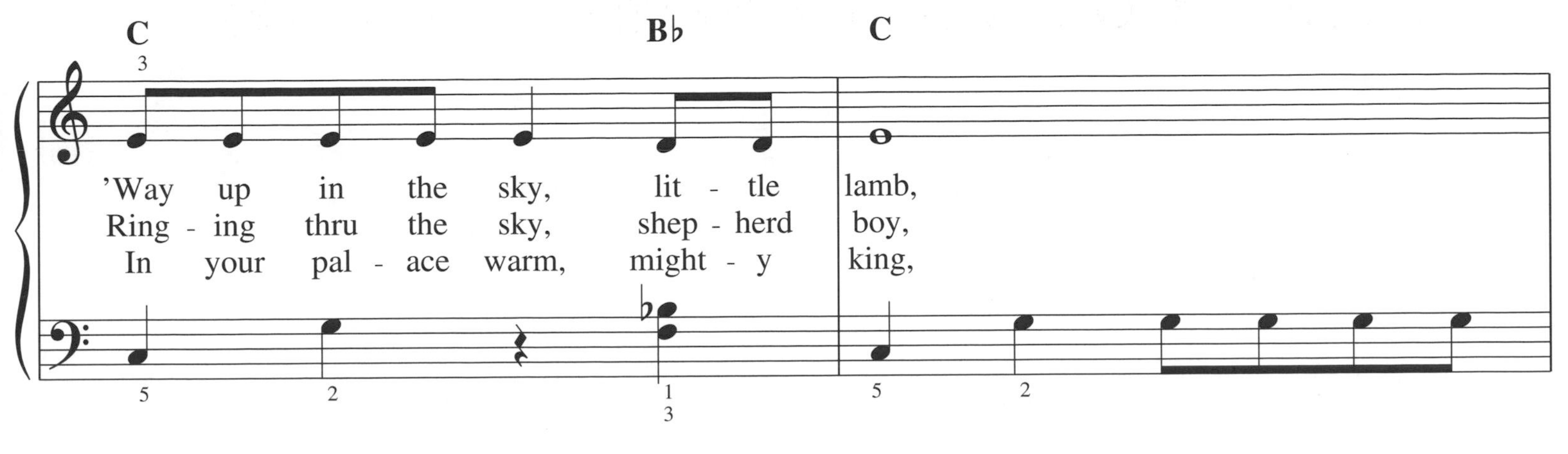
C
B♭
C
'Way up in the sky, lit - tle lamb,
Ring - ing thru the sky, shep - herd boy,
In your pal - ace warm, might - y king,

G F G C G F G
Do you see what I see?
Do you hear what I hear?
Do you know what I know?
A
A
A

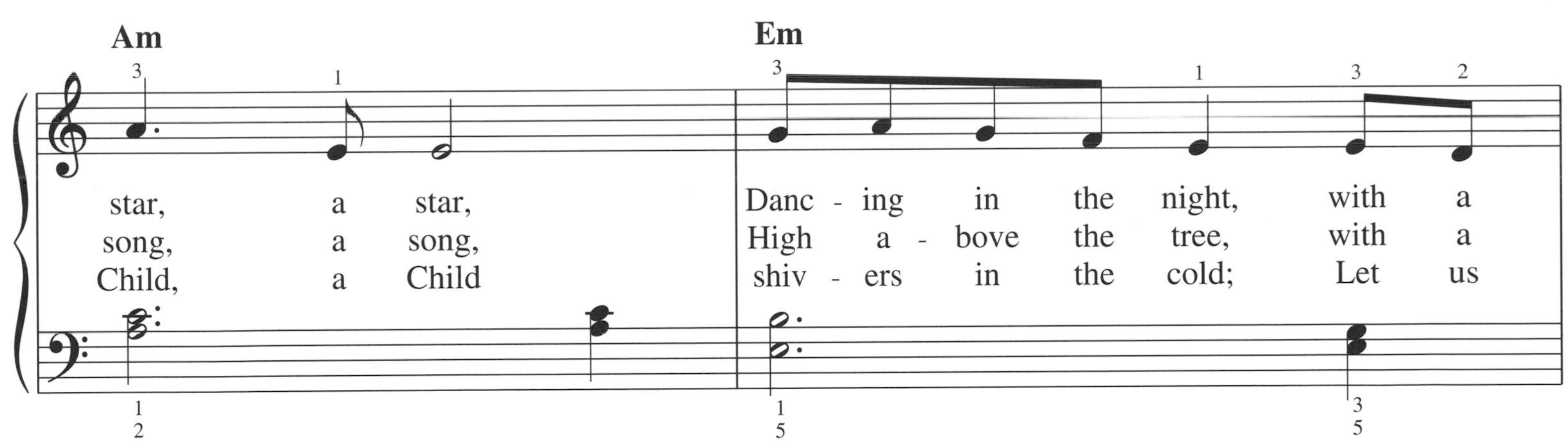
Am
Em
star, a star, Danc - ing in the night, with a
song, a song, High a - bove the tree, with a
Child, a Child shiv - ers in the cold; Let us

F G F E Am
tail as big as a kite, With a
voice as big as the sea, With a
bring Him sil - ver and gold, Let us

F C/E Dm G C B♭
1.,2.
C
tail as big as a kite.
voice as big as the sea.
bring Him sil - ver and gold.
Said the
Said the
3.
C B♭ C
Said the king to the peo - ple ev - 'ry - where,
G F G C G F G C B♭
Lis - ten to what I say!
Pray for peace, peo - ple ev - 'ry -
C G F G C G F G
where,
Lis - ten to what I say!
The

Am
Em
Child, The Child, sleep - ing in the night, He will
F
G
F
E
Am
bring us good - ness and light, He will
F
C/E
Dm
G
G7
C
B♭/C
bring us good - ness and light.
C
B♭/C
C
rall.

THE FIRST CHANUKAH NIGHT

Words by ENID FUTTERMAN
Music by MICHAEL COHEN

Moderately fast

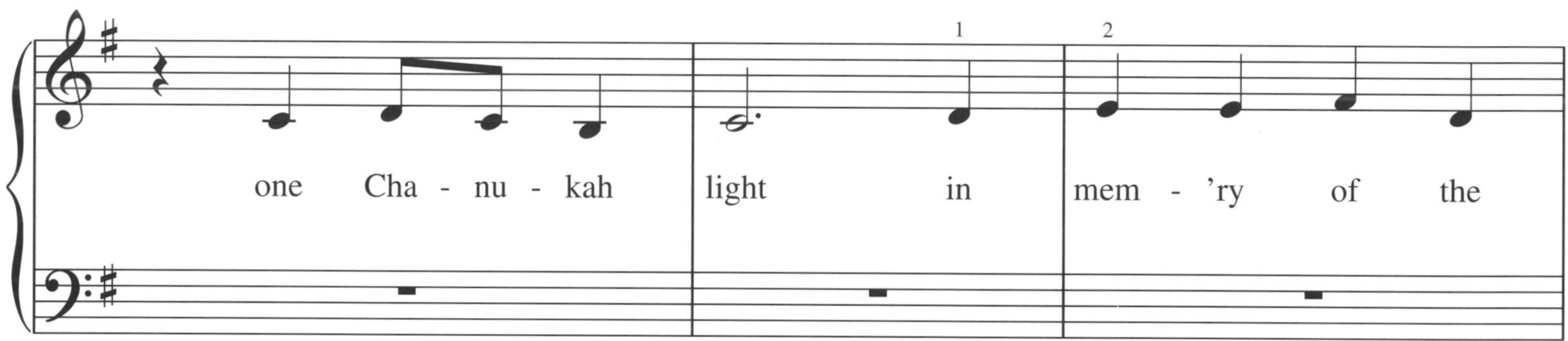

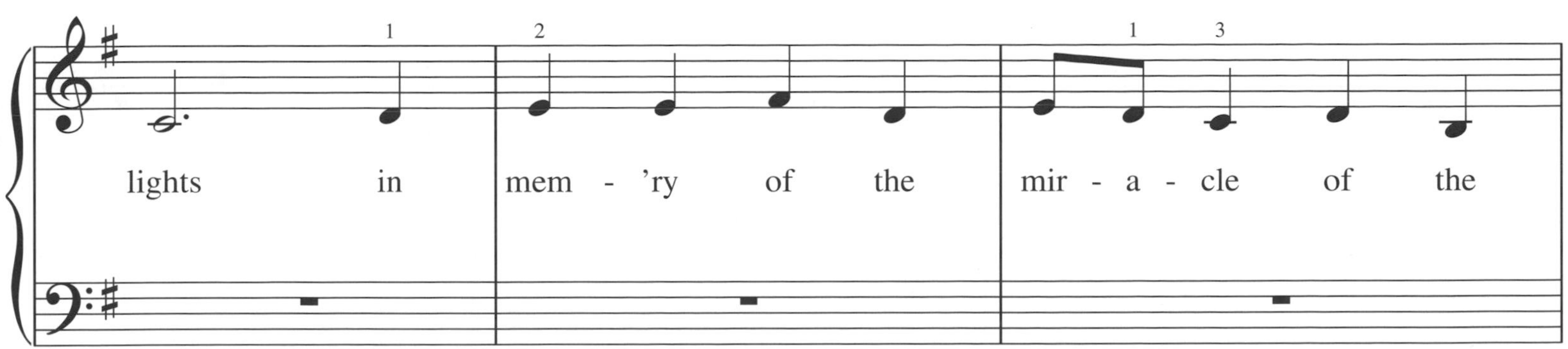
1
2
1 3
lights in mem - 'ry of the mir - a - cle of the

Em
4 1 2
3 1 4
sec - ond Cha - nu - kah night. On the third Cha - nu - kah
5 1

B7
night we light three Cha - nu - kah lights in
(On the fourth Cha - nu - kah night we light

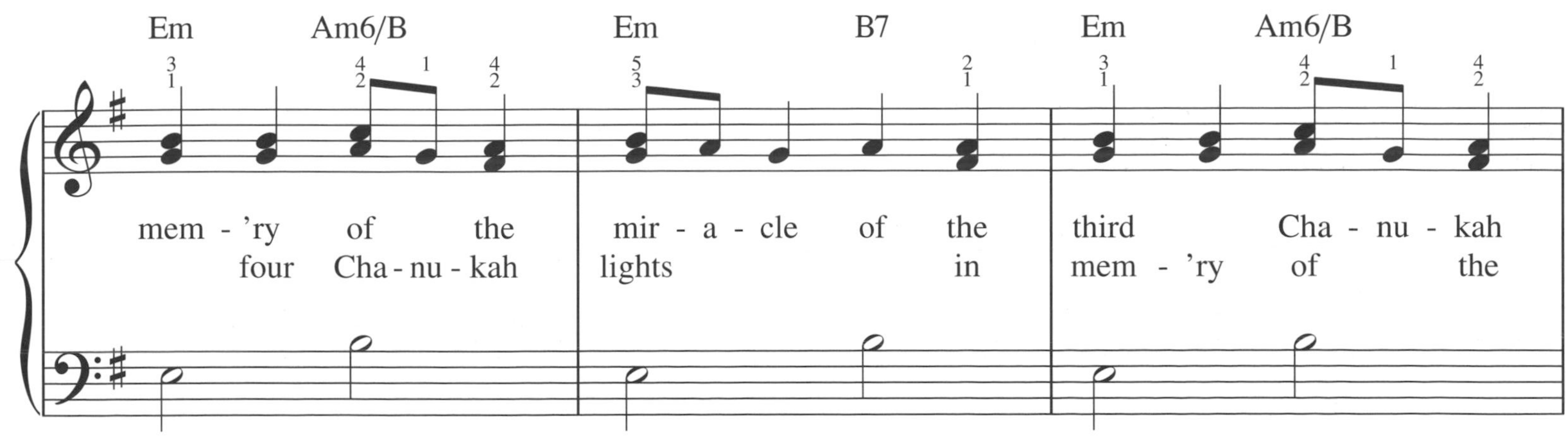
Em Am6/B Em B7 Em Am6/B
mem - 'ry of the mir - a - cle of the third Cha - nu - kah
four Cha - nu - kah lights in mem - 'ry of the

Em
Am6/B
Em
B7
Em
Am/E
E7/G♯
night.
On the
mir - a - cle of the fourth Cha - nu - kah night.)

Am
Am/E
D7
G
fifth Cha - nu - kah night we light five Cha - nu - kah

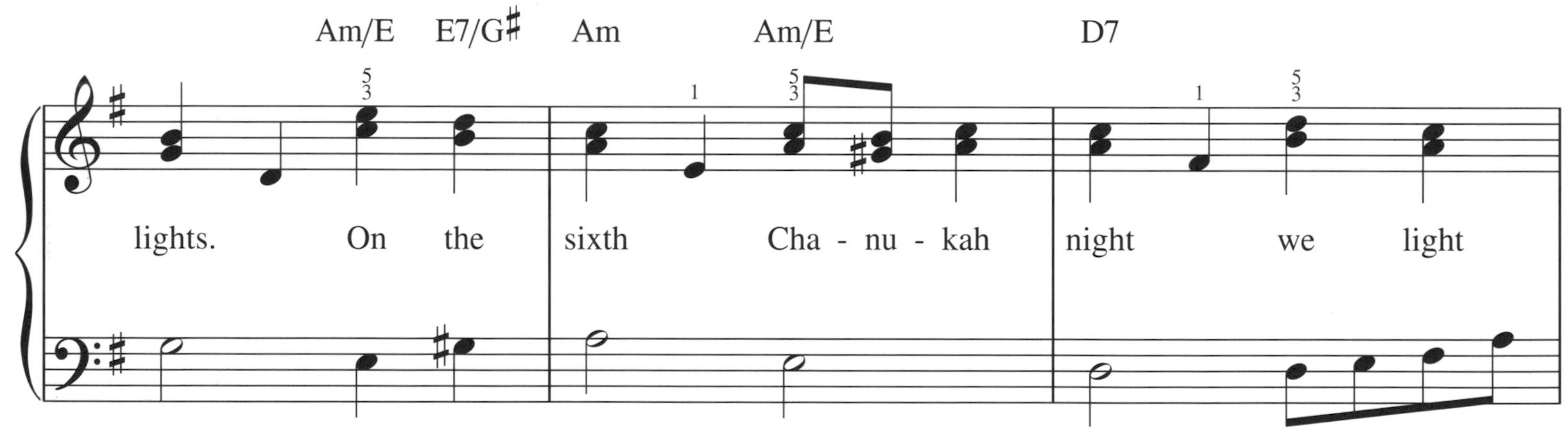
Am/E
E7/G♯
Am
Am/E
D7
lights. On the sixth Cha - nu - kah night we light

G
F
six Cha - nu - kah lights. We will sur - vive we're

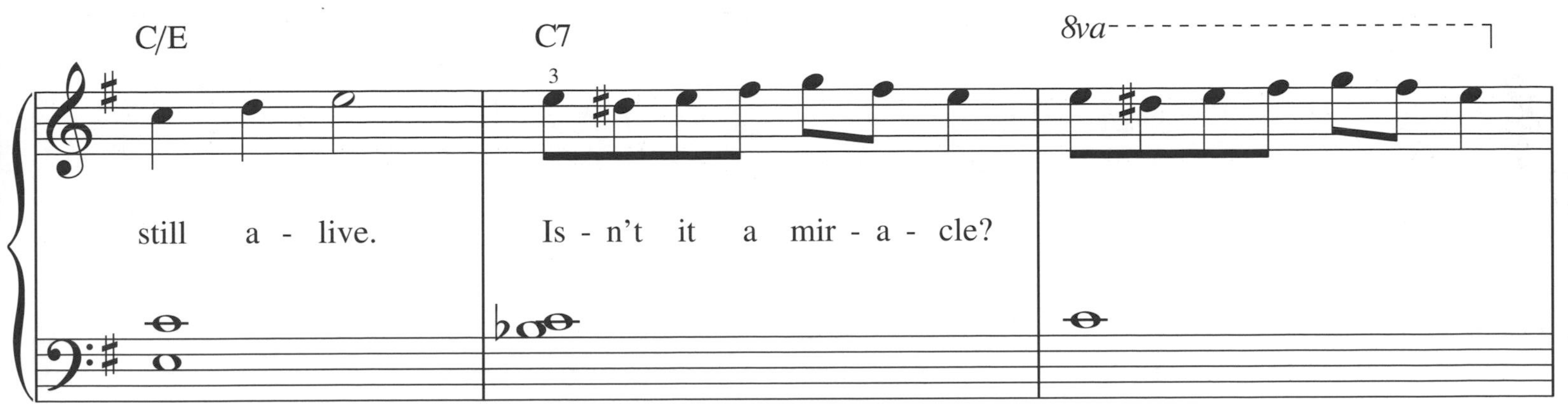
C/E
C7
8va
still a - live.
Is - n't it a mir - a - cle?

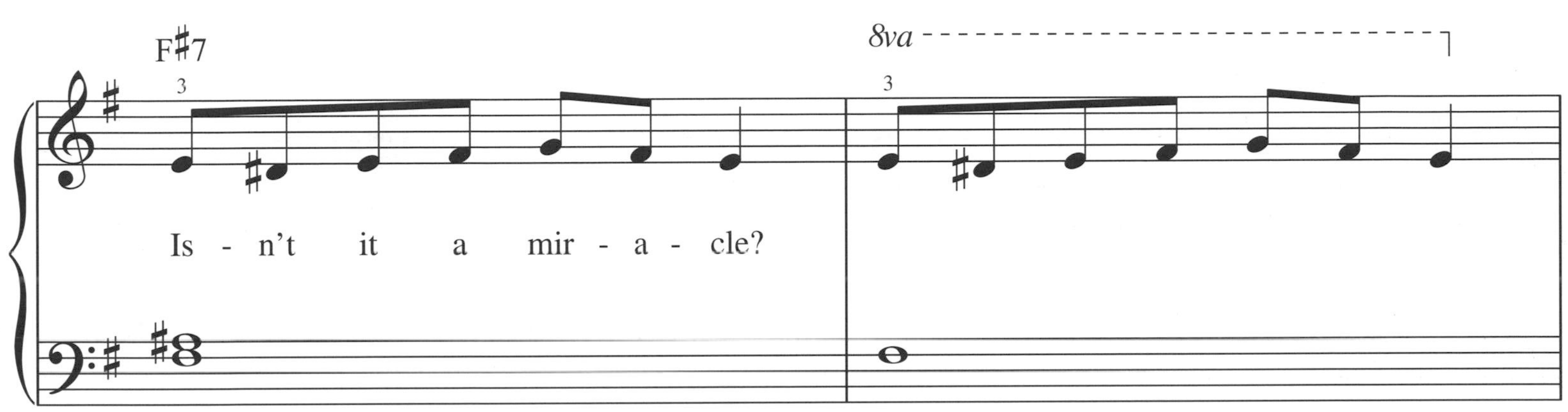
F♯7
8va
Is - n't it a mir - a - cle?

B7
Em
Is - n't it a mir - a - cle?
On the
sev - enth Cha - nu - kah

night we light
sev - en Cha - nu - kah
lights.

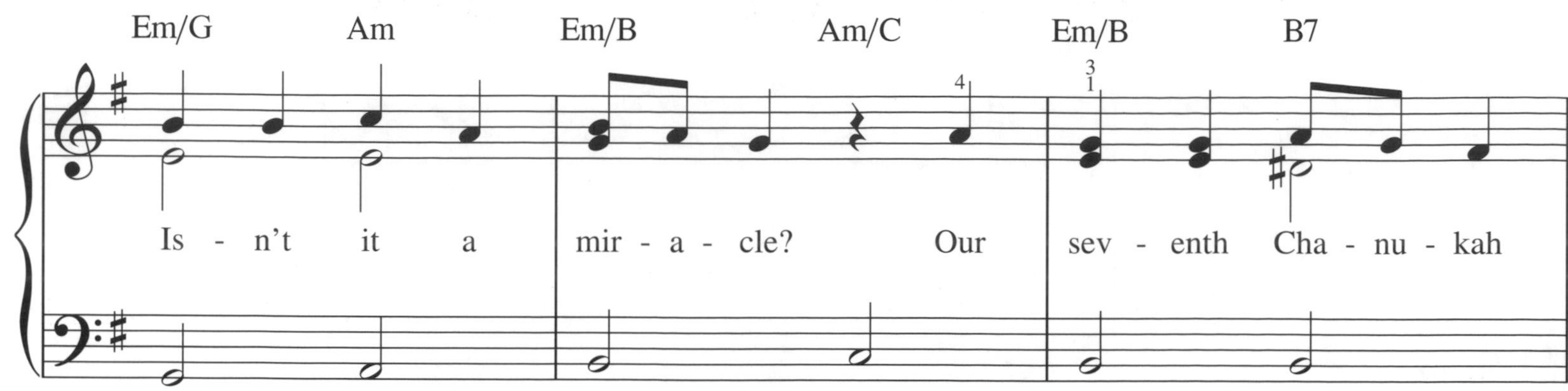
Em/G
Am
Em/B
Am/C
Em/B
B7
Is - n't it a mir - a - cle? Our sev - enth Cha - nu - kah

Em
Em/B
Em
B7
Em
night. On the eighth Cha - nu - kah night we light

Em/G
Am
eight Cha - nu - kah lights in mem - 'ry of the

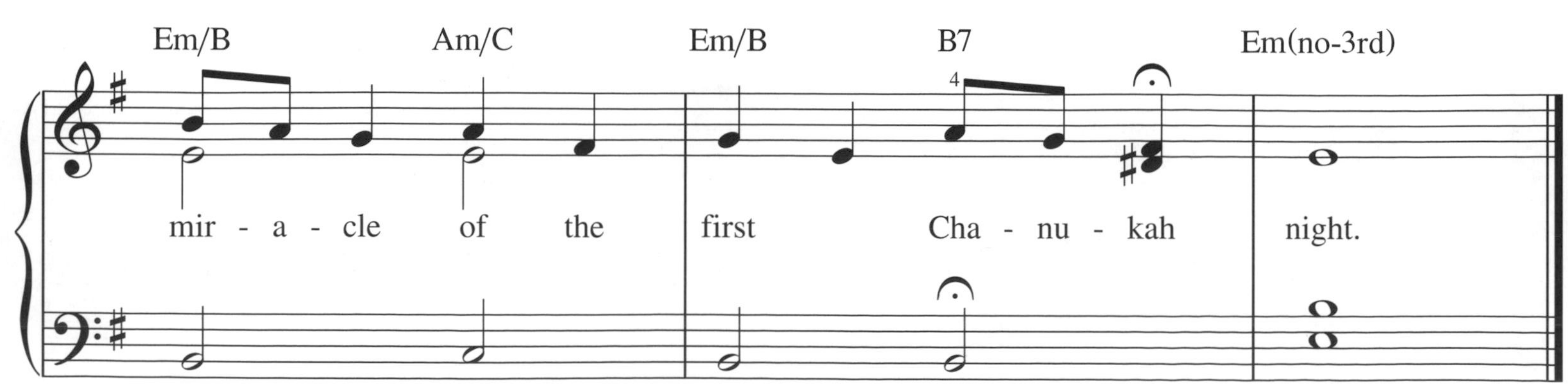
Em/B
Am/C
Em/B
B7
Em(no-3rd)
mir - a - cle of the first Cha - nu - kah night.

FIRST DAY OF THE SON

Words and Music by
DERRICK PROCELL

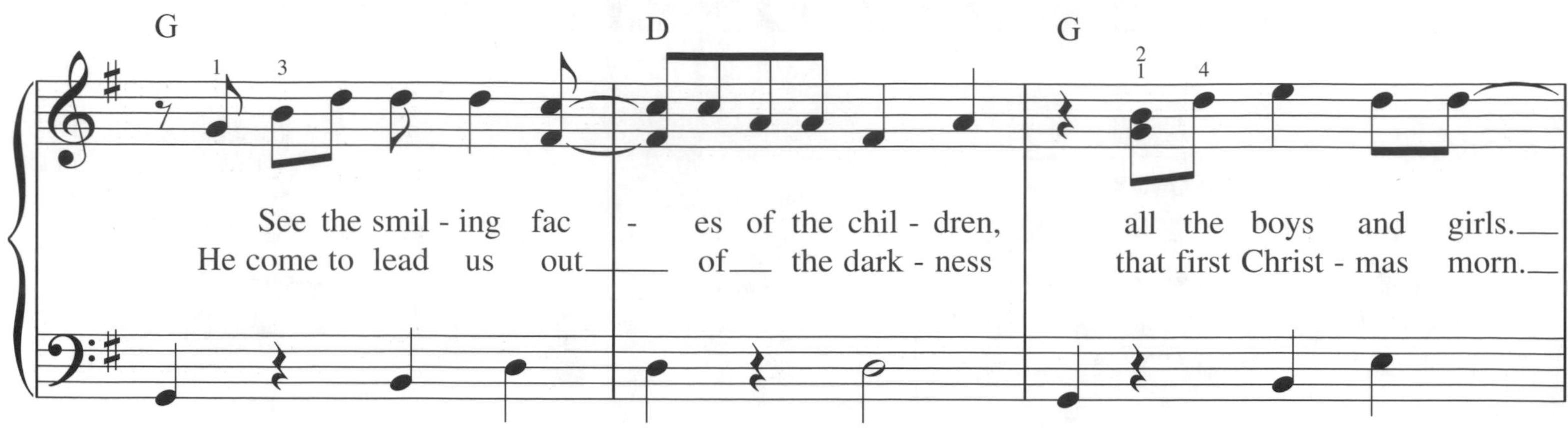
G
D
G
See the smil - ing fac - es of the chil - dren,
He come to lead us out of the dark - ness
all the boys and girls.
that first Christ - mas morn.

Cmaj9
Gmaj9
And e - ven in the dark - est cor - ner
So let Him fill your heart with glad - ness;

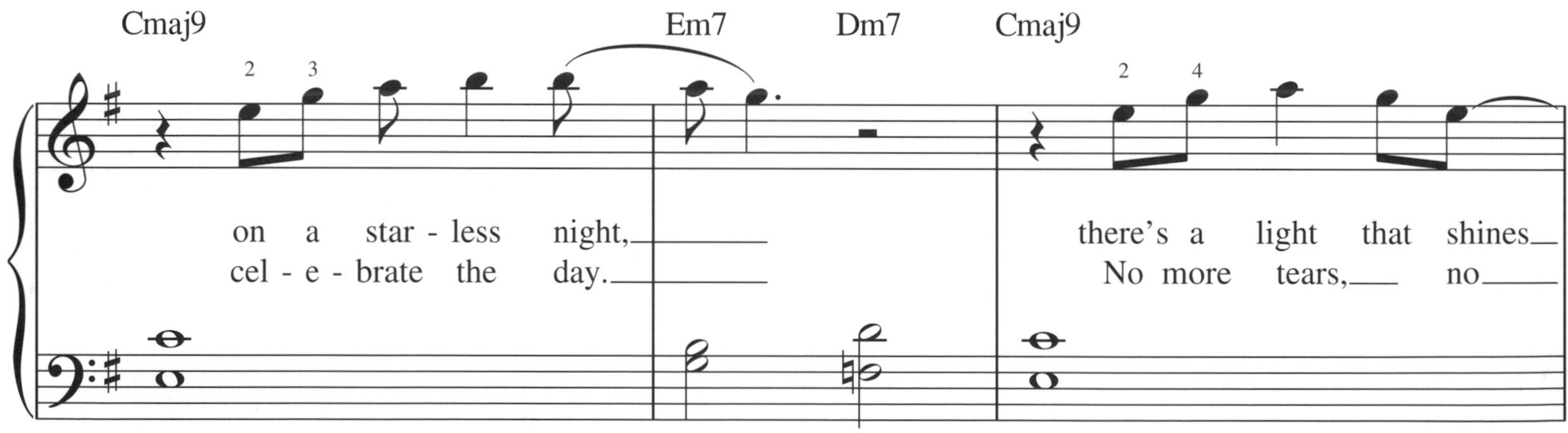
Cmaj9
Em7
Dm7
Cmaj9
on a star - less night,
cel - e - brate the day.
there's a light that shines
No more tears, no

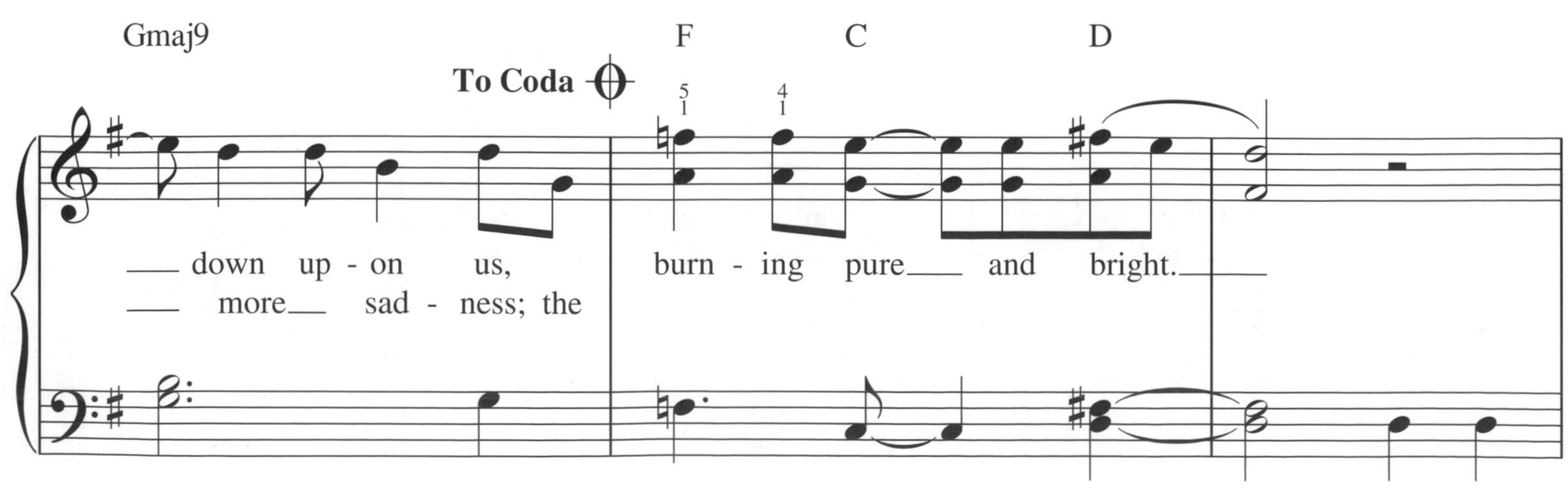
Gmaj9
To Coda
F
C
D
down up - on us,
more sad - ness; the
burn - ing pure and bright.

G
C
G
Christ - mas,
Christ - mas,
first day of the Son.
D
C
G
C
Christ - mas,
Christ - mas,
sun - ny
G
D
G
N.C.
G
days for ev - 'ry - one.
D
G
D
D.S. al Coda

CODA
F
C
D
Son is here to stay.
The
Son is here to stay.
G
C
Christ - mas,
Choir: (Christ - mas)
Christ - mas,
(Christ - mas)
G
D
C
G
first day of the Son.
Christ - mas,
(Christ - mas)
C
G
D
G
1.
Christ - mas,
sun - ny
(Christ - mas)
days for ev - 'ry - one.

Em
D/E
Em
Now's the time for all men to treat each oth - er like
D/E
Em
D/E
good friends. Peace on earth, mer - cy too!
C
C/D
D
C/D
D/E
Just wan - na say "Mer - ry Christ - mas" to you!
2.
D
G
N.C.
Sun - ny days for ev - 'ry - one.

FROSTY THE SNOW MAN

Words and Music by STEVE NELSON
and JACK ROLLINS

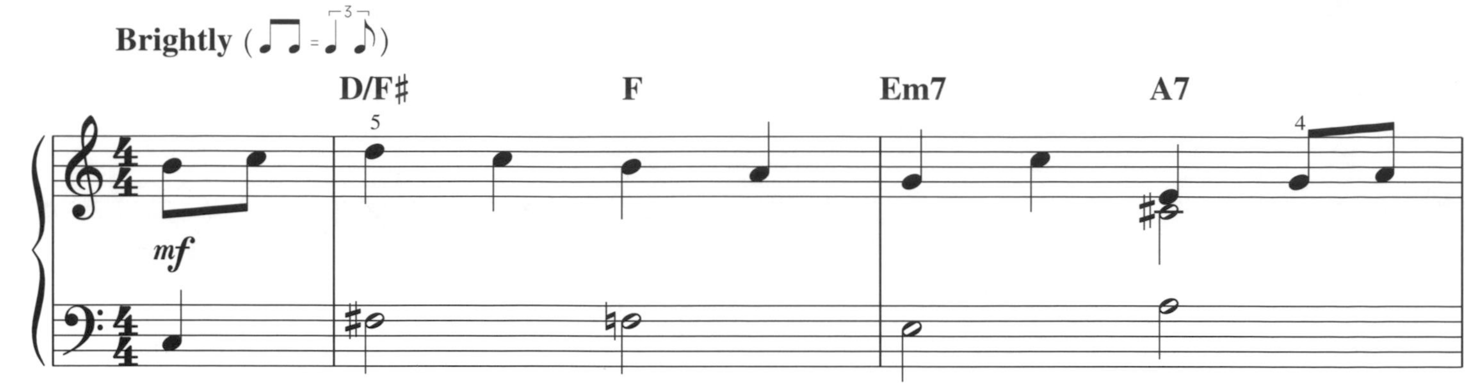

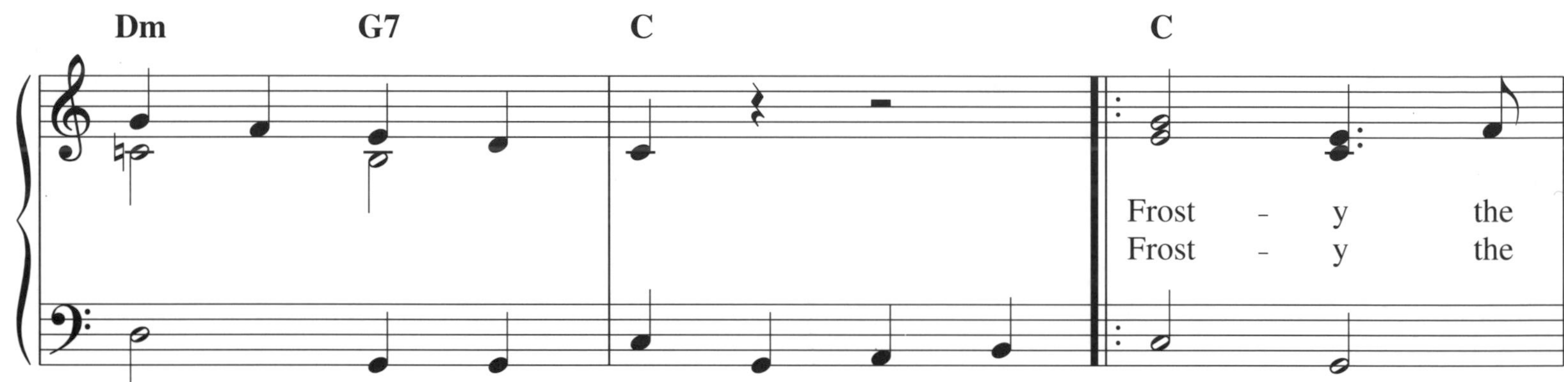

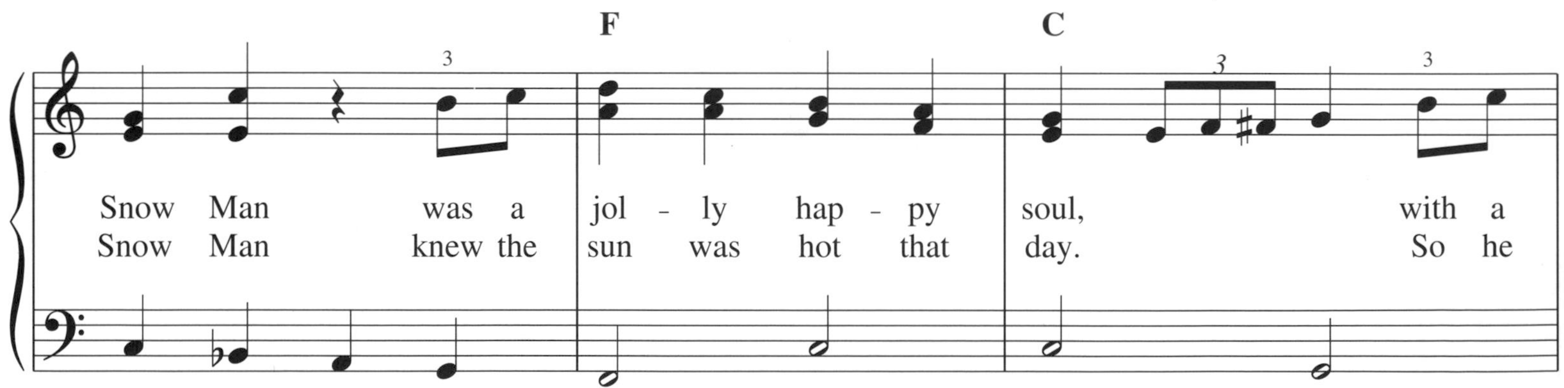

C
C7
coal.
way."
Frost - y the Snow Man is a
Down to the vil - lage with a

F
C
F
F♯dim7
fair - y tale they say; he was made of snow, but the
broom - stick in his hand, run - ning here and there all a -

C/G
A7
Dm
G7
C
chil - dren know how he came to life one day. There
round the square, say - in' "Catch me if you can." He

F/A
Fm/A♭
Em/G
A7/E
Dm7
G7
must have been some mag - ic in that old silk hat they
led them down the streets of town to the left and to the

C
G/D
found, for when they placed it on his head, he be -
right. He ran so fast he dis - ap - peared, yep,

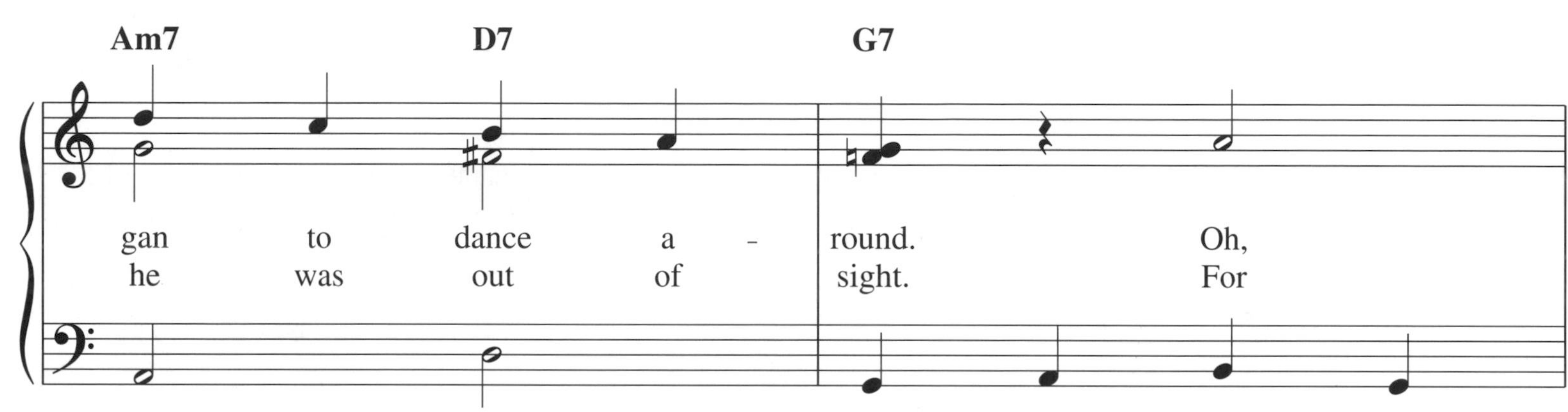
Am7
D7
G7
gan to dance a - round. Oh,
he was out of sight. For

C
C7
F
F♯dim7
Frost - y the Snow Man was a - live as he could
Frost - y the Snow Man had to hur - ry on his
1

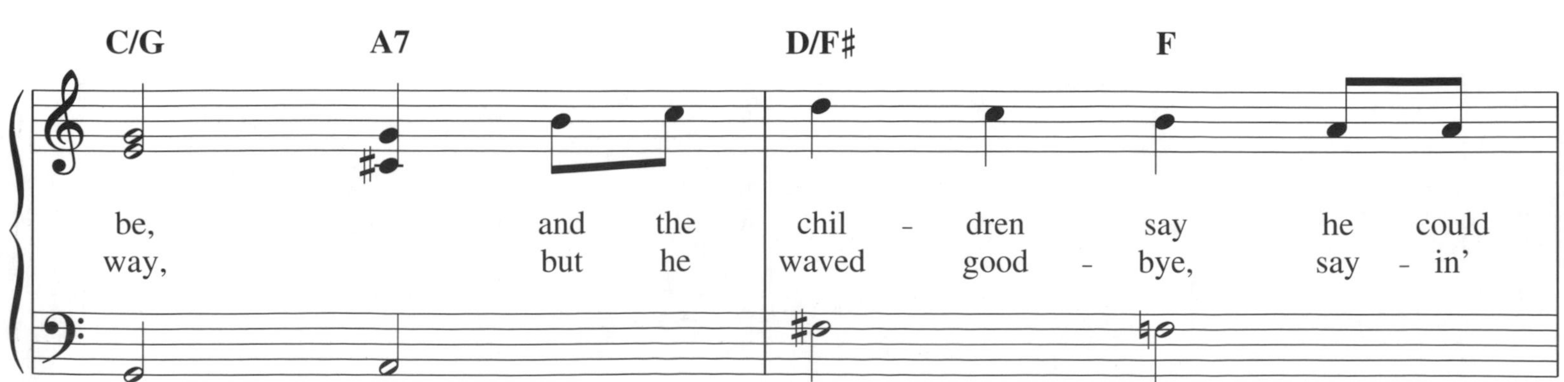
C/G
A7
D/F♯
F
be, and the chil - dren say he could
way, but he waved good - bye, say - in'

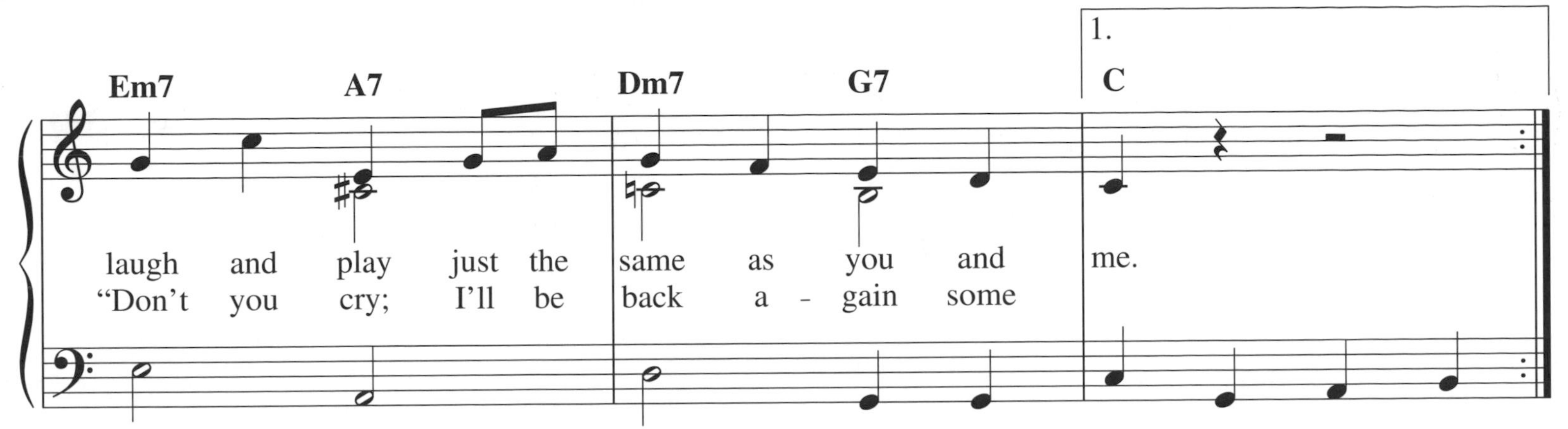
1.
Em7
A7
Dm7
G7
C
laugh and play just the same as you and me.
"Don't you cry; I'll be back a - gain some

2.
C
day."
Thump-e - ty thump thump thump-e - ty thump thump,
5 1 5 1

G7
look at frost - y go!
Thump-e - ty thump thump
4

C
thump-e - ty thump thump o - ver the hills of snow!

THE GIFT

Words and Music by TOM DOUGLAS
and JIM BRICKMAN

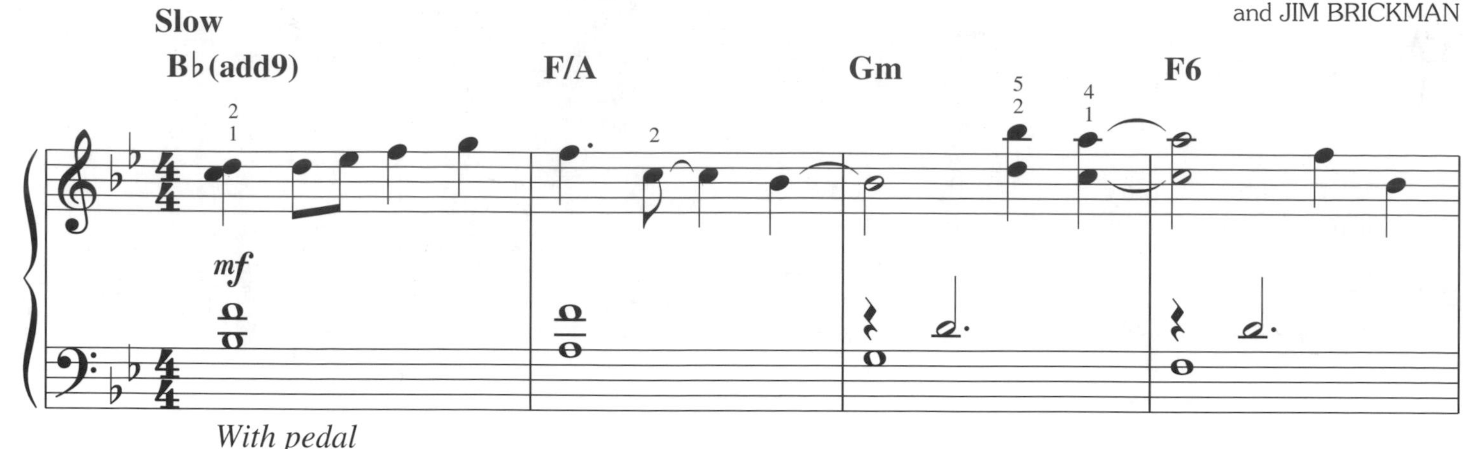

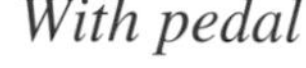

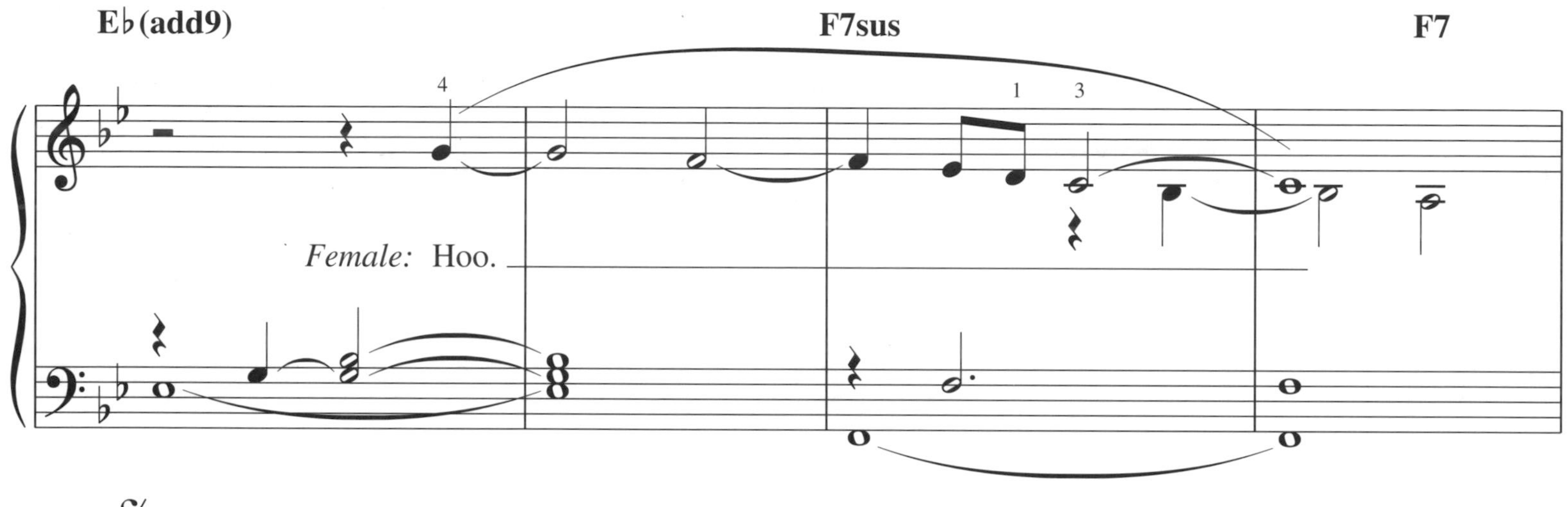

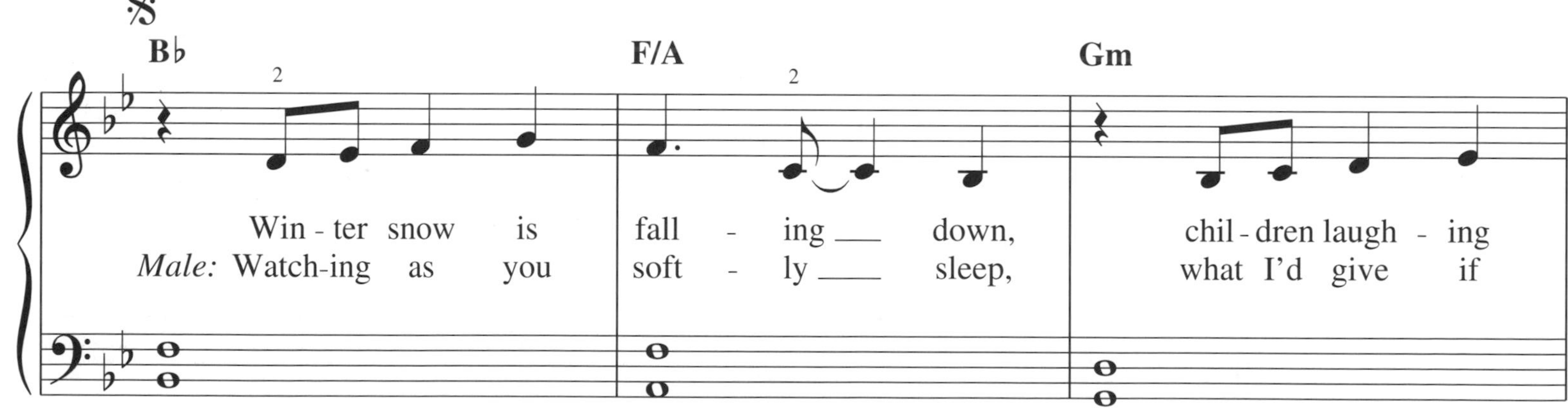

Cm7
Fsus
F
B♭
fair - y tale come true.
on - ly time stood still.
Sit - ting by the fire
But the col - ors fade

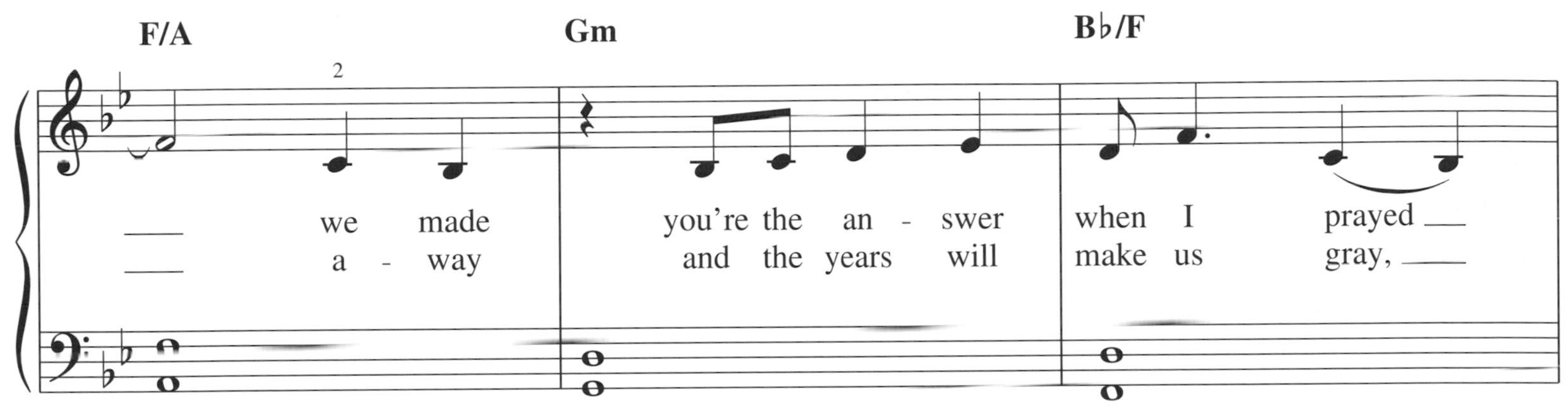
F/A
Gm
B♭/F
we made
a - way
you're the an - swer
and the years will
when I prayed
make us gray,

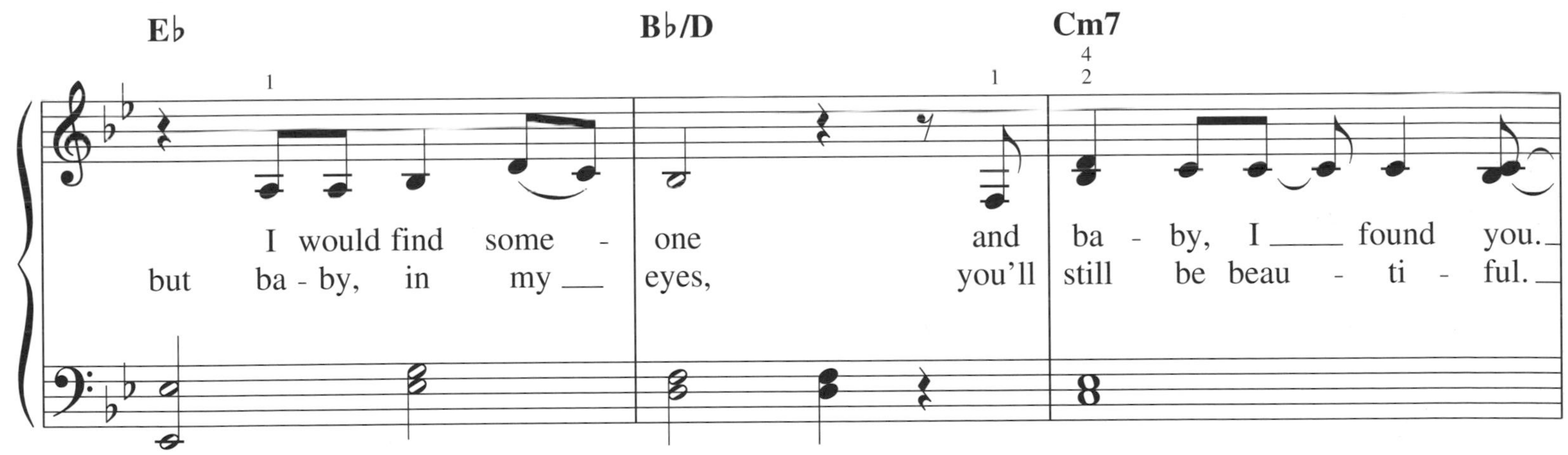
E♭
B♭/D
Cm7
I would find some - one
but ba - by, in my eyes,
and ba - by, I found you.
you'll still be beau - ti - ful.

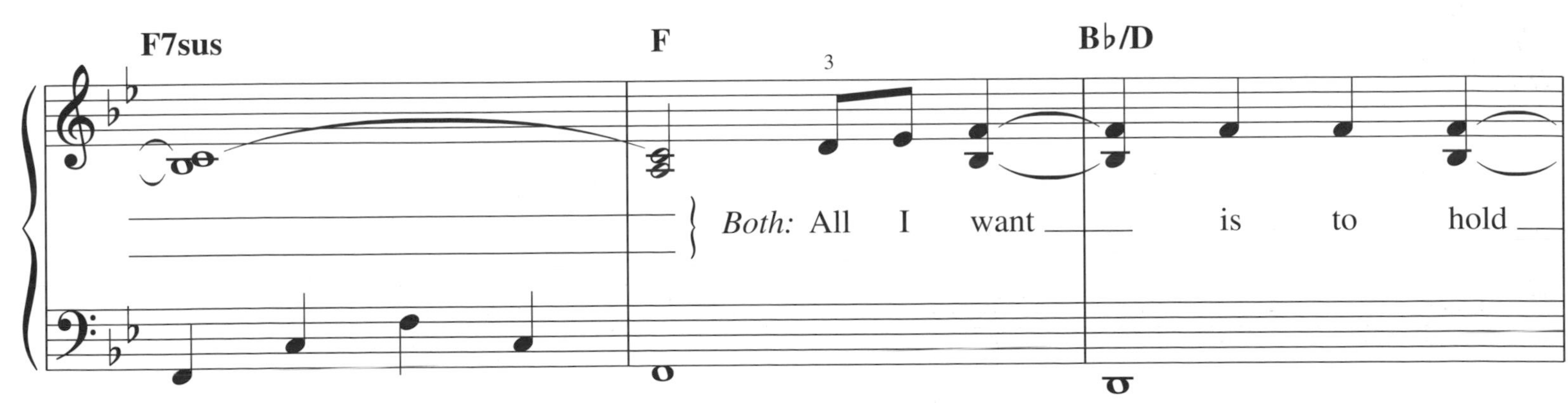
F7sus
F
B♭/D
Both: All I want is to hold

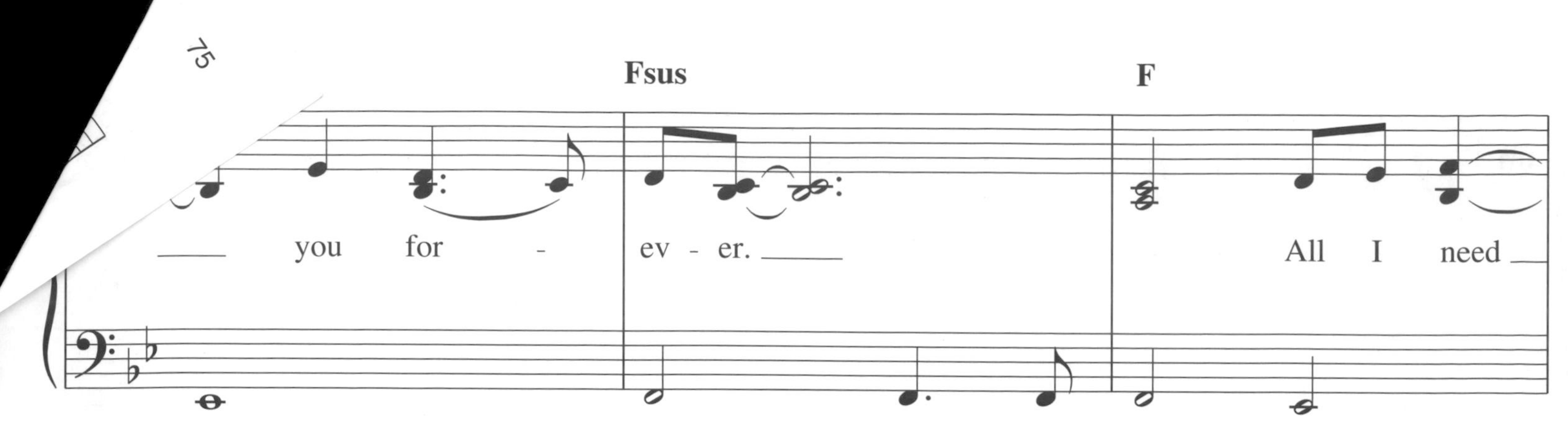
75
Fsus
F
you for - ev - er.
All I need
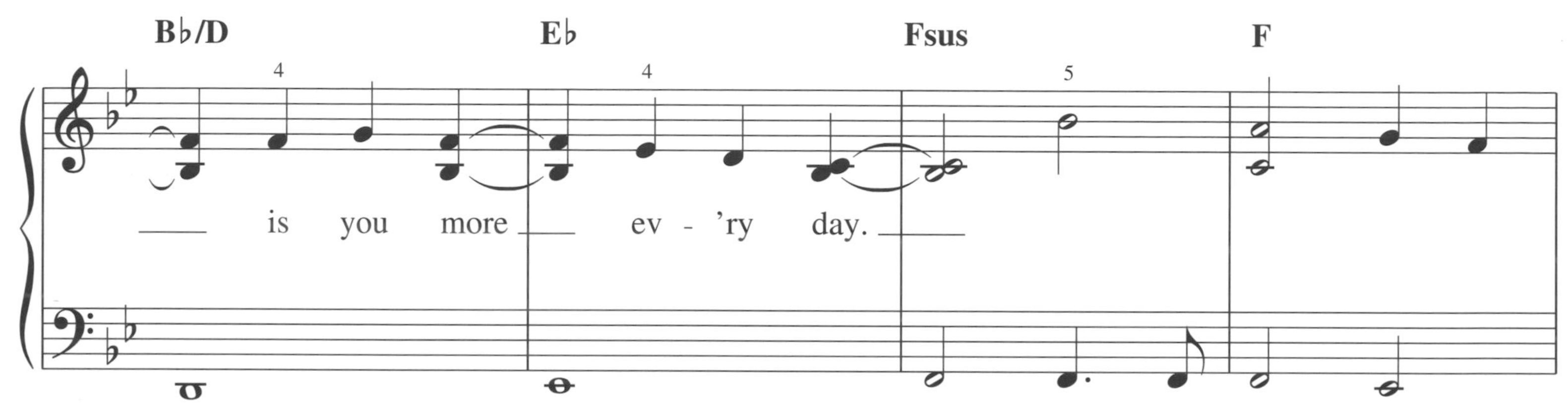
B♭/D
E♭
Fsus
F
is you more ev - 'ry day.
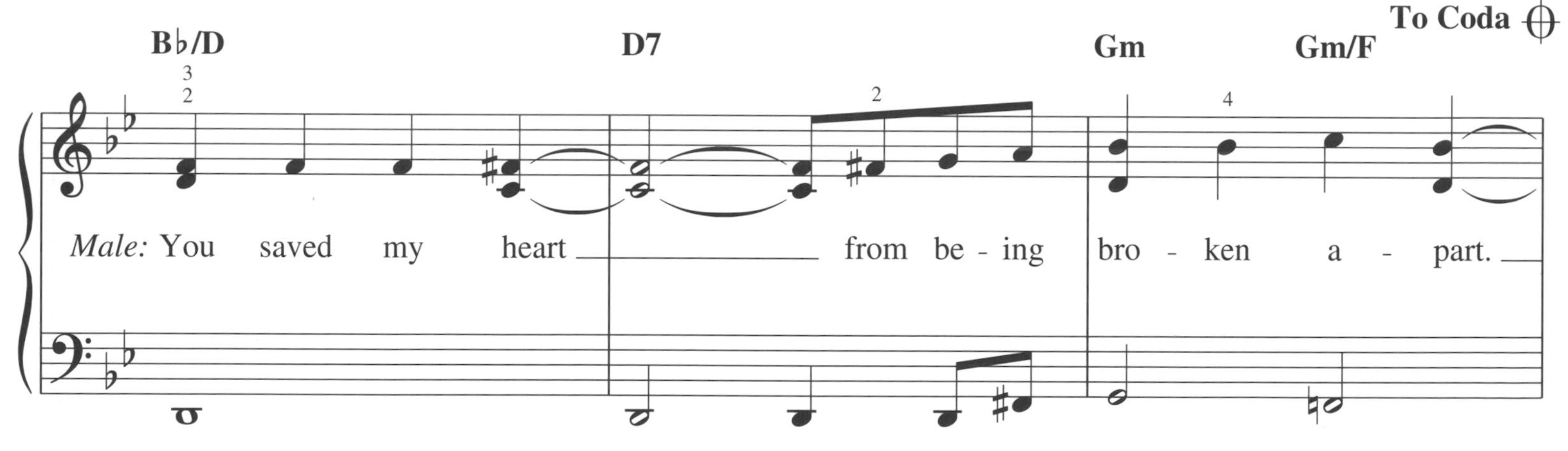
B♭/D
D7
Gm
Gm/F
To Coda
Male: You saved my heart from be - ing bro - ken a - part.
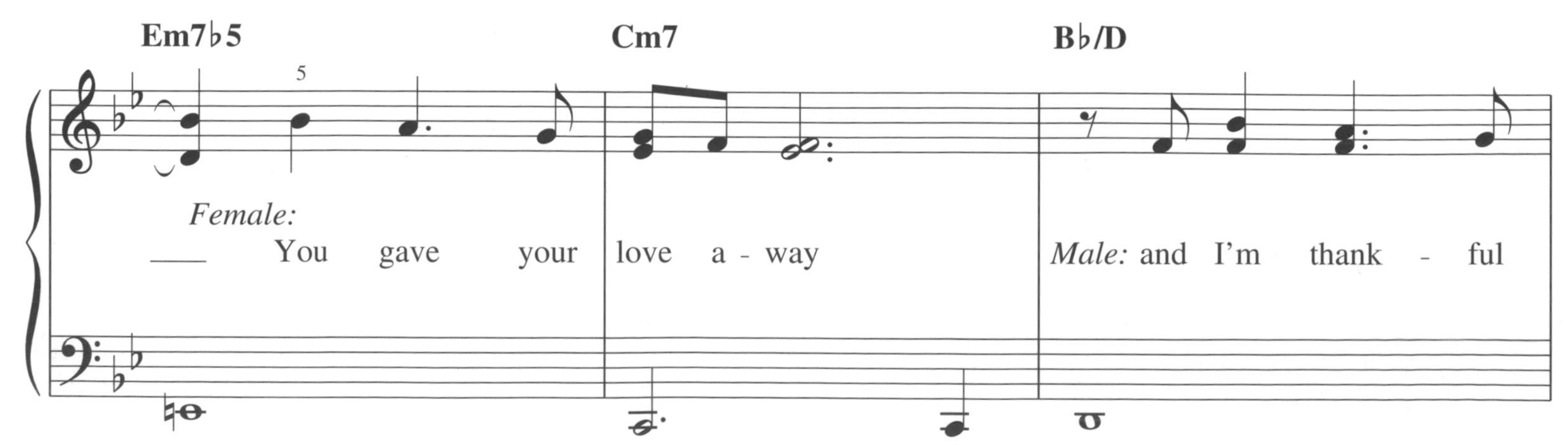
Em7♭5
Cm7
B♭/D
Female:
You gave your love a - way
Male: and I'm thank - ful

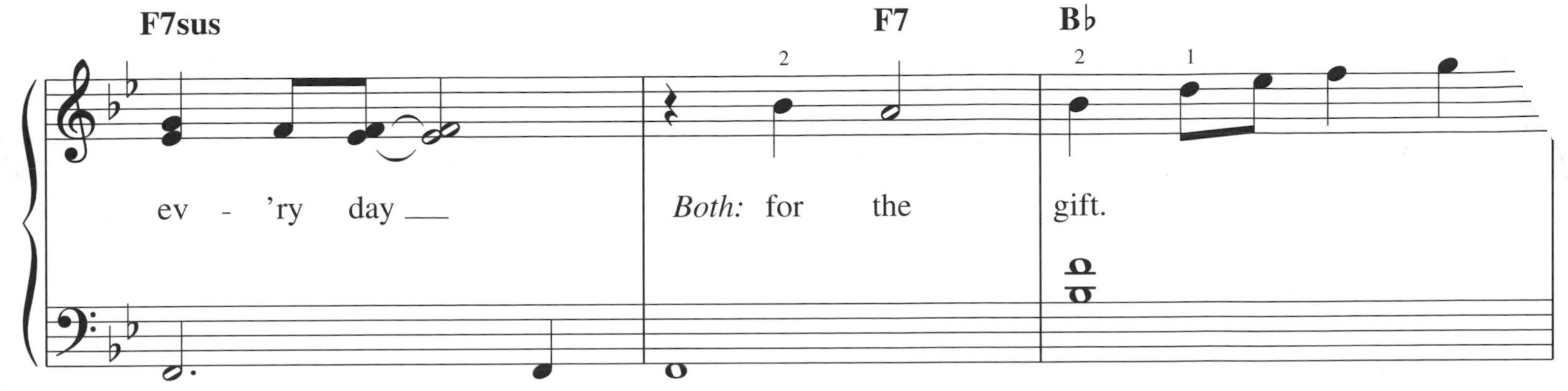
F7sus
F7
B♭
ev - 'ry day
Both: for the
gift.

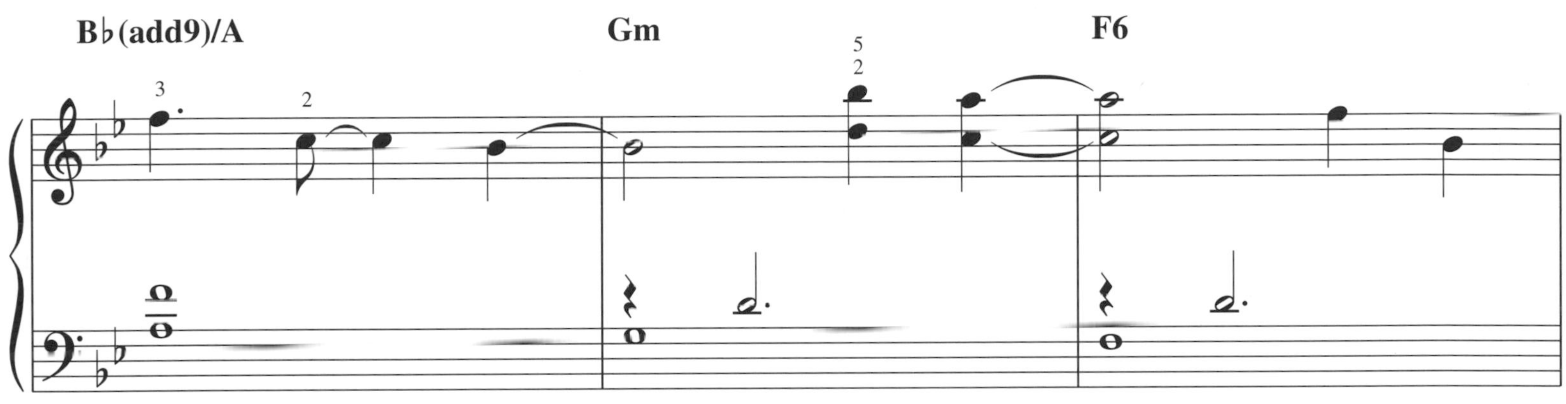
B♭(add9)/A
Gm
F6

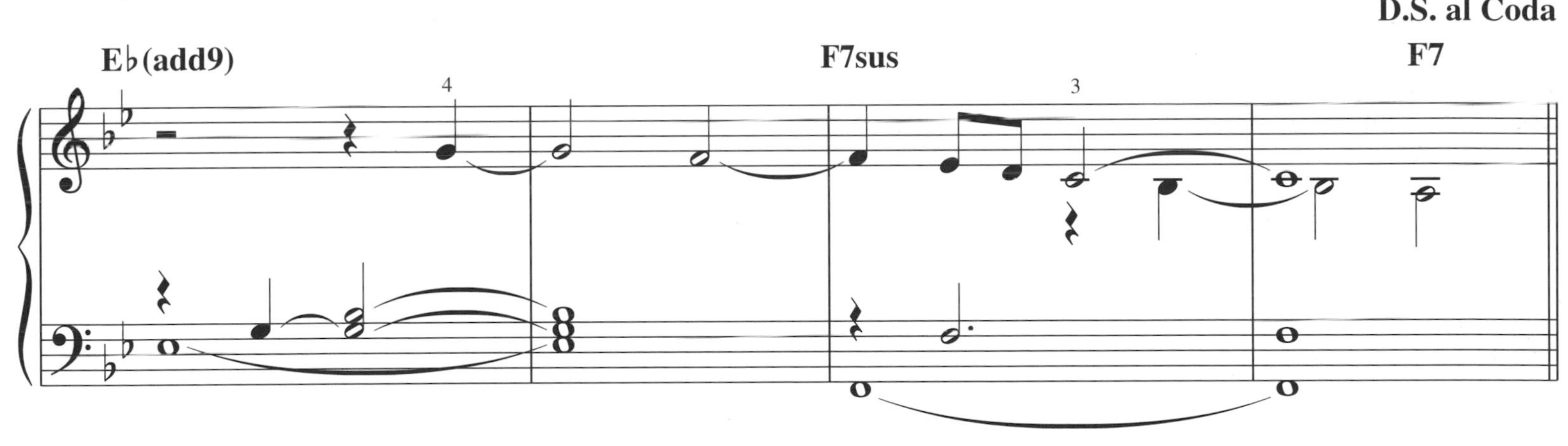
D.S. al Coda
E♭(add9)
F7sus
F7

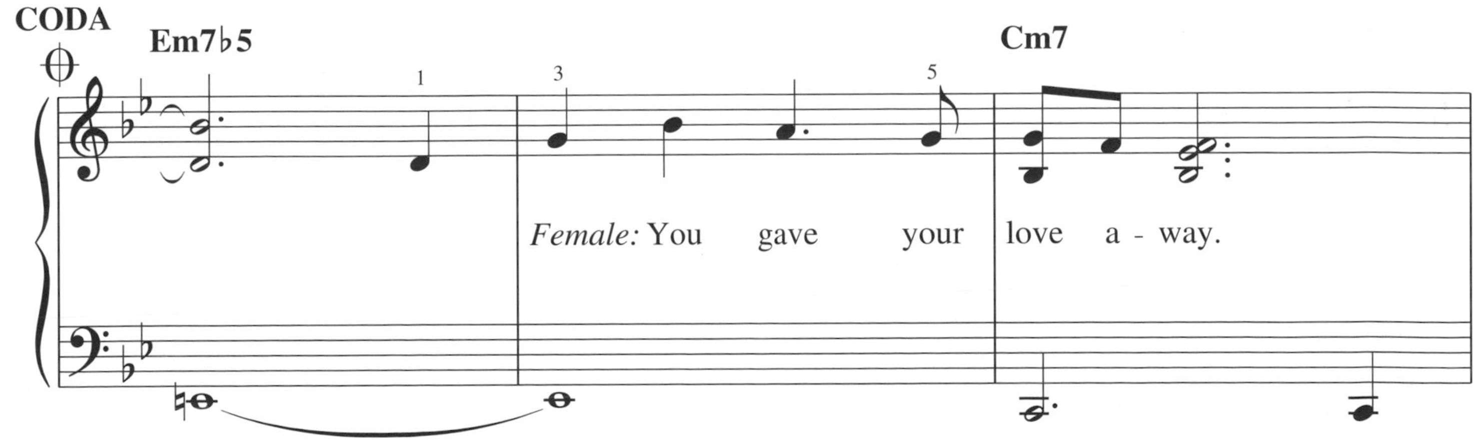
CODA
Em7♭5
Cm7
Female: You gave your
love a - way.

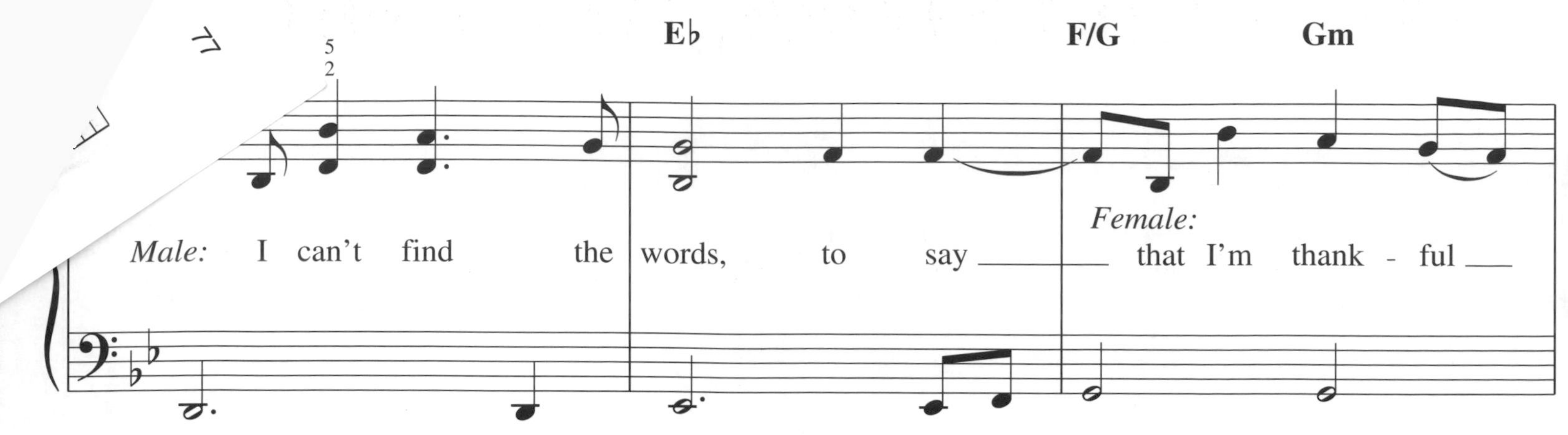
Eb
F/G
Gm
Male: I can't find the words, to say
Female: that I'm thank - ful

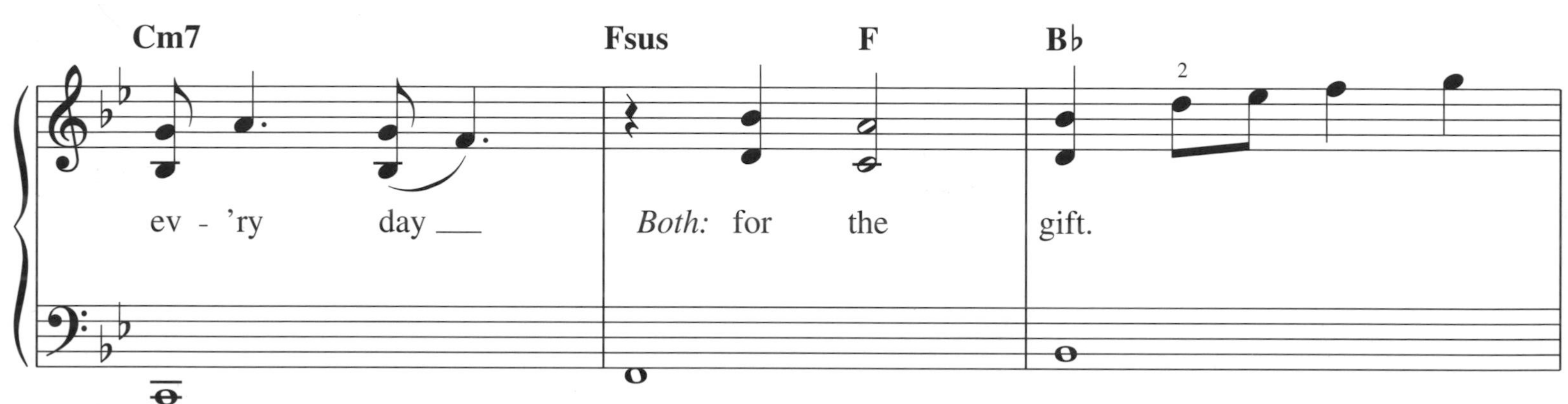
Cm7
Fsus
F
Bb
ev - 'ry day
Both: for the
gift.

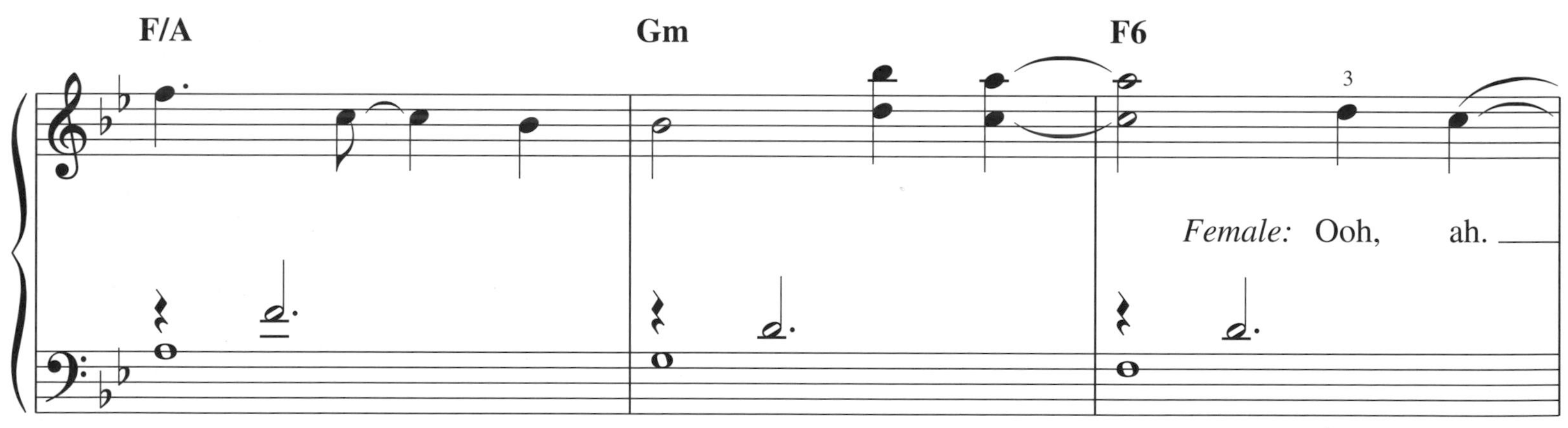
F/A
Gm
F6
Female: Ooh, ah.

Eb(add9)
Fsus
Bb(add9)
Male: Ah,
ooh,
ooh.

HAPPY CHRISTMAS, LITTLE FRIEND

Lyrics by OSCAR HAMMERSTEIN II
Music by RICHARD RODGERS

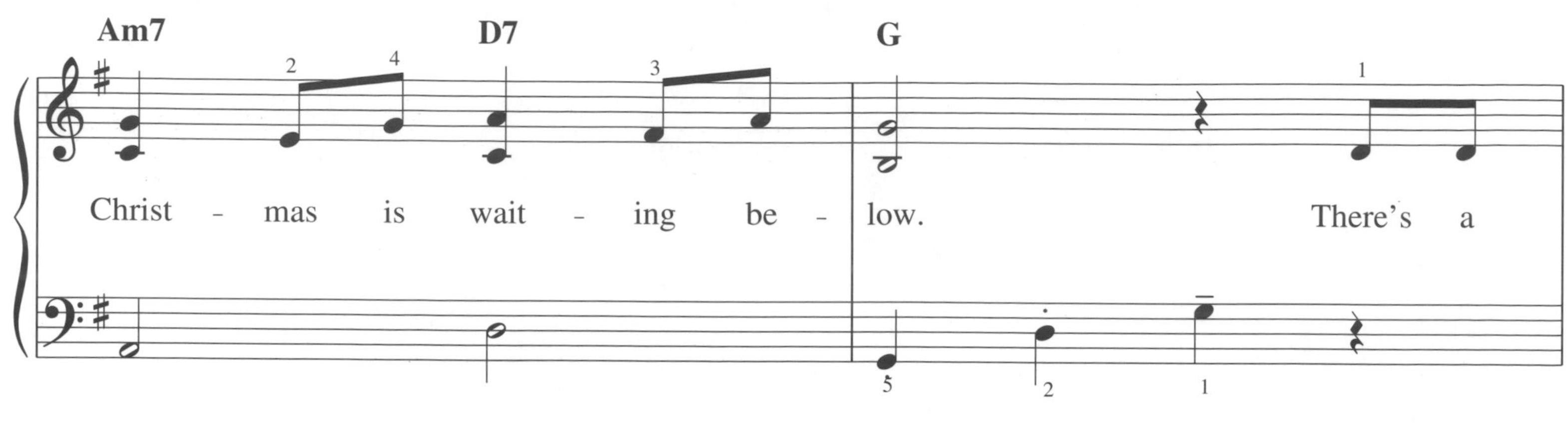
Am7
D7
G
Christ - mas is wait - ing be - low. There's a

D
G
D
G
tree in the room run - ning o - ver with stars that

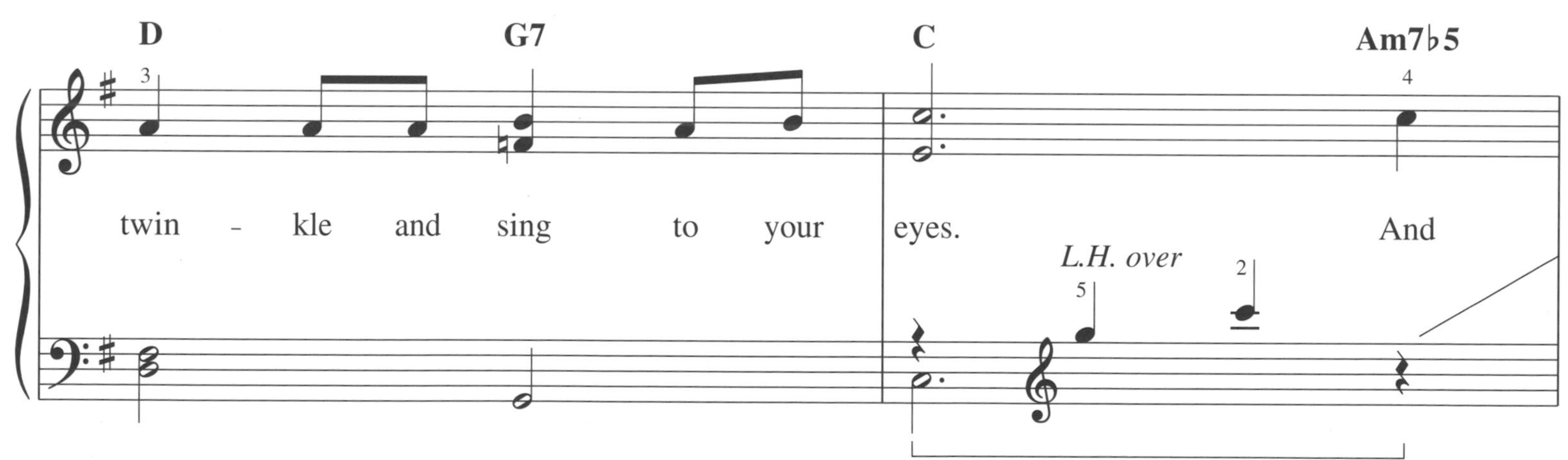
D
G7
C
Am7♭5
twin - kle and sing to your eyes. And
L.H. over

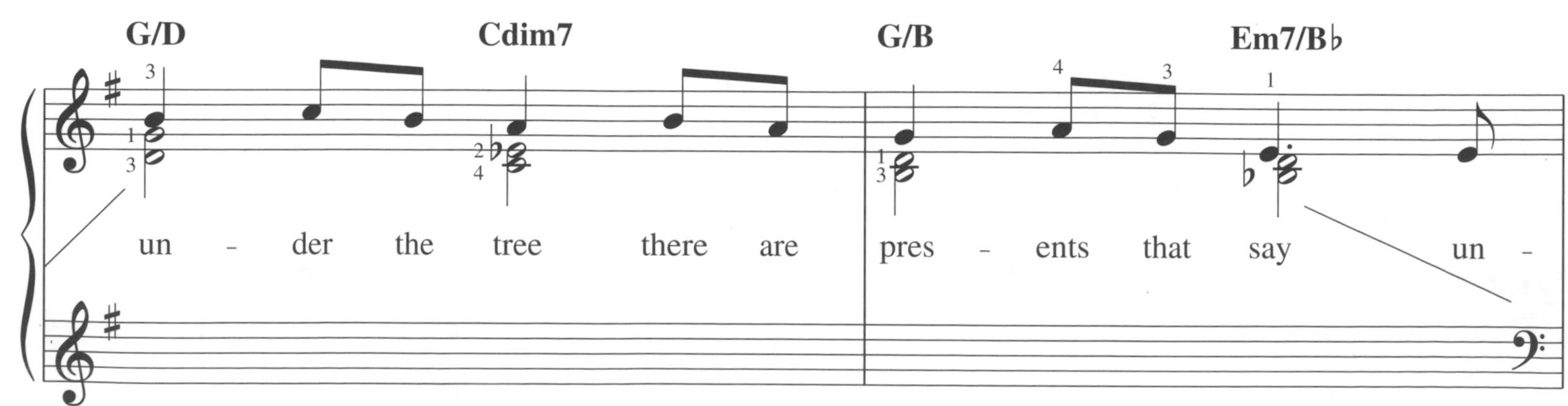
G/D
Cdim7
G/B
Em7/B♭
un - der the tree there are pres - ents that say un -

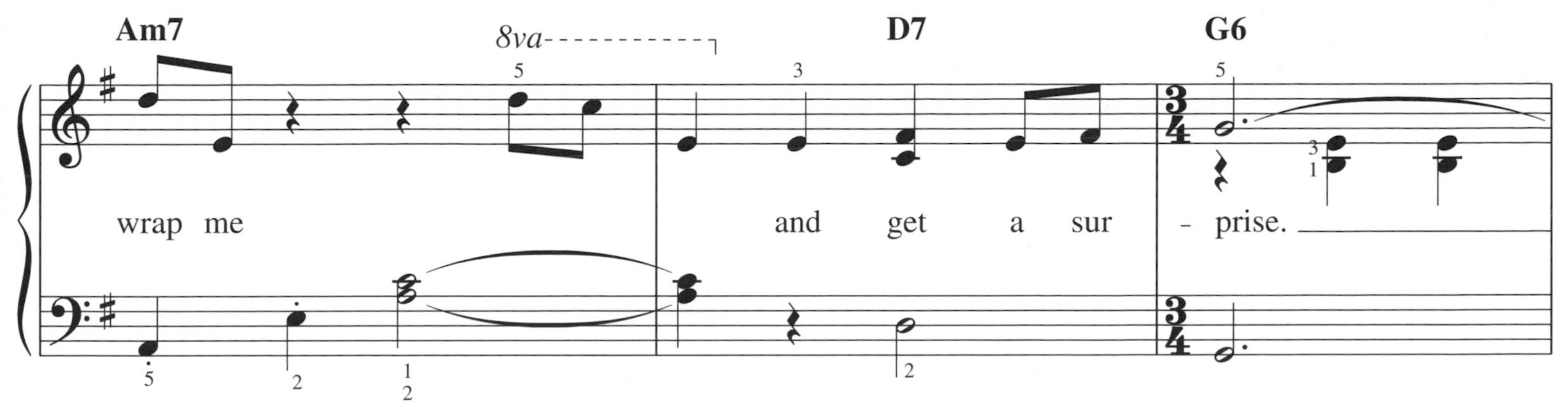
Am7
8va
D7
G6
wrap me
and get a sur
- prise.

Slowly
G
G6
G
Am7
Hap - py

D
G
Am7
Christ - mas,
lit - tle
friend,
may your
heart
be

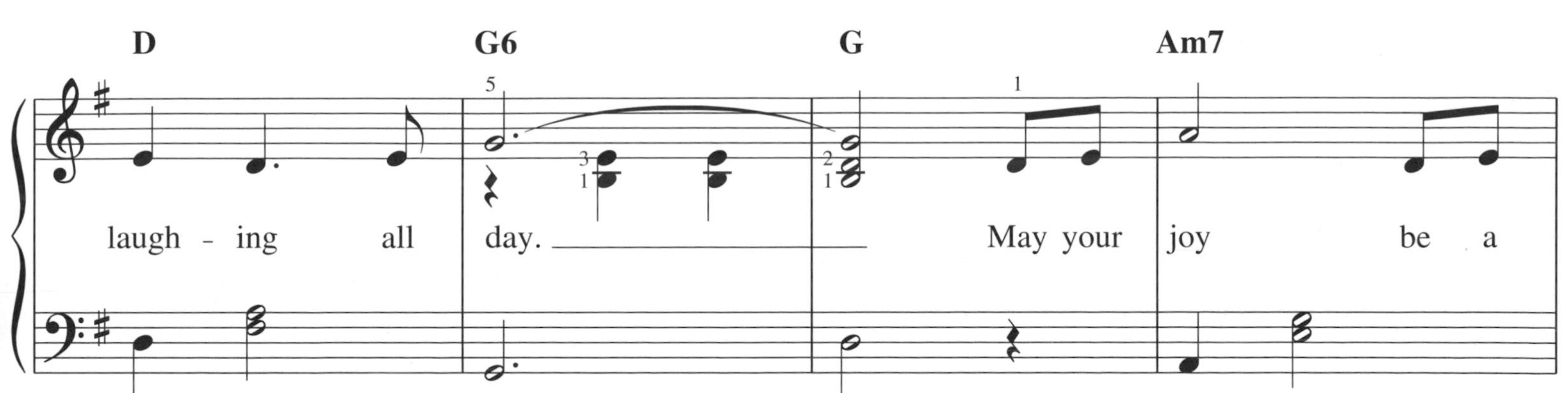
D
G6
G
Am7
laugh - ing
all
day.
May your
joy
be a

D
G/B
Am7
dream you'll re - mem - ber as the years roll a -

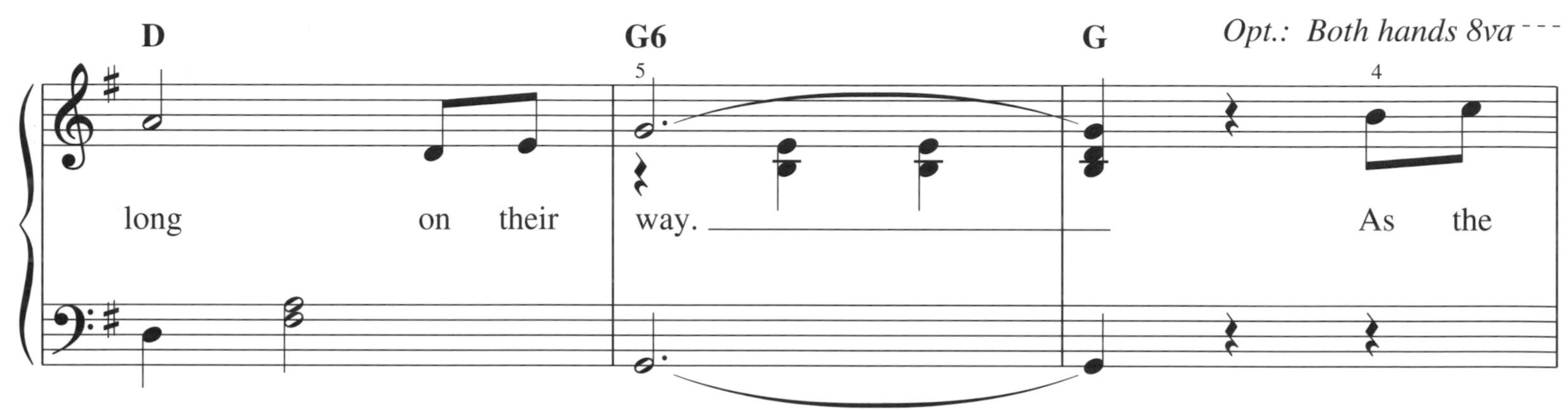
D
G6
G
Opt.: Both hands 8va
long on their way. As the

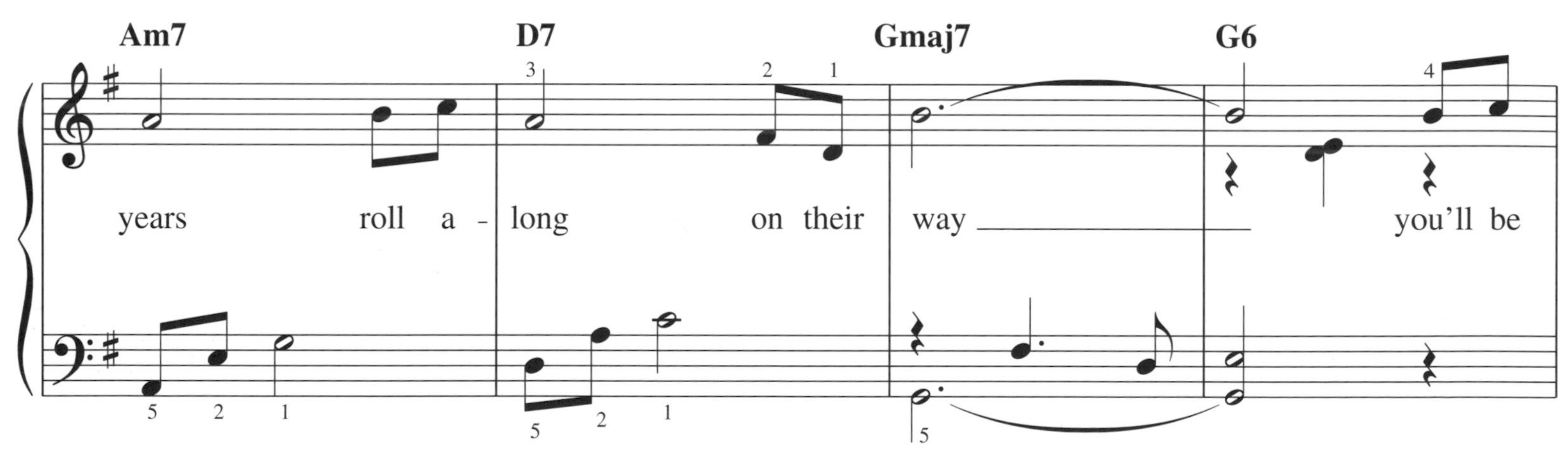
Am7
D7
Gmaj7
G6
years roll a - long on their way you'll be

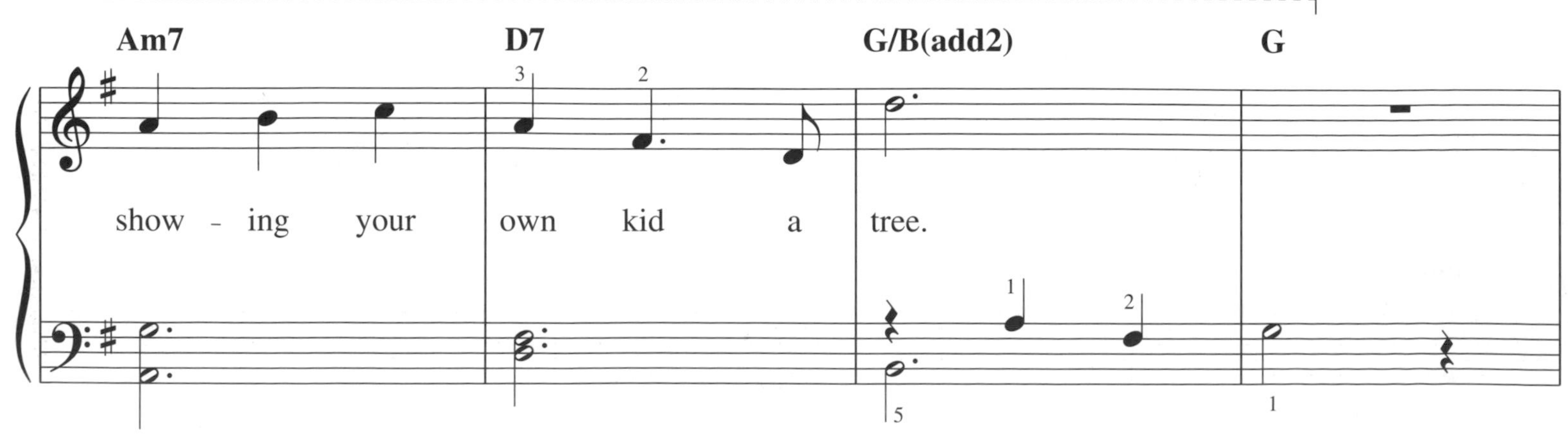
Am7
D7
G/B(add2)
G
show - ing your own kid a tree.

Am7
D7
G
Then at last, my friend, you'll know how

Am7
D7
G/F
G
hap - py a Christ - mas can be, how

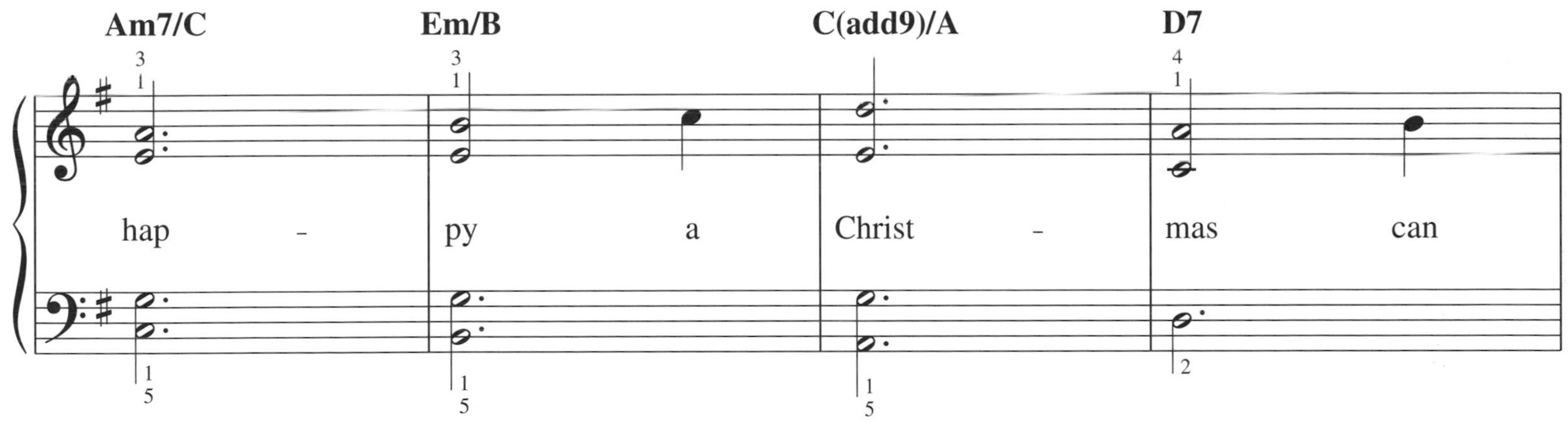
Am7/C
Em/B
C(add9)/A
D7
hap - py a Christ - mas can

G
C
G
be.
8vb

GOD BLESS US EVERYONE

from A CHRISTMAS CAROL

Music by ALAN MENKEN
Lyrics by LYNN AHRENS

G Bm C6 G/B Bm
In your heart there's a light as
C6 G/B Bm C D G Bm
bright as a star in heav - en. Let it
C6 G/B Bm C D7sus D7 G(add9)
shine through the night, and God bless us, ev - 'ry - one.
D D7/C G/B C
'Til each child is fed,

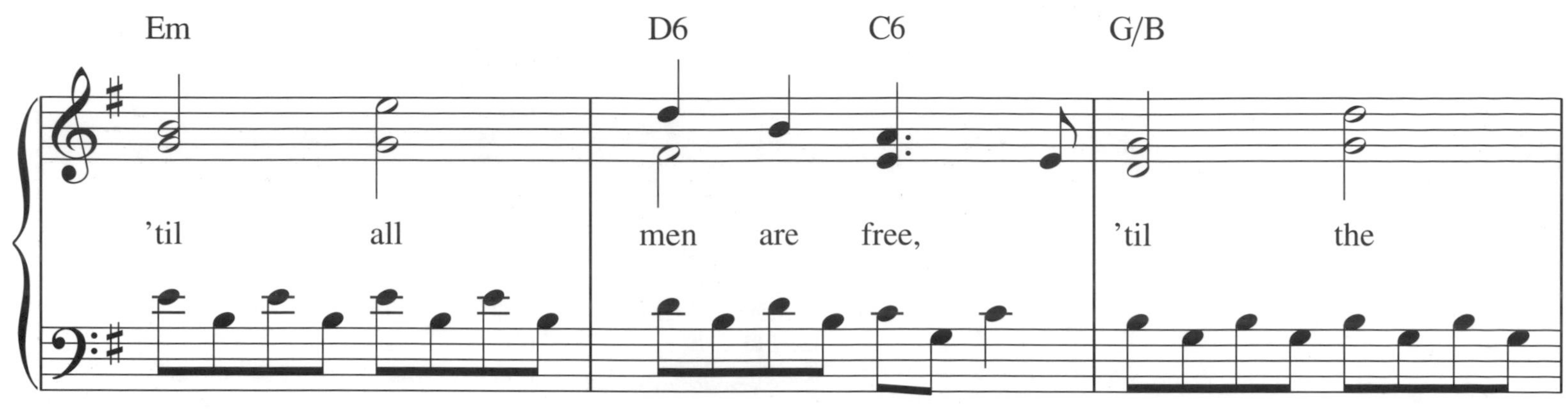
Em
D6
C6
G/B
'til all
men are free,
'til the

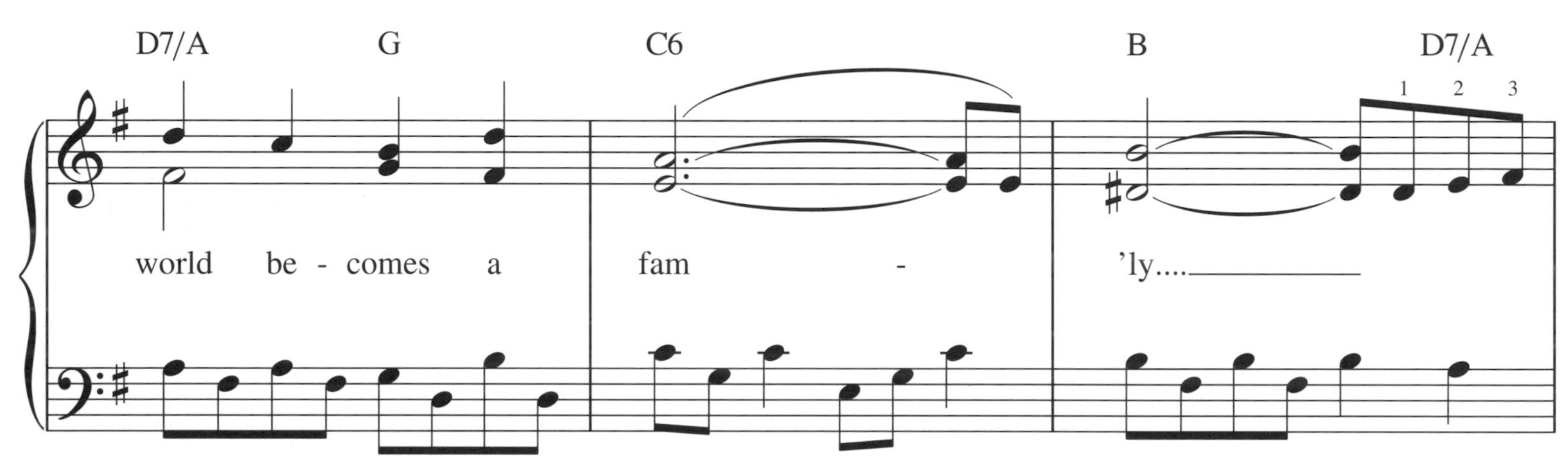
D7/A
G
C6
B
D7/A
world be - comes a
fam -
'ly....

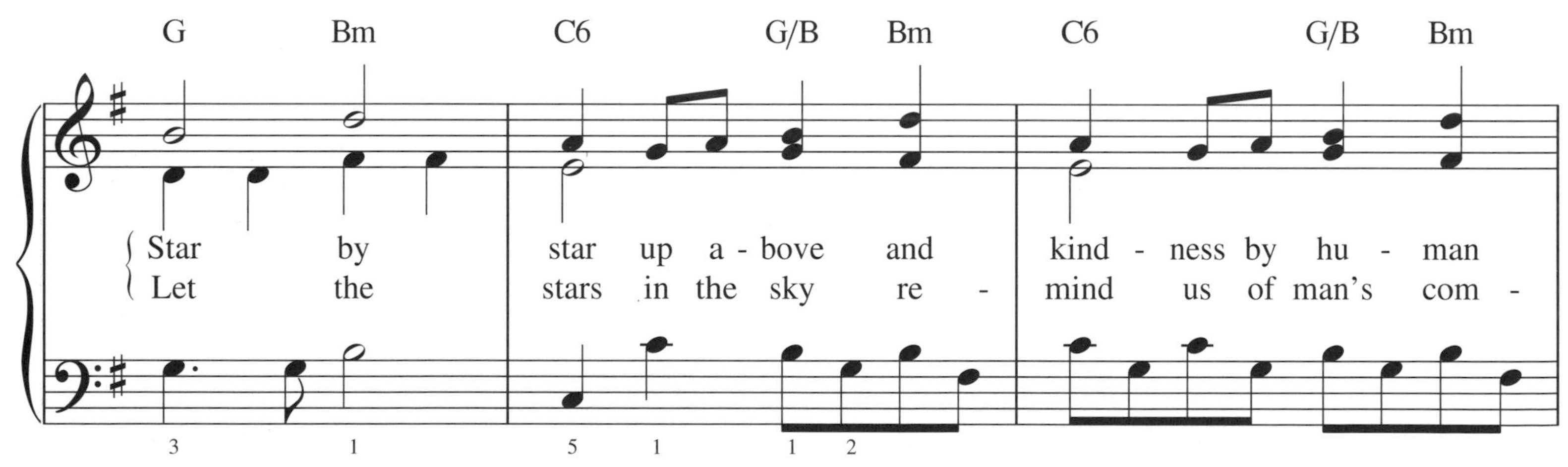
G
Bm
C6
G/B
Bm
C6
G/B
Bm
Star by
star up a - bove and
kind - ness by hu - man
Let the
stars in the sky re -
mind us of man's com -

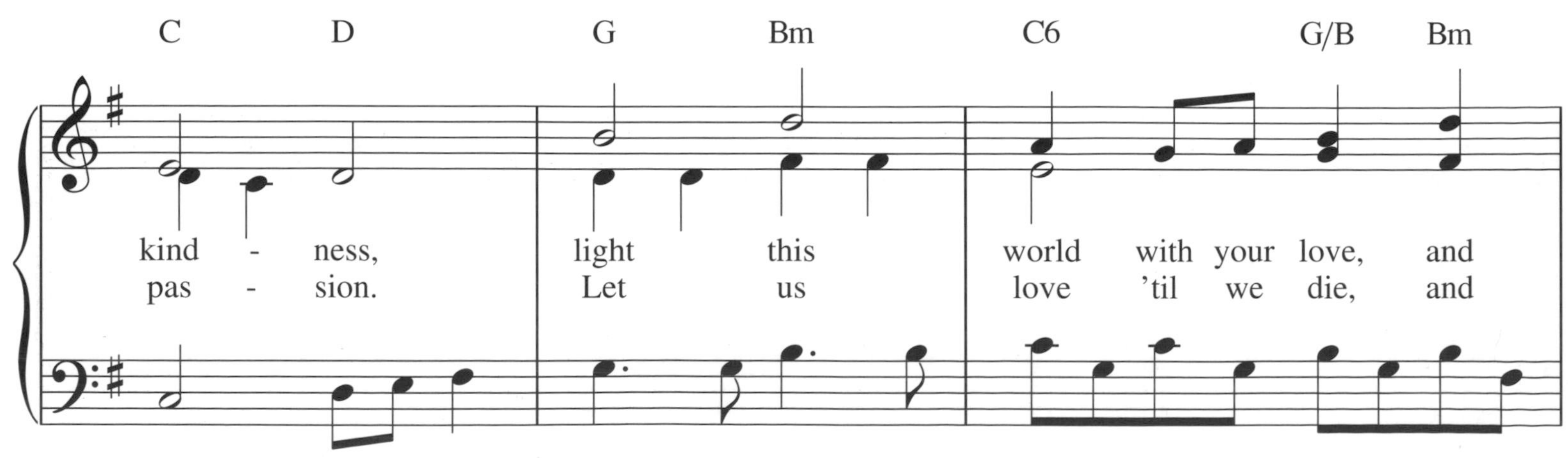
C
D
G
Bm
C6
G/B
Bm
kind - ness,
light this
world with your love, and
pas - sion.
Let us
love 'til we die, and

To Coda
C
G/B
D7sus
D7
G(add9)
God bless us, ev - 'ry - one.
God bless us,
D.S. al Coda
CODA
Cmaj7/D
D7
ev - 'ry -
G
Bm
C6
G/B
C
Bm7
one.
God bless_ us,
Cmaj7/D
Am/D
G
ev - 'ry - one.
8vb

HAPPY HANUKKAH, MY FRIEND

(The Hanukkah Song)

Words and Music by JUSTIN WILDE
and DOUGLAS ALAN KONECKY

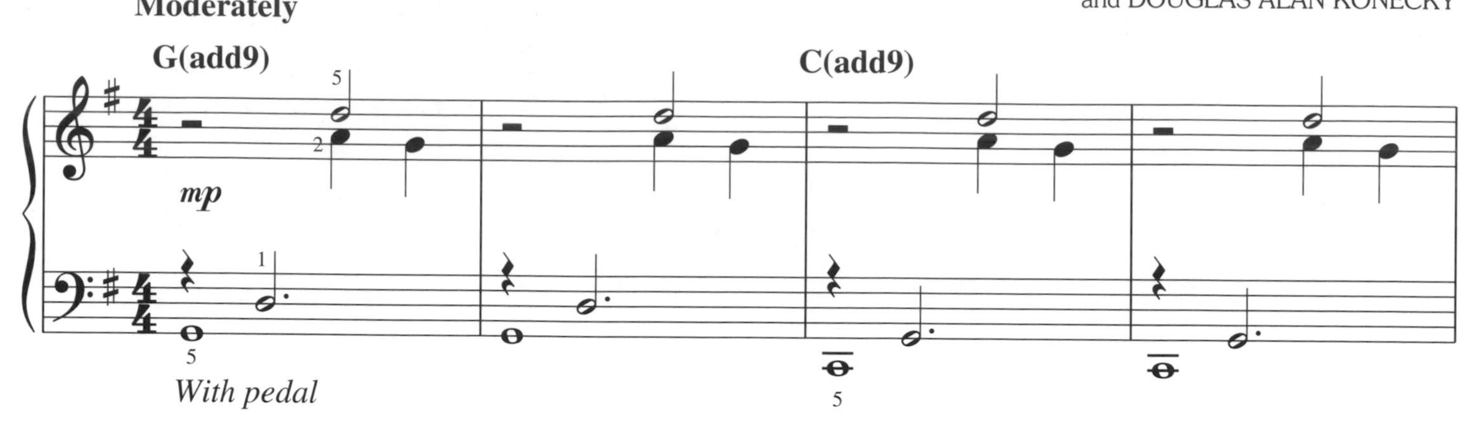

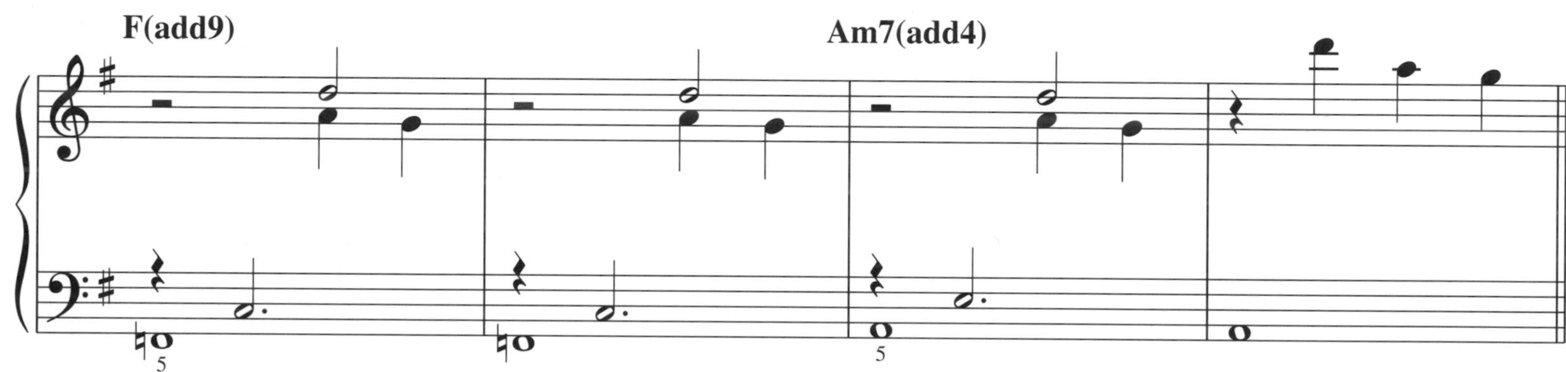

C/G
G
F
Am
G
geth - er.
broth - ers.
As
So
twi - light greets the set - ting sun
let's be - gin with you and me,

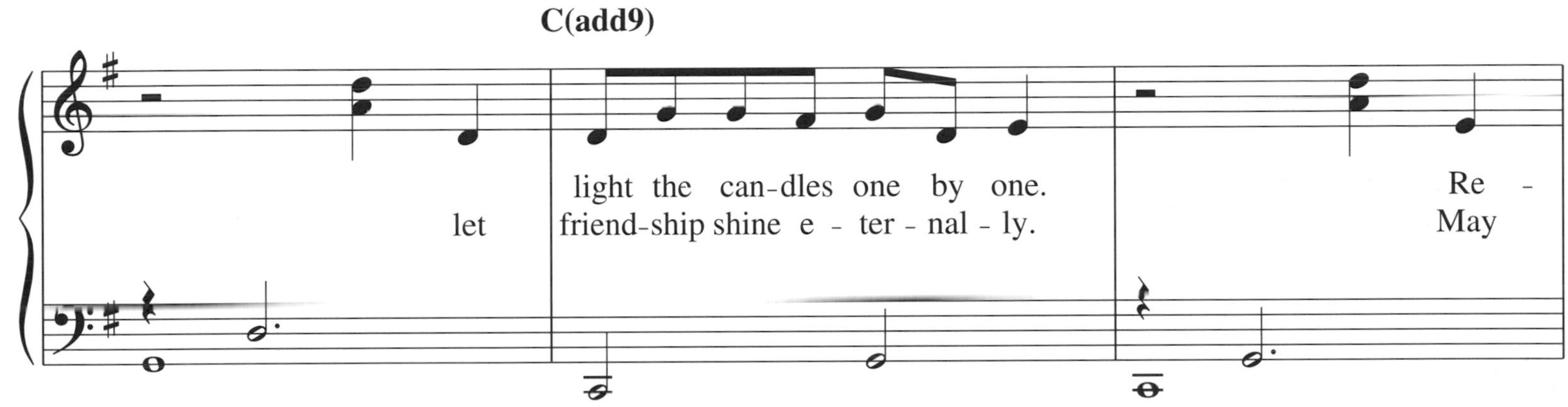
C(add9)
let
light the can - dles one by one.
friend - ship shine e - ter - nal - ly.
Re -
May

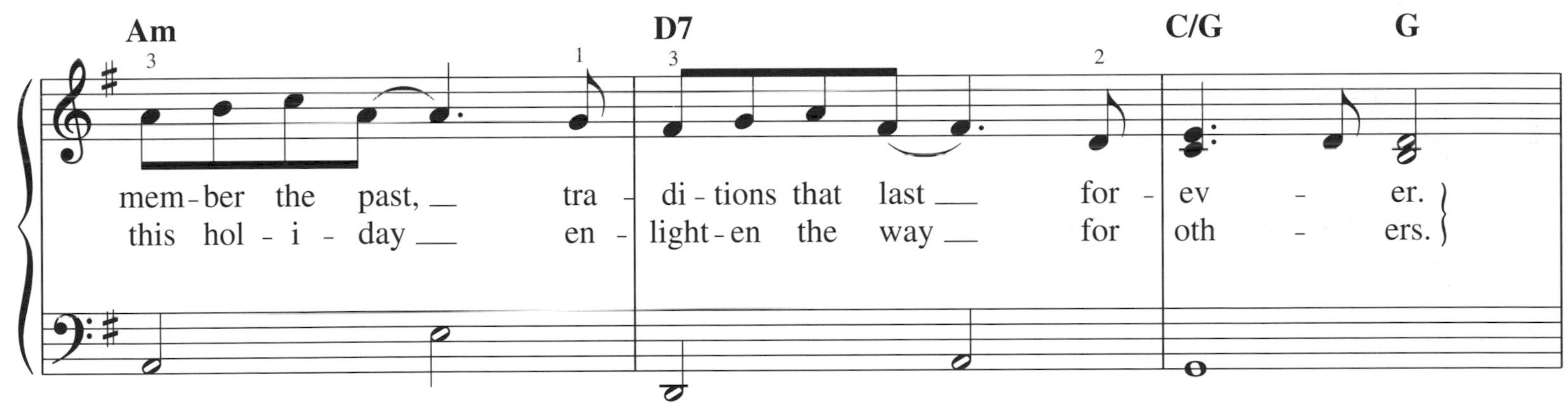
Am
D7
C/G
G
mem - ber the past,
this hol - i - day
tra -
en -
di - tions that last
light - en the way
for -
for
ev - er.
oth - ers.

C
G
Em
Come, let's
share the joy of

Am G D F♯m♭5 B7
Ha - nuk - kah. May our friend-ship grow, as the

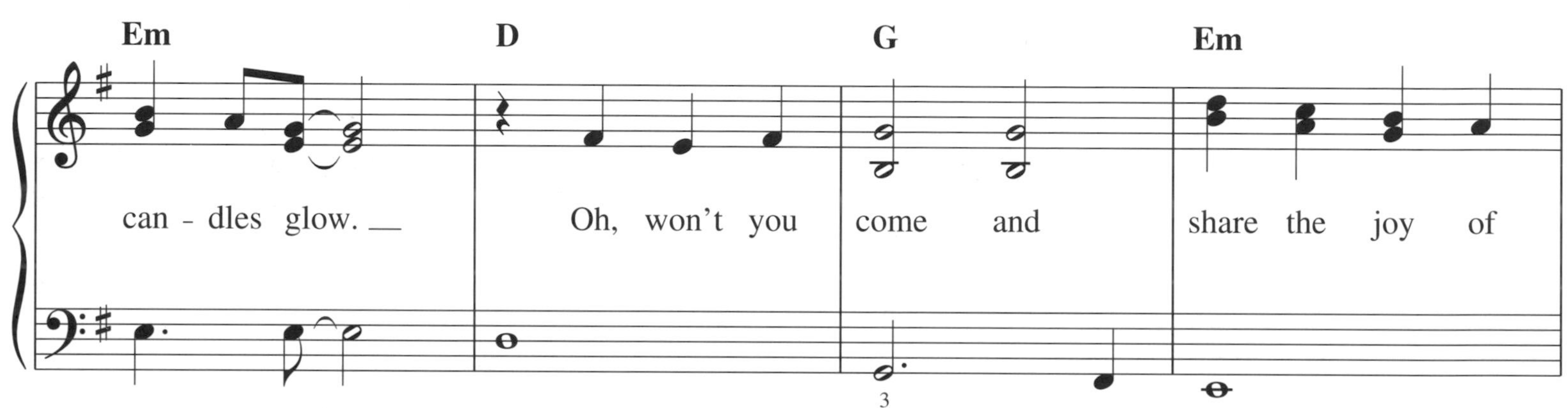
Em D G Em
can - dles glow. Oh, won't you come and share the joy of

Am G F♯m♭5 B7 Em
Ha - nuk - kah; and we'll cel - e - brate as
and we're hop - ing all you're

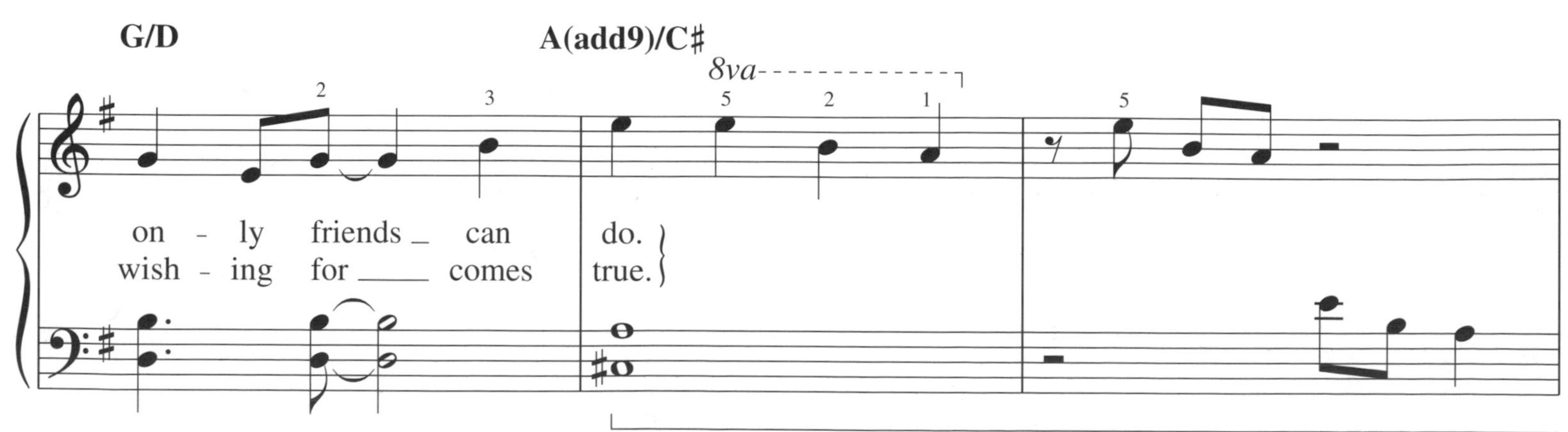
G/D A(add9)/C♯
8va
on - ly friends can do.
wish - ing for comes true.

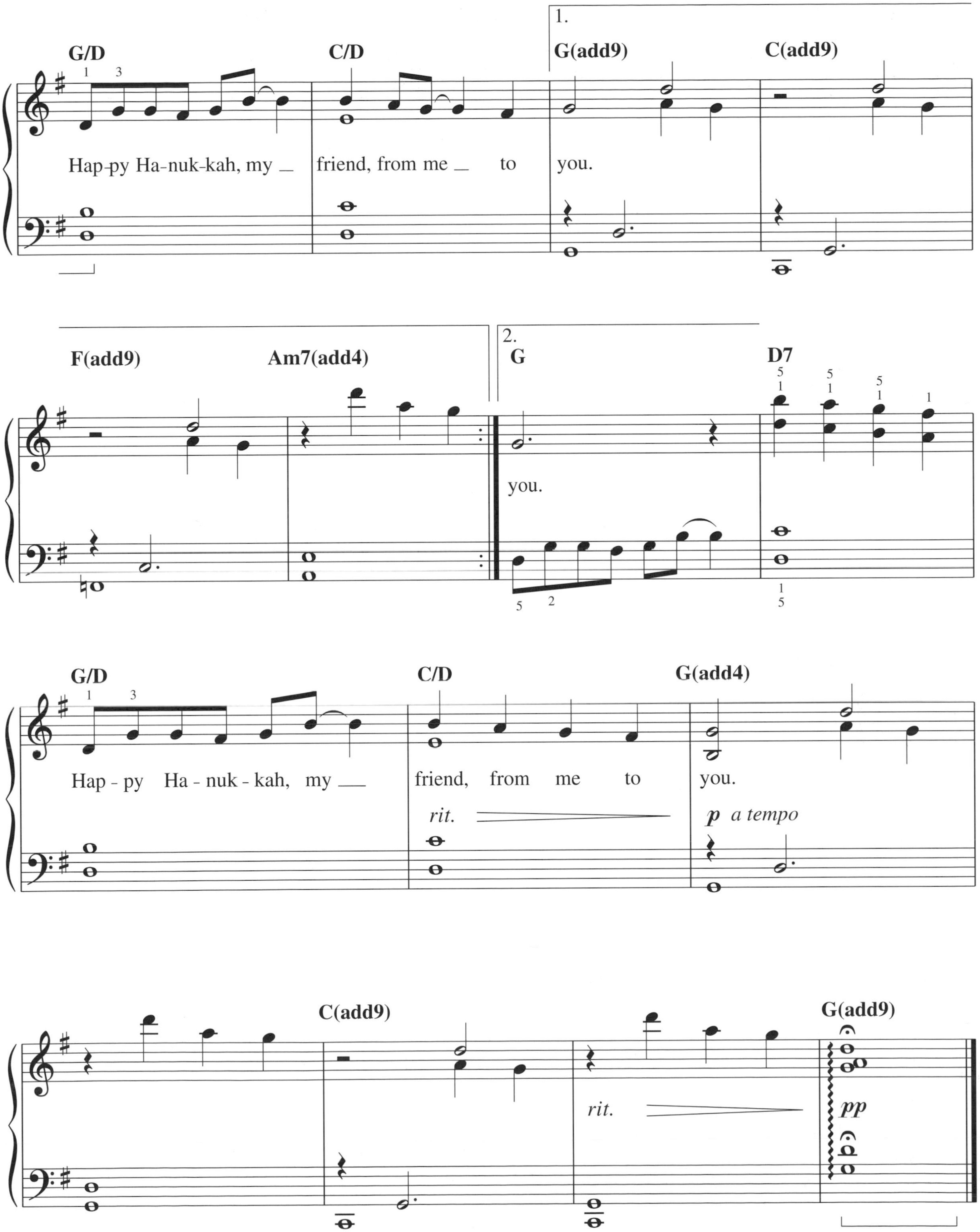

1.

G/D C/D G(add9) C(add9)

Hap-py Ha-nuk-kah, my _ friend, from me _ to you.

F(add9) Am7(add4)

2.

G D7

you.

G/D C/D G(add4)

Hap - py Ha - nuk - kah, my _ friend, from me to you.

rit. **p** *a tempo*

HAPPY HOLIDAY

from the Motion Picture Irving Berlin's HOLIDAY INN

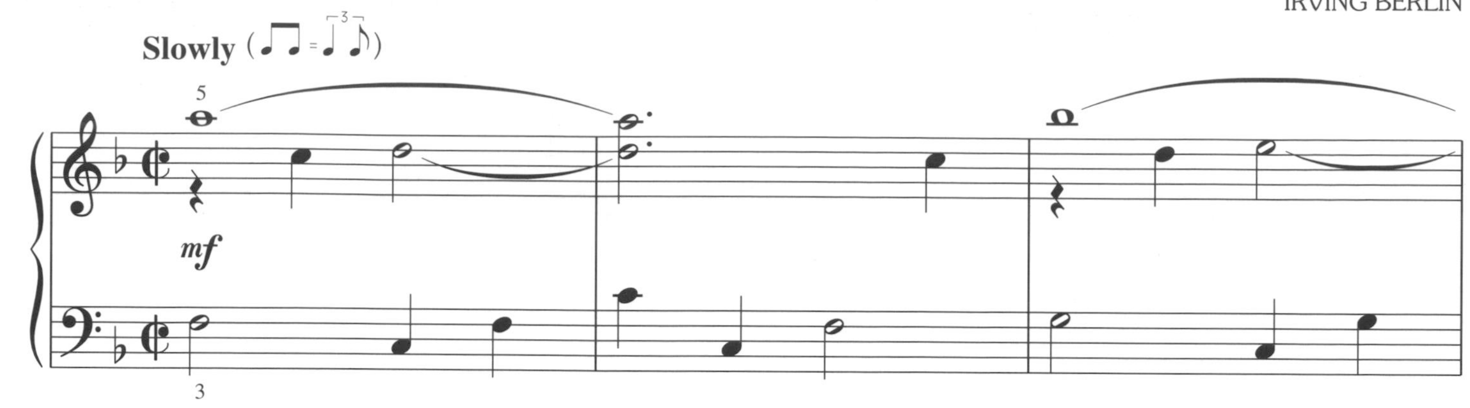

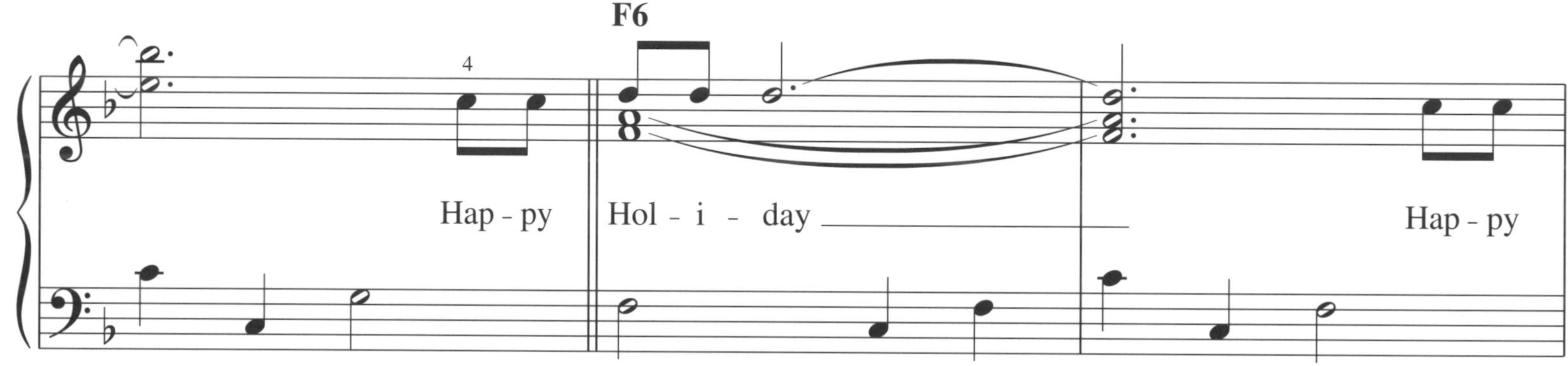

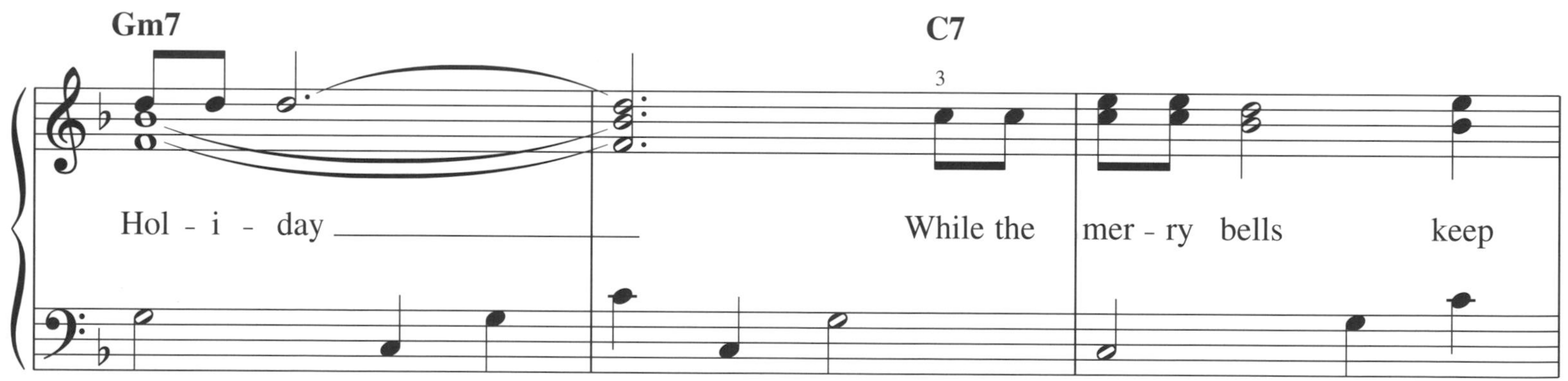

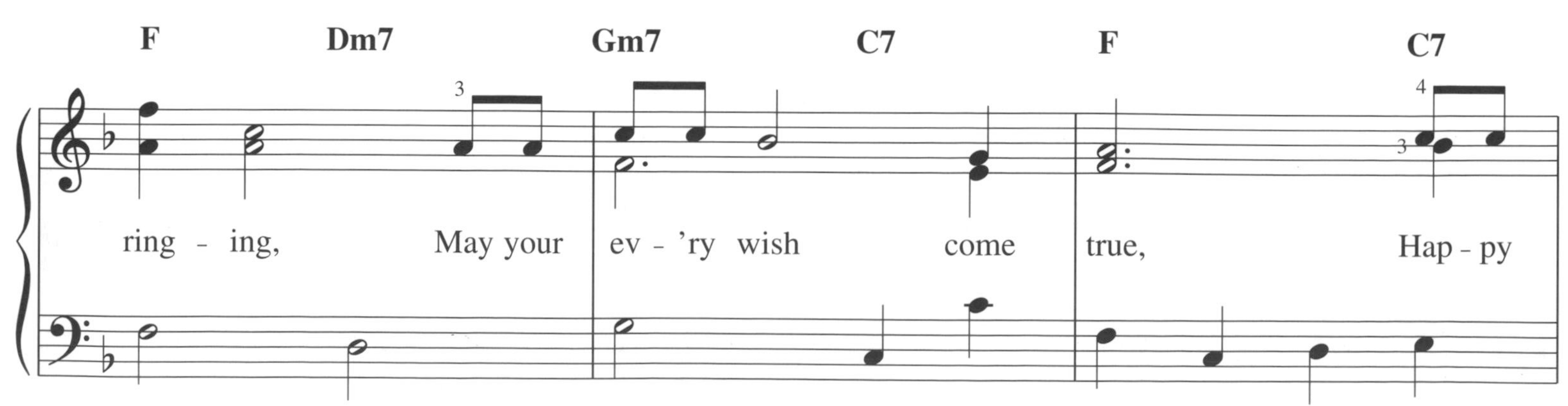

F6
Gm7
Hol - i - day
Hap - py
Hol - i - day

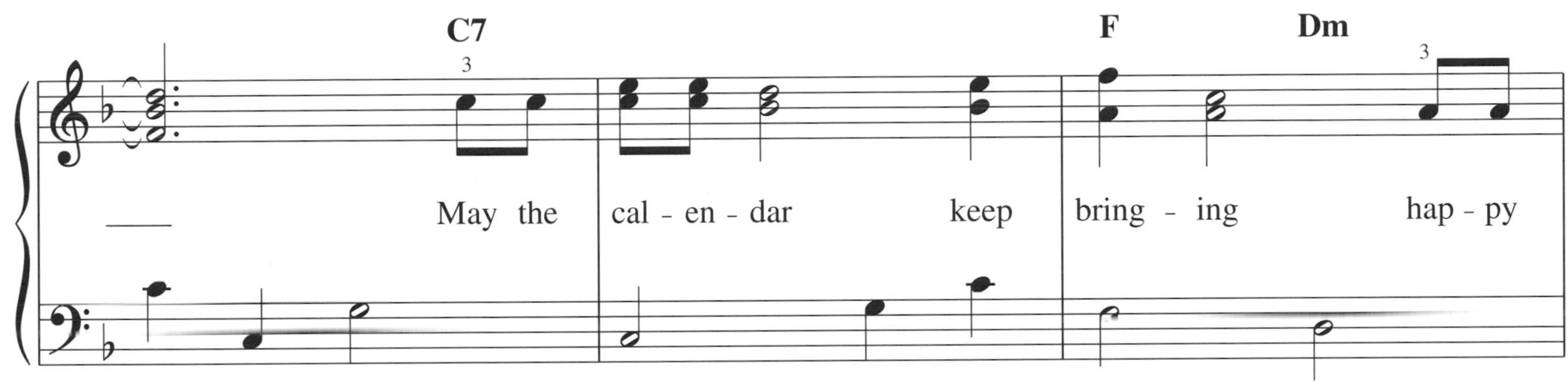
C7
F
Dm
May the
cal - en - dar
keep
bring - ing
hap - py

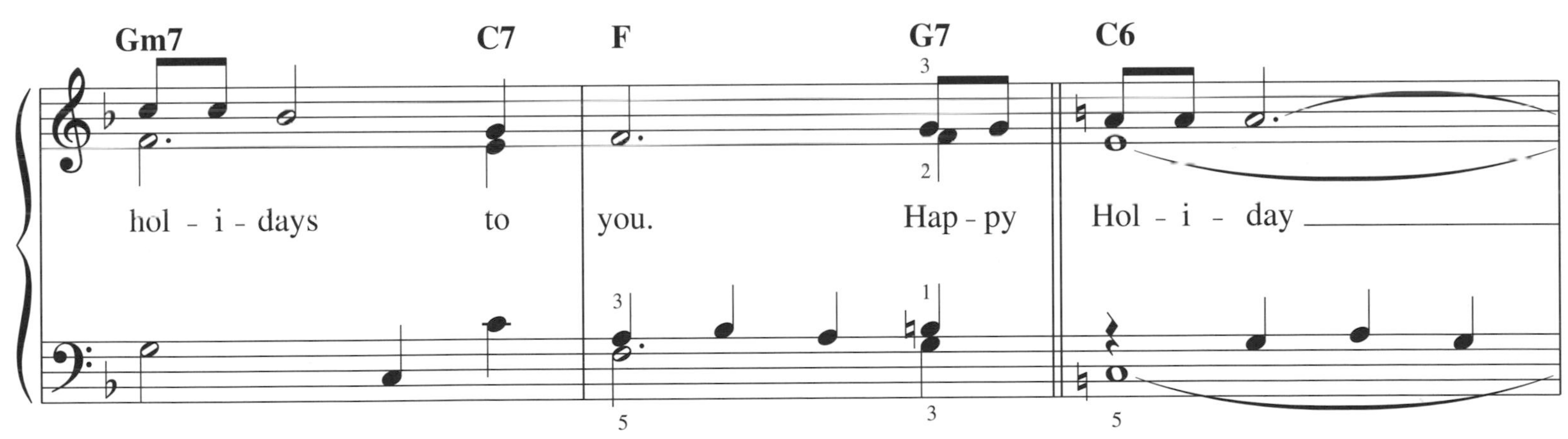
Gm7
C7
F
G7
C6
hol - i - days
to
you.
Hap - py
Hol - i - day

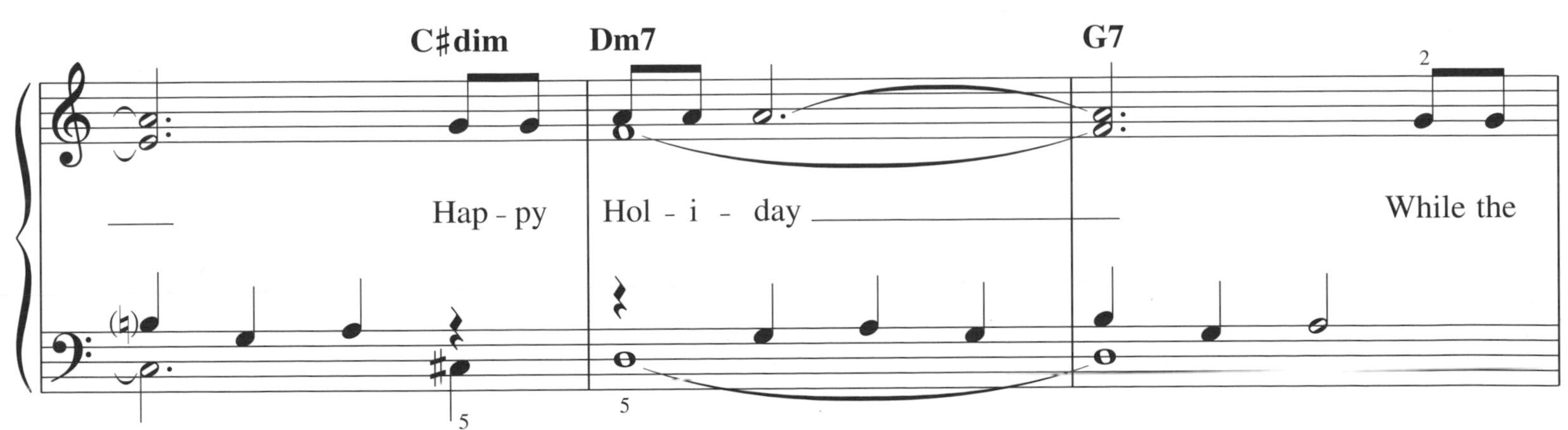
C♯dim
Dm7
G7
Hap - py
Hol - i - day
While the

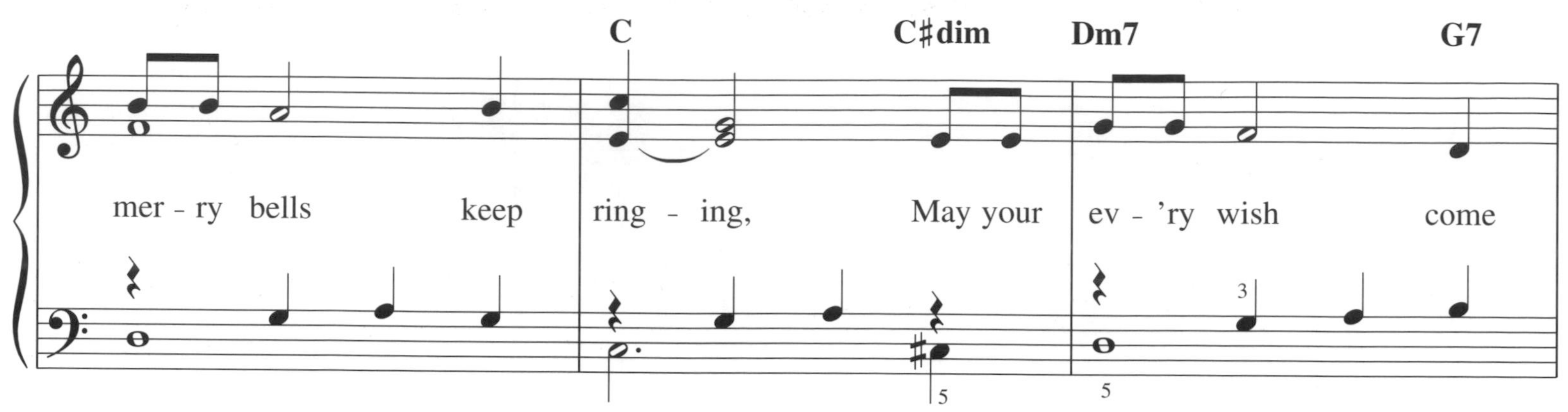
C
C#dim
Dm7
G7
mer - ry bells keep
ring - ing, May your
ev - 'ry wish come

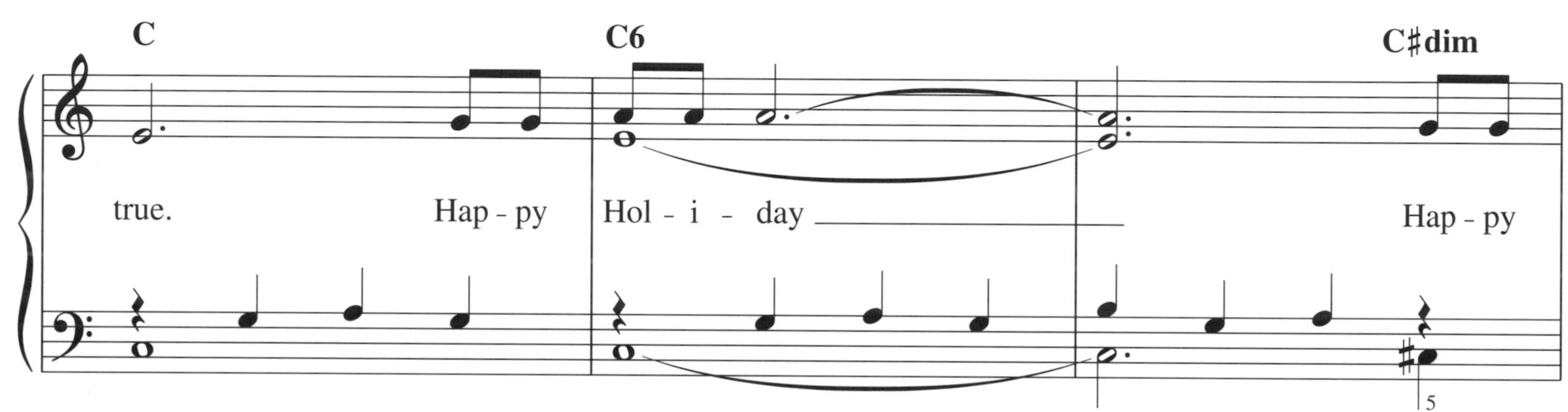
C
C6
C#dim
true. Hap - py
Hol - i - day
Hap - py

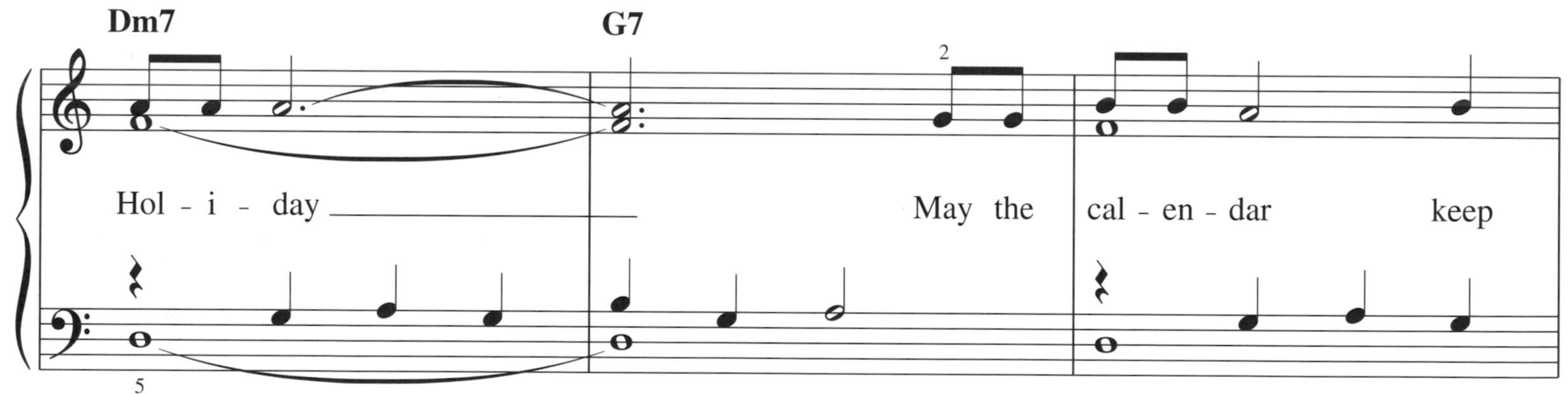
Dm7
G7
Hol - i - day
May the
cal - en - dar keep

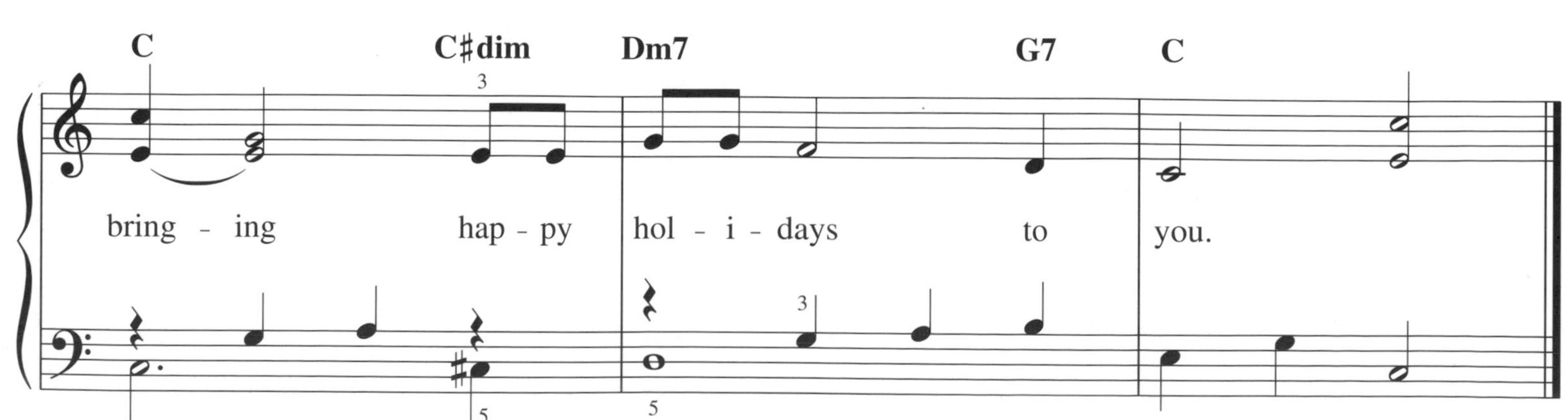
C
C#dim
Dm7
G7
C
bring - ing hap - py
hol - i - days to
you.

I YUST GO NUTS AT CHRISTMAS

Words and Music by
HARRY STEWART

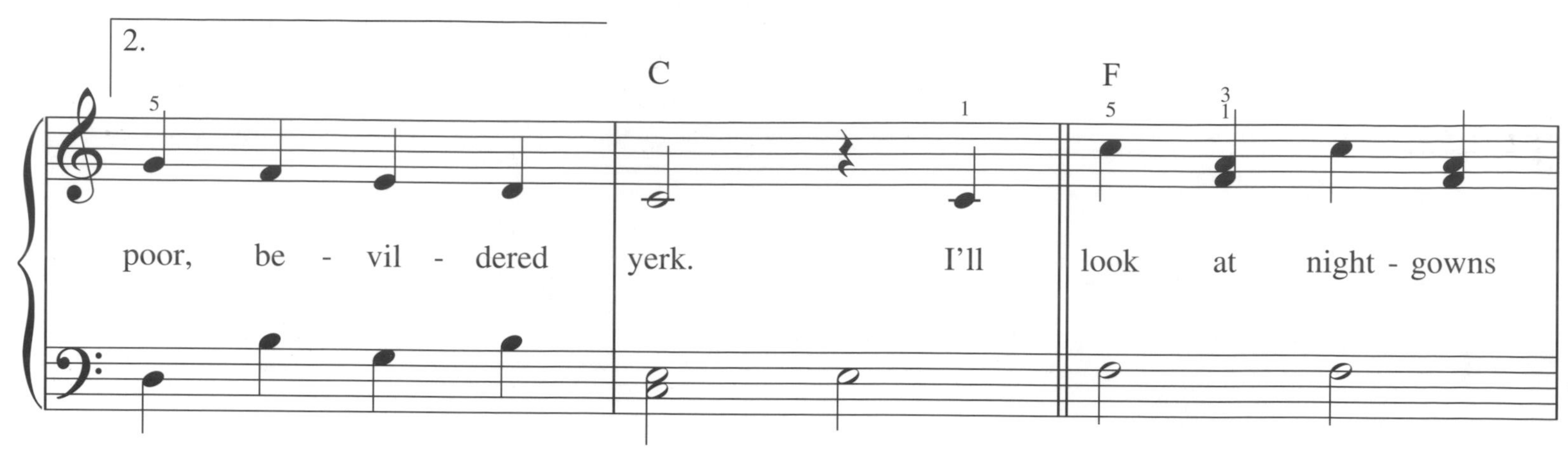
2.
C
F
poor, be - vil - dered
yerk. I'll
look at night - gowns

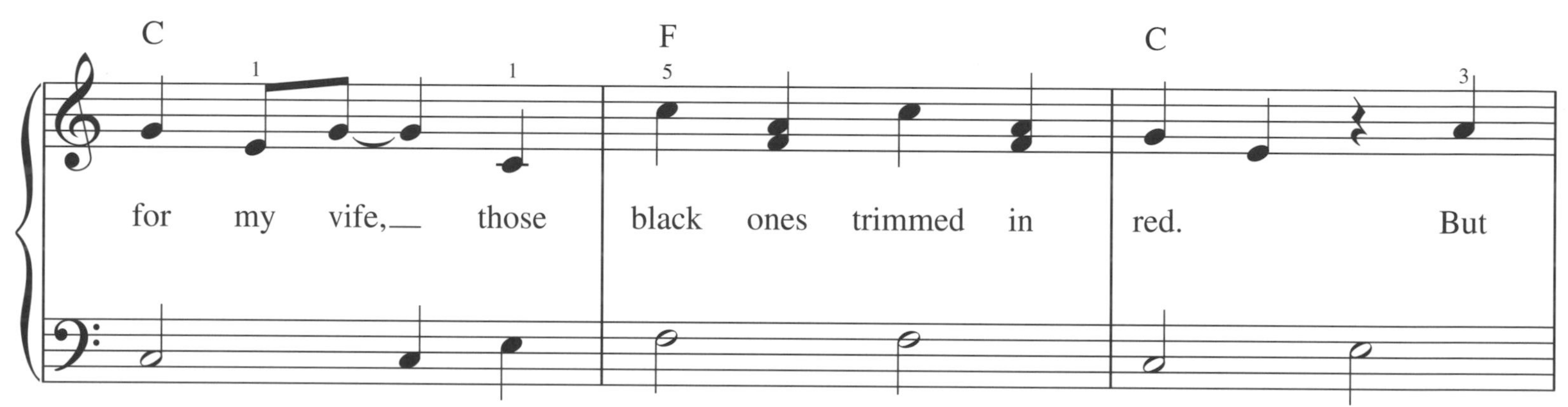
C
F
C
for my vife, those
black ones trimmed in
red. But

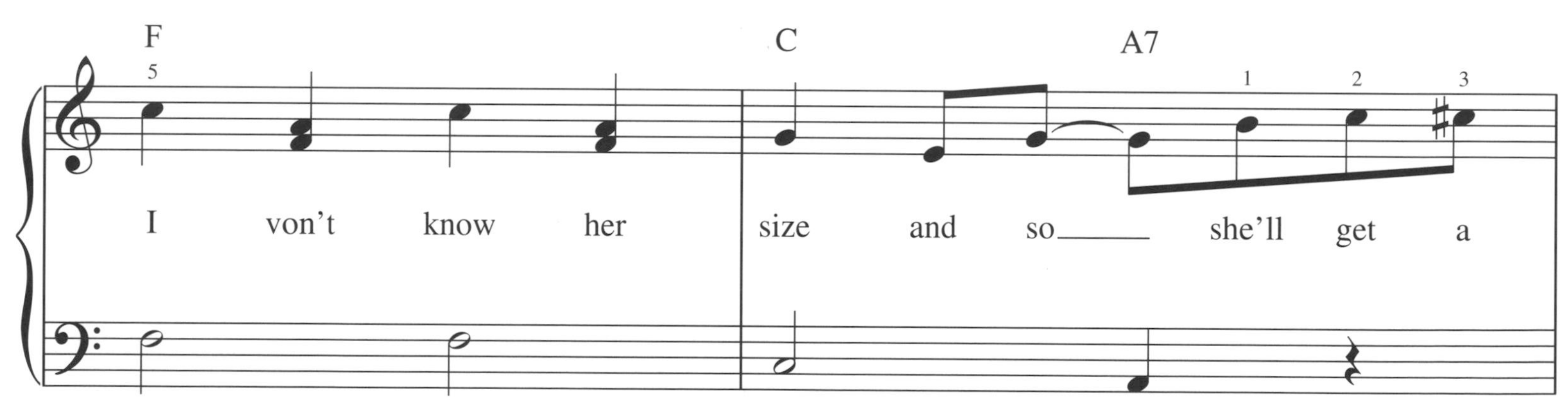
F
C
A7
I von't know her
size and so she'll get a

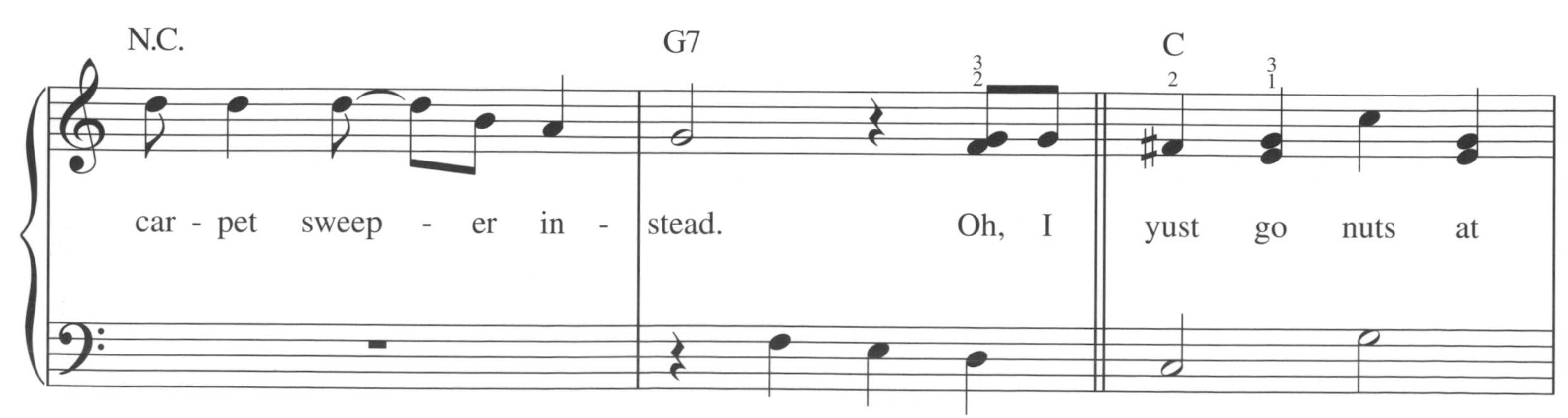
N.C.
G7
C
car - pet sweep - er in -
stead. Oh, I
yust go nuts at

C♯dim
G7
Christ - mas, when each kid hangs up his sock. It's a

time for kids to flip their lids while their

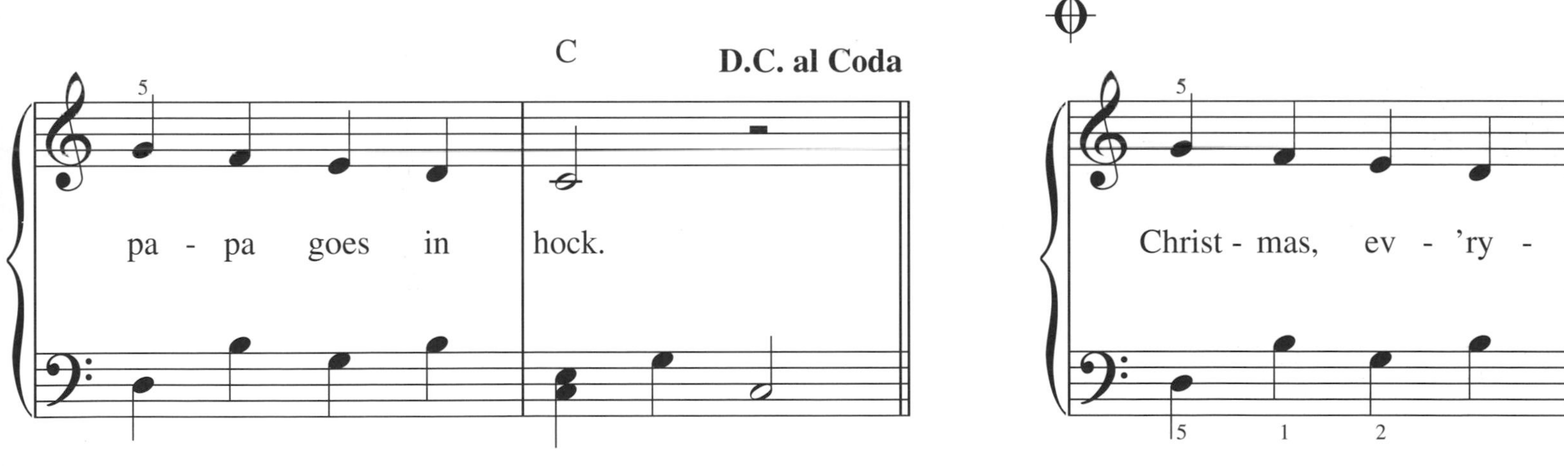
C
D.C. al Coda
CODA
pa - pa goes in hock.
Christ - mas, ev - 'ry -

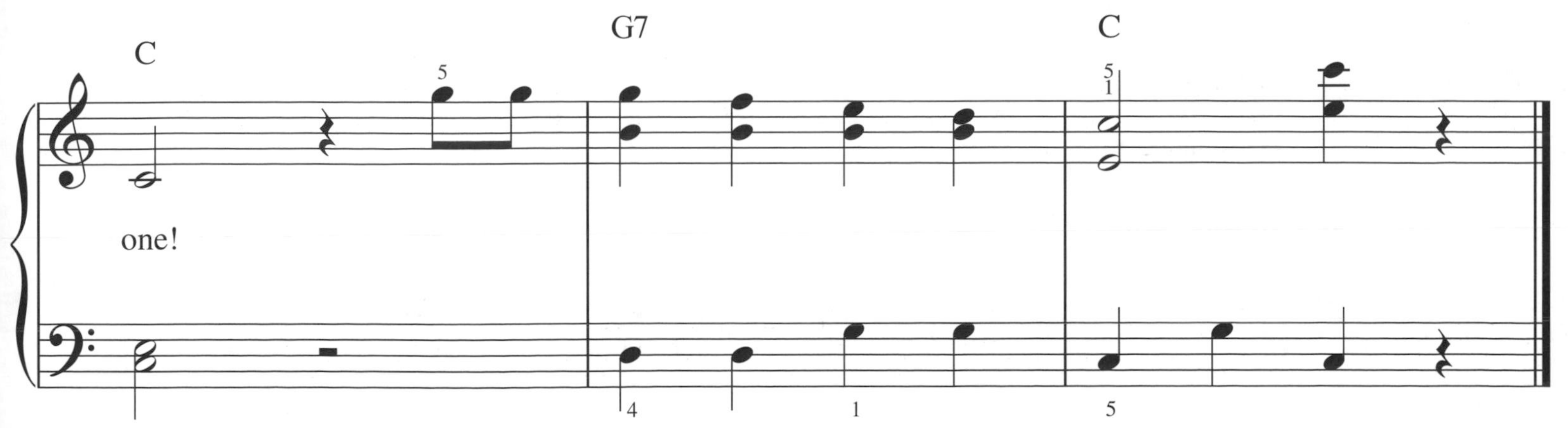
C
G7
C
one!

HAPPY XMAS
(War Is Over)

Words and Music by JOHN LENNON
and YOKO ONO

C
Dm
G
I hope you have fun, the near and the dear ones,
we hope you have fun, the near and the dear ones,

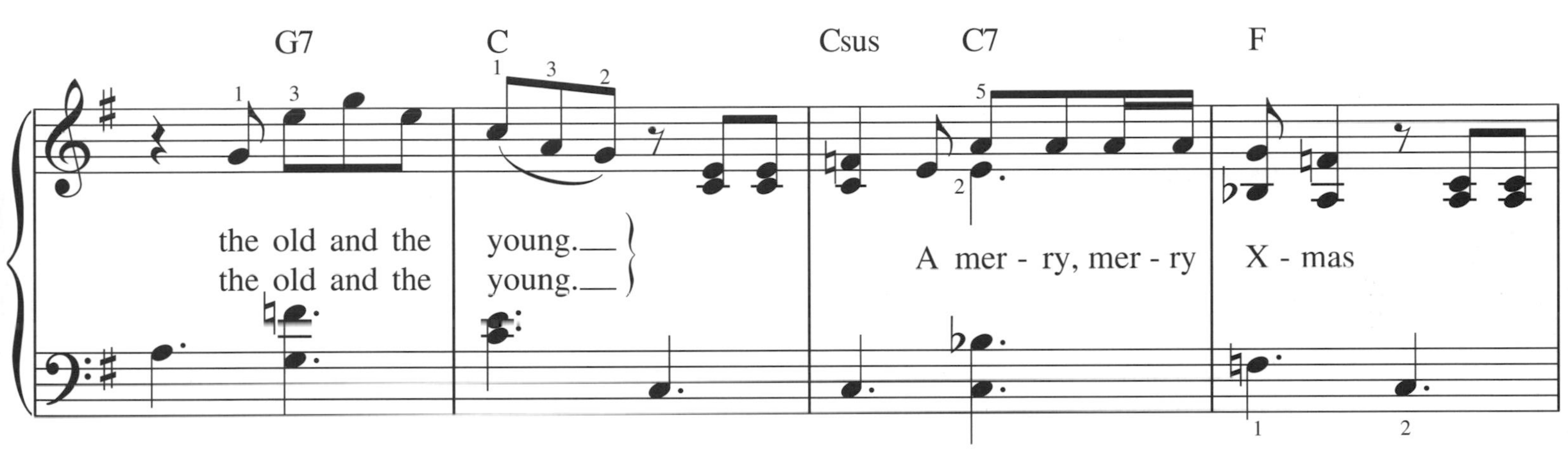
G7
C
Csus
C7
F
the old and the young.
the old and the young.
A mer - ry, mer - ry X - mas

G
Dm
and a hap - py New Year. Let's hope it's a good one

To Coda
G7
C
D
D7
G
with - out an - y fear. And so this is X - mas
(War is

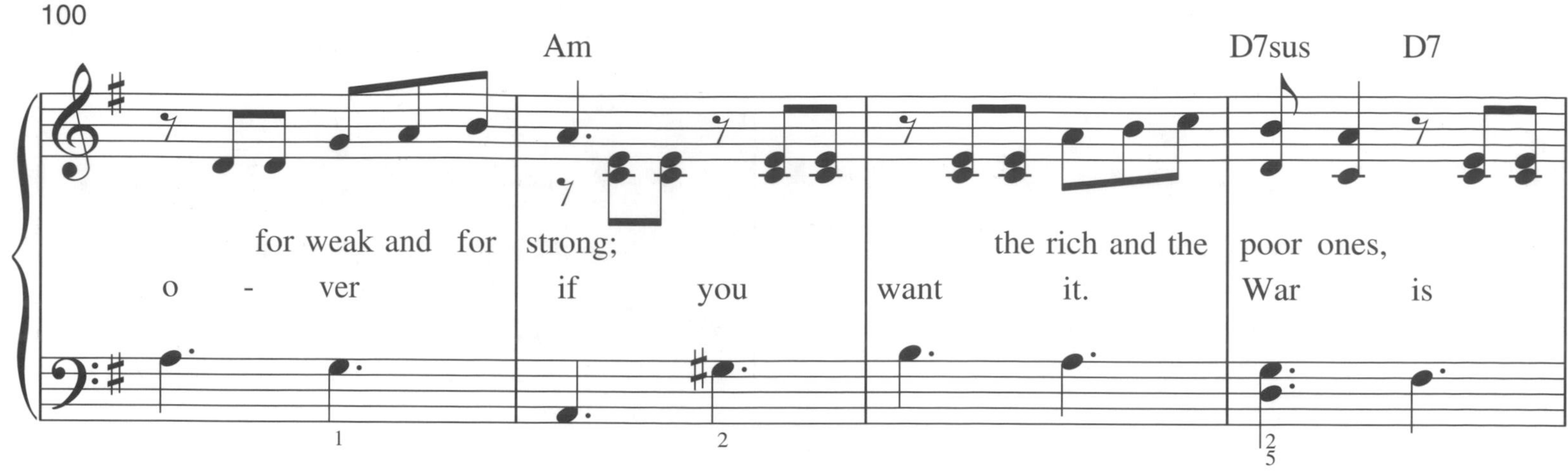
Am
D7sus
D7
for weak and for
strong;
the rich and the
poor ones,
o - ver
if you
want it.
War is

G
C
the road is so
long.
And so hap-py
X - mas
o - ver
now.)
(War is

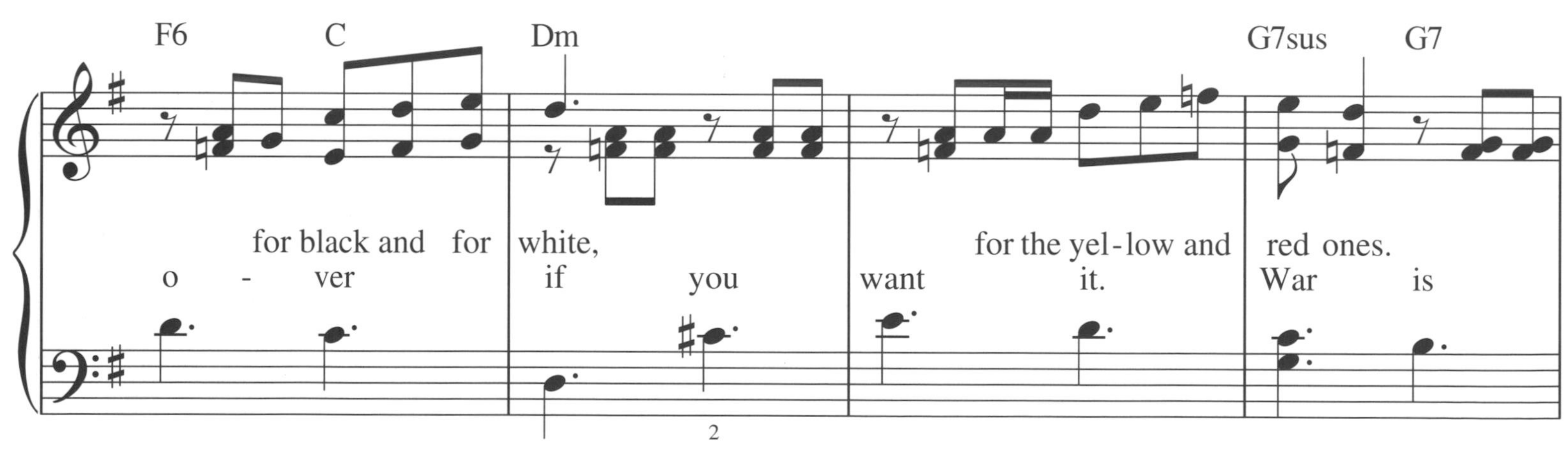
F6
C
Dm
G7sus
G7
for black and for
white,
for the yel-low and
red ones.
o - ver
if you
want it.
War is

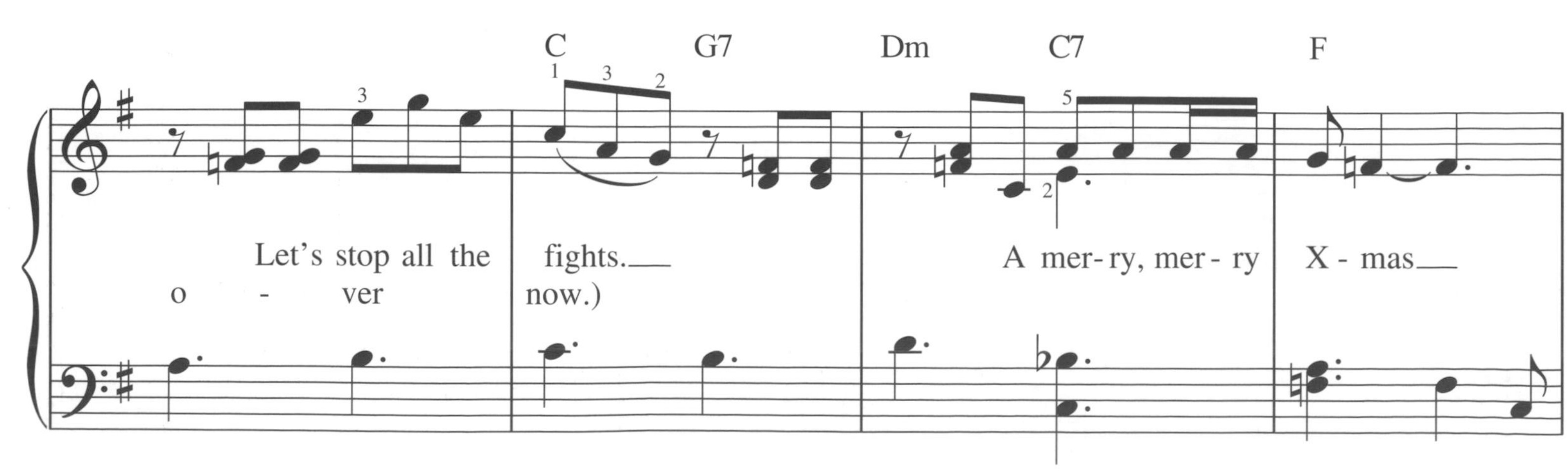
C
G7
Dm
C7
F
Let's stop all the
fights.
A mer-ry, mer-ry
X - mas
o - ver
now.)

G
Dm
and a hap-py New Year.
Let's hope it's a good one
2

D.S. al Coda
CODA
F
C
D
D7
C
with - out an - y fear.
And so this is
fear.

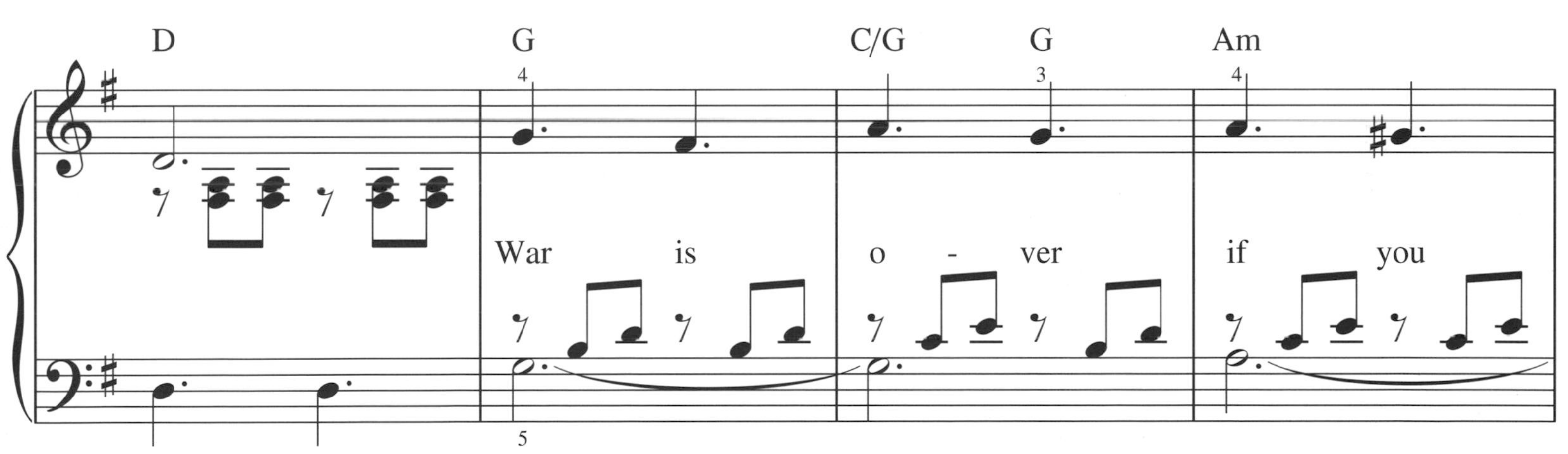
D
G
C/G
G
Am
War is o - ver if you

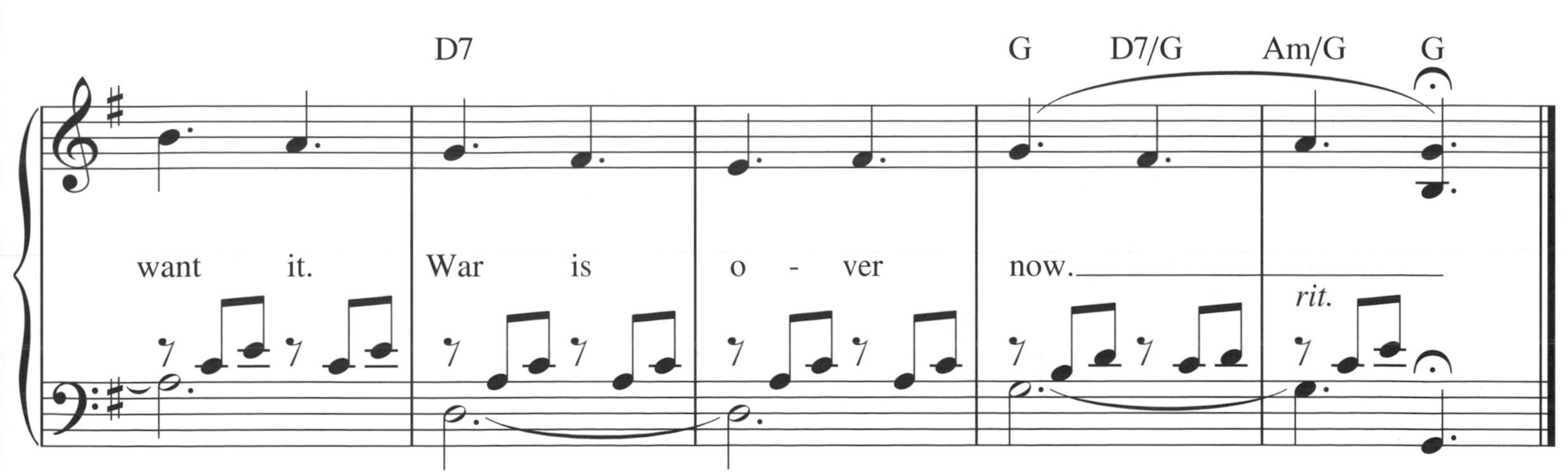
D7
G
D7/G
Am/G
G
want it. War is o - ver now.
rit.

HERE COMES SANTA CLAUS
(Right Down Santa Claus Lane)

Words and Music by GENE AUTRY
and OAKLEY HALDEMAN

Bb Bdim F D7 Gm7 C7
Bells are ring - ing, chil - dren sing - ing, all is mer - ry and
Hear those sleigh - bells jin - gle jan - gle, what a beau - ti - ful
San - ta knows that we're God's chil - dren, that makes ev - 'ry - thing
Peace on earth will come to all if we just fol - low the
mf

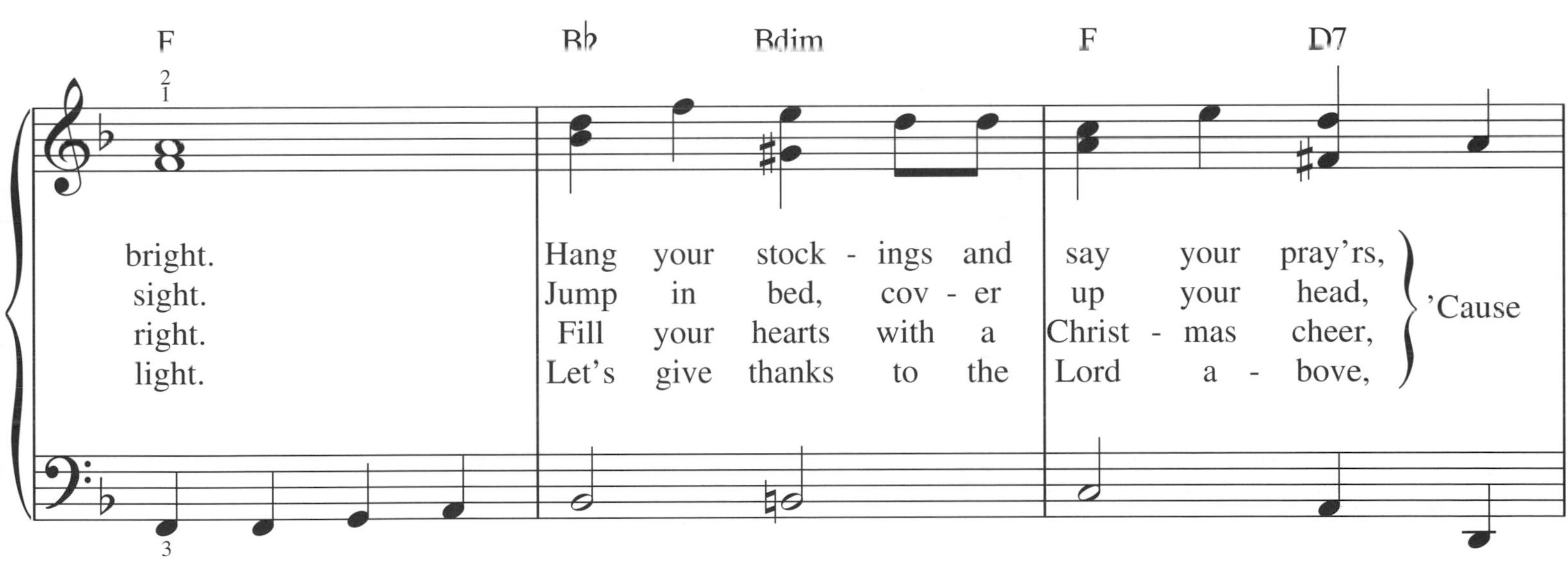
F Bb Bdim F D7
bright. Hang your stock - ings and say your pray'rs,
sight. Jump in bed, cov - er up your head,
right. Fill your hearts with a Christ - mas cheer,
light. Let's give thanks to the Lord a - bove,
'Cause

Gm7 C7 1. - 3. F 4. F
San - ta Claus comes to - night. night.

THE HOLIDAY SEASON

D7
F/G
C6
D7
F/G
To Coda
com - in' down the chim - ney, down. (He'll be com- in' down the chim- ney, down.)
com - in' down the chim - ney, down. (When he's com- in' down the chim- ney, down.)
com - in' down the chim - ney, down. (He'll be com- in' down the chim- ney, down.)
1. C6
2. C6
F/C
C
It's the
He'll have a big fat pack up -
F/C
C
F/C
C
F/C
C
on his back and lots of good-ies for you and for me. So leave a
F/C
C
F/C
C
D7
pep - per-mint stick for old Saint Nick hang - in' on the Christ-mas tree.

G9
D.S. al Coda
It's the
CODA
C6
F
C/E
He'll have a big fat pack up - on
Dm7
C
F
C/E
Dm7
C
his back and lots of good-ies for you and for me. So leave a
F
C/E
Dm7
C
D7
pep - per-mint stick for old Saint Nick hang - in' on the Christ-mas tree.
G9
C6
It's the hol - i - day sea - son, so,

Dm7 G13 Dm7 G13 Dm7 G13
whoop - de - doo and dick - o - ry dock, a - don't for - get to
Em7 A7 Dm7 G13 C6 A7
hang up your sock, 'cause just ex - act - ly at twelve o' - clock he'll be
D7 F/G D7 F/G D7
com - in' down the chim - ney, com - in' down the chim - ney, com -
F/G C6
- in' down the chim - ney, down.

HOLLY LEAVES AND CHRISTMAS TREES

Words and Music by RED WEST
and GLEN SPREEN

C
Dm
home-ward bound.
That's the way it's
al-ways been; the

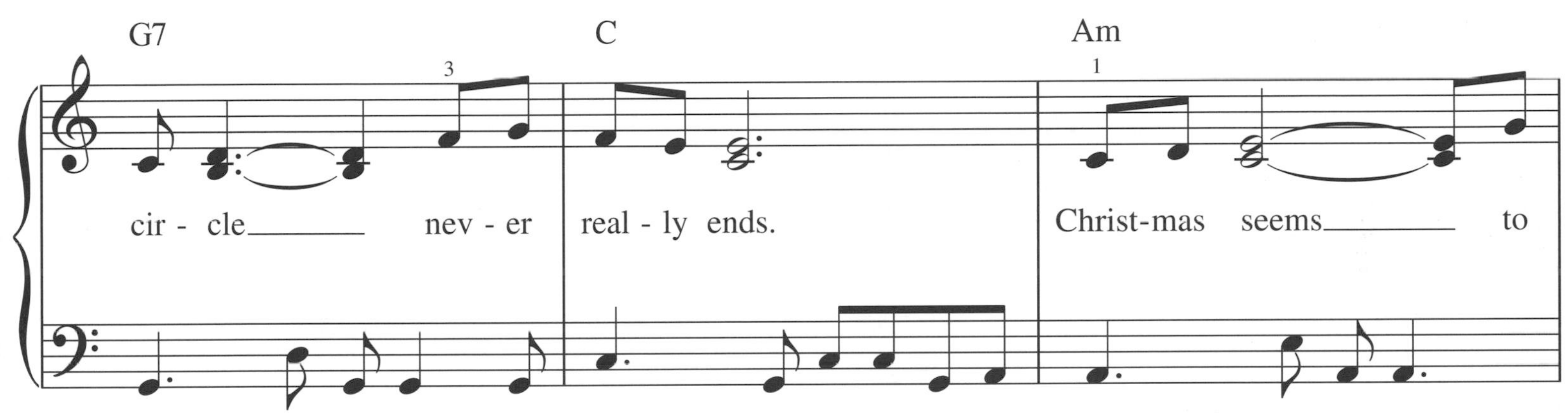
G7
C
Am
cir - cle nev - er
real - ly ends.
Christ-mas seems to

Dm
F
C
come and go
home's a place that
I don't know.

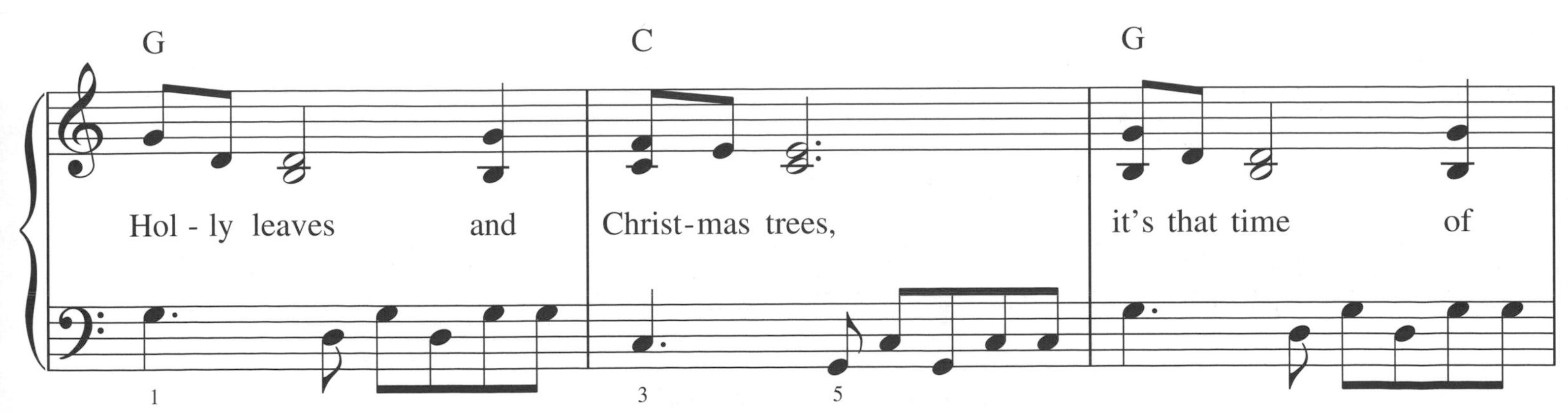
G
C
G
Hol - ly leaves and
Christ-mas trees,
it's that time of

C
Am
Em
year,
lights a - glow and
mis - tle - toe don't

F
G
C
mean a thing when you're not
here.
As I walk, walk this

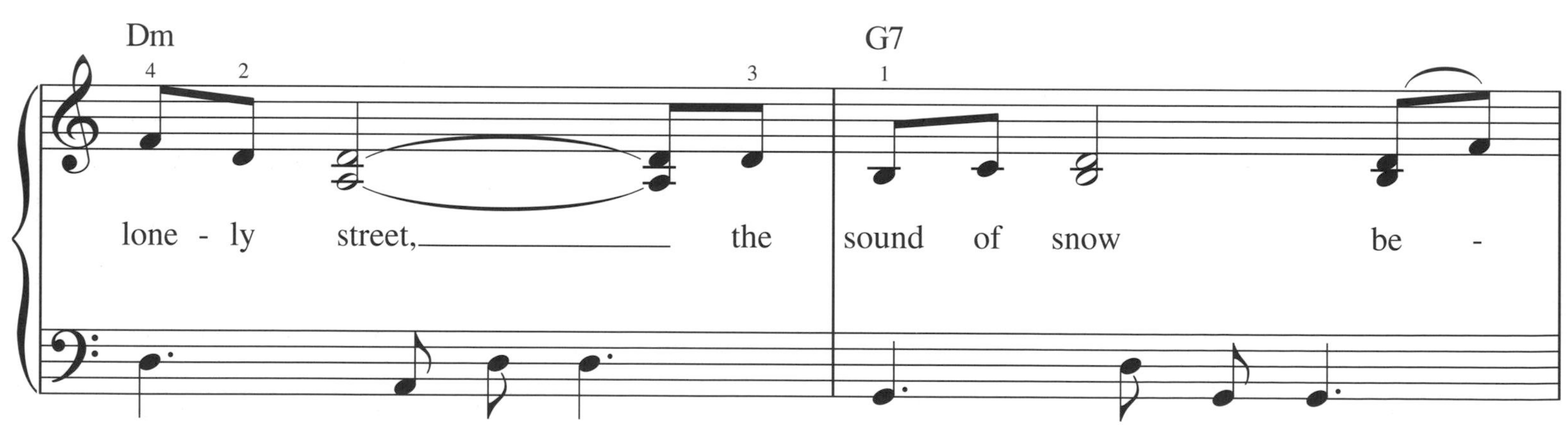

Dm
G7
lone - ly street, the
sound of snow be -

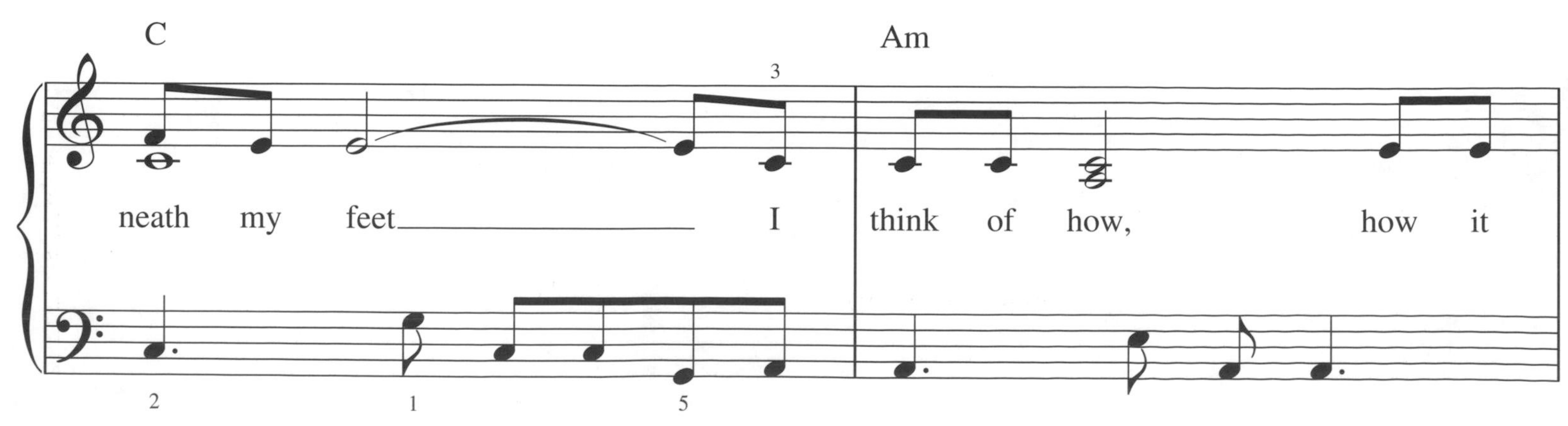

C
Am
neath my feet I
think of how, how it

Dm
F
used to be, when hol - ly leaves and
G7
F
Christ - mas trees used to mean so
C
F/C
much to me.
C

I WONDER AS I WANDER

By JOHN JACOB NILES

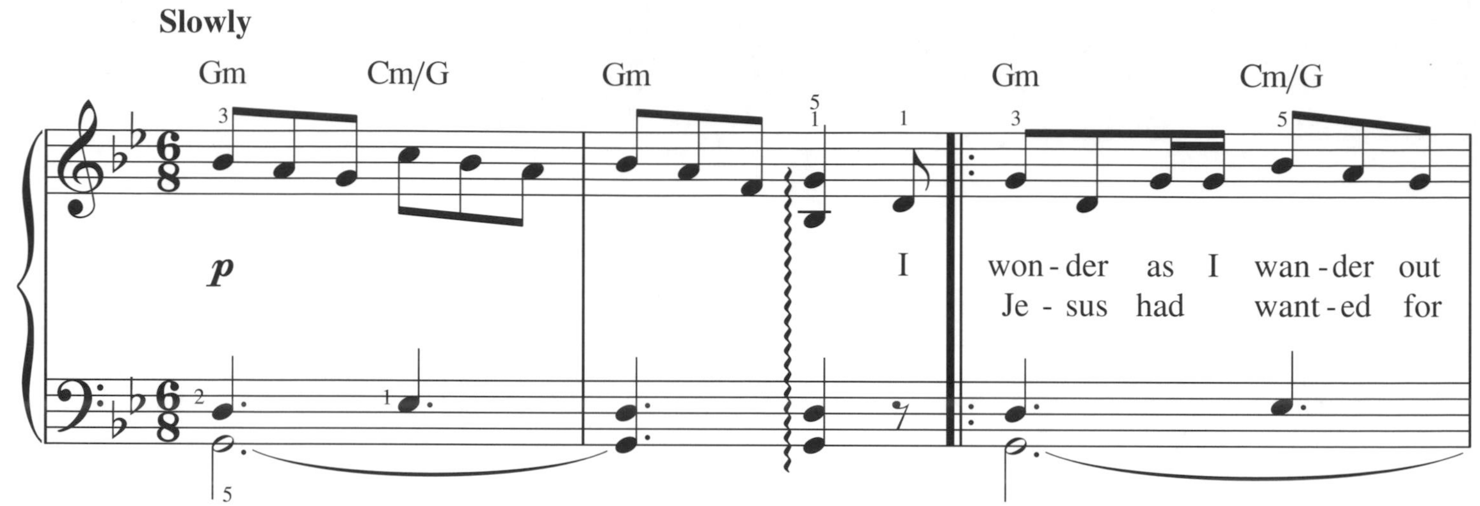

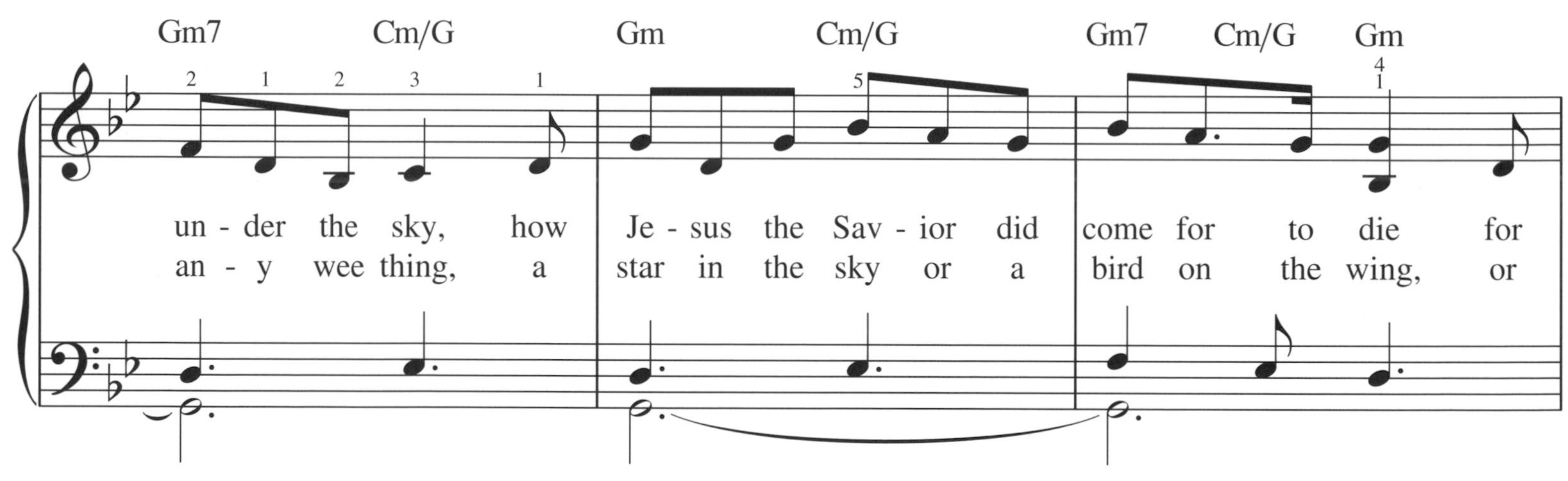

Gm Cm Gm Cm/G Gm7 D7/F♯
un - der the sky. When Mar - y birthed Je - sus, 'twas in a cow's stall, with
He was the King. I won - der as I wan - der, out un - der the sky, how
Gm Cm/G Gm7 Cm/G Gm Cm/G
wise men and farm - ers and shep - herds and all. But high from God's heav - en a
Je - sus the Sav - ior did come for to die for poor on - 'ry peo - ple like
Gm7 G7/D Cm Gm/B♭ Cm7 B♭/D Cm7
star's light did fall, and the prom - ise of ag - es it
you and like I... I won - der as I wan - der out
1. Gm7 Cm
then did re - call. If
2. Gm Cm Gm
un - der the sky.

I'D LIKE TO GO BACK HOME FOR CHRISTMAS

Words and Music by
LOONIS McGLOHON

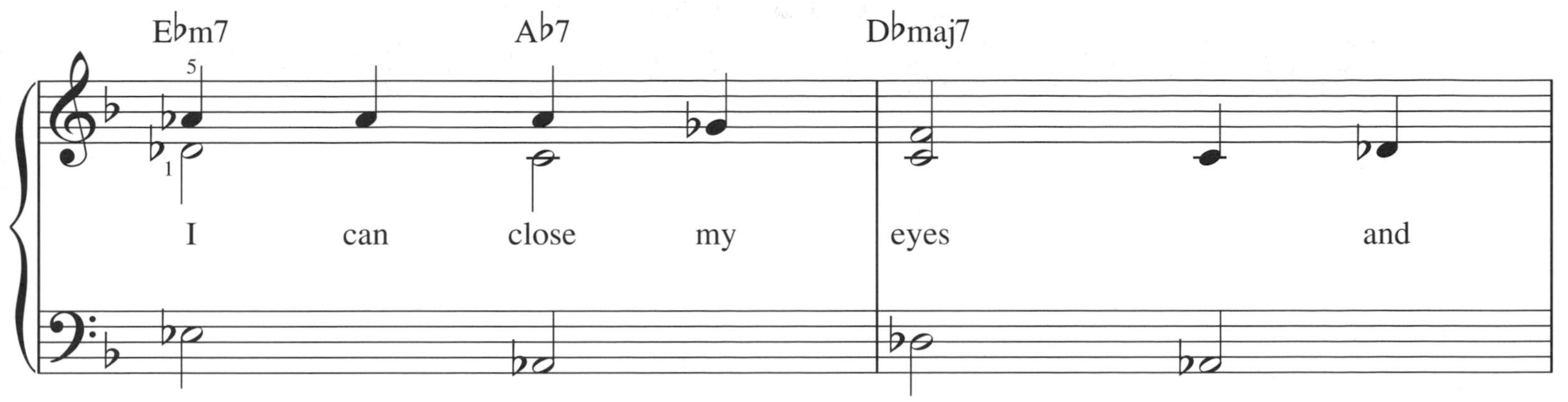
E♭m7
A♭7
D♭maj7
5
1
I can close my eyes and

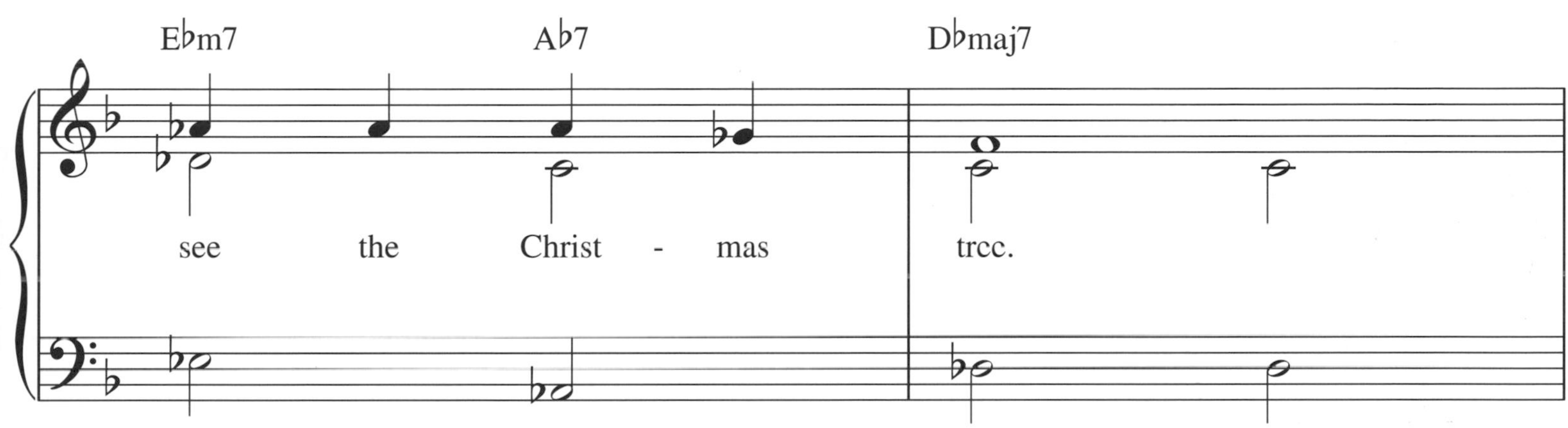
E♭m7
A♭7
D♭maj7
see the Christ - mas trcc.

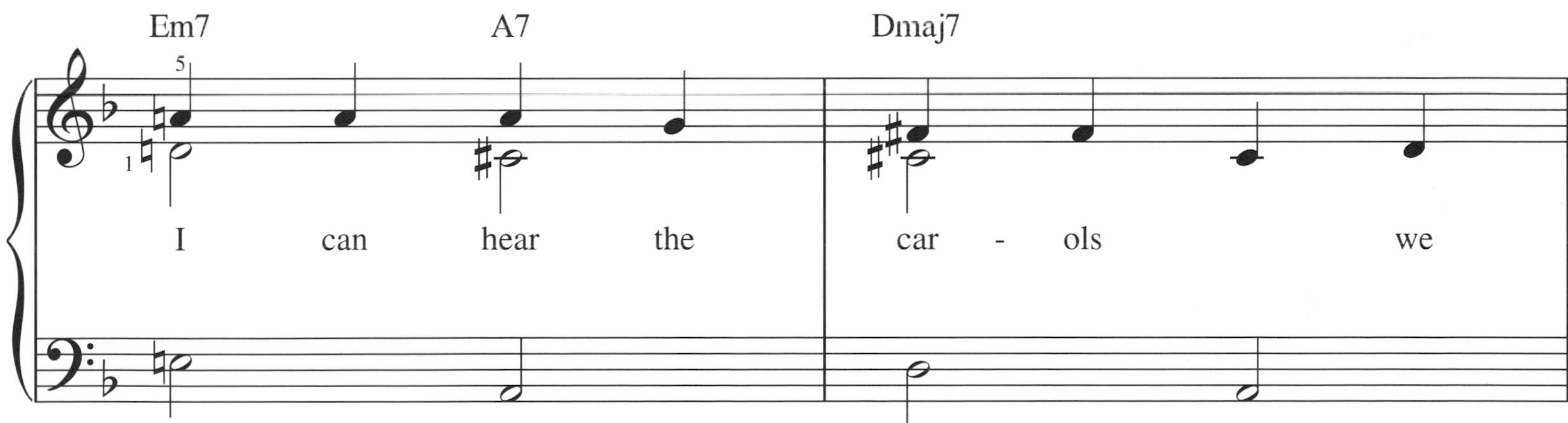
Em7
A7
Dmaj7
5
1
I can hear the car - ols we

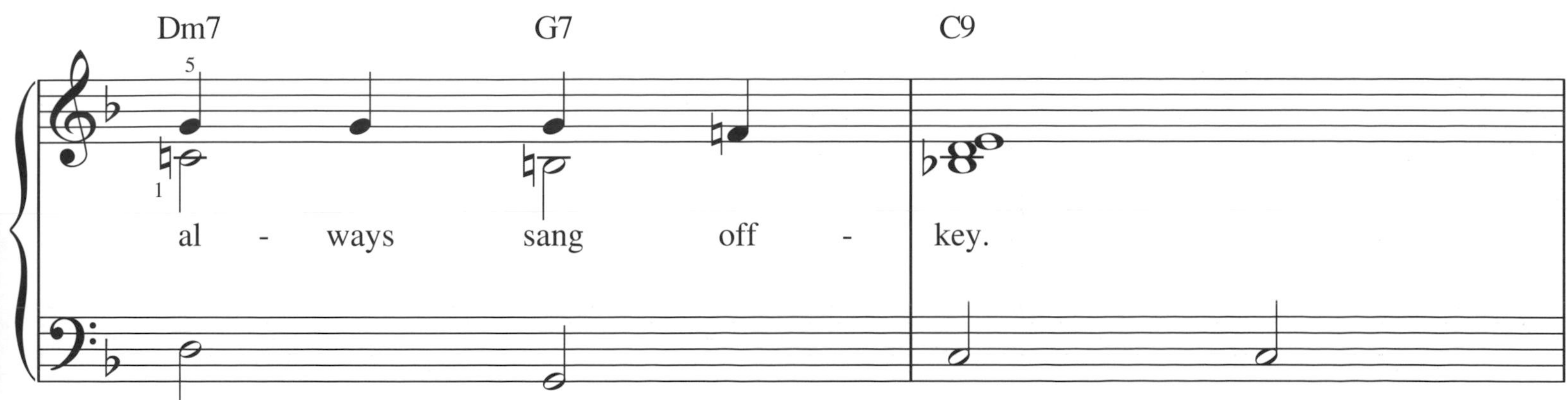
Dm7
G7
C9
5
1
al - ways sang off - key.

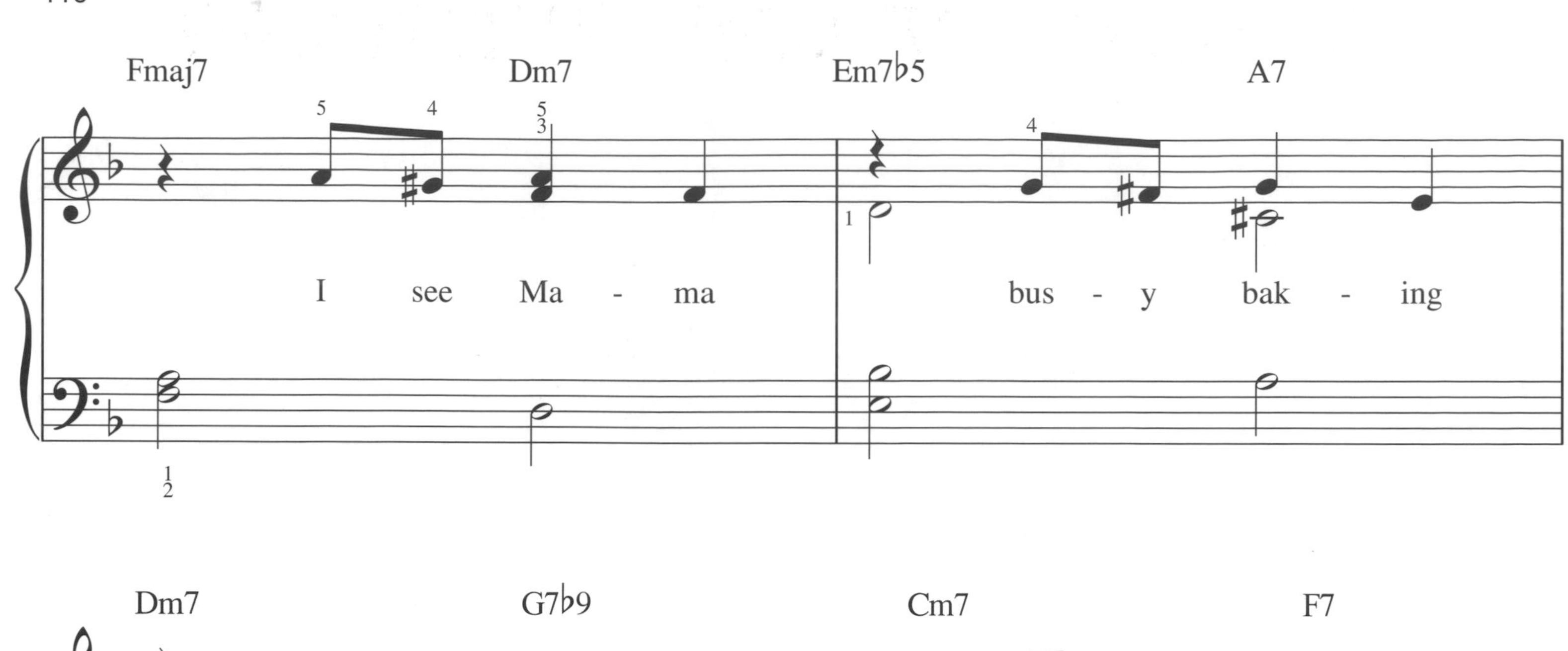
Fmaj7
Dm7
Em7♭5
A7
I see Ma - ma
bus - y bak - ing

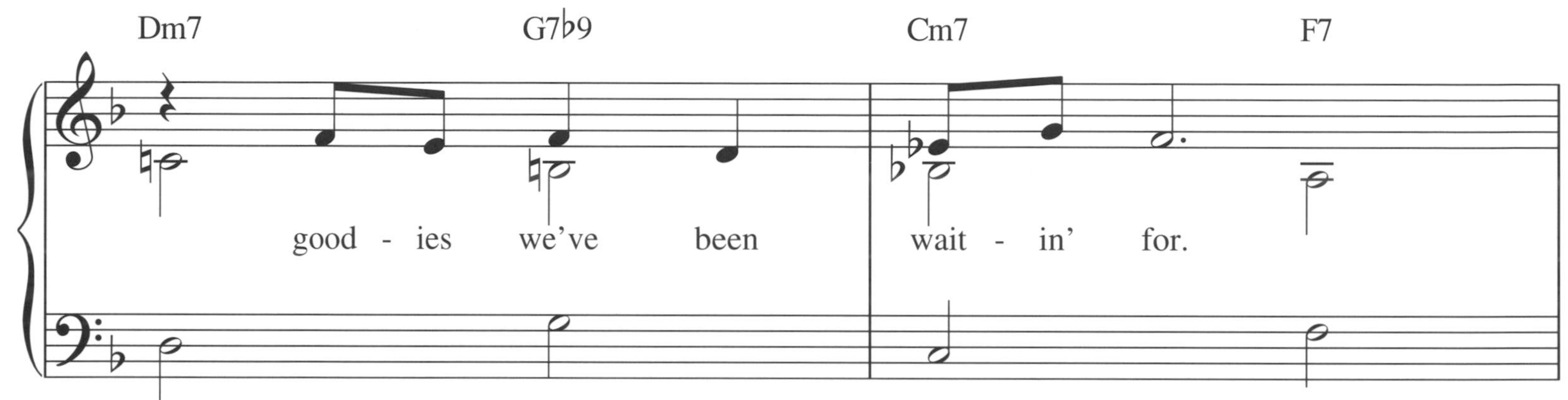
Dm7
G7♭9
Cm7
F7
good - ies we've been
wait - in' for.

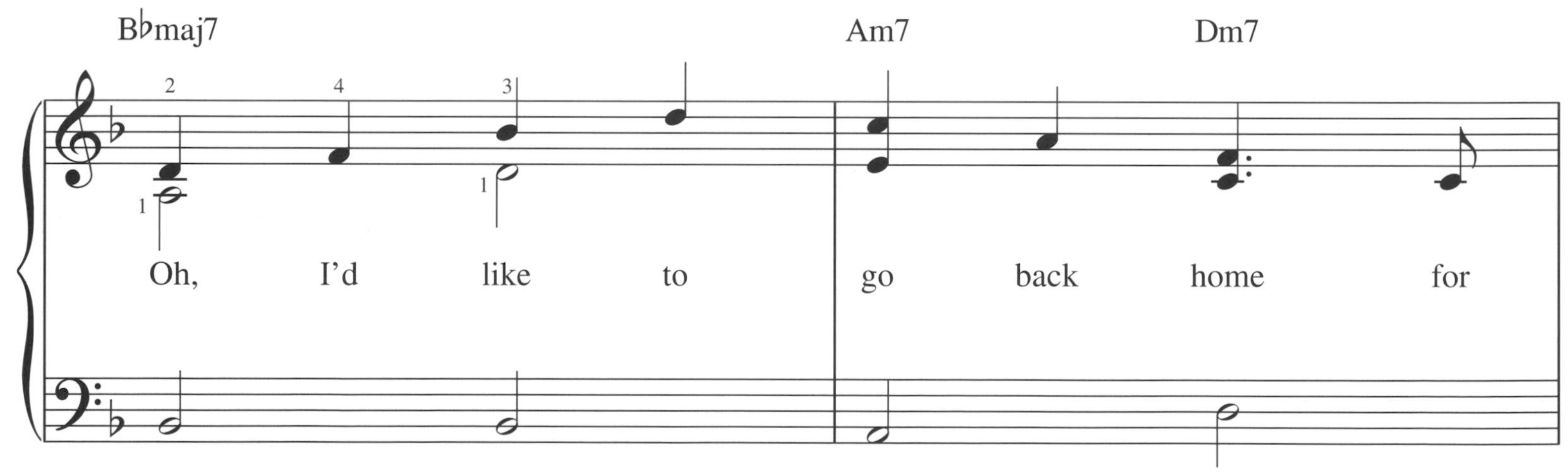
B♭maj7
Am7
Dm7
Oh, I'd like to
go back home for

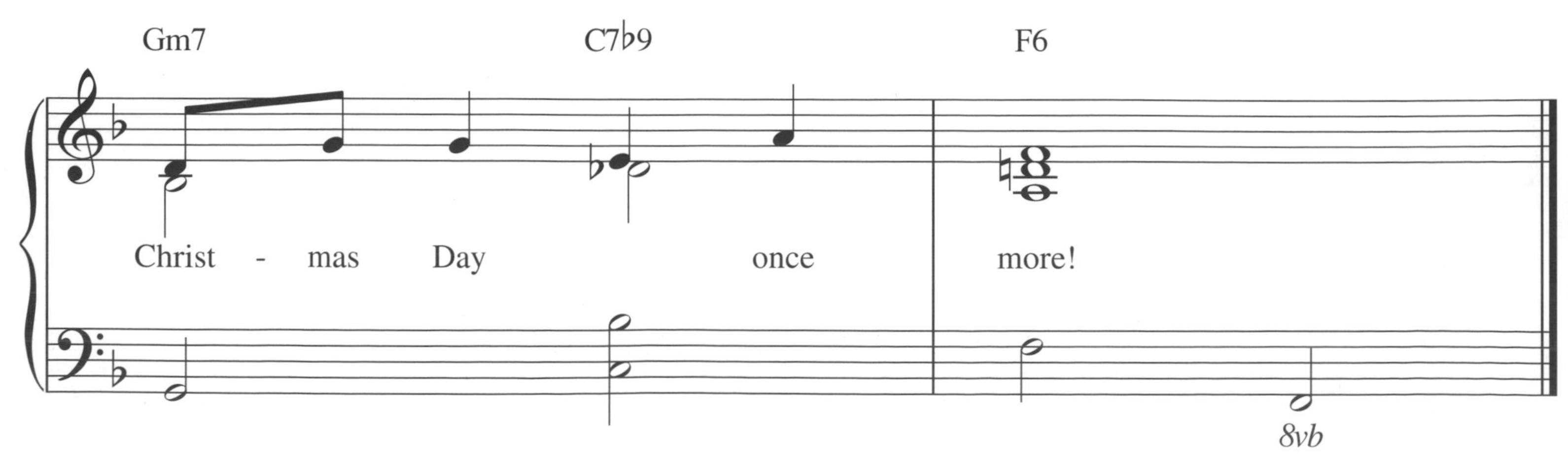
Gm7
C7♭9
F6
Christ - mas Day once
more!
8vb

I'LL BE HOME FOR CHRISTMAS

Words and Music by KIM GANNON
and WALTER KENT

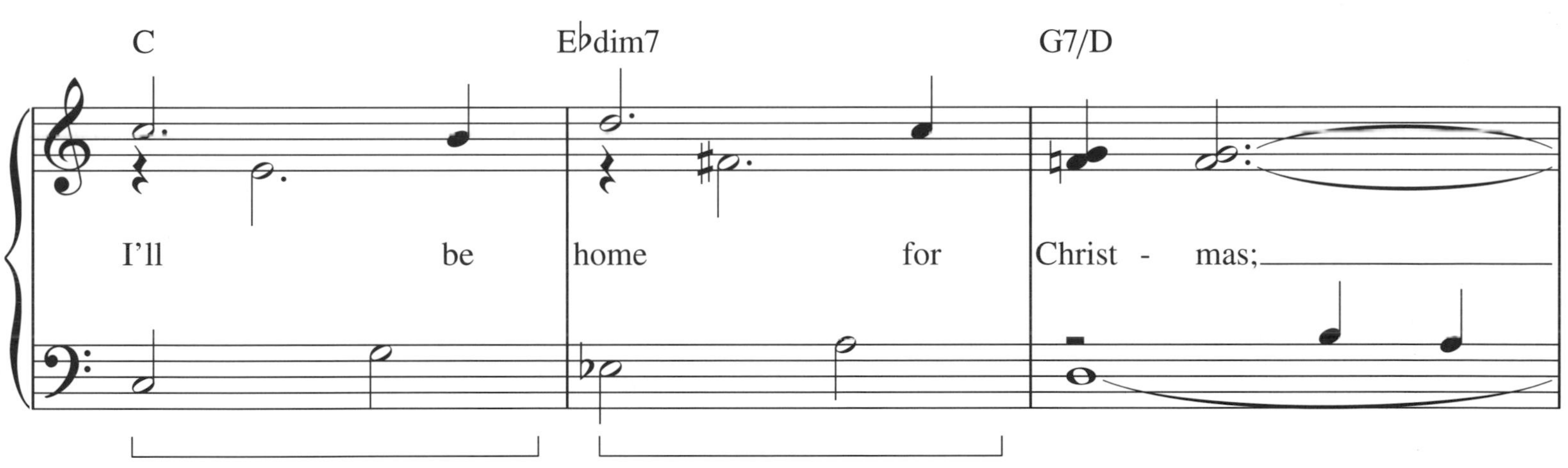

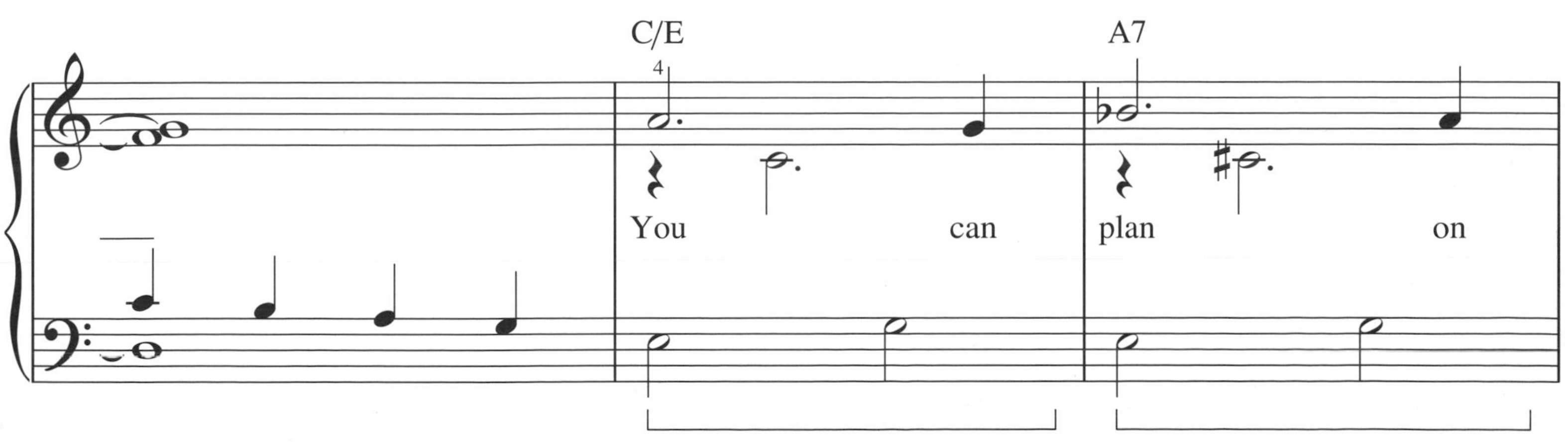

Dm
F
me.
Please
have

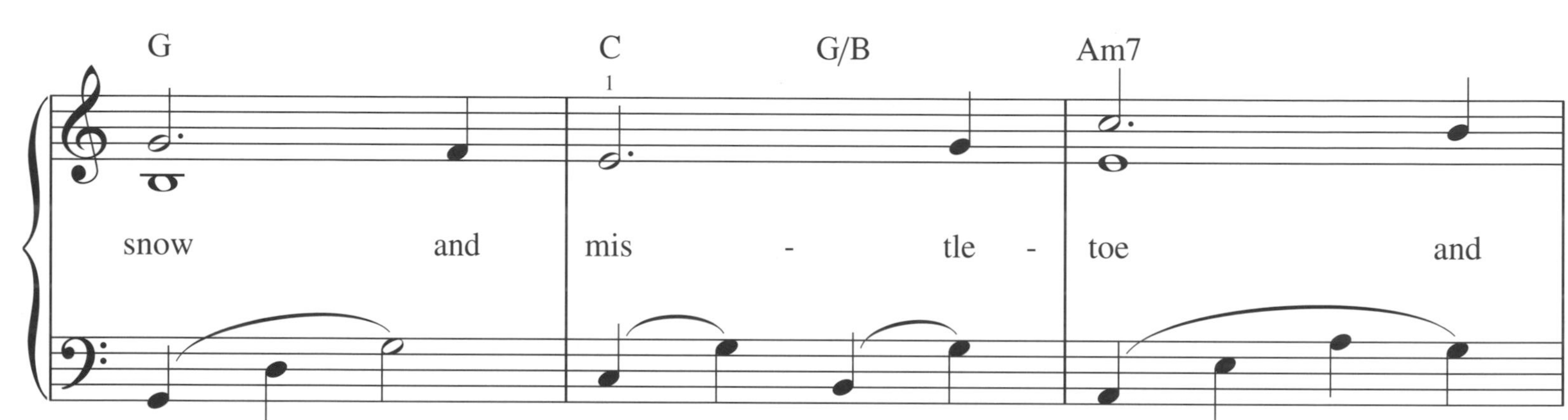
G
C
G/B
Am7
snow
and
mis - tle - toe
and

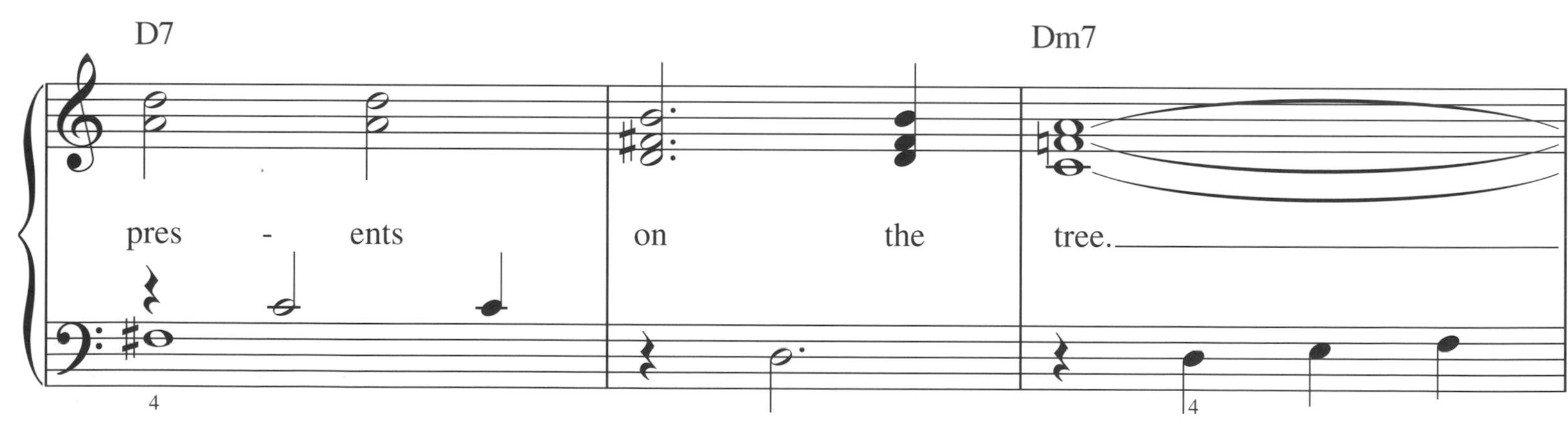
D7
Dm7
pres - ents
on
the
tree.

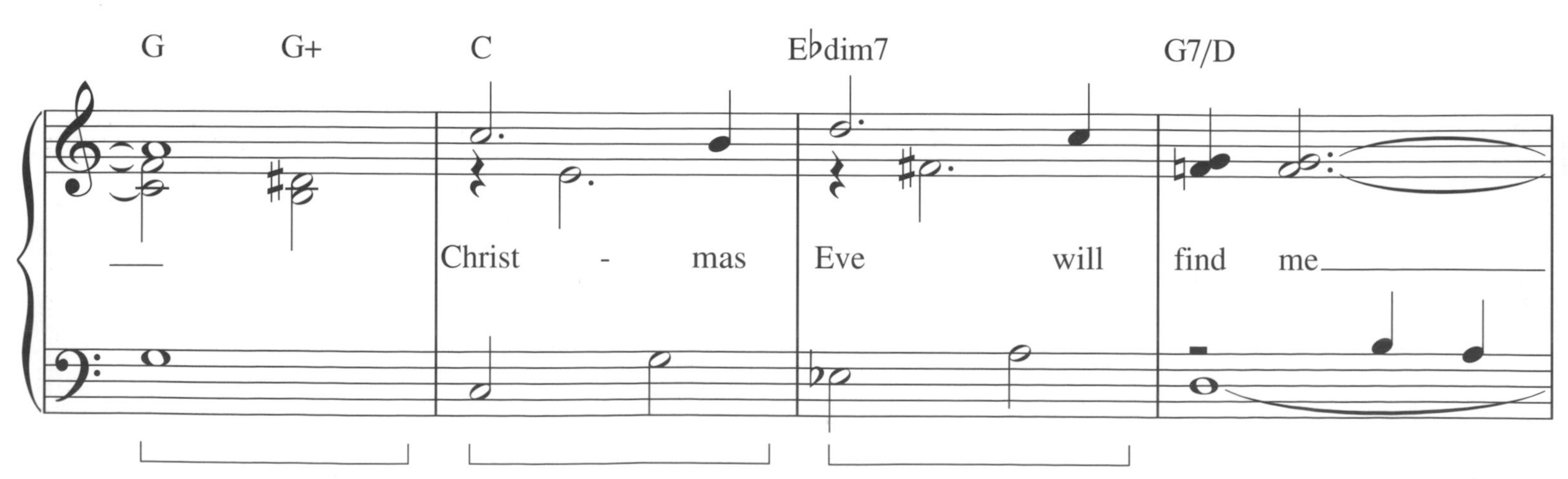
G
G+
C
E♭dim7
G7/D
Christ - mas
Eve
will
find
me

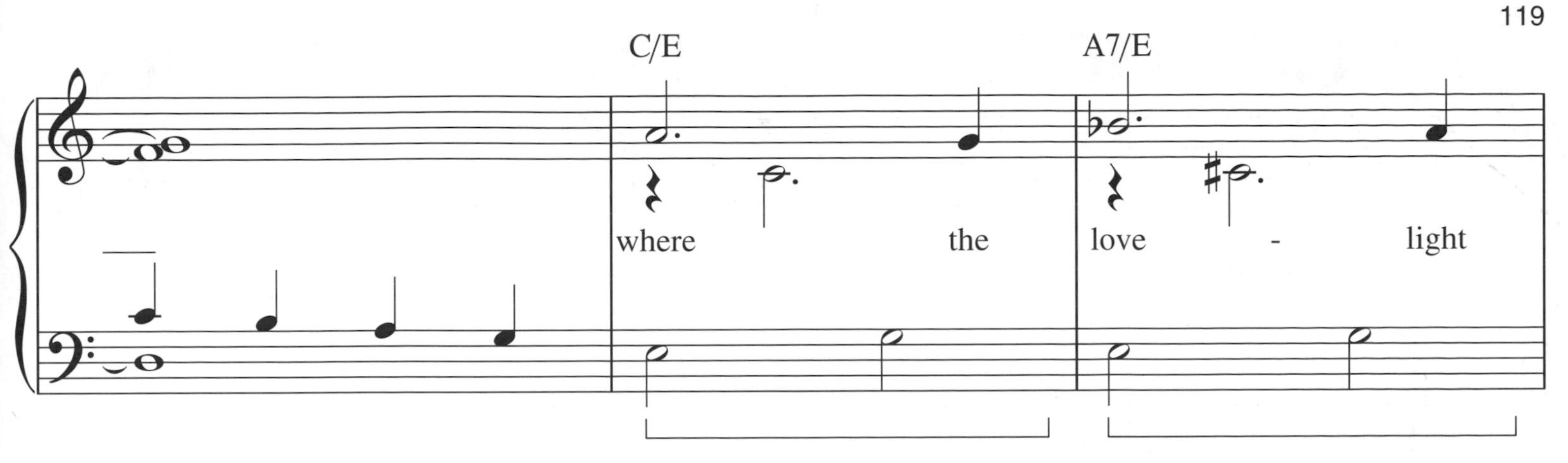
C/E
A7/E
where the love - light

Dm
F
gleams.
I'll be

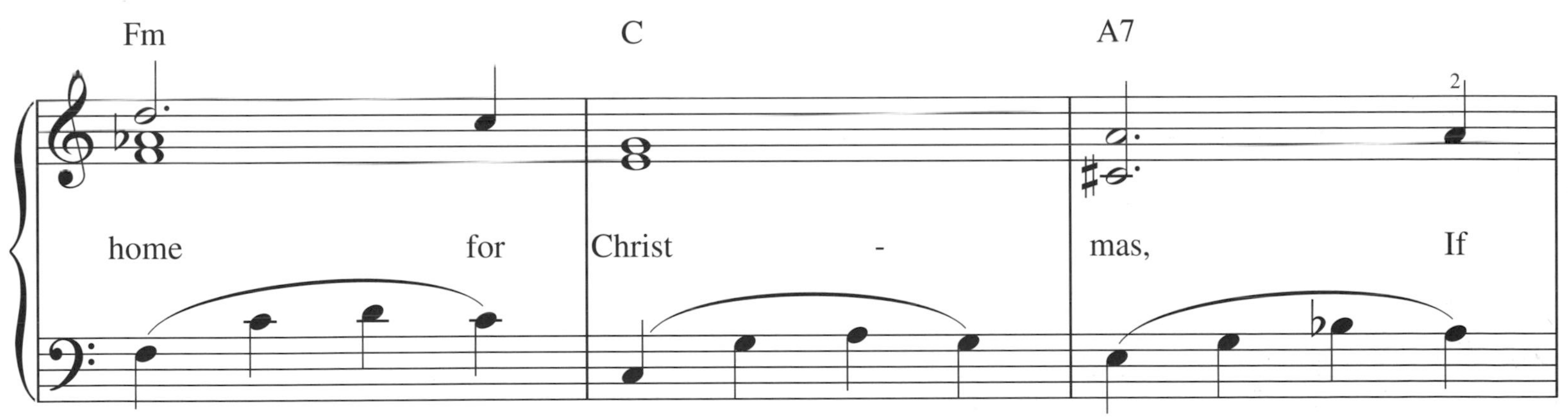
Fm
C
A7
home for Christ - mas, If

D7
Dm
G7
C
B♭
A♭
C
on - ly in my dreams.

IF I GET HOME ON CHRISTMAS DAY

Words and Music by
TONY MACAULEY

D7♭9
G
Bm
I
miss you and I
can
will
stay a

Em
G/D
C
while.
You'll
see it in my eyes

Am
D7
and when I
smile.
If I

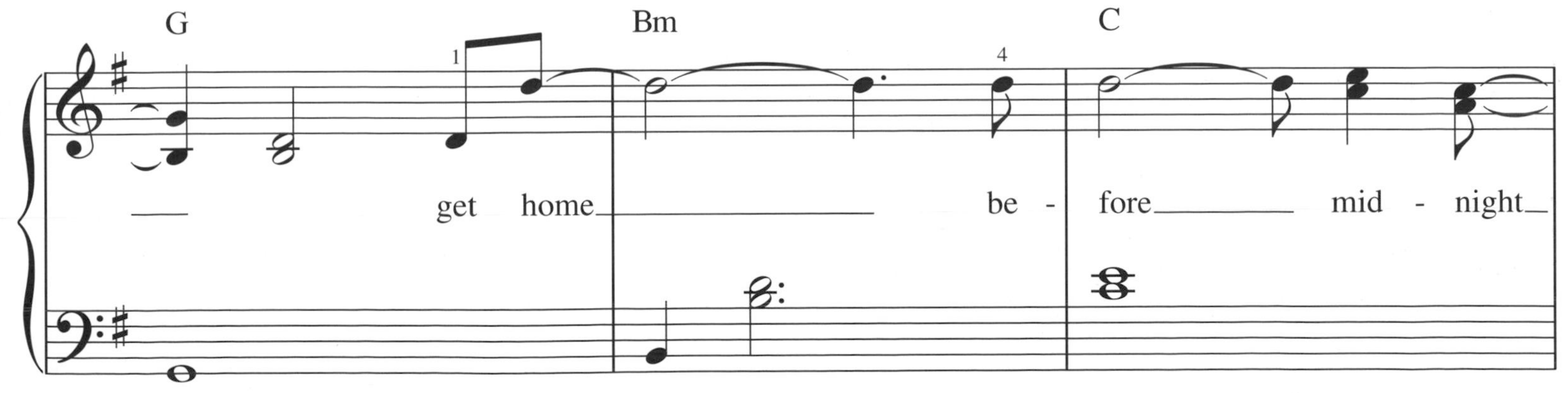
G
Bm
C
get home
be - fore mid - night

Am
Bm
Em
while
and
you're
still

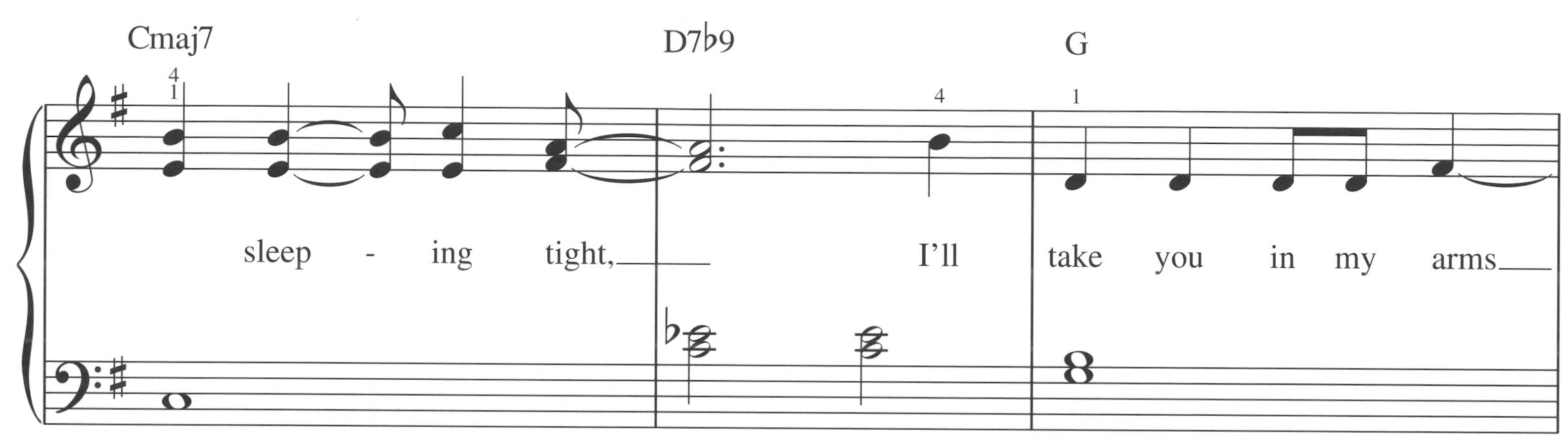
Cmaj7
D7♭9
G
sleep - ing tight,
I'll
take you in my arms

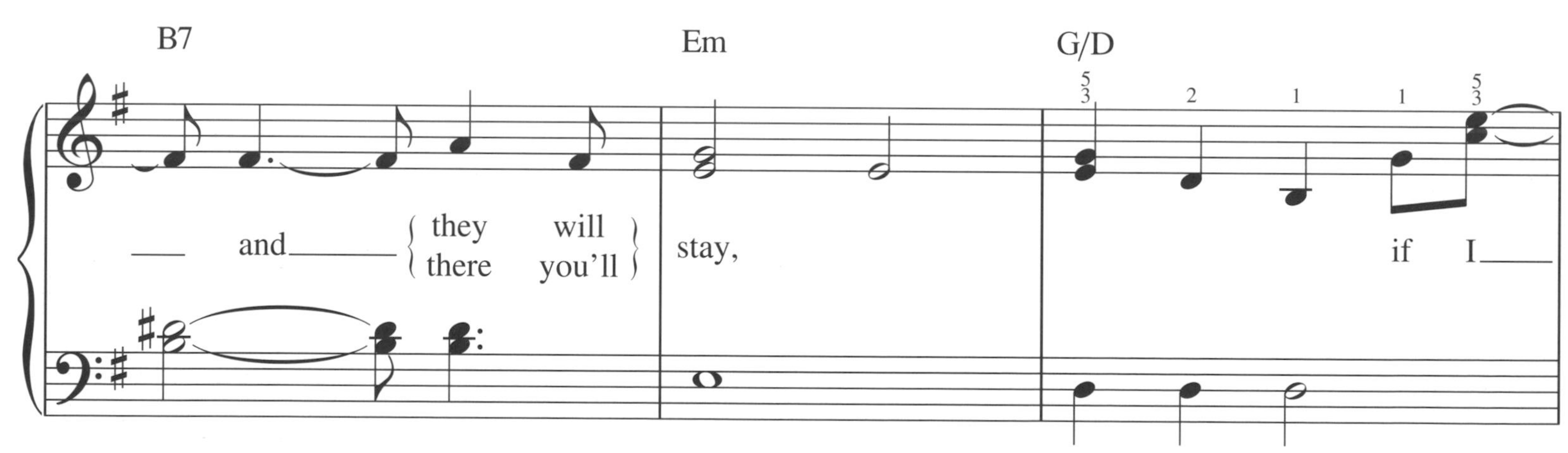
B7
Em
G/D
and
they will
there you'll
stay,
if I

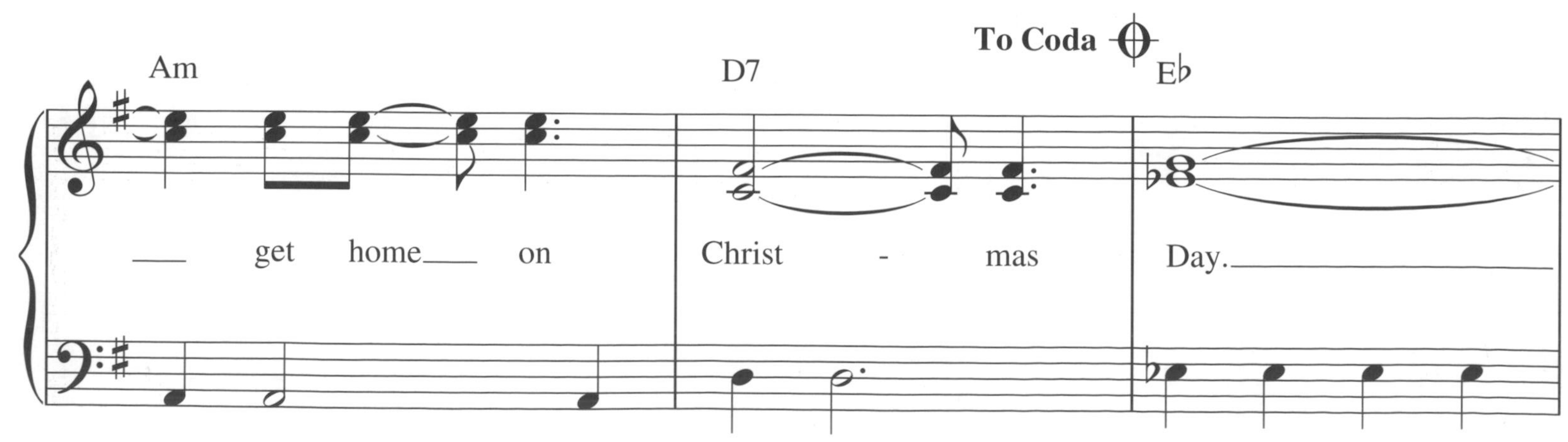
Am
D7
To Coda
E♭
get home on
Christ - mas
Day.

G
3
3
2
1

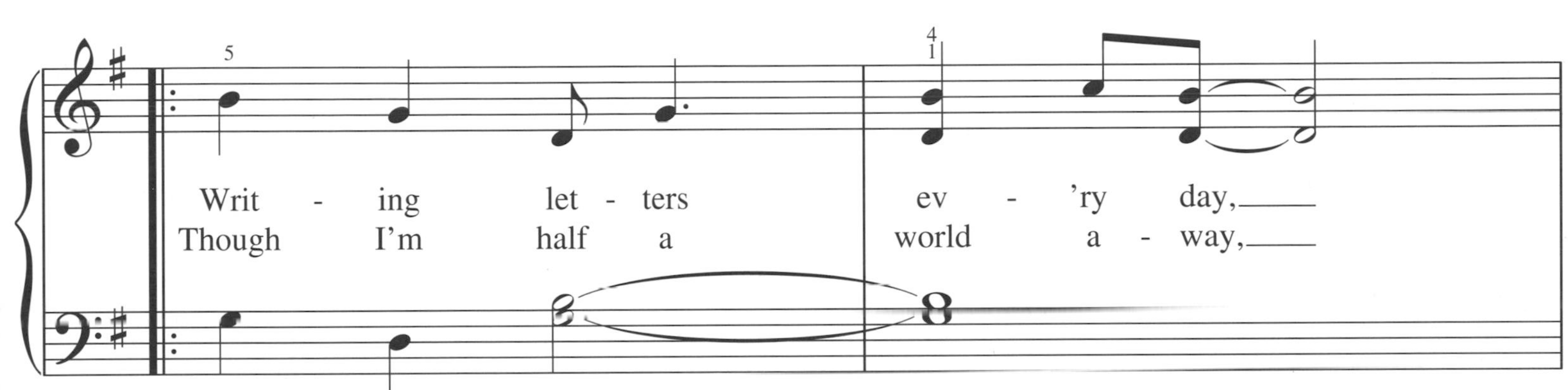
5
4
1
Writ - ing let - ters ev - 'ry day,
Though I'm half a world a - way,

Cmaj7/G
4
1
1
1.
Am
5
3
nev - er real - ly seem to say the way I feel you
if we're pa - tient and we pray, I

D7
3
G
in this heart of mine.

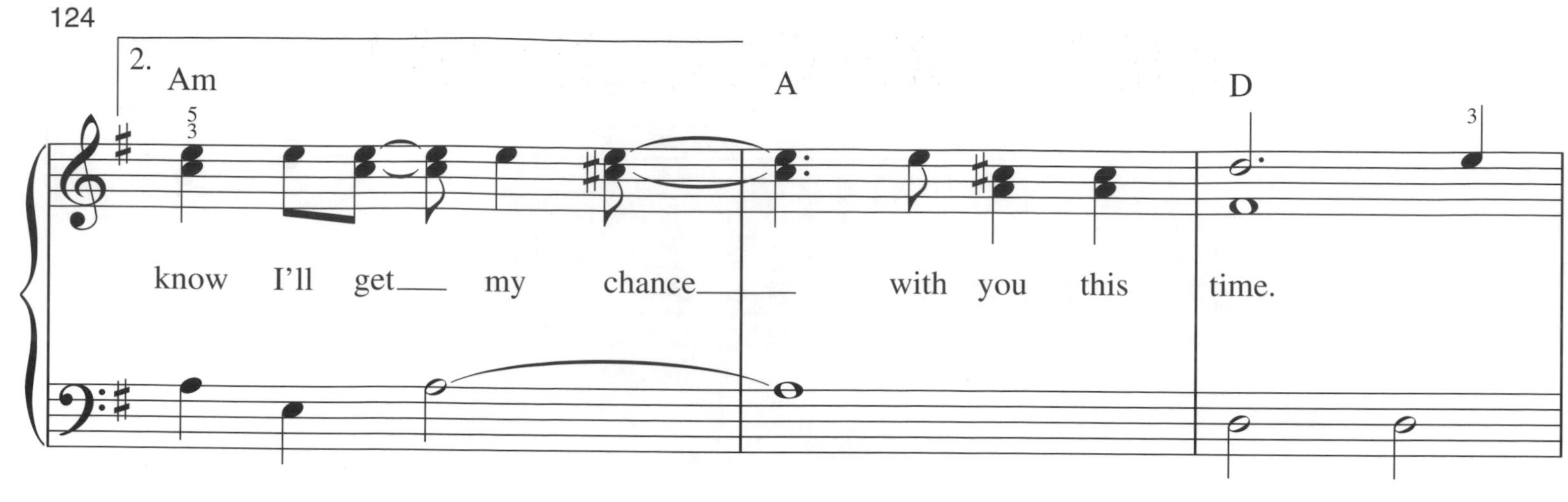
2.
Am
A
D
know I'll get my chance with you this time.

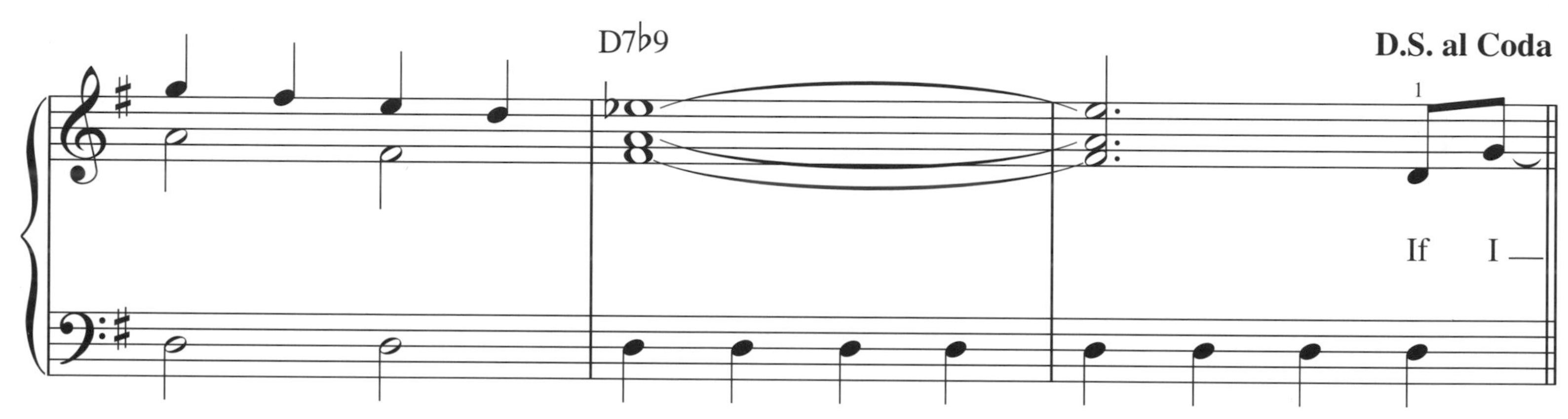
D7♭9
D.S. al Coda
If I

CODA
E♭
Cm
Day.

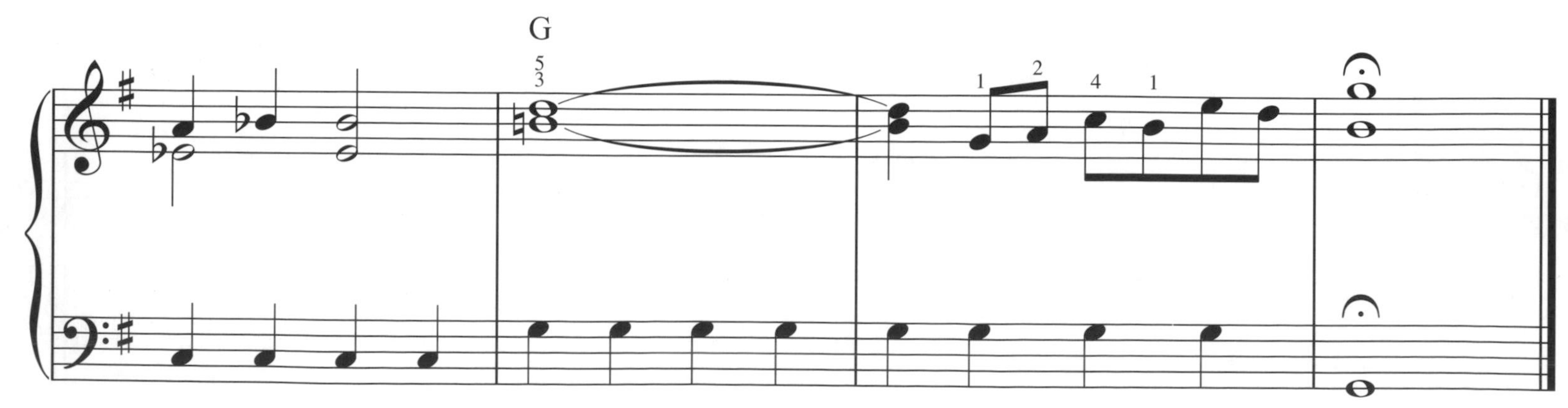
G

JINGLE, JINGLE, JINGLE

Music and Lyrics by
JOHNNY MARKS

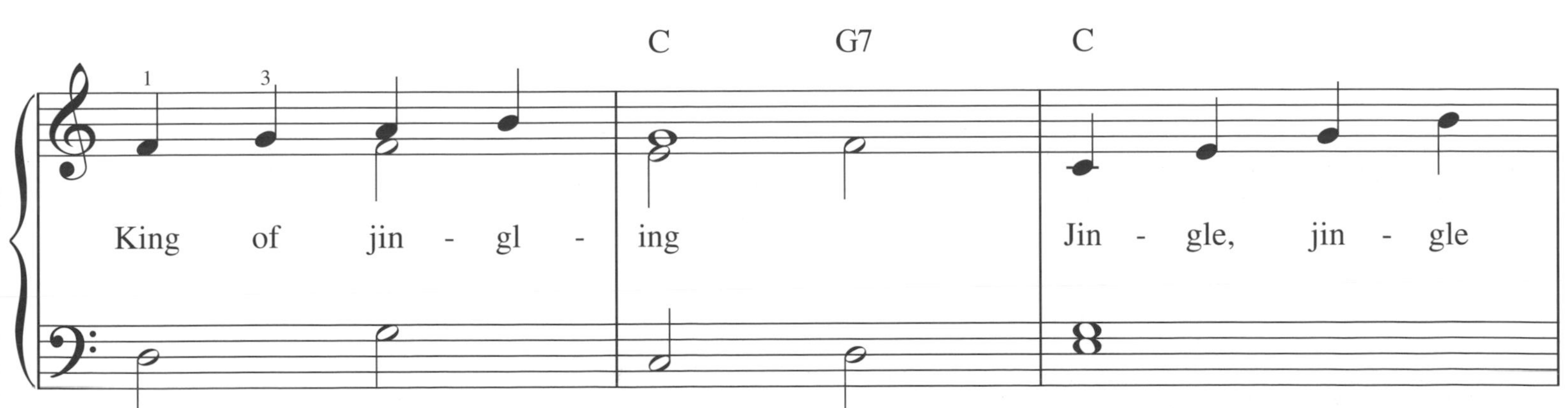

G7
rein - deer, through the frost - y air they'll go,

They are not just plain deer, they're the fast - est deer I

C
F
C
know. You must be - lieve that on Christ - mas Eve

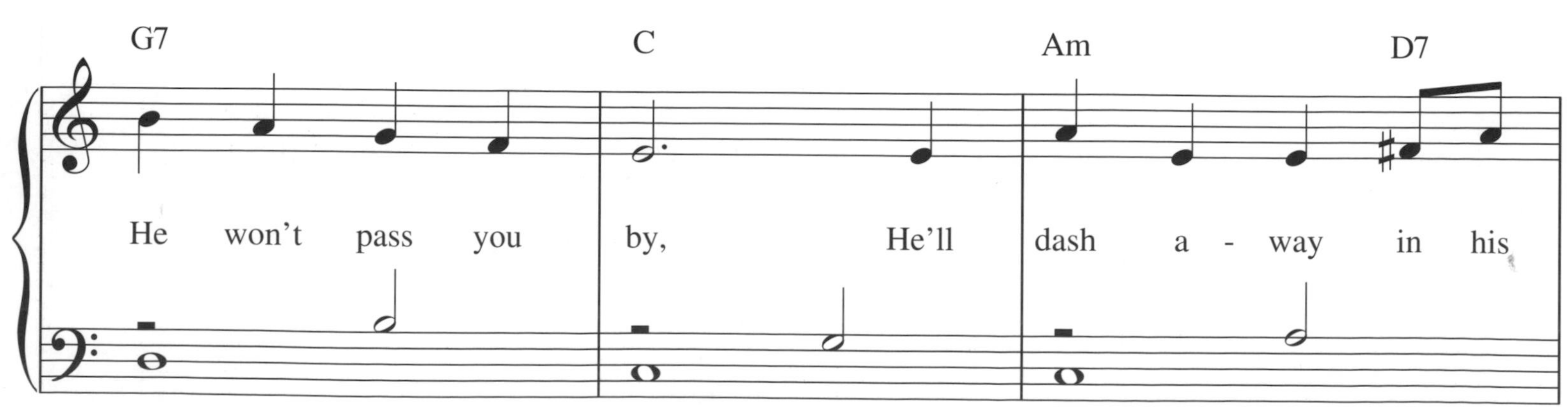
G7
C
Am
D7
He won't pass you by, He'll dash a - way in his

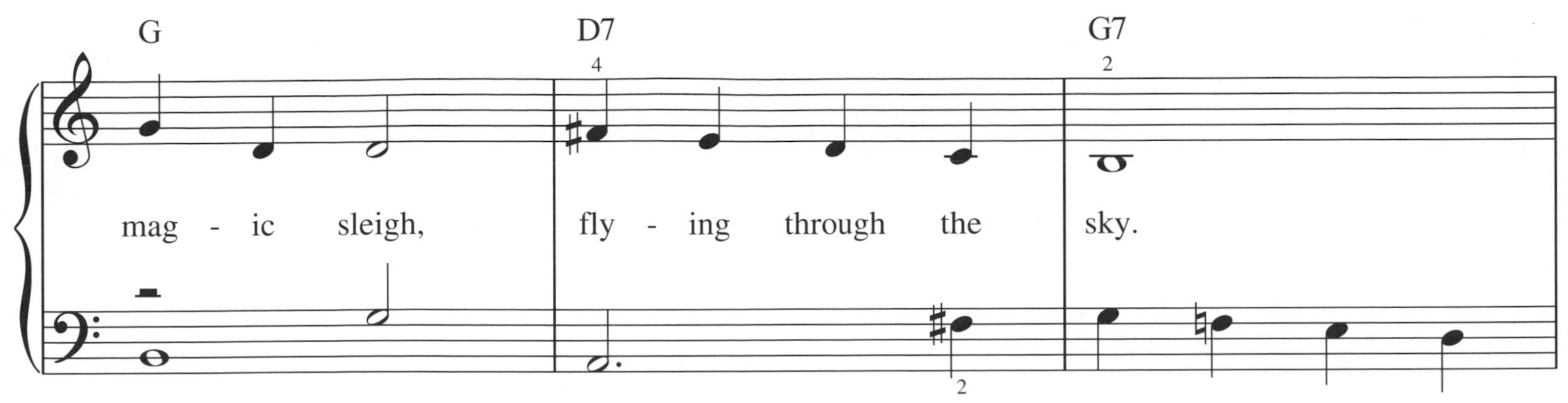
G
D7
G7
4
2
mag - ic sleigh,
fly - ing through the
sky.
2

C
1
Jin - gle, jin - gle,
jin - gle, you will
hear his sleigh bells

G7
ring,
Jol - ly old Kris
Kin - gle is the

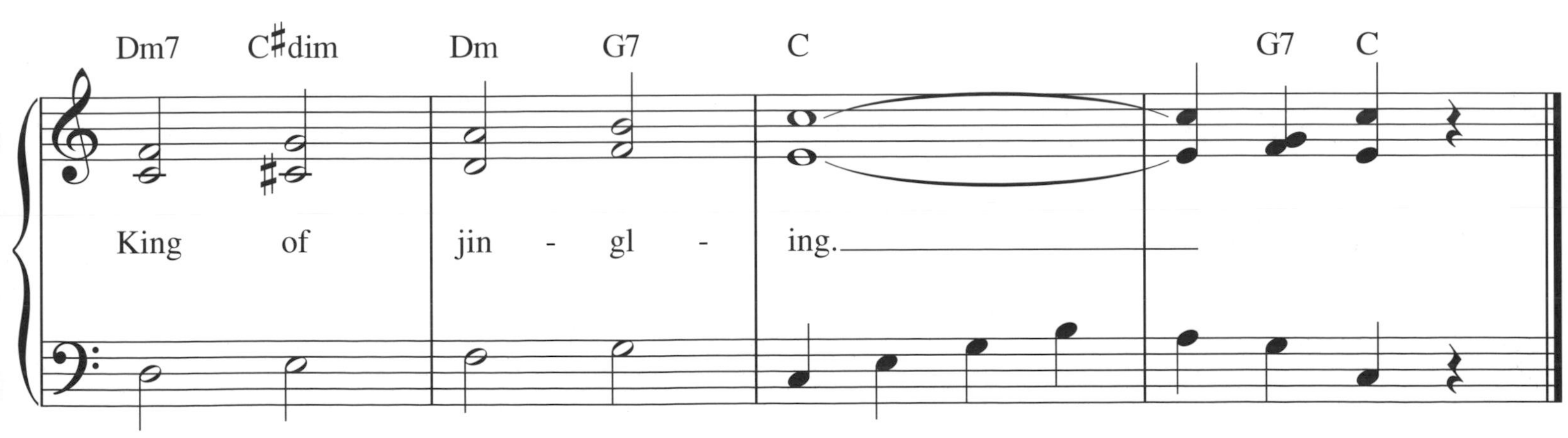
Dm7 C♯dim
Dm G7
C
G7 C
King of
jin - gl -
ing.

IT MUST HAVE BEEN THE MISTLETOE

(Our First Christmas)

By JUSTIN WILDE
and DOUG KONECKY

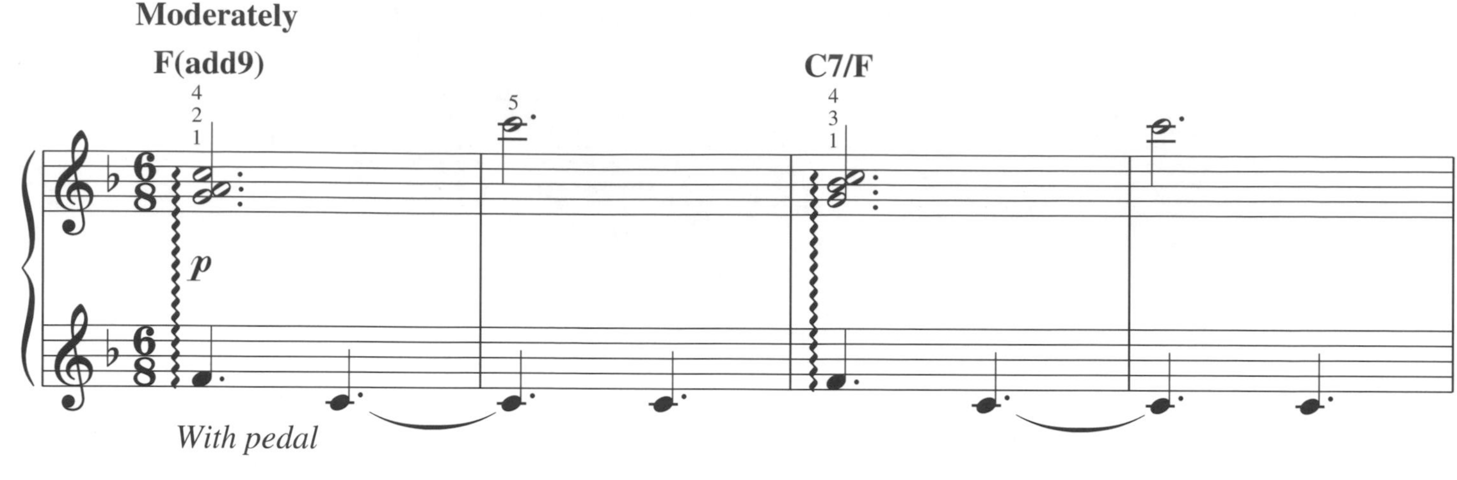

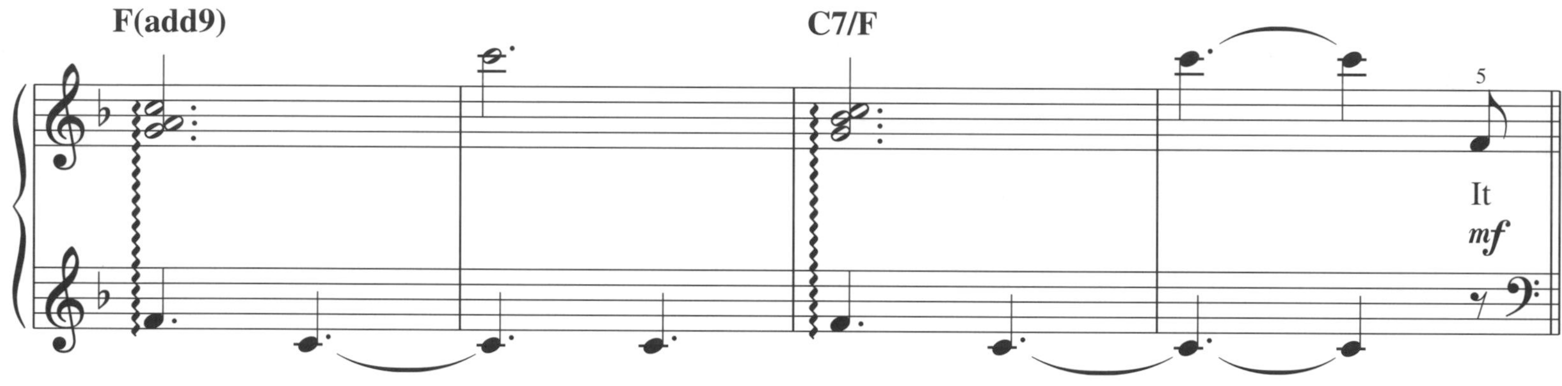

B♭/C
F(add9)
feel - ing
ev - 'ry - where. It
must have been ___ the

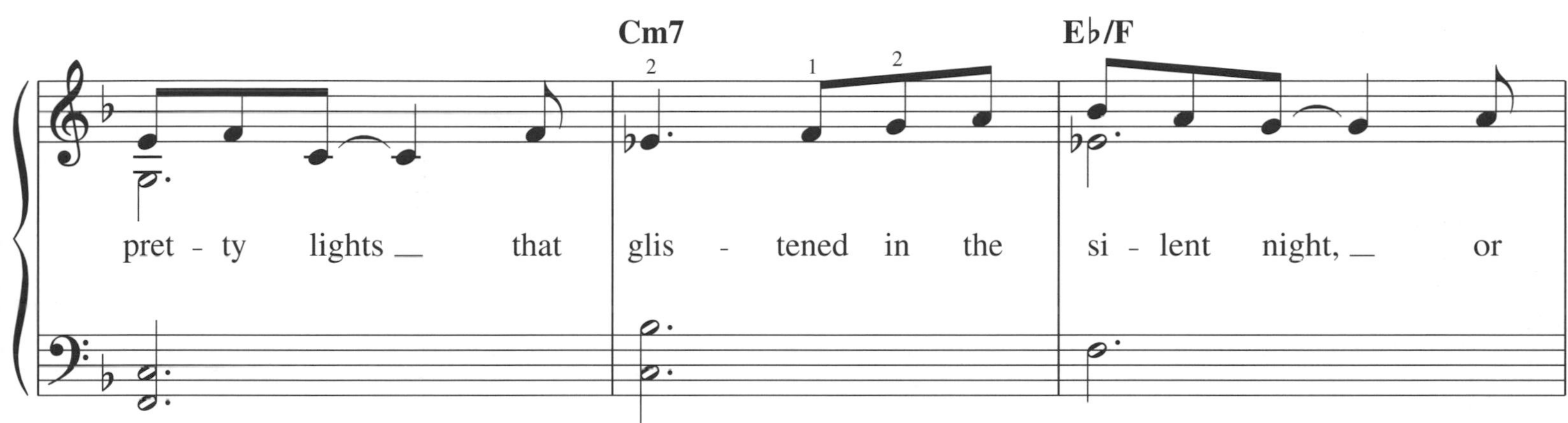
Cm7
E♭/F
pret - ty lights ___ that
glis - tened in the
si - lent night, ___ or

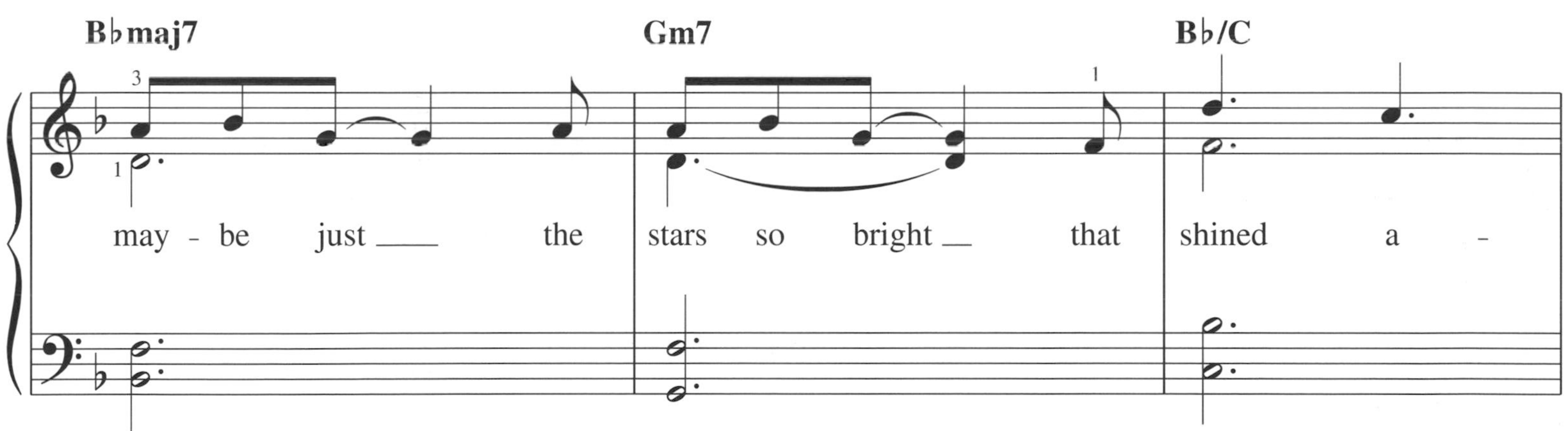
B♭maj7
Gm7
B♭/C
may - be just ___ the
stars so bright ___ that
shined a -

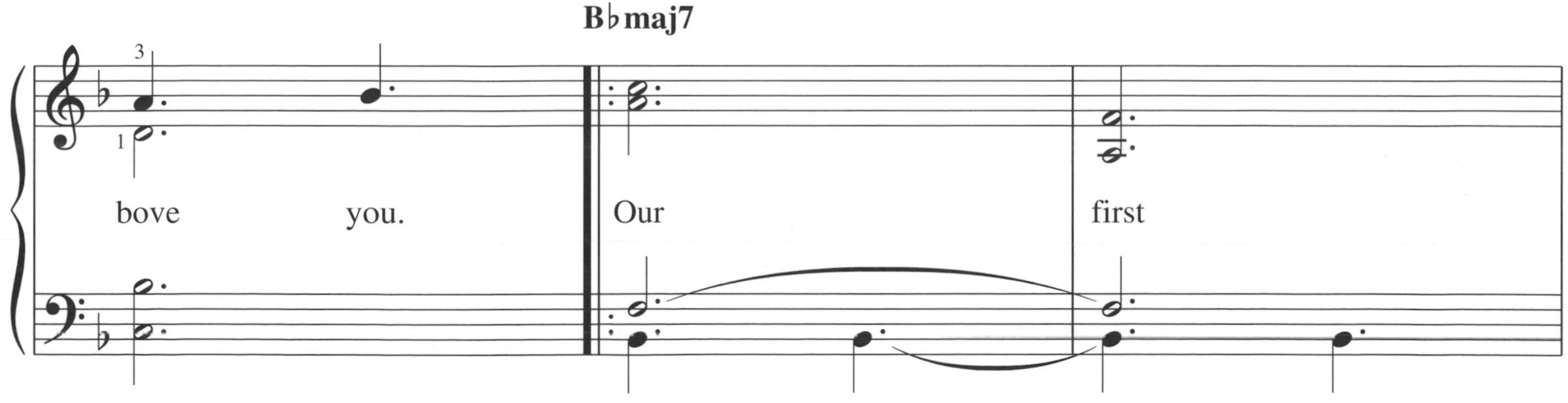
B♭maj7
bove you.
Our
first

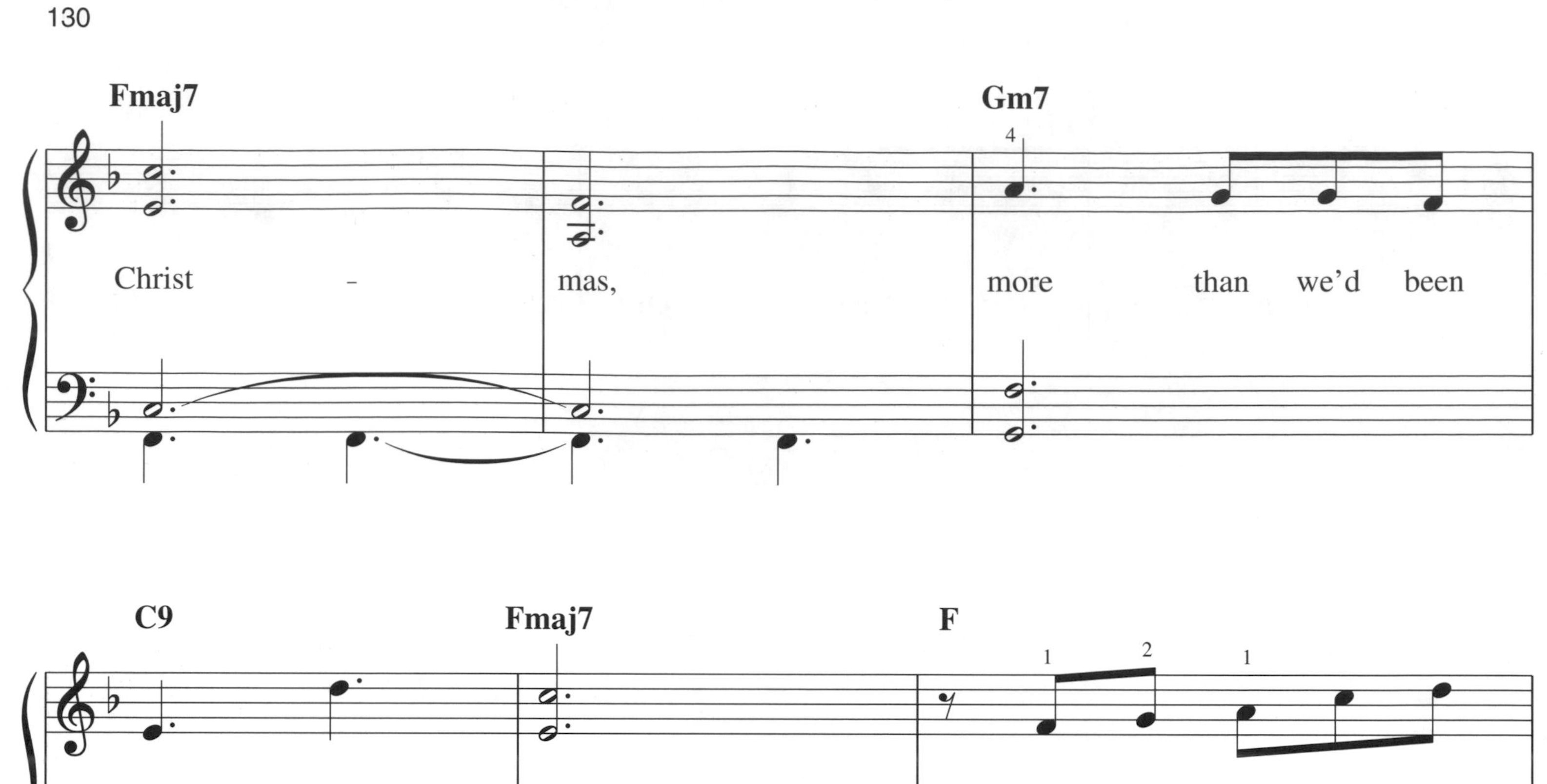
Fmaj7
Gm7
Christ - mas, more than we'd been
C9
Fmaj7
F
dream - ing of.

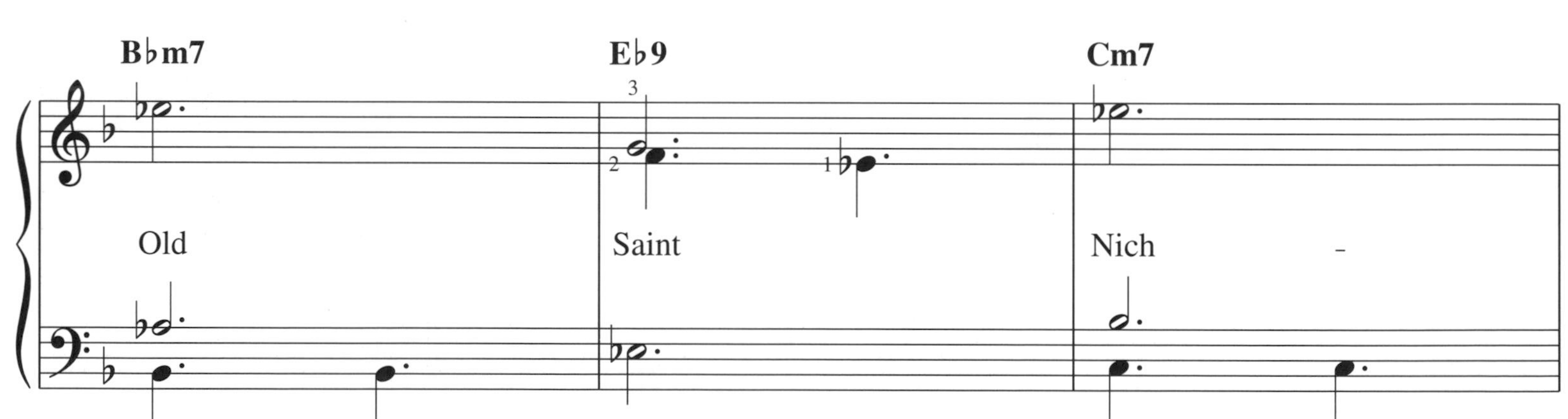
B♭m7
E♭9
Cm7
Old Saint Nich -

Fm7
B♭7sus
B♭7
'las had his fin - gers crossed that
must have known that kiss would

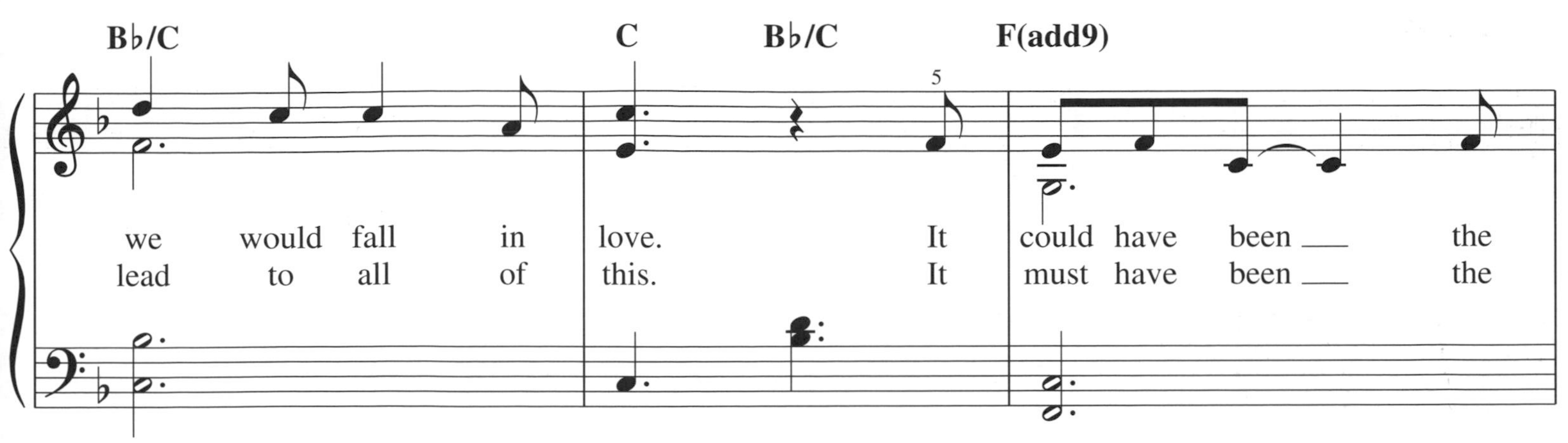
B♭/C
C
B♭/C
F(add9)
5
we would fall in love. It could have been the
lead to all of this. It must have been the

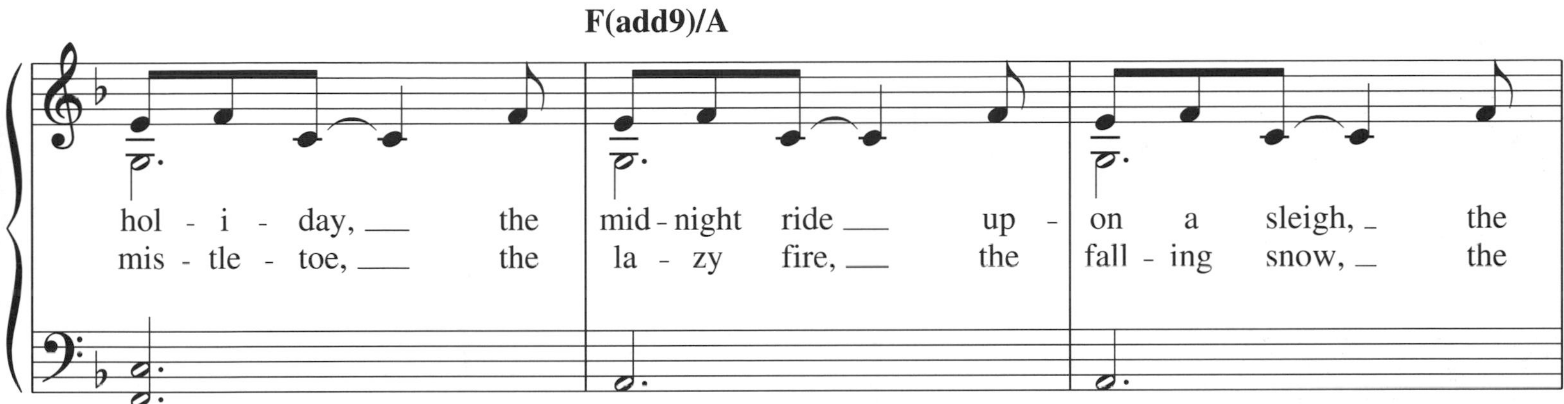
F(add9)/A
hol - i - day, the mid - night ride up - on a sleigh, the
mis - tle - toe, the la - zy fire, the fall - ing snow, the

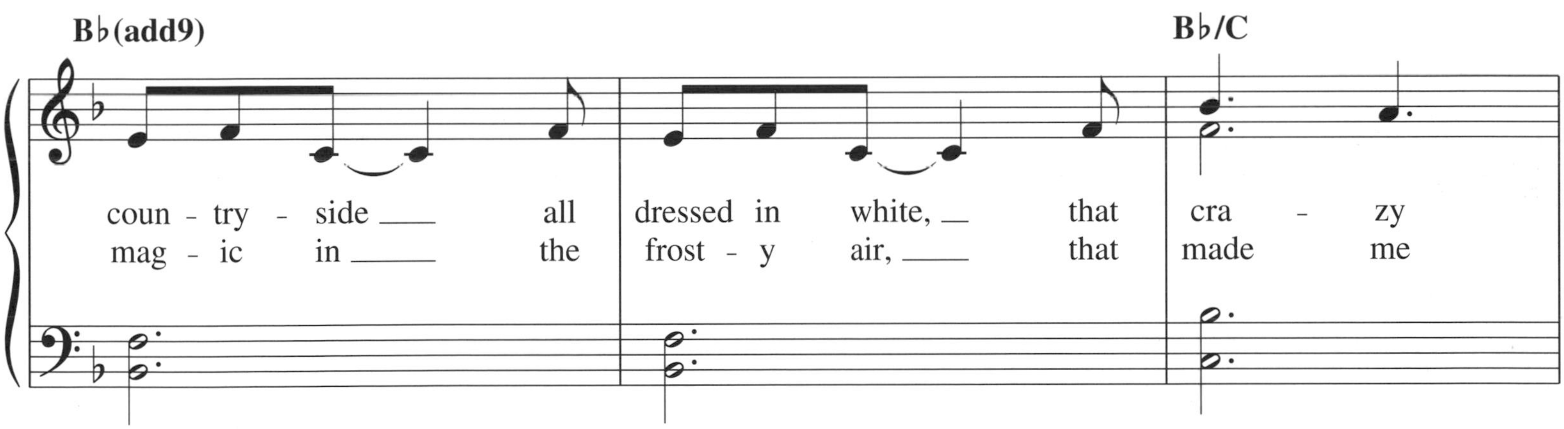
B♭(add9)
B♭/C
coun - try - side all dressed in white, that cra - zy
mag - ic in the frost - y air, that made me

F(add9)
snow - ball fight. It could have been the stee - ple bell that
love you. On Christ - mas Eve a wish come true, that

Cm7
E♭/F
B♭maj7
wrapped us up with - in its spell. __ It on - ly took one
night I fell in love with you. __ It on - ly took one

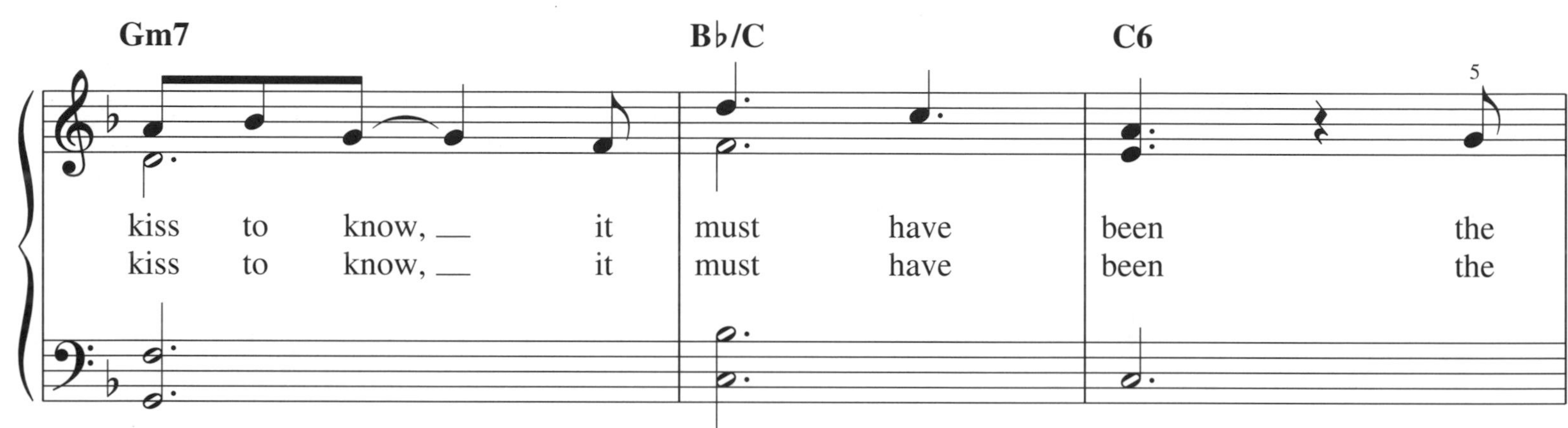
Gm7
B♭/C
C6
kiss to know, __ it must have been the
kiss to know, __ it must have been the

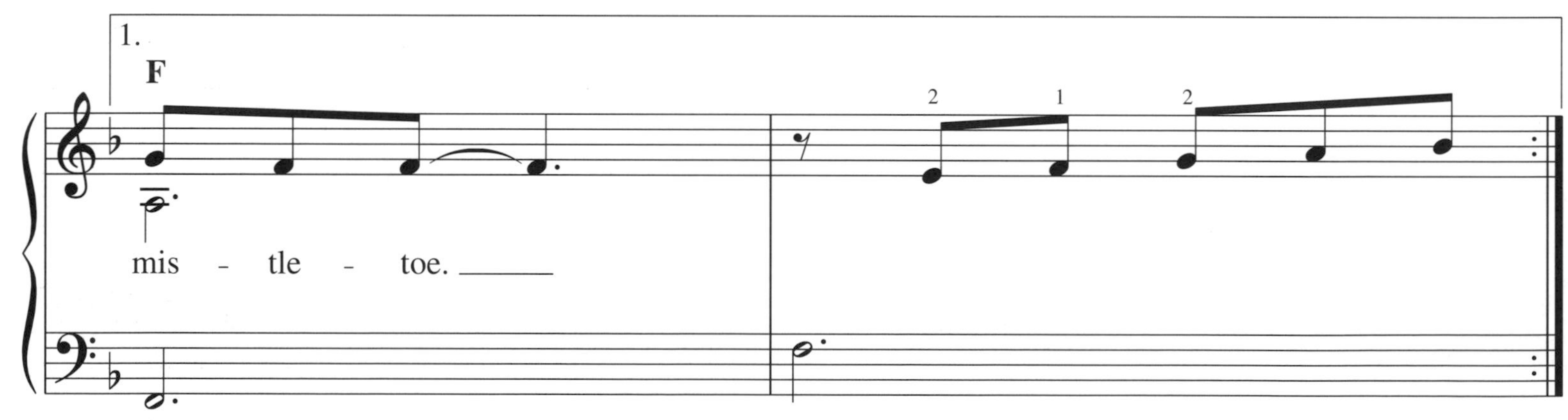
1.
F
mis - tle - toe. ___

2.
F
F(add9)/C
mis - tle - toe! ___ It

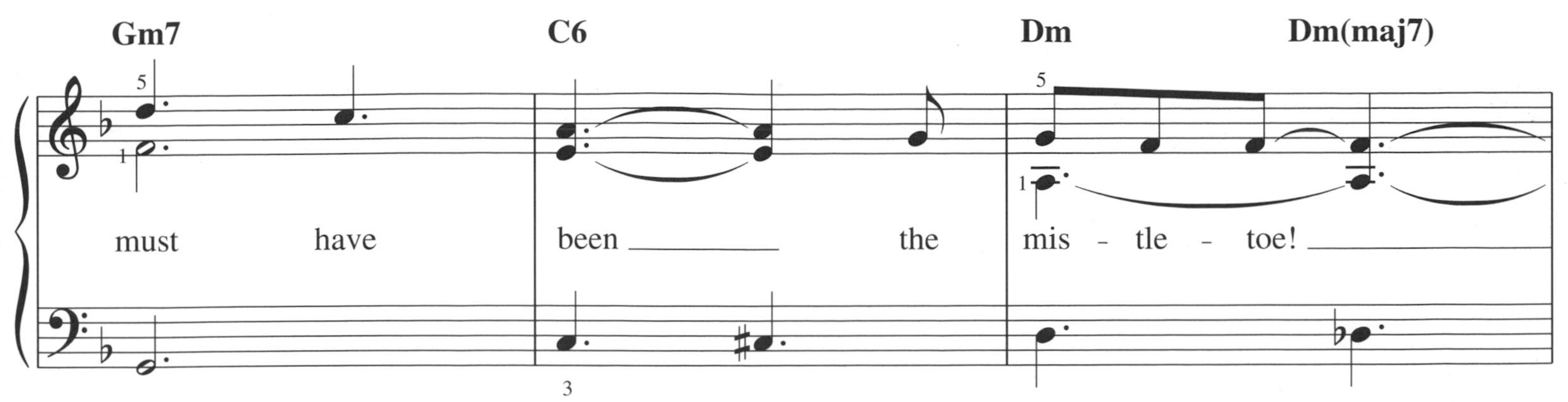
Gm7
C6
Dm
Dm(maj7)
must have been the mis - tle - toe!

Freely
Dm7
Dm6
Gm7/B♭
B♭/C
It must have been the

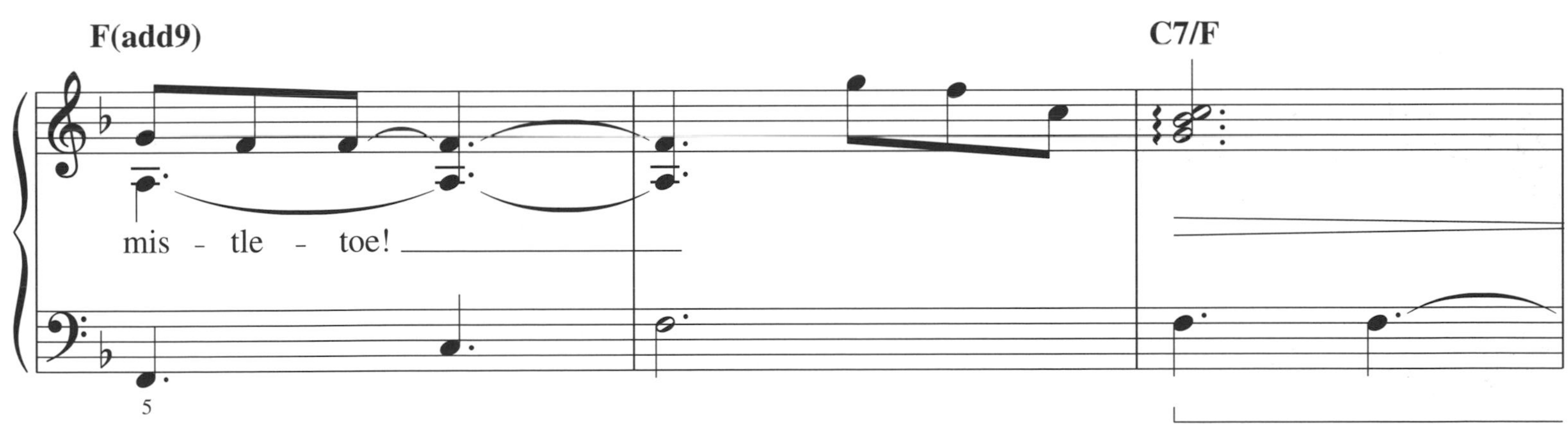
F(add9)
C7/F
mis - tle - toe!

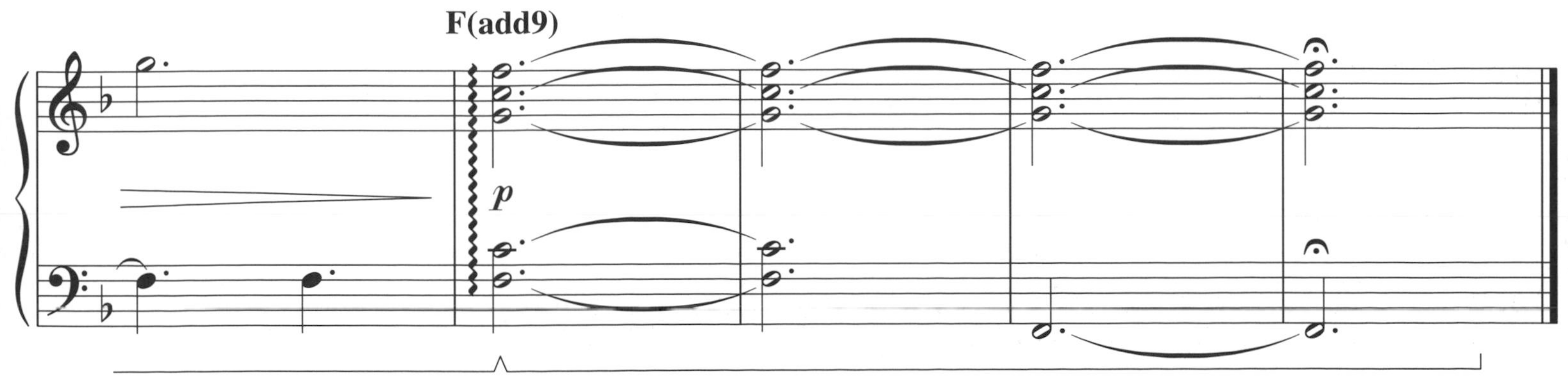
F(add9)
p

THE LAST MONTH OF THE YEAR
(What Month Was Jesus Born In?)

Words and Music by VERA HALL
Adapted and Arranged by RUBY PICKENS TARTT
and ALAN LOMAX

Additional Lyrics

2. Well, they laid Him in a manger,
Last month of the year!
(Repeat)
Chorus

3. Wrapped Him up in swaddling clothes,
Last month of the year!
(Repeat)
Chorus

4. He was born of the Virgin Mary,
Last month of the year!
(Repeat)
Chorus

LITTLE SAINT NICK

Words and Music by BRIAN WILSON
and MIKE LOVE

G
G6
G♯dim7
tale a - bout Christ - mas that you've all been told. And a
walk a to - bog - gan with a four - speed stick. She's

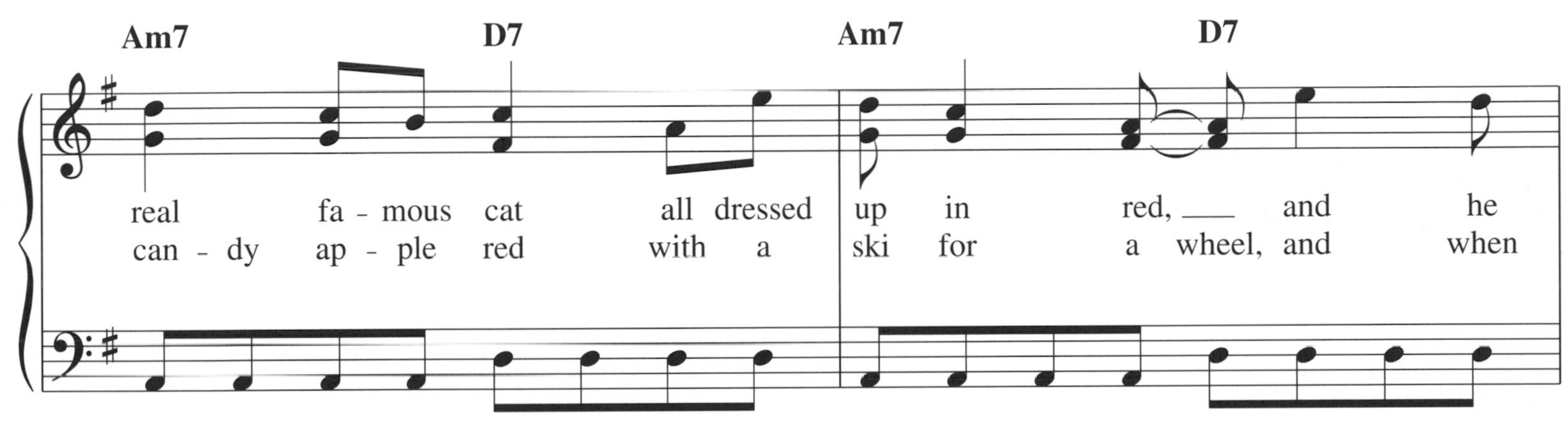
Am7
D7
Am7
D7
real fa - mous cat all dressed up in red, and he
can - dy ap - ple red with a ski for a wheel, and when

G
G6
G7
spends the whole year work - in' out on his sled.
San - ta hits the gas, man, just watch her peel.
It's the

C
To Coda
Lit - tle Saint Nick. (Lit - tle Saint Nick.) It's the

Am7
D
D
1.
2.
Lit-tle Saint Nick. (Lit-tle Saint Nick.) Just a Saint Nick.)
C F/C C F B♭/F F
Run, run, rein - deer. Run, run, rein - deer.
C F/C C
Oh, run, run, rein - deer.
A N.C. D.S. al Coda
Run, run, rein - deer. He don't miss no one. And

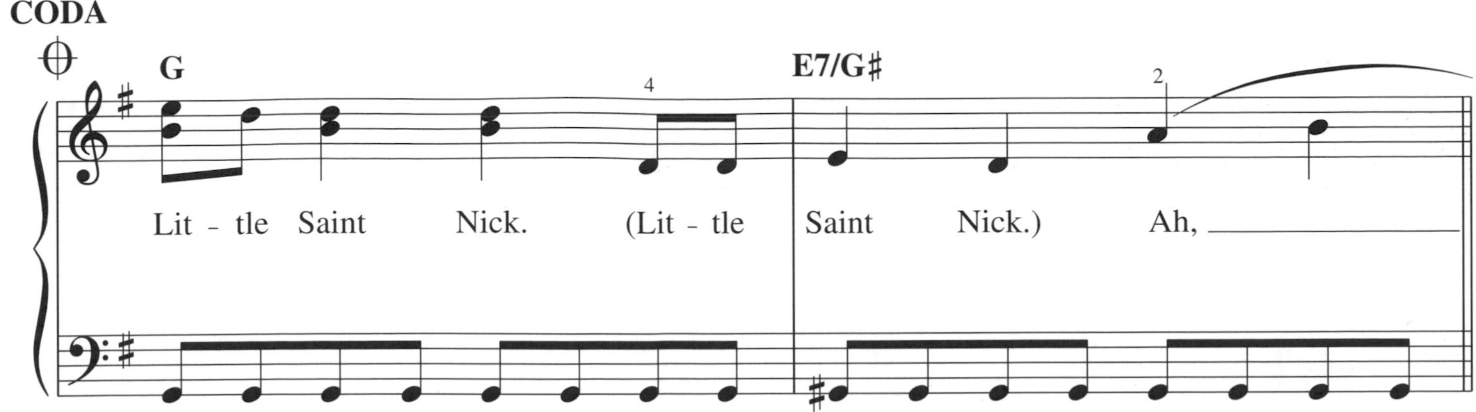

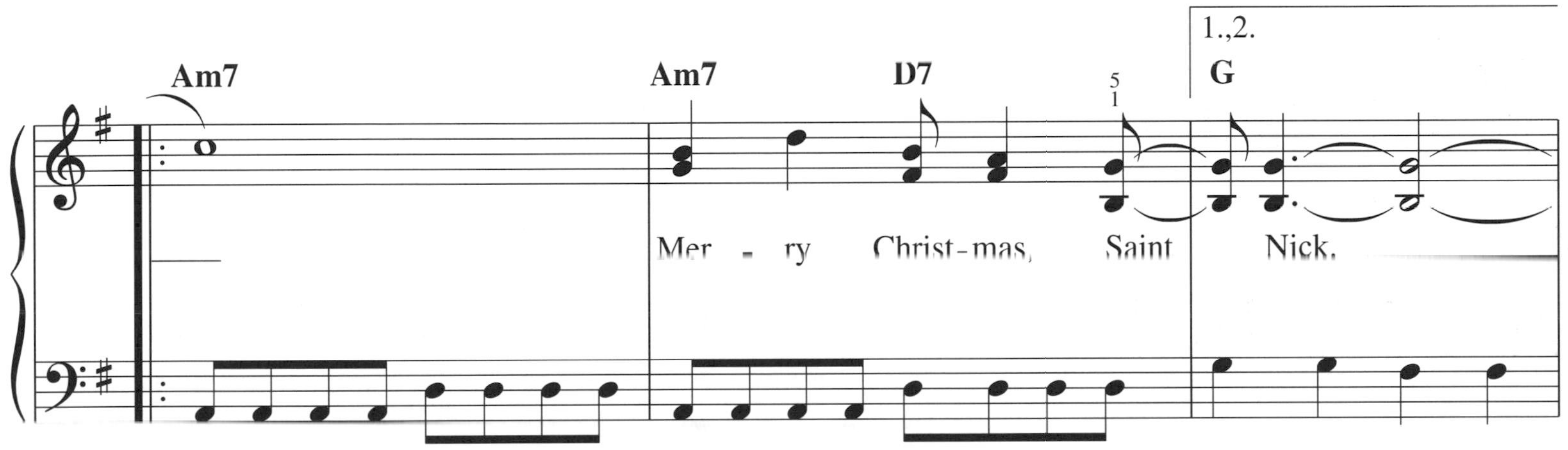

Additional Lyrics

3. Haulin' through the snow at a fright'nin' speed,
   With a half a dozen deer with Rudy to lead,
   He's gotta wear his goggles 'cause the snow really flies,
   And he's cruisin' ev'ry pad with a little surprise.

MERRY CHRISTMAS, DARLING

Words and Music by RICHARD CARPENTER
and FRANK POOLER

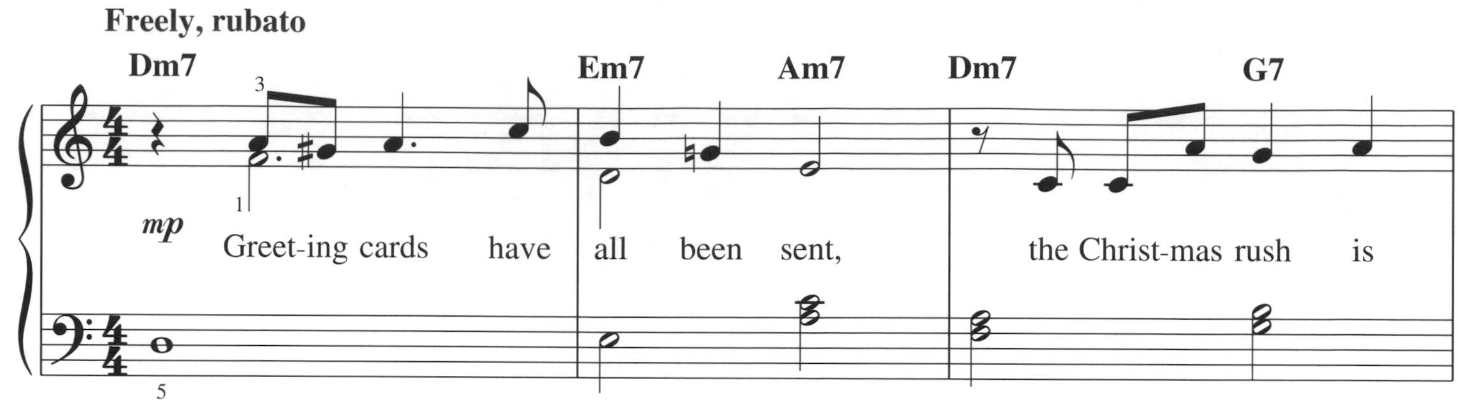

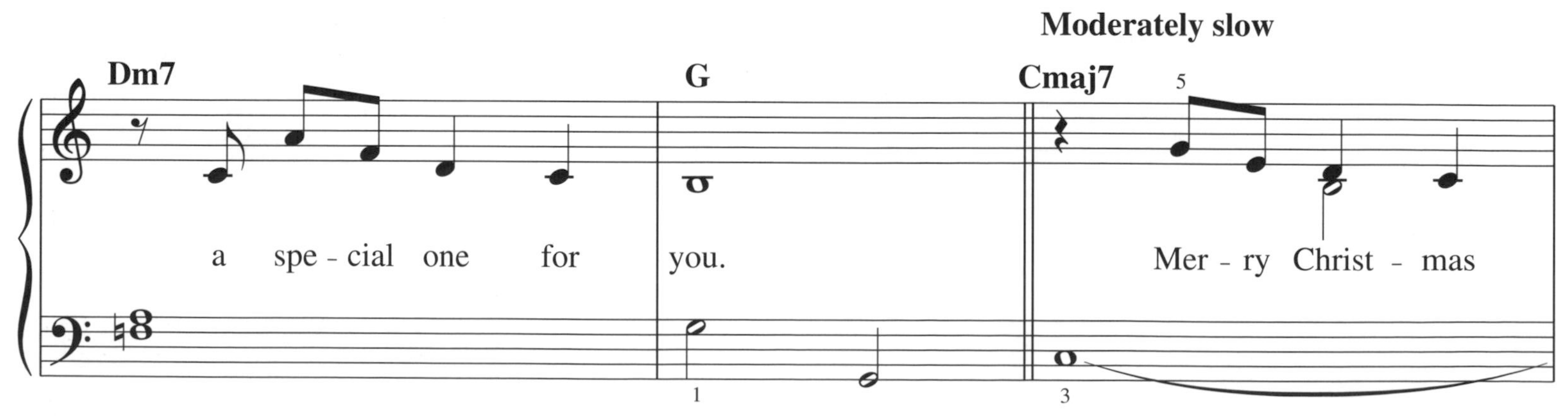

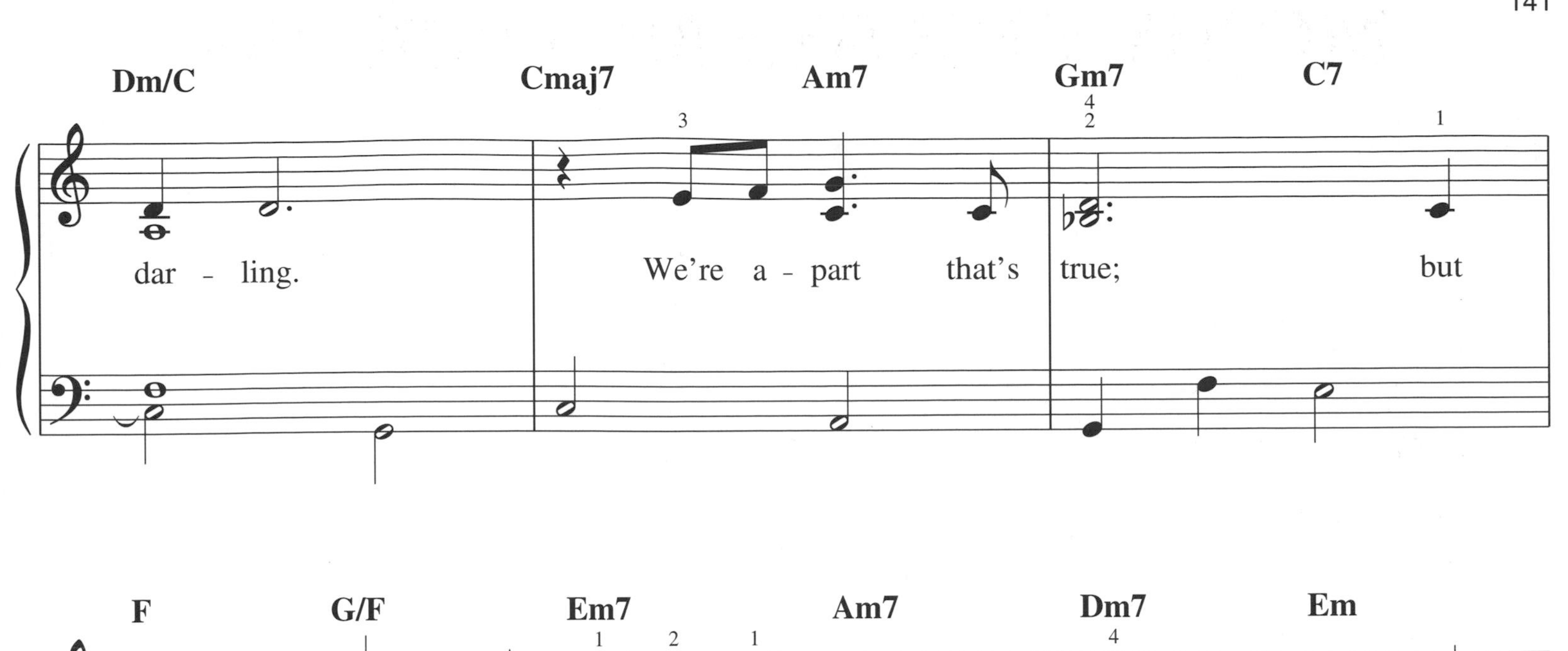
Dm/C
Cmaj7
Am7
Gm7
C7
dar - ling.
We're a - part that's
true;
but

F
G/F
Em7
Am7
Dm7
Em
I can dream and
in my dreams, I'm
Christ - mas - ing with

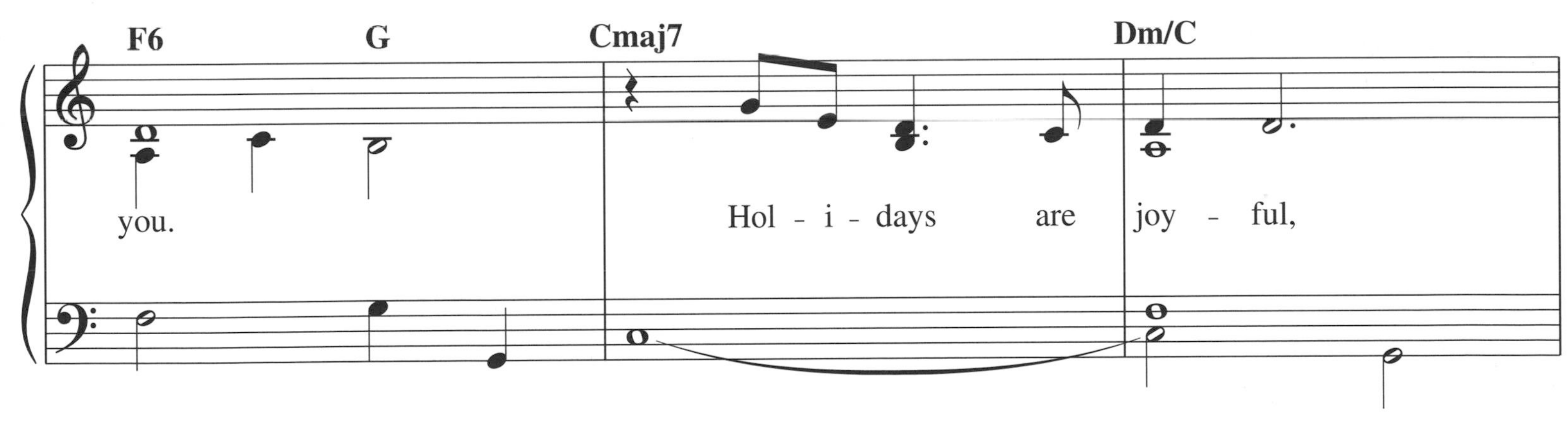
F6
G
Cmaj7
Dm/C
you.
Hol - i - days are
joy - ful,

Cmaj7
Gm7
C7
F
G/F
there's al - ways some - thing
new. But
ev - 'ry day's a

Em7
Am7
D/F♯
Fm6
B♭9
hol - i - day
when I'm near to
you.
The

E♭
F/E♭
Dm7
Gm
Cm7
F7
lights on my tree I
wish you could see,
I wish it ev - 'ry

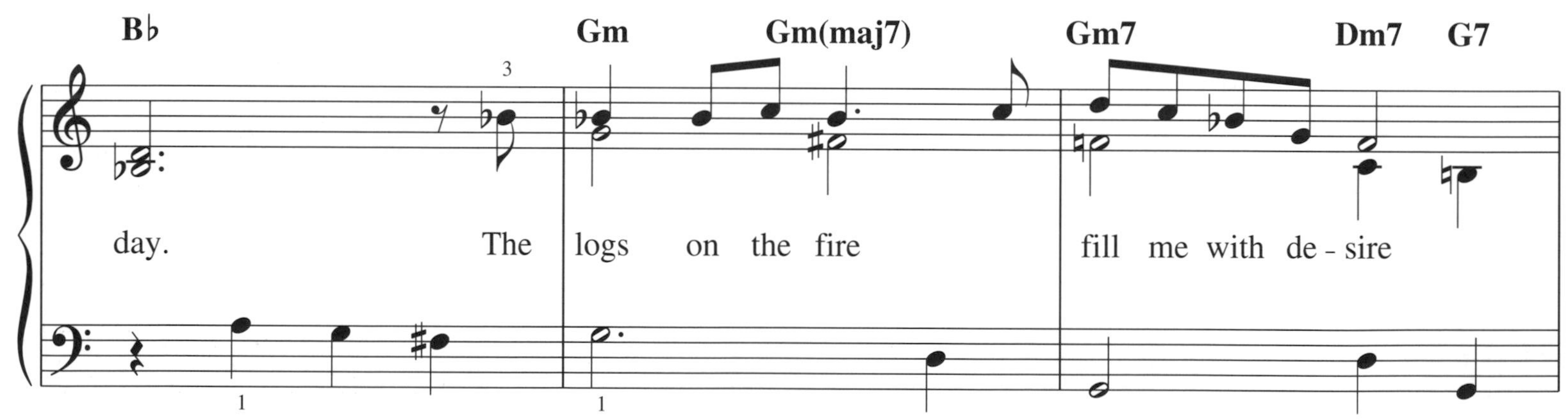
B♭
Gm
Gm(maj7)
Gm7
Dm7
G7
day.
The
logs on the fire
fill me with de - sire

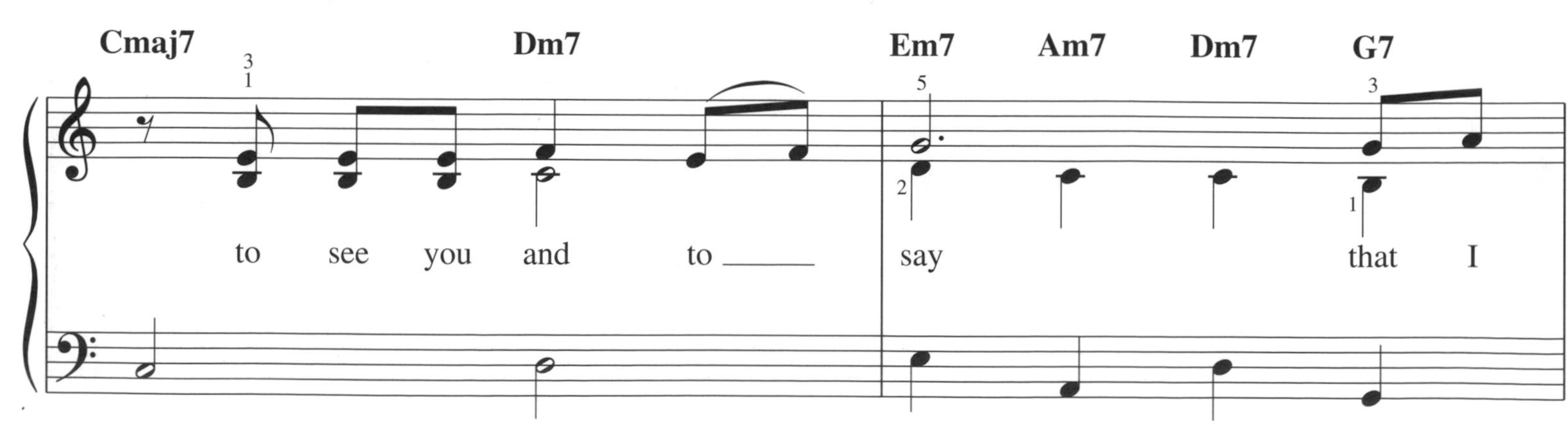
Cmaj7
Dm7
Em7
Am7
Dm7
G7
to see you and to
say
that I

Cmaj7
Dm/C
Cmaj7
wish you mer - ry Christ - mas, hap - py New Year
Gm7
C7
F
G/F
Em7
Am7
too. I've just one wish on this Christ-mas Eve;
1.
2.
Dm7
G7
C
B♭9
Dm7
G7
I wish I were with you. The
I wish I were with
Em7♭5
A7
Dm7
G7
N.C.
B♭
C
you. I wish I were with you.
rit.

A MERRY CHRISTMAS TO ME

Words and Music by DAN RODOWICZ
and PHILLIP KEVEREN

G(add2)/B
B♭9
Am7
D13
me.
Scenes of
2.
D
G
A/G
Cm/G
Christ - mas to
me.
G
E♭7
Dm7
G13♭9
Cmaj7
For hard - ened hearts can love a - gain,
Em7
E♭7
Dm7
G7♯5
C6/9
and smiles that have fad - ed shine bright;

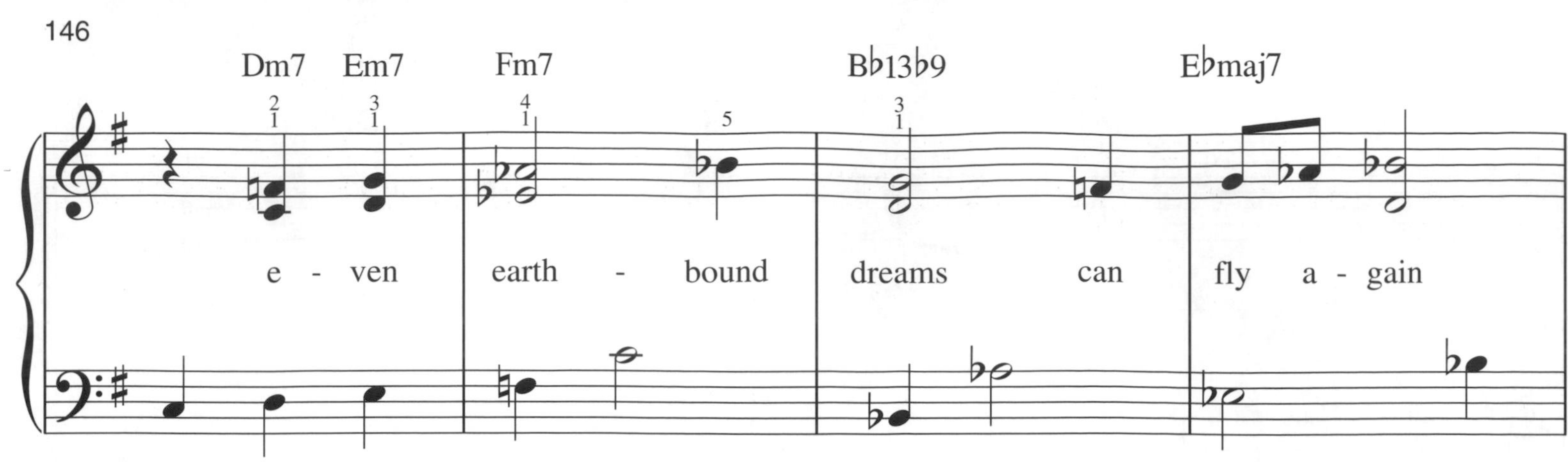
Dm7 Em7 Fm7 B♭13♭9 E♭maj7
e - ven earth - bound dreams can fly a - gain

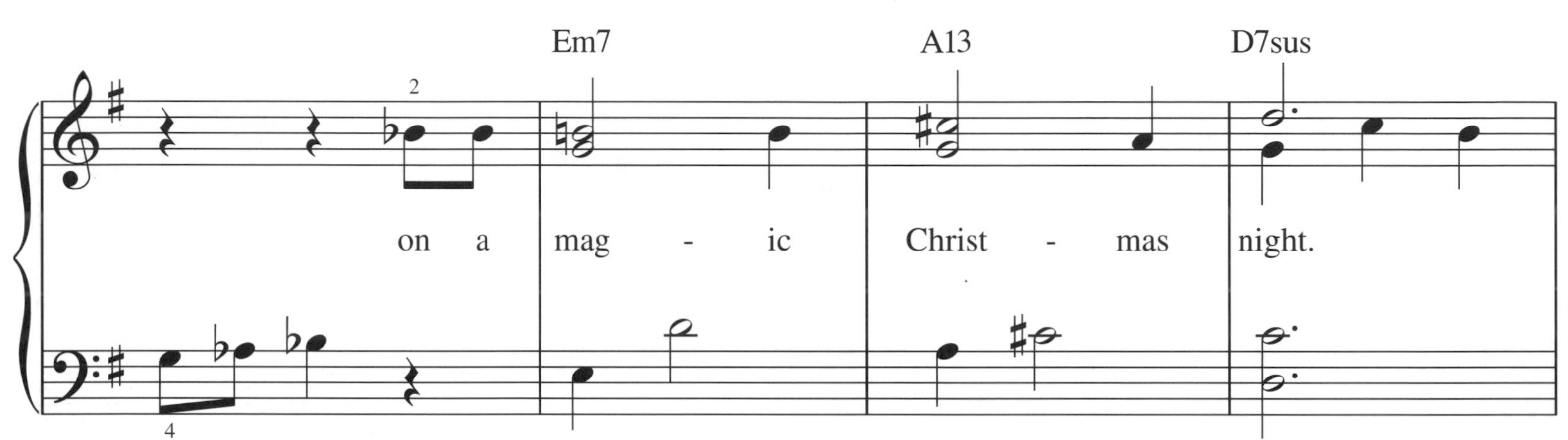
Em7 A13 D7sus
on a mag - ic Christ - mas night.

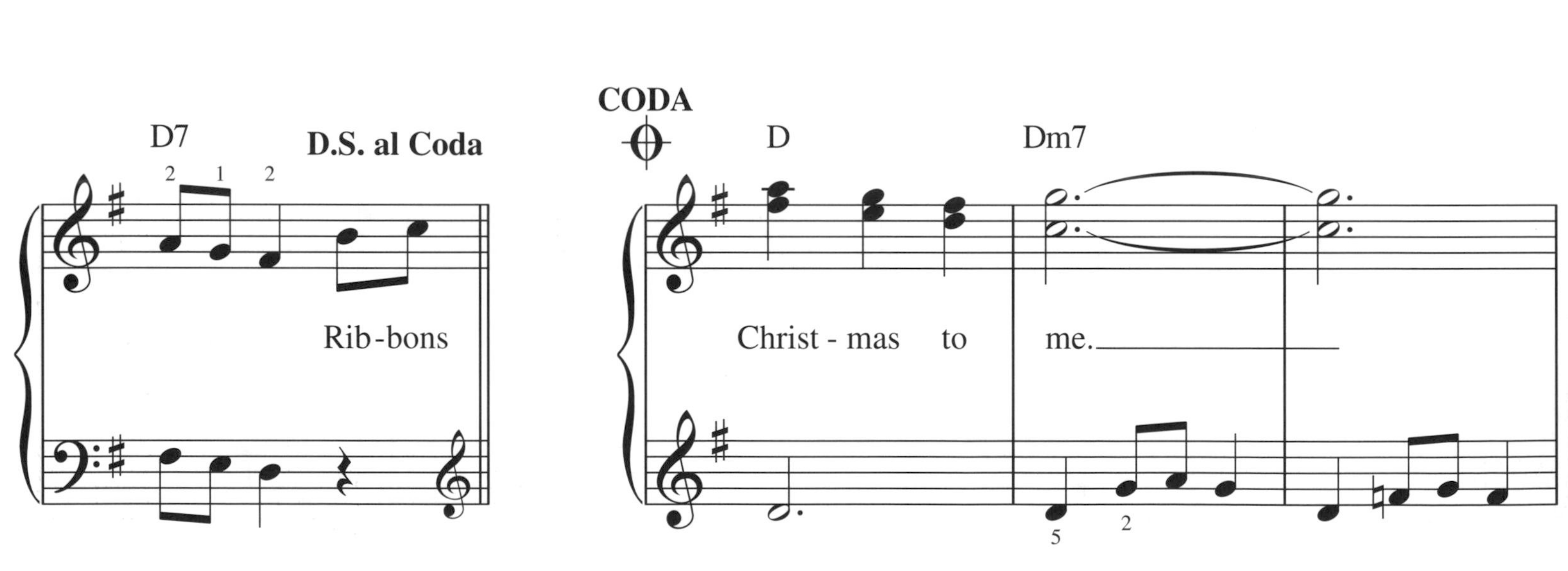
D7 D.S. al Coda
Rib-bons
CODA
D Dm7
Christ-mas to me.

G13 G7♭9 Cmaj7
But what I long to see won't be

A/B
B7♭9
Em
Em(maj7)
un - der my tree, though my wish is most sin -

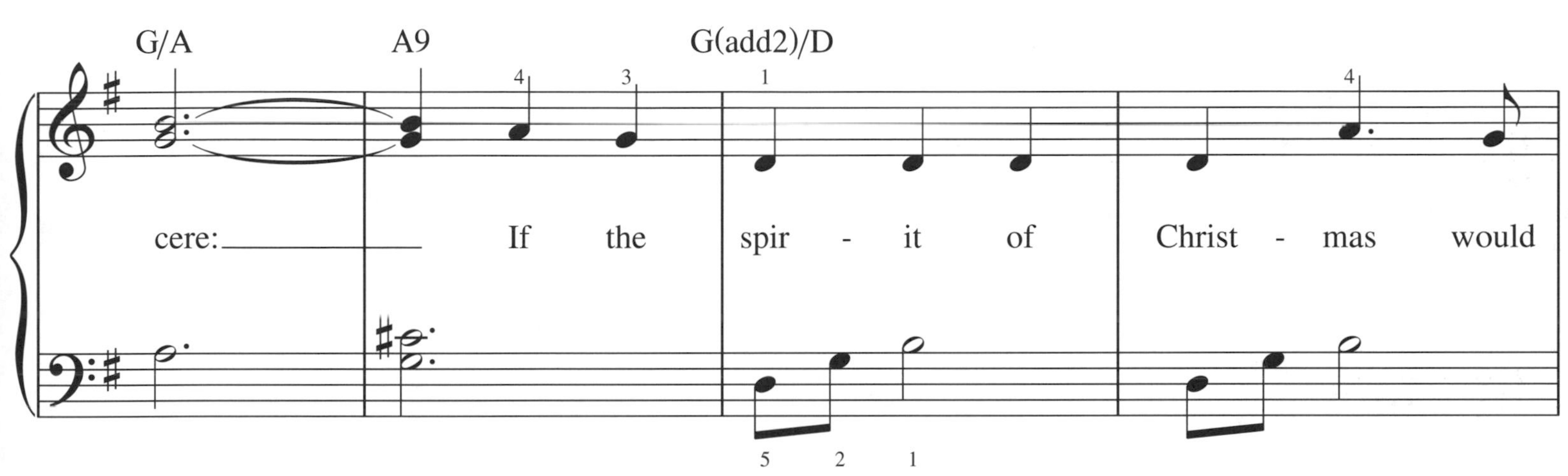
G/A
A9
G(add2)/D
cere: If the spir - it of Christ - mas would

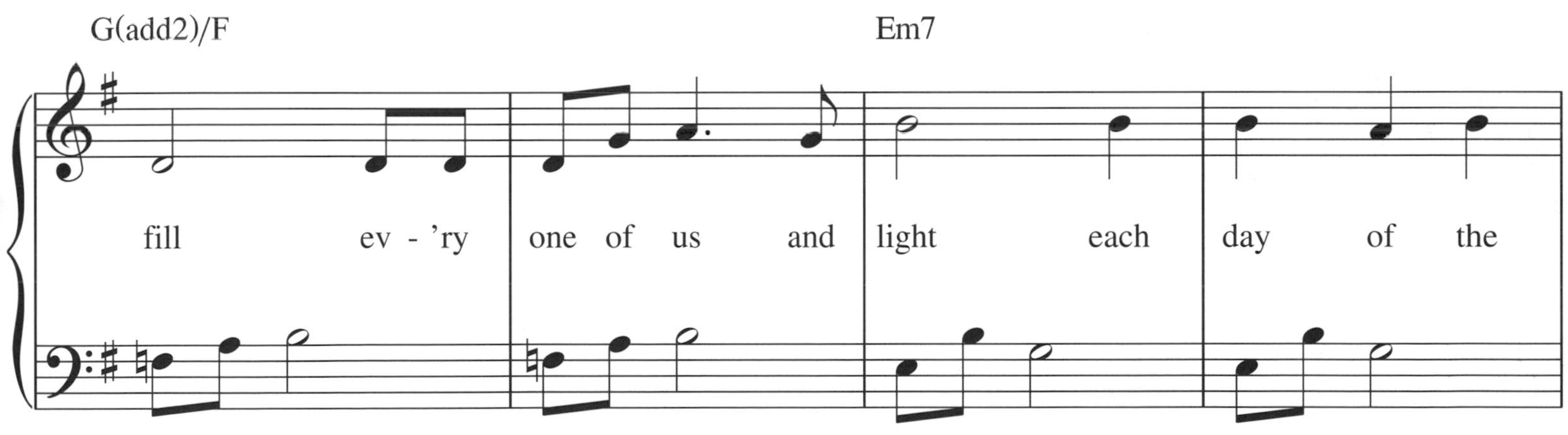
G(add2)/F
Em7
fill ev - 'ry one of us and light each day of the

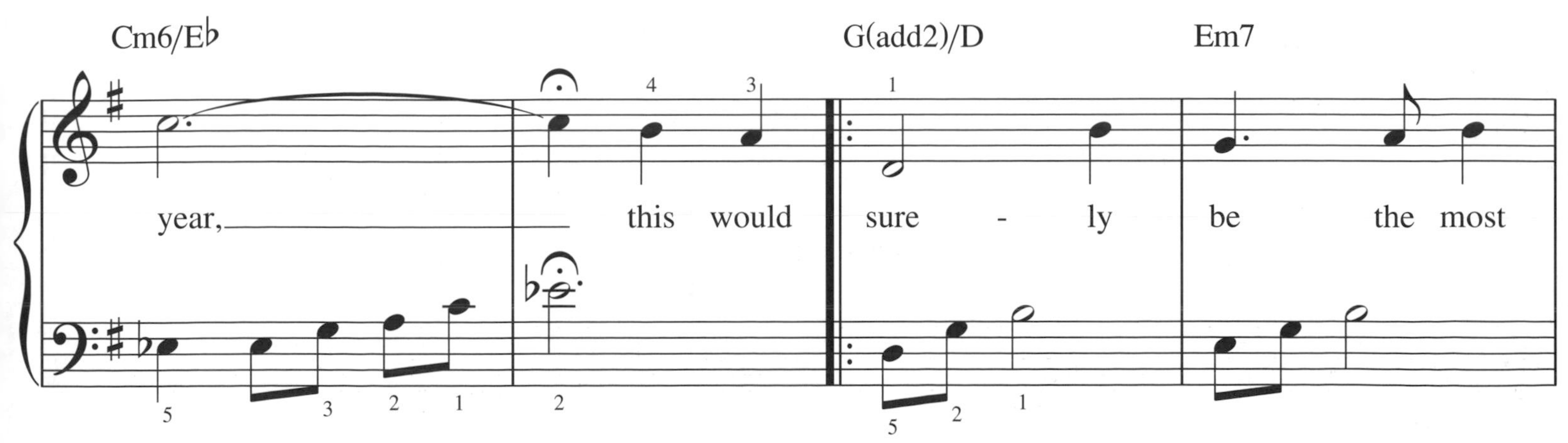
Cm6/E♭
G(add2)/D
Em7
year, this would sure - ly be the most

Am7
D7
1.
C♯m7♭5
Mer - ry Christ - mas to me.
Cm9
F13
This would
2.
G
B/G
A/G
me.
E♭sus2/G
G(add2)

MERRY CHRISTMAS WALTZ

Words and Music by BOB BATSON
and INEX LOEWER

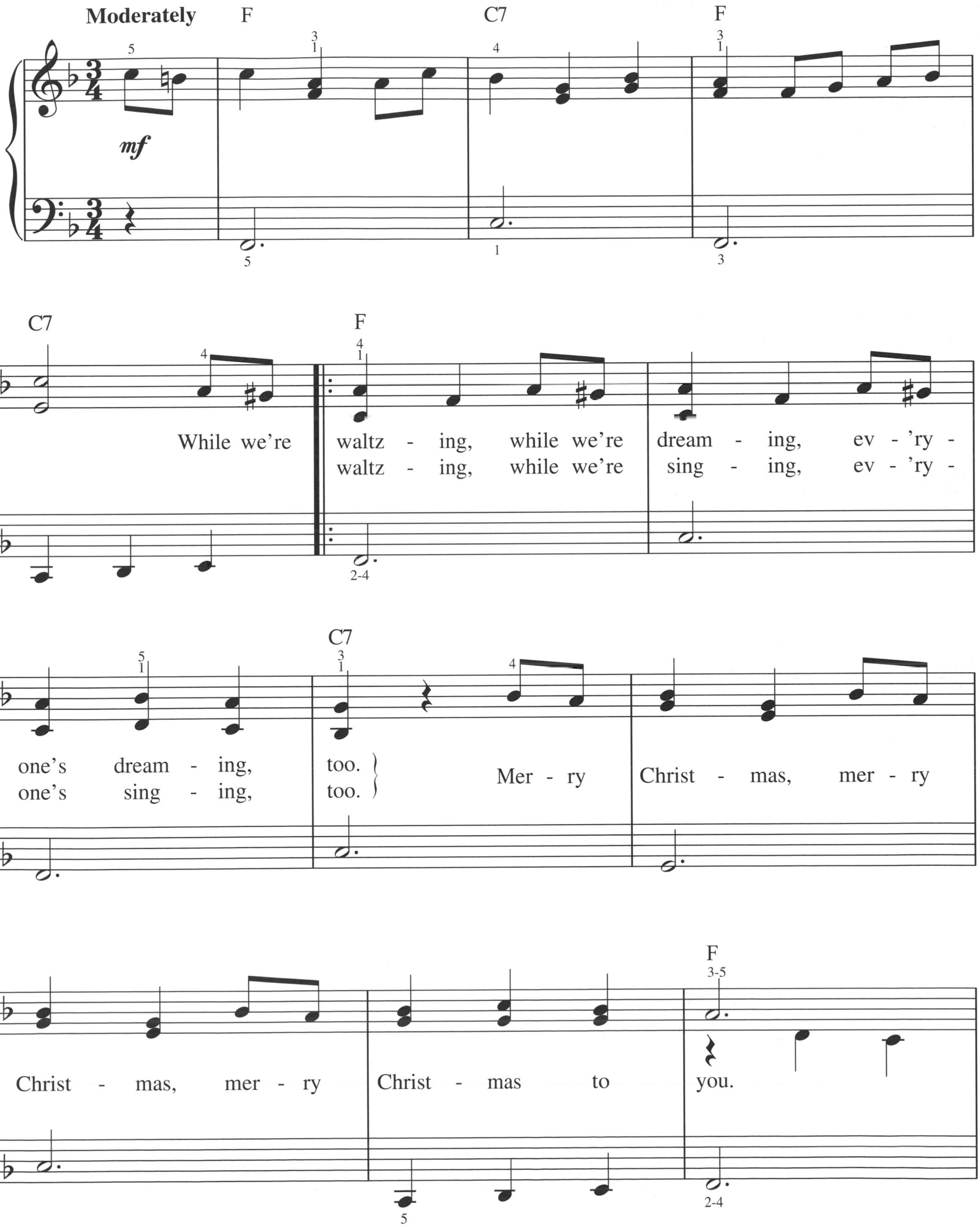

Moderately

F C7 F

mf

C7 F

While we're waltz - ing, while we're dream - ing, ev - 'ry -
waltz - ing, while we're sing - ing, ev - 'ry -

C7

one's dream - ing, too.
one's sing - ing, too.
Mer - ry Christ - mas, mer - ry

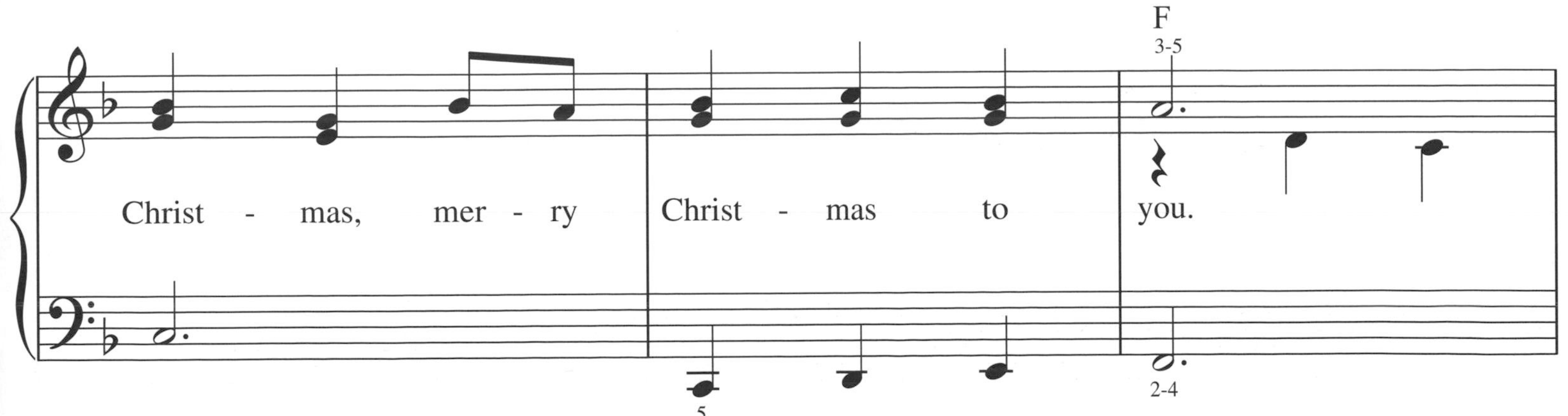

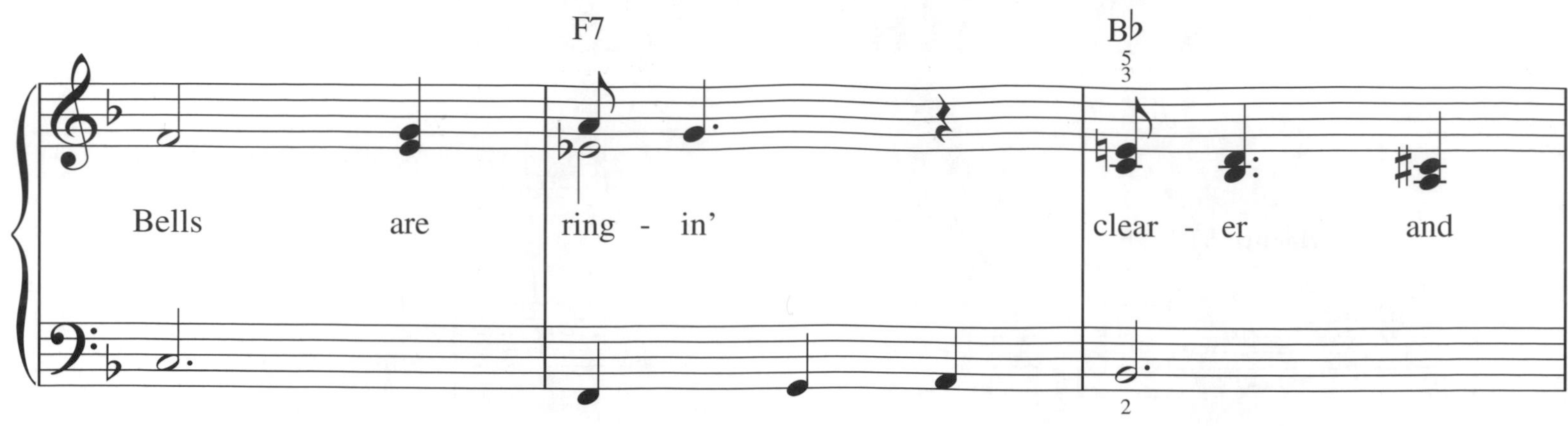
F7
B♭
Bells are ring - in' clear - er and

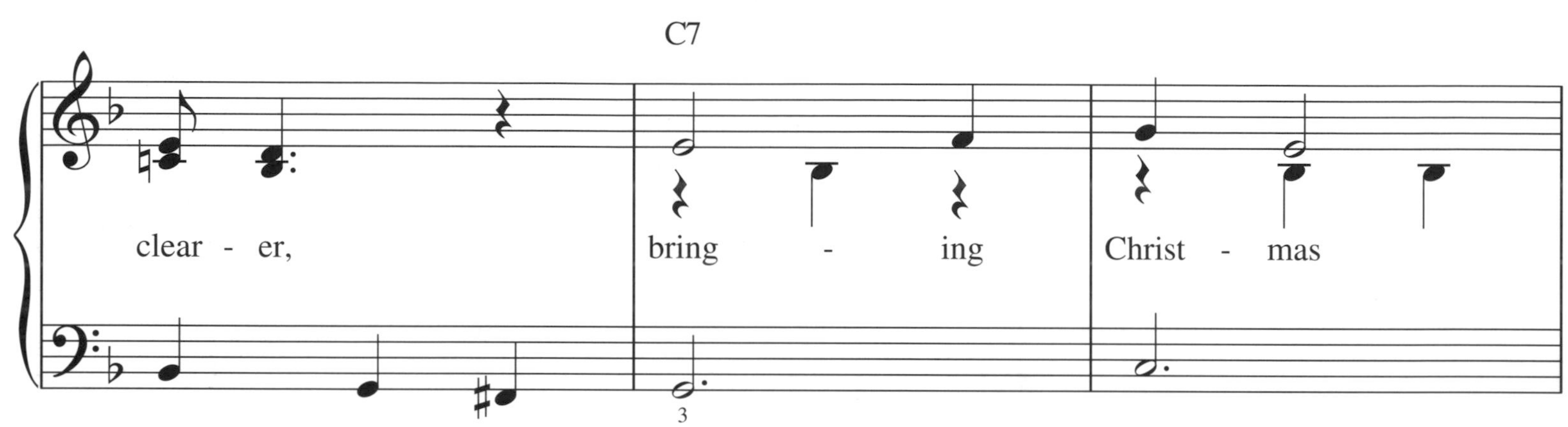
C7
clear - er, bring - ing Christ - mas

F
near - er and near - er. Mu - sic play - ing, cou - ples

C7
sway - ing, what a beau - ti - ful sight and the

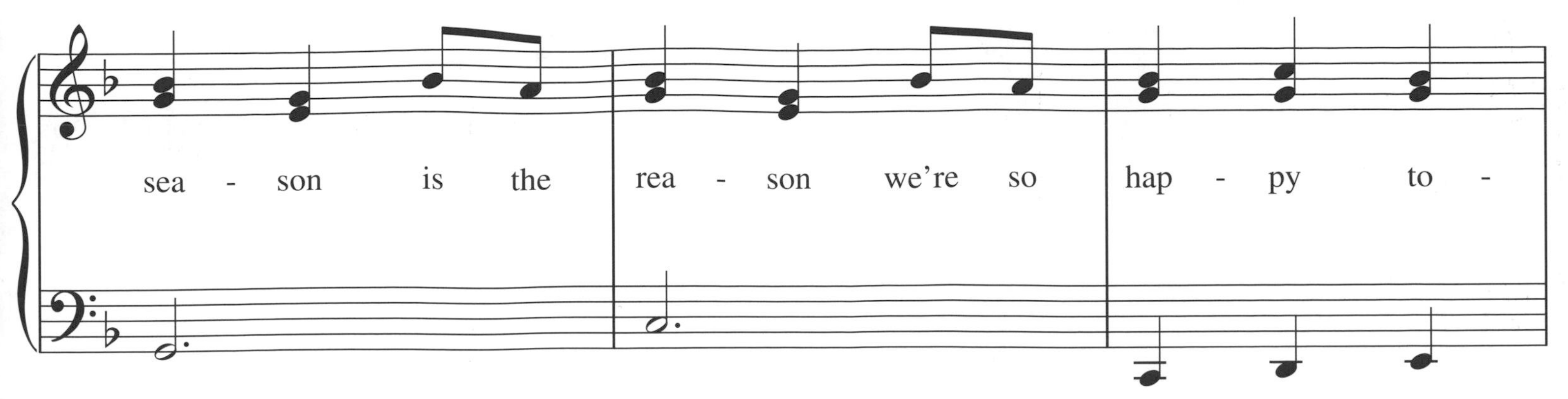

sea - son is the rea - son we're so hap - py to -

F
3-5
3 1
4 1
5 1
night. So stay in my arms, dar - lin',

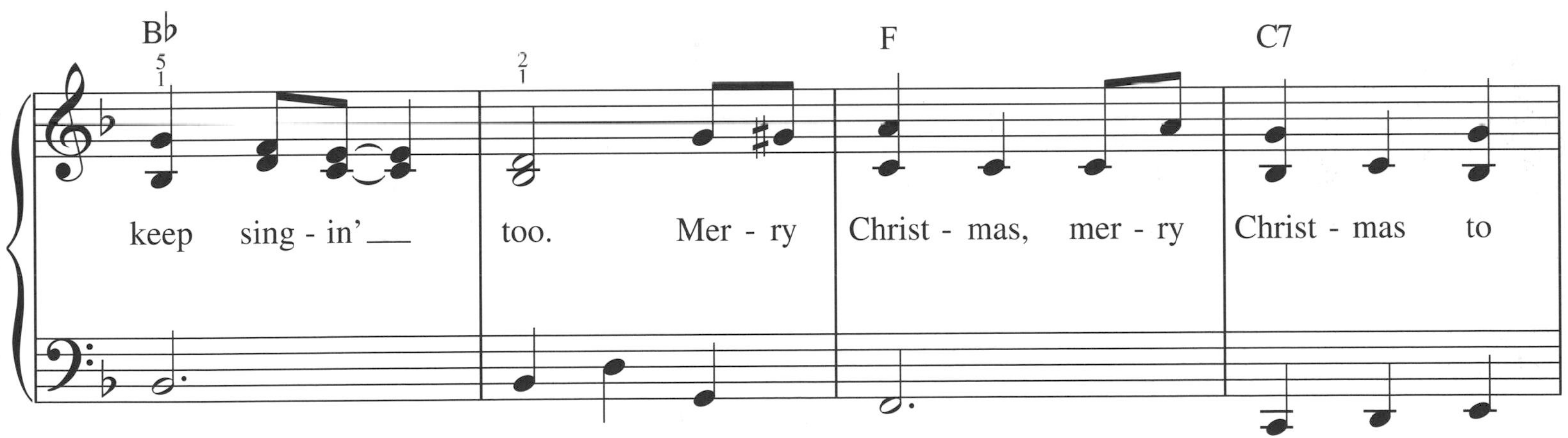

B♭
5 1
2 1
F
C7
keep sing - in' too. Mer - ry Christ - mas, mer - ry Christ - mas to

1.
F F/A A♭dim C7
5 1
you. While we're
2.
F B♭m/F F
you.

THE MOST WONDERFUL TIME OF THE YEAR

Words and Music by EDDIE POLA
and GEORGE WYLE

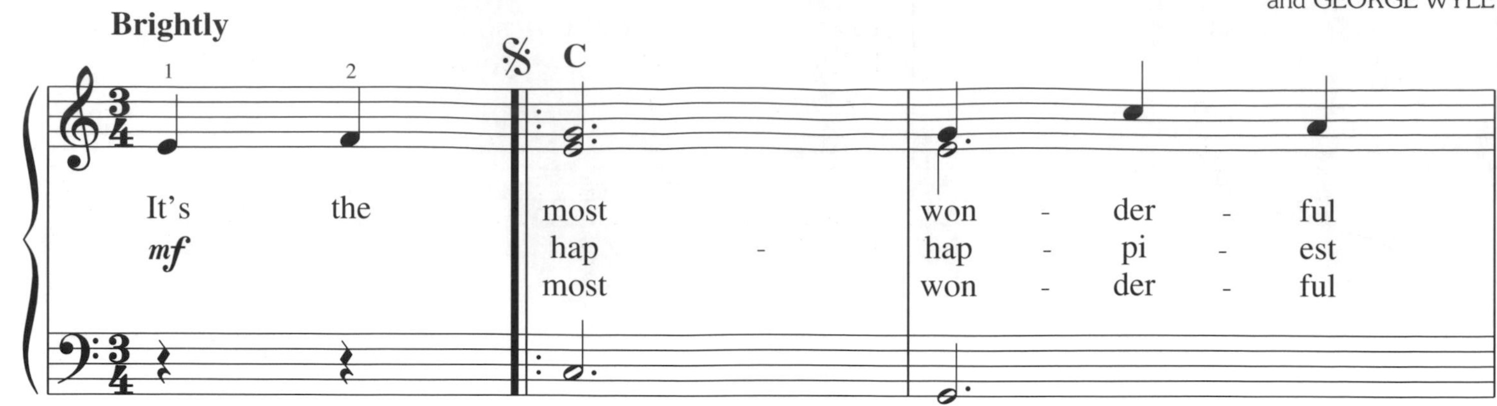

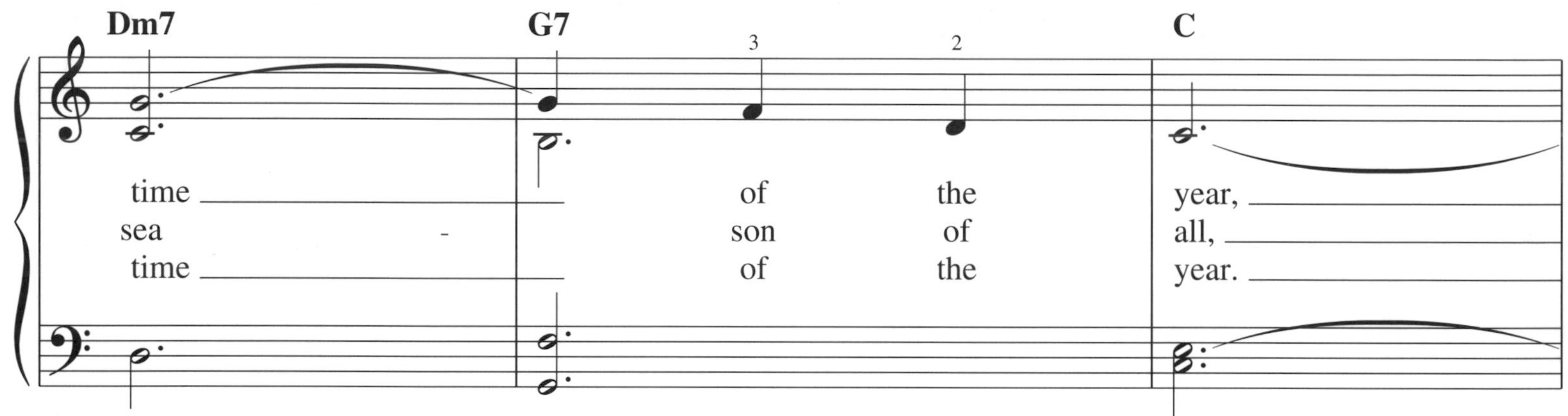

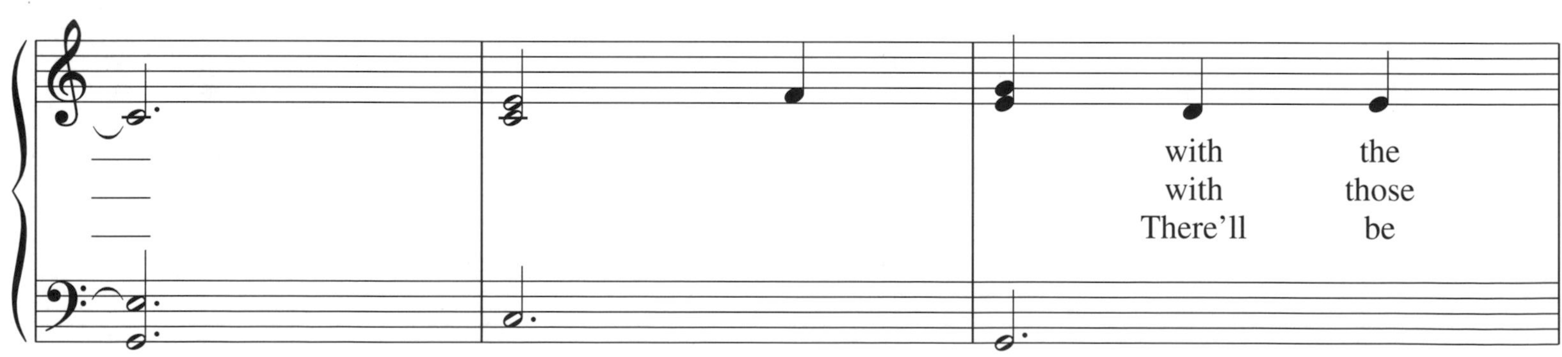

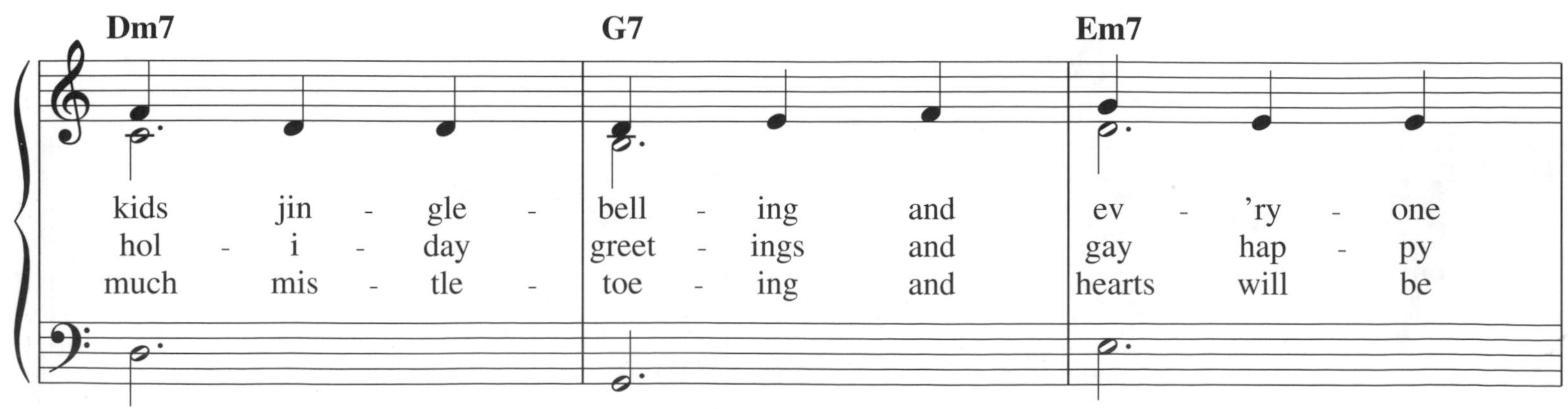

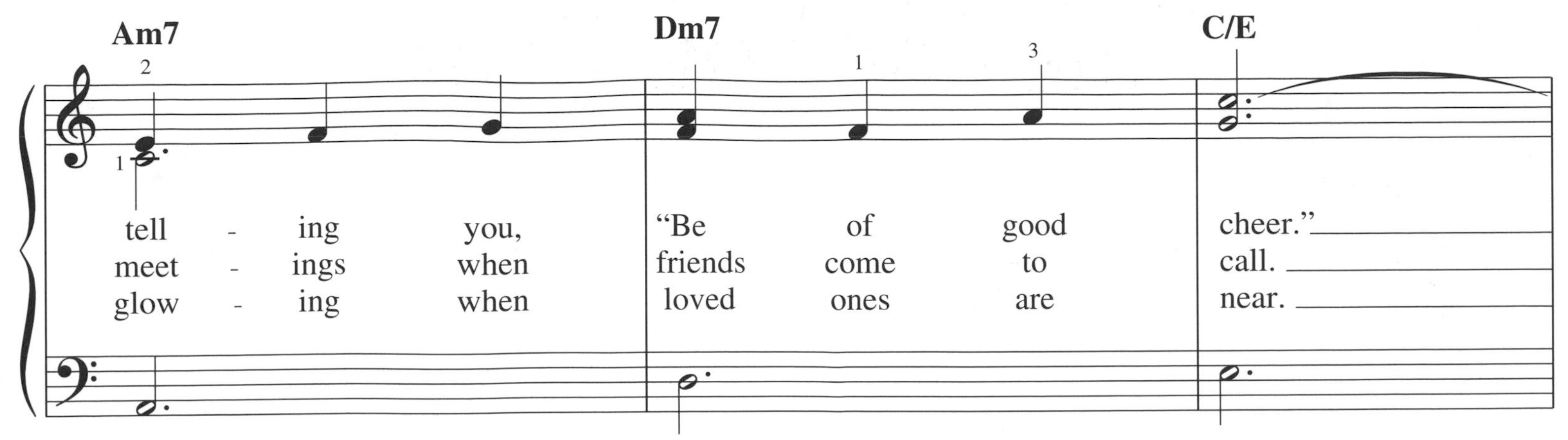
Am7
Dm7
C/E
tell - ing you, "Be of good cheer."
meet - ings when friends come to call.
glow - ing when loved ones are near.

F
F♯dim
To Coda
1.
C/G
It's the most
It's the
It's the

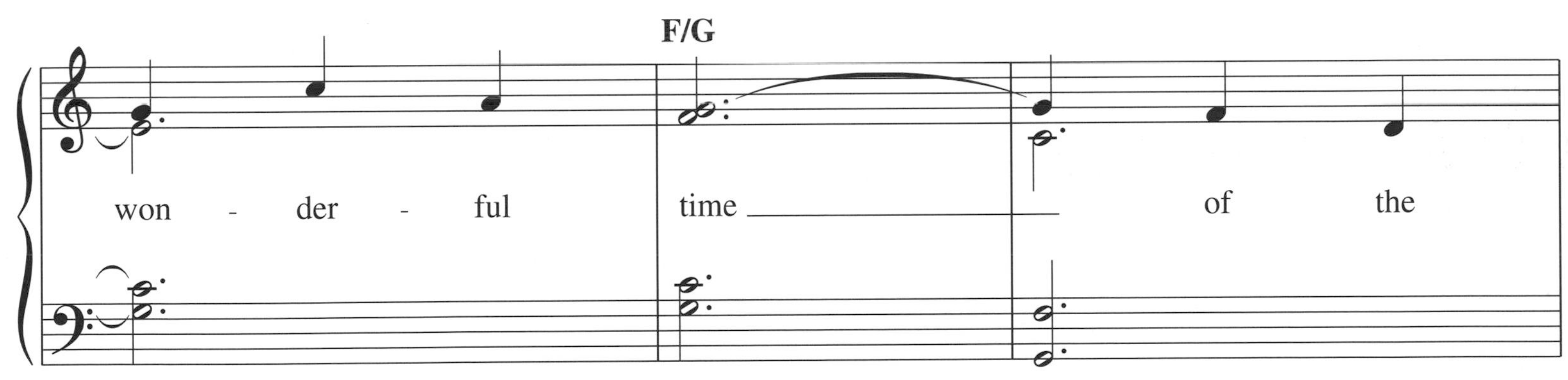
F/G
won - der - ful time of the

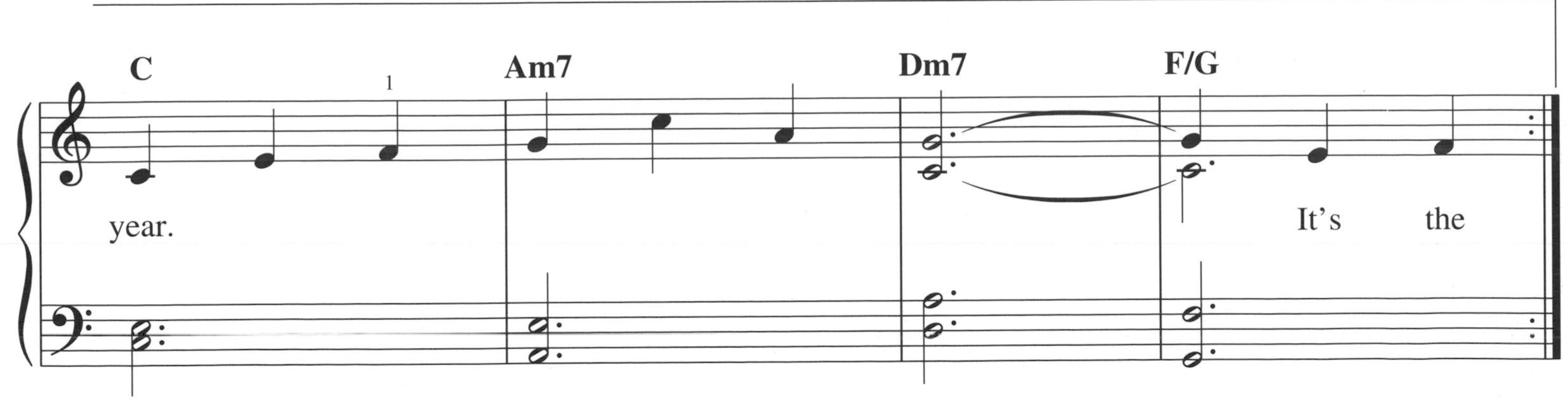
C
Am7
Dm7
F/G
year. It's the

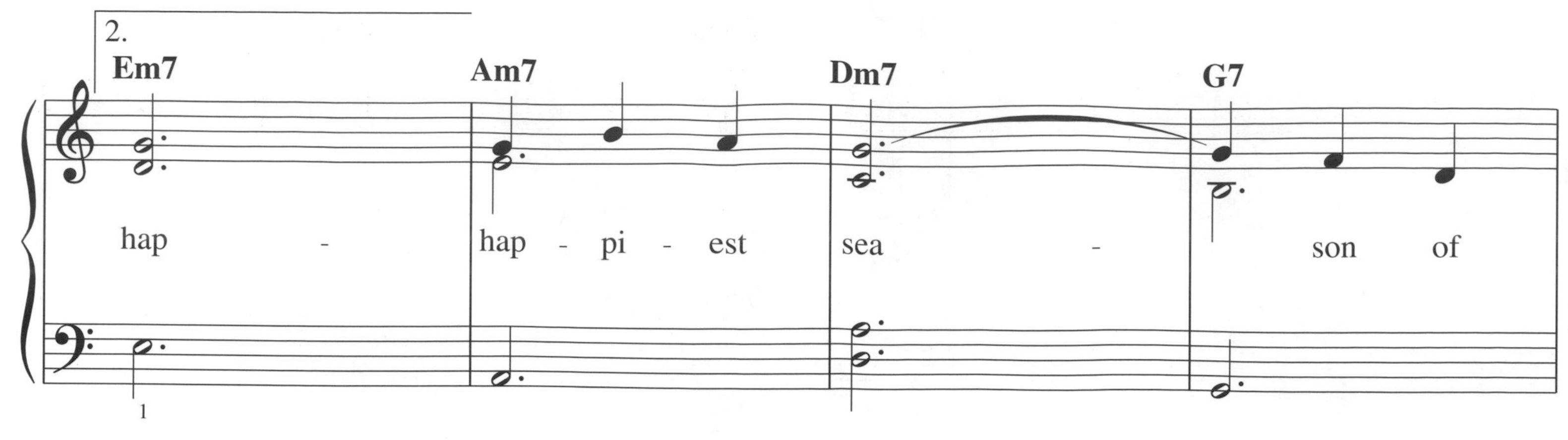
2.
Em7
Am7
Dm7
G7
hap - hap - pi - est sea - son of
1

Gm7
5
1
C7
all.
There'll be
1
1

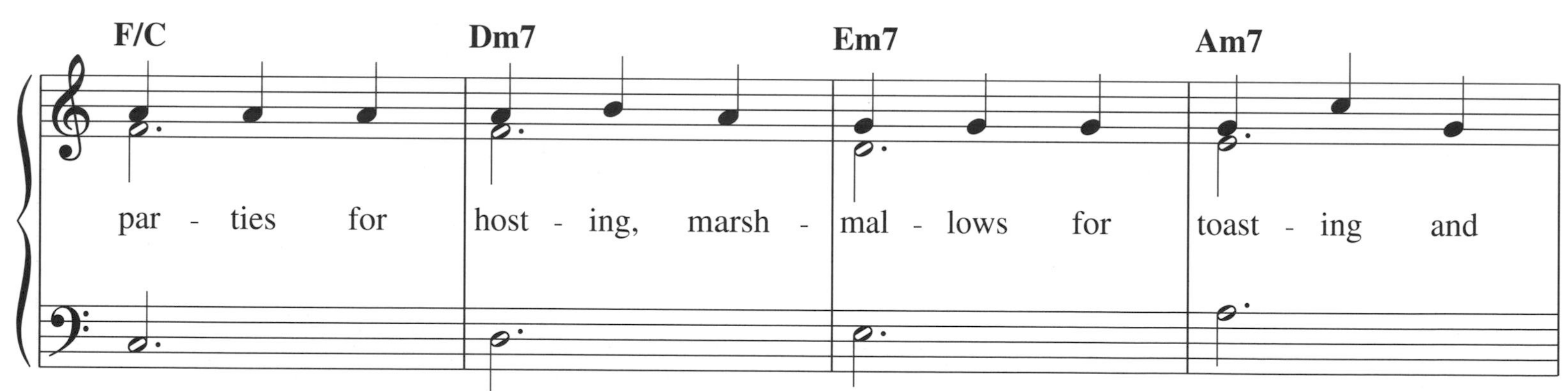
F/C
Dm7
Em7
Am7
par - ties for host - ing, marsh - mal - lows for toast - ing and

Dm7
3
1
G7
C
car - ol - ing out in the snow.
There'll be

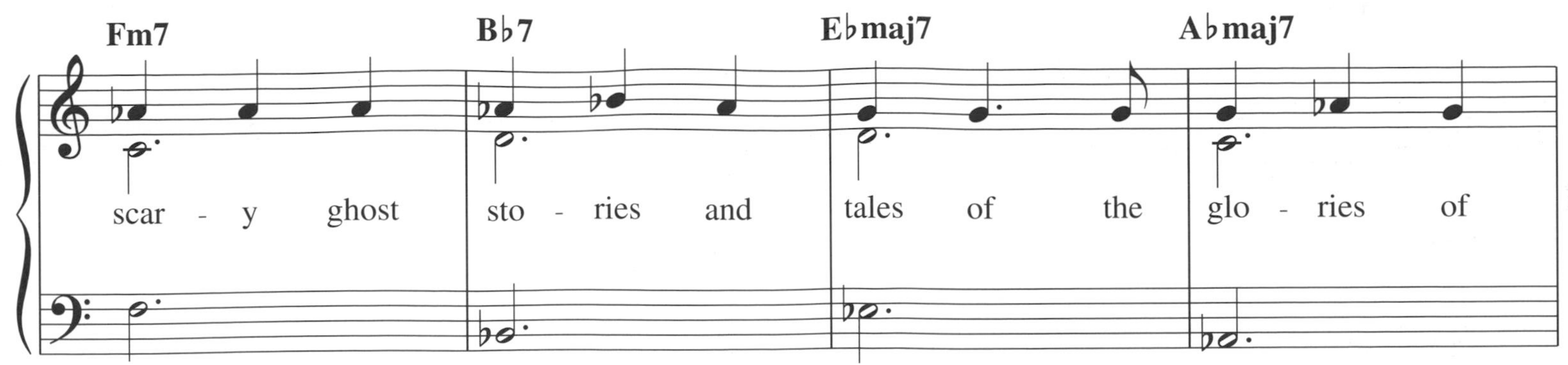
Fm7
B♭7
E♭maj7
A♭maj7
scar - y ghost sto - ries and tales of the glo - ries of

Fm
Dm7
F/G
G7
D.S. al Coda
Christ - mas - es long, long a - go. It's the

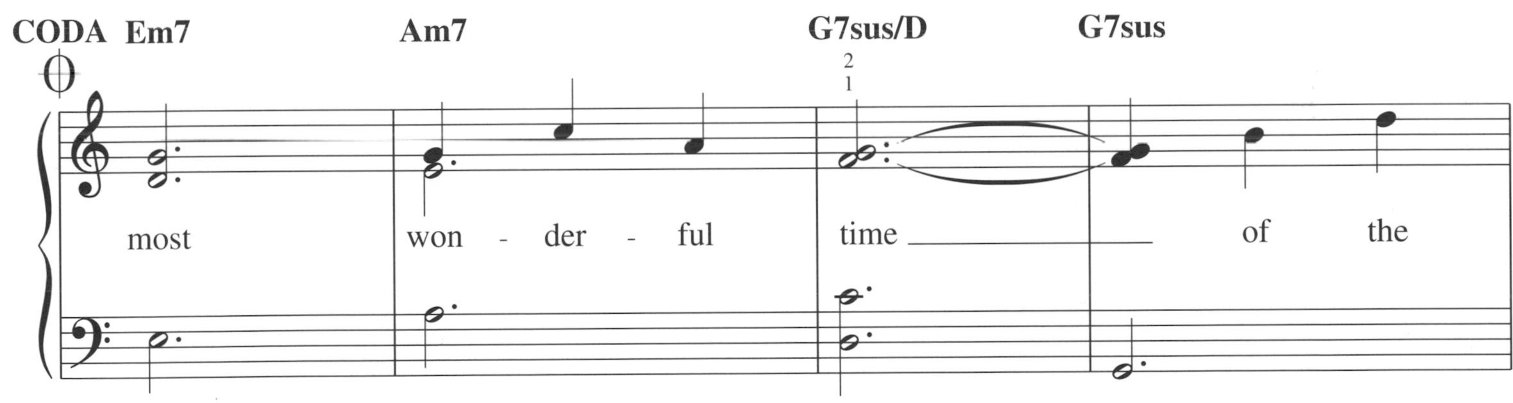
CODA
Em7
Am7
G7sus/D
G7sus
2
1
most won - der - ful time of the

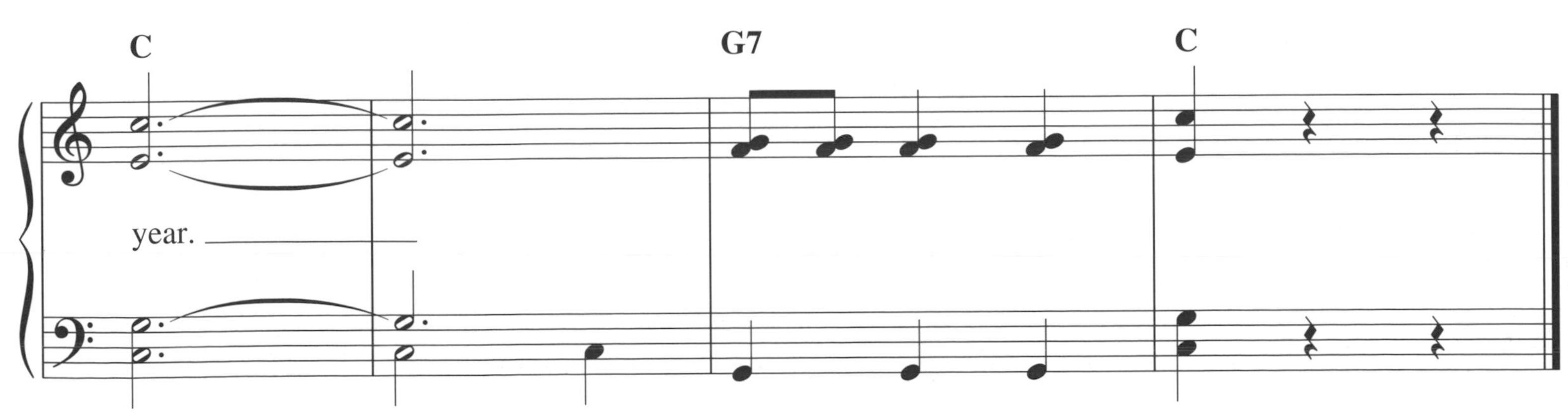
C
G7
C
year.

NO MORE BLUE CHRISTMASES

Words and Music by GERRY GOFFIN
and MICHAEL MASSER

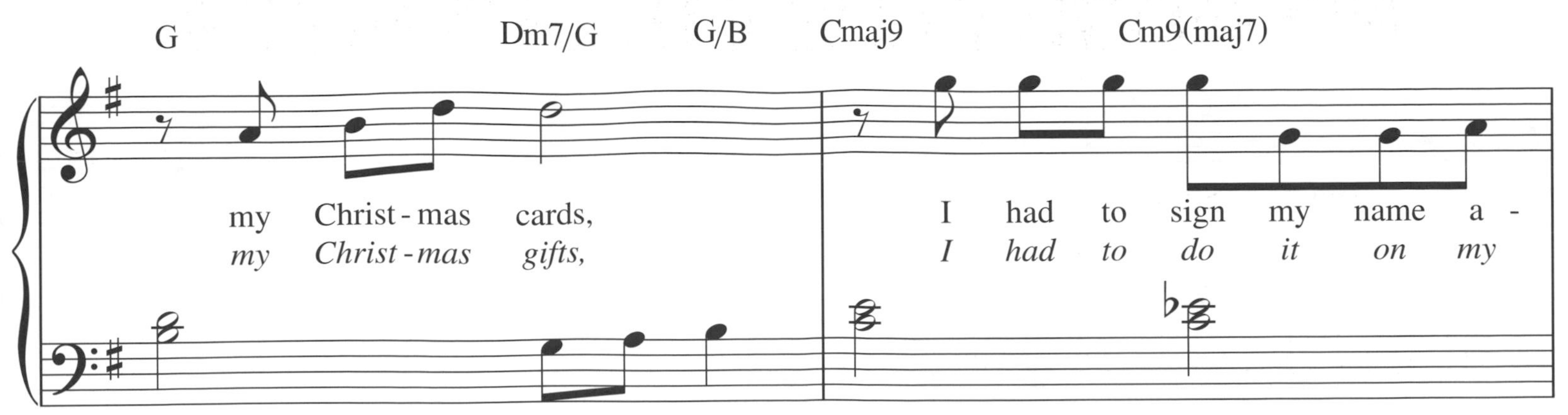
G
Dm7/G
G/B
Cmaj9
Cm9(maj7)
my Christ - mas cards,
my Christ - mas gifts,
I had to sign my name a -
I had to do it on my

G
Fmaj7/G
G/B
Cmaj9
lone. But
own. (Sung:)
now your name is next to mine, and
Cham - pagne par - ties ev - 'ry - where; till

To Coda
Cm9(maj7)
G/D
D/E
there's more love in ev - 'ry line; I'm
I met you I did - n't care. Now
wish - in' a Mer - ry Christ - mas to
there's more than just a Christ - mas tree to

Am7
D7sus
G(add2)
Em9
Am7
D
D/C
ev - 'ry - one I've known.
No more blue Christ-mas - es;

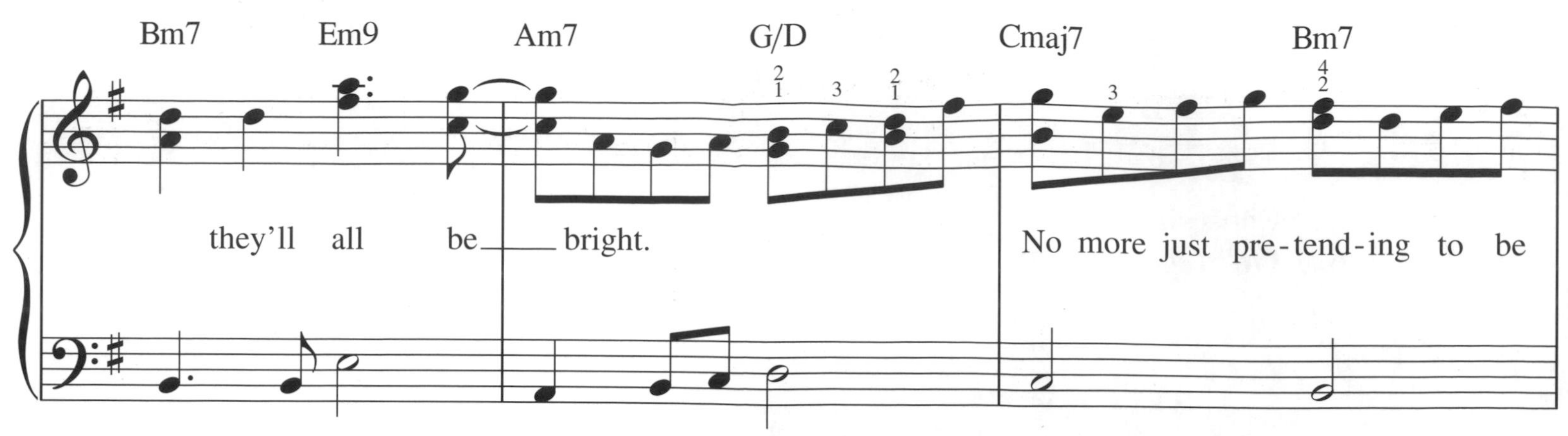
Bm7
Em9
Am7
G/D
Cmaj7
Bm7
they'll all be bright.
No more just pre-tend-ing to be

Am7
D/F♯
G
F♯m7♭5
B7/D♯
Em
hap - py when I'm sad,
go - ing through the mo - tions while

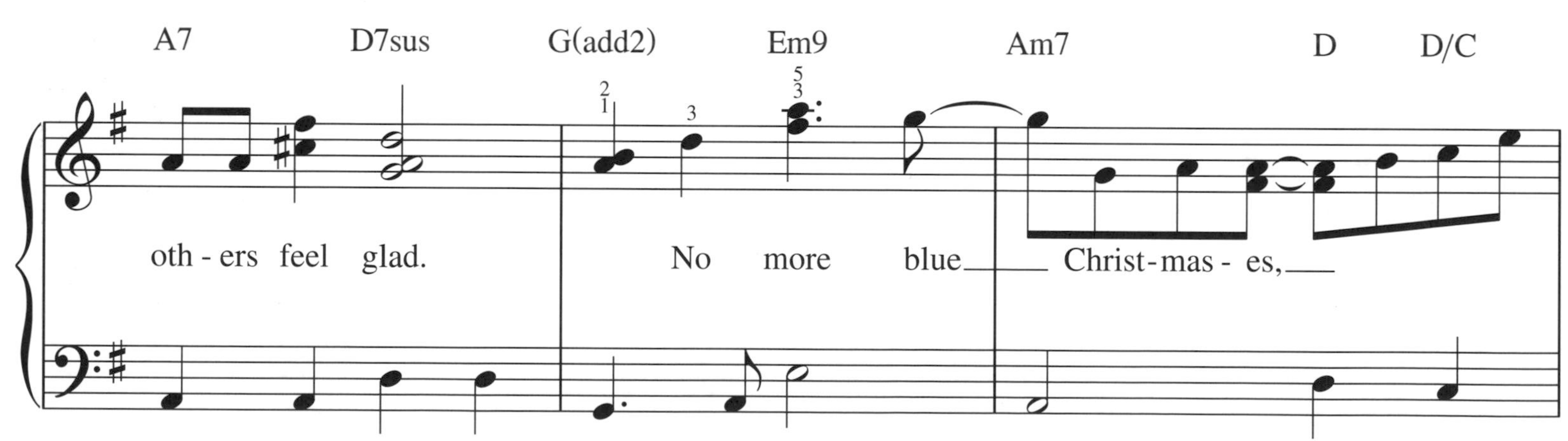
A7
D7sus
G(add2)
Em9
Am7
D
D/C
oth - ers feel glad.
No more blue Christ-mas - es,

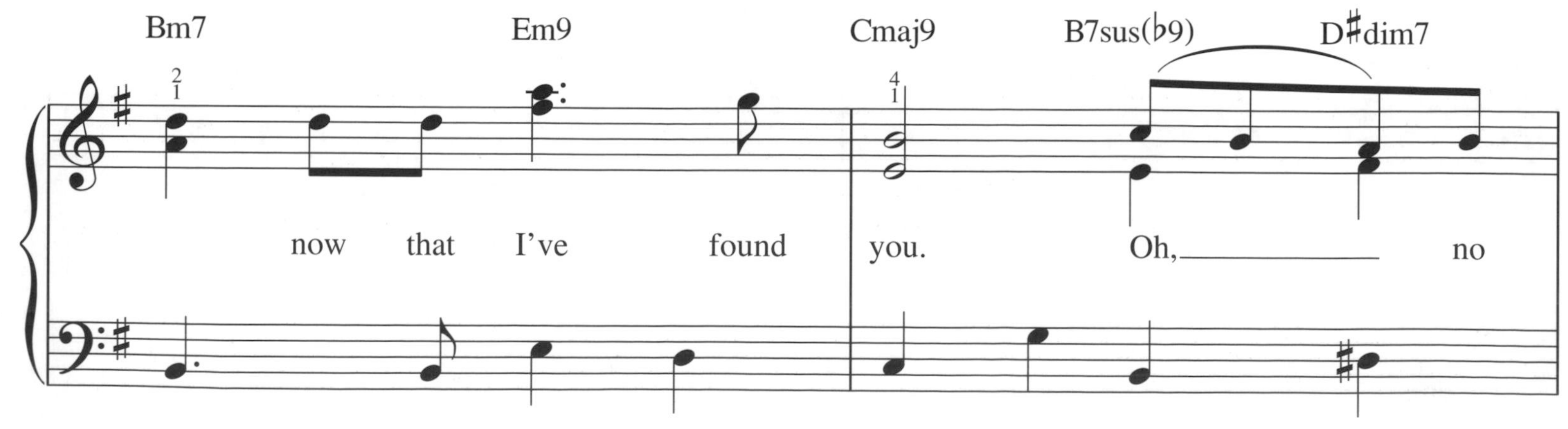
Bm7
Em9
Cmaj9
B7sus(♭9)
D♯dim7
now that I've found you.
Oh, no

Em7
Dm7/G
G7/B
C
E♭maj7
won - der that I thought that they were go - ing out of style;

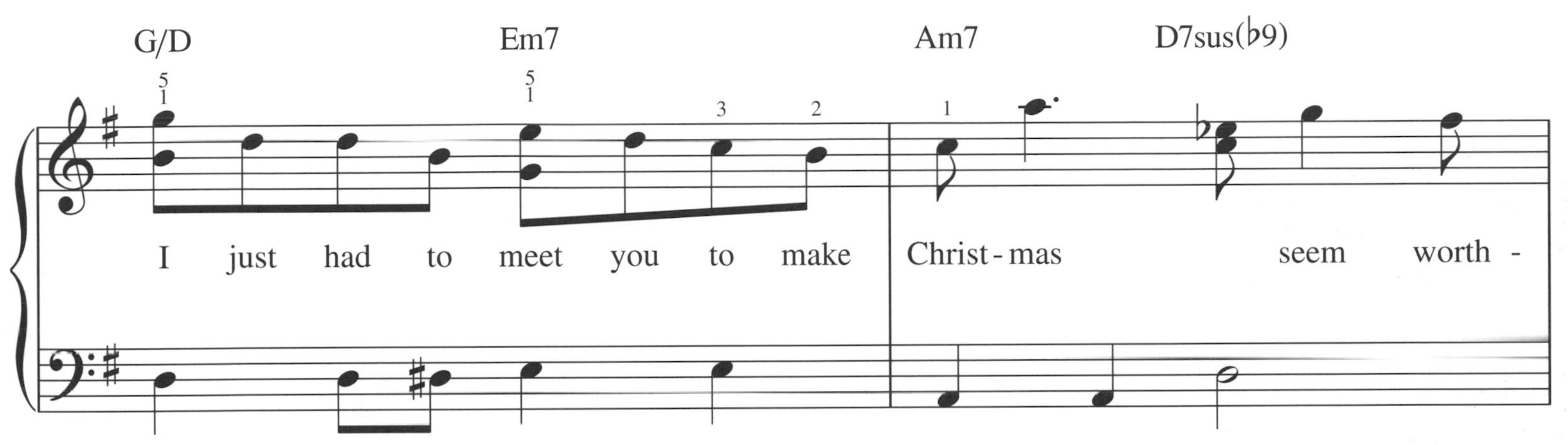
G/D
Em7
Am7
D7sus(♭9)
I just had to meet you to make Christ - mas seem worth -

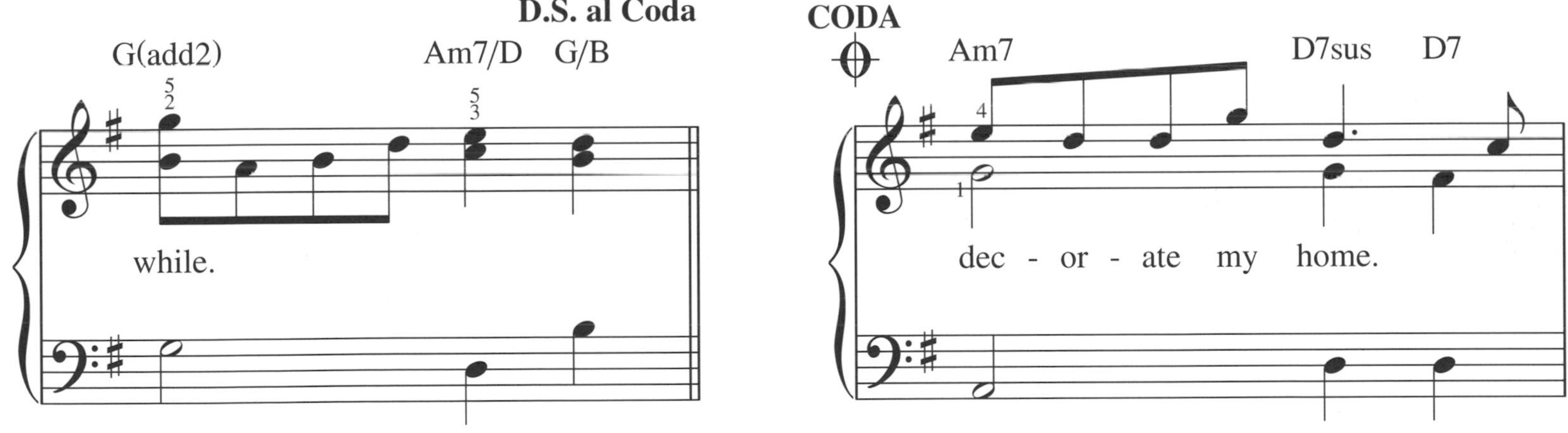
D.S. al Coda
G(add2)
Am7/D
G/B
while.
CODA
Am7
D7sus
D7
dec - or - ate my home.

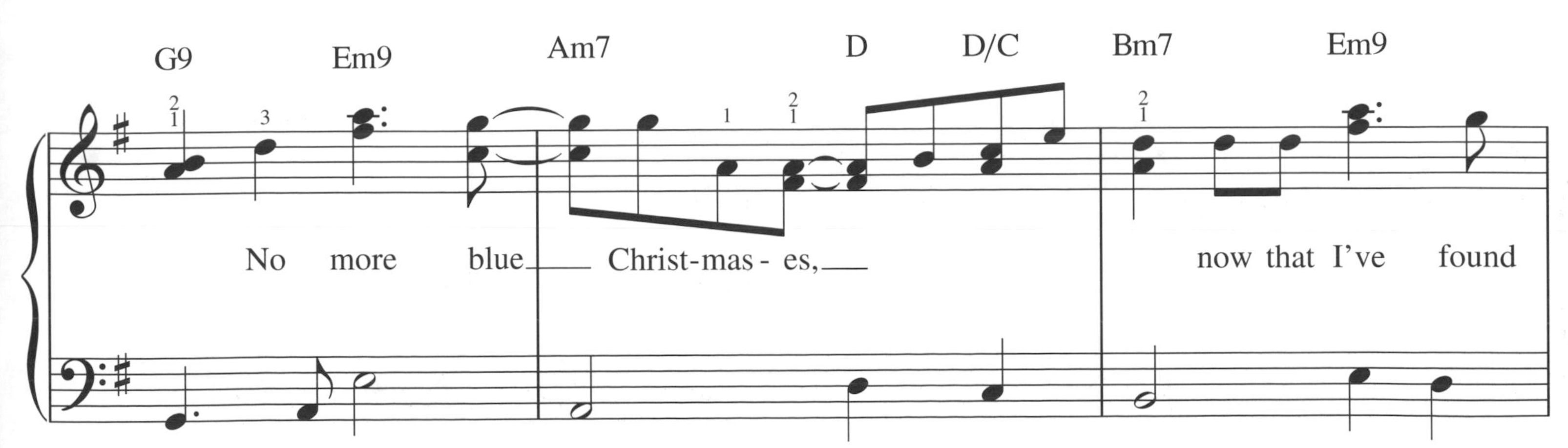
G9
Em9
Am7
D
D/C
Bm7
Em9
No more blue Christ-mas - es, now that I've found

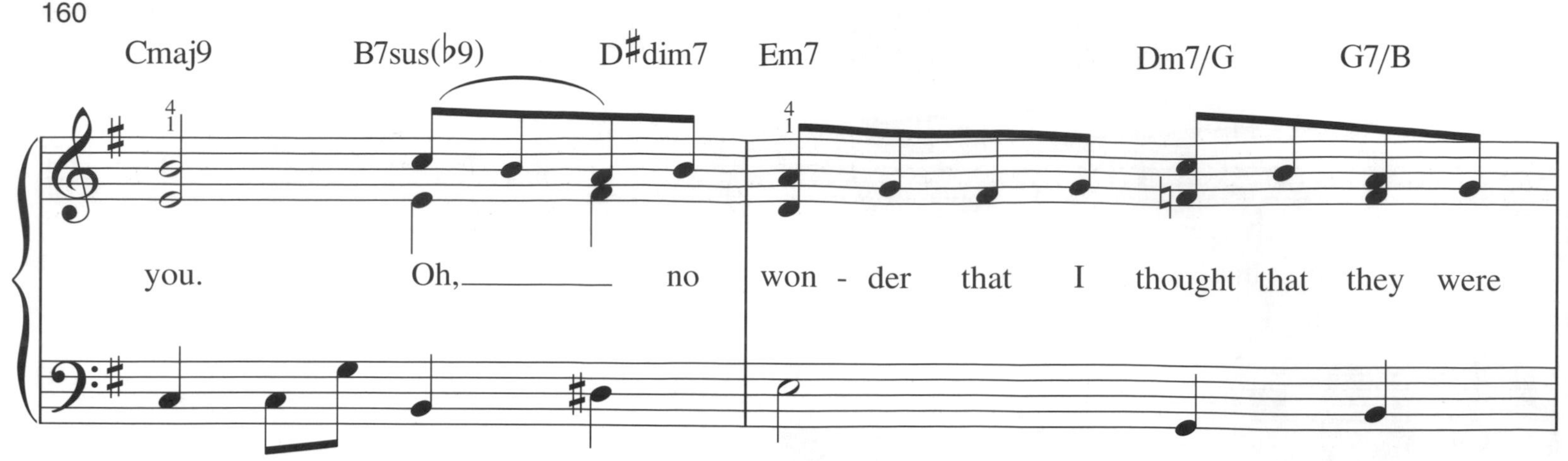
Cmaj9
B7sus(♭9)
D♯dim7
Em7
Dm7/G
G7/B
you. Oh, no won - der that I thought that they were

C(add2)
E♭maj7
G/D
Em7
go - ing out of style; I just had to meet you to make

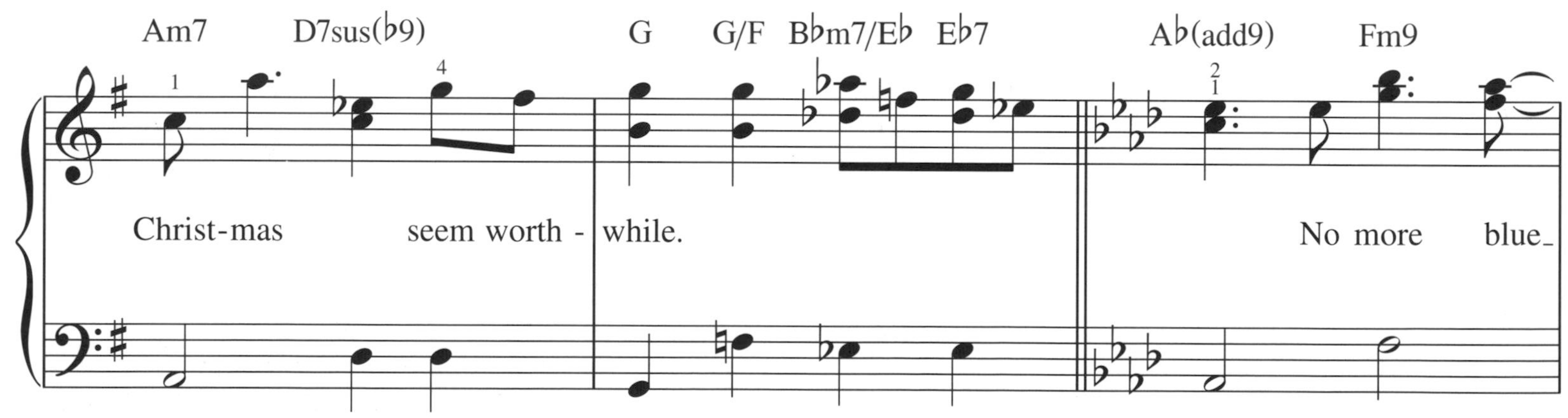
Am7
D7sus(♭9)
G
G/F
B♭m7/E♭
E♭7
A♭(add9)
Fm9
Christ-mas seem worth - while. No more blue

B♭m7
E♭
E♭/D♭
Cm7
Fm9
D♭maj9
C7sus(♭9)
Edim7
Christ-mas - es, now that I've found you. Oh, no

Fm7
Ebm7/Ab
Ab7/C
Db
Emaj7
won - der that I thought that they were go - ing out of style;
Ab/Eb
Fm7
Bbm7
Bbm7/Eb
Ebm7
Ebm7/Ab
I just had to meet you to make Christ - mas seem worth - while.
Dbmaj9
Ab(add2)/C
Bbm7
Bbm7/Eb
Absus2
Fm7
I just had to meet you to make Christ-mas seem worth - while.
Bbm7
Bbm7/Eb
Ab(add2)

A PLACE CALLED HOME

from A CHRISTMAS CAROL

Music by ALAN MENKEN
Lyrics by LYNN AHRENS

To Coda

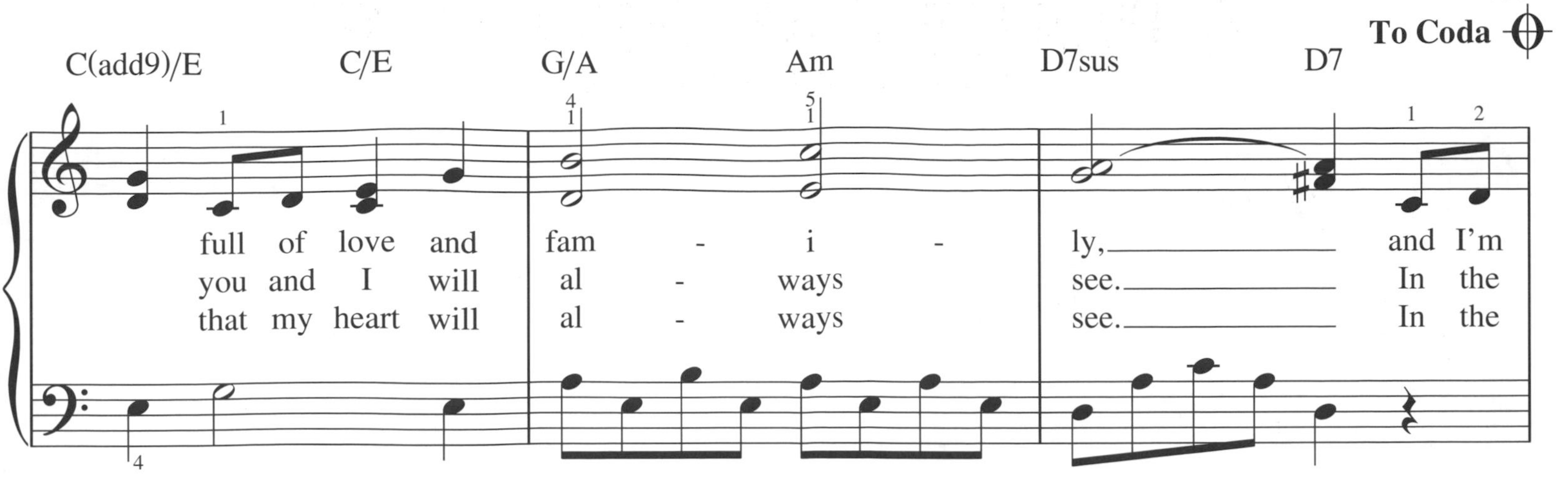
C(add9)/E
C/E
G/A
Am
D7sus
D7
full of love and fam - i - ly, and I'm
you and I will al - ways see. In the
that my heart will al - ways see. In the

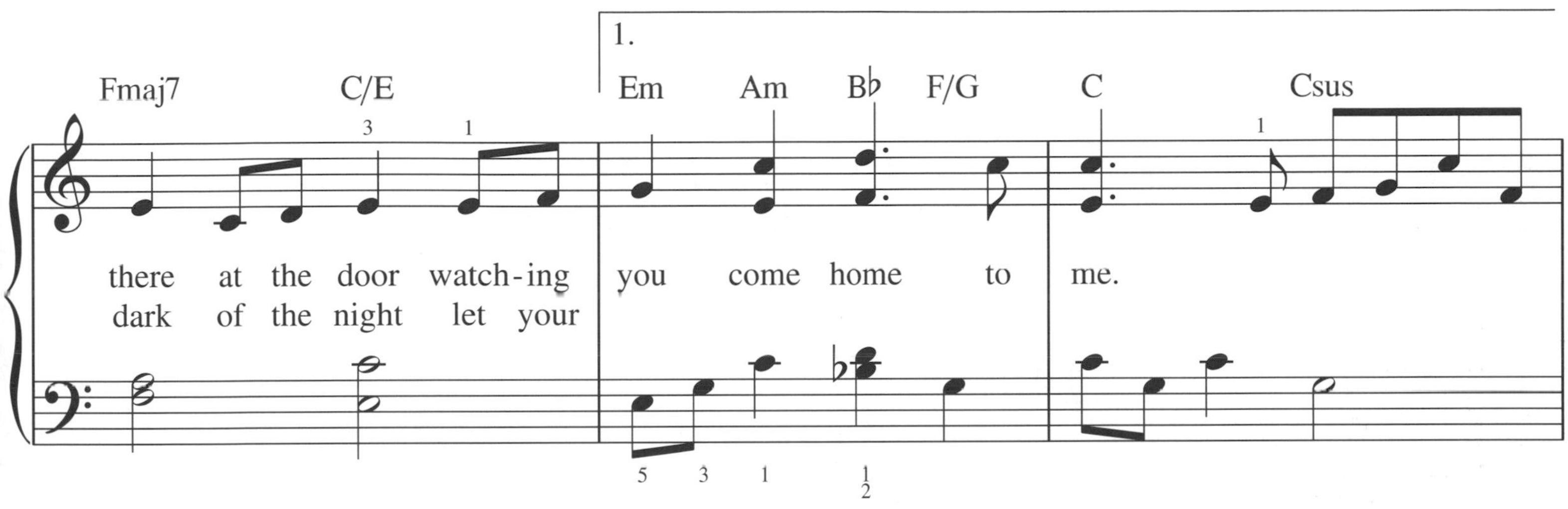
1.
Fmaj7
C/E
Em
Am
B♭
F/G
C
Csus
there at the door watch-ing you come home to me.
dark of the night let your

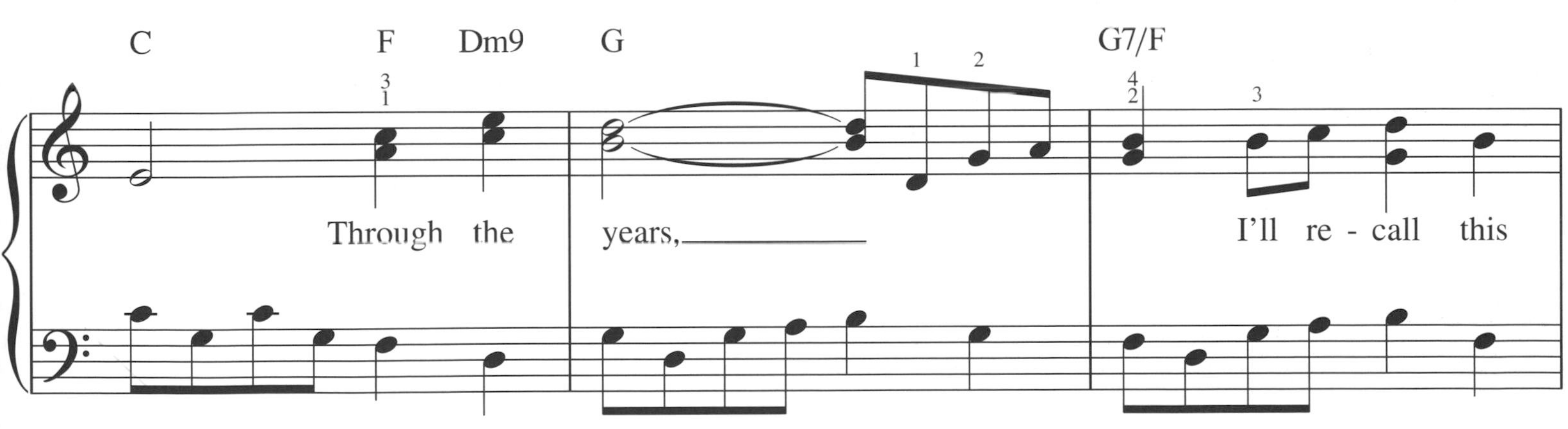
C
F
Dm9
G
G7/F
Through the years, I'll re - call this

C(add9)/E
Am
C/D
day, in your arms,

D9
Dm/G
Em/G
G7sus
when I fin - 'lly found my way to a place called

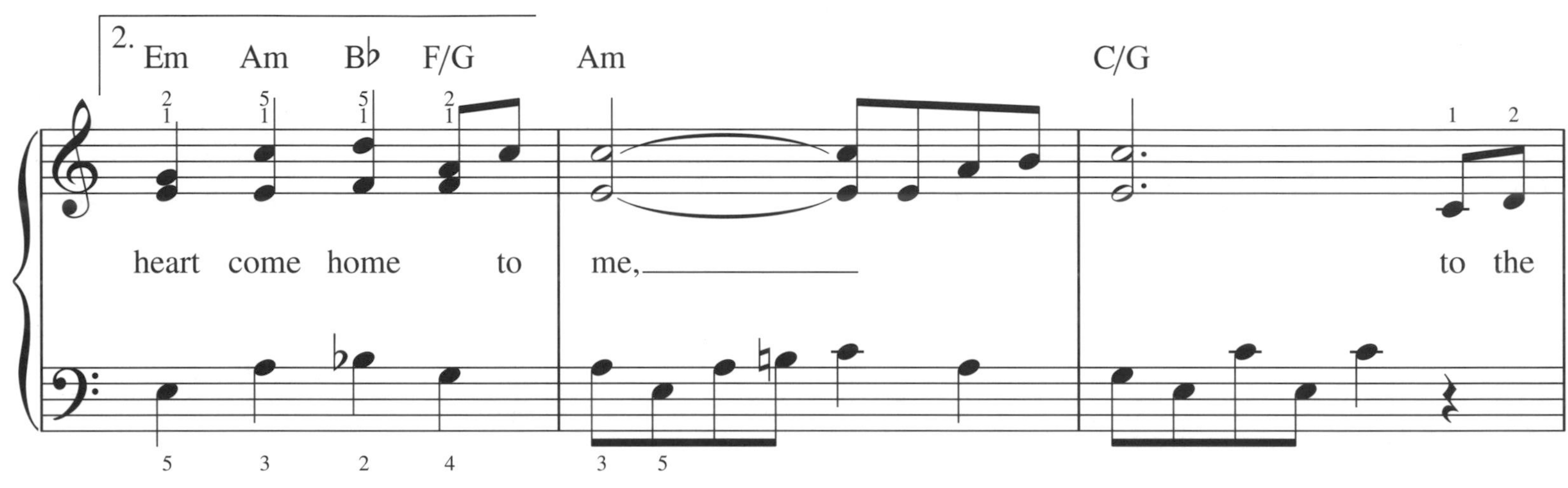
2.
Em Am B♭ F/G
Am
C/G
heart come home to me, to the

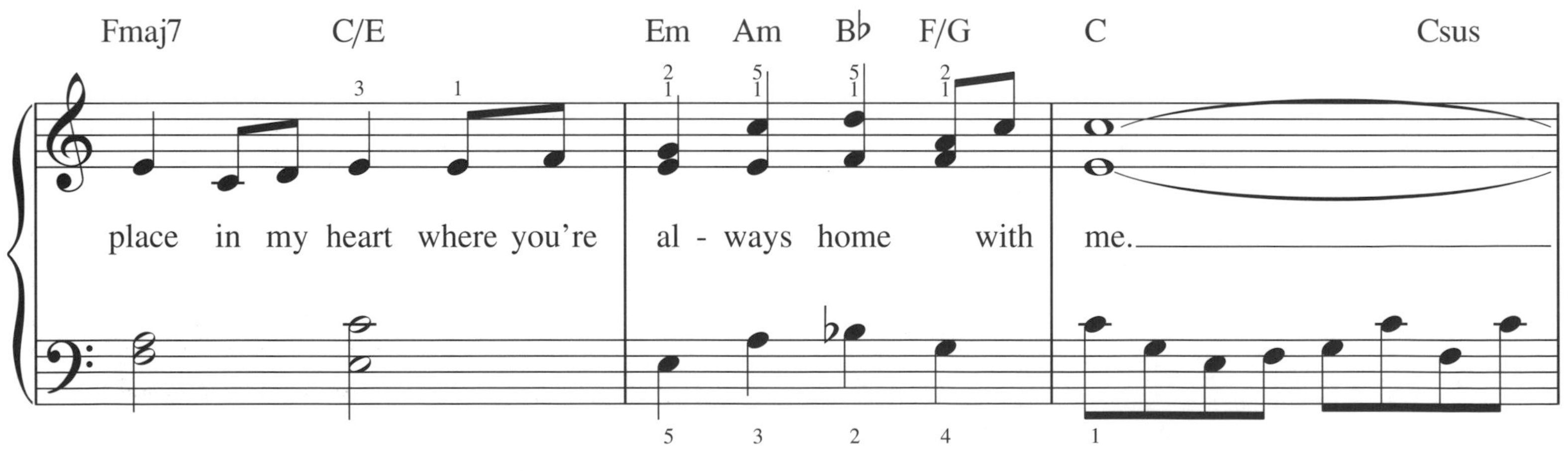
Fmaj7 C/E
Em Am B♭ F/G
C Csus
place in my heart where you're al - ways home with me.

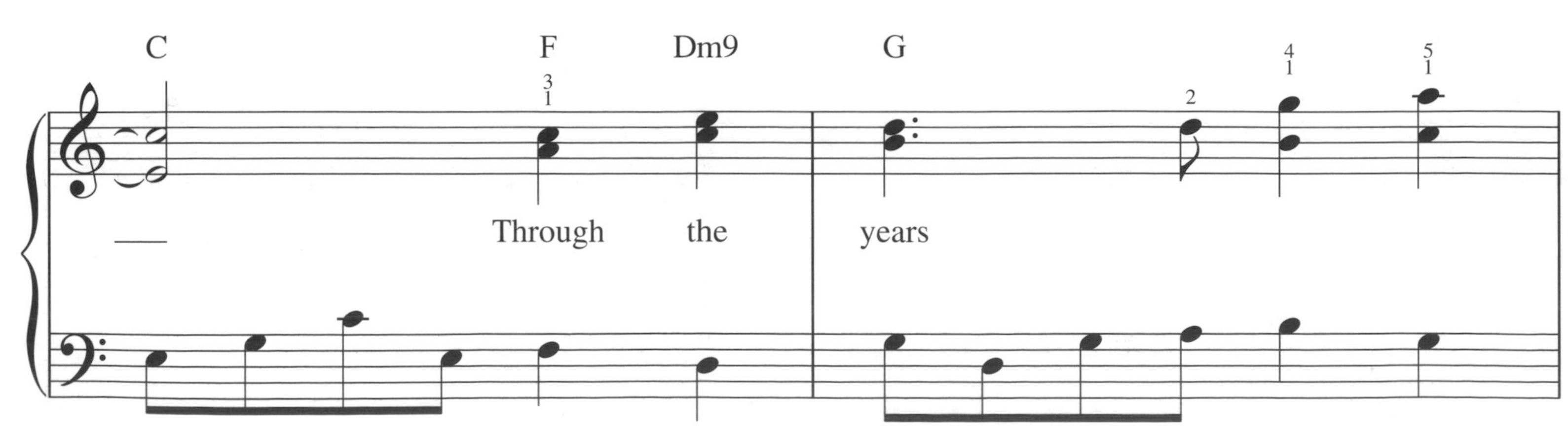
C F Dm9
G
Through the years

G7/F
C(add9)/E
I'll re - call this
day,
Am
C/D
in your
arms,
D9
Dm/G
Em/G
when I fin - 'lly
found
my
G7sus
Em/G
D.S. al Coda
G7sus
CODA
Fmaj7
C/E
way
to a place
called
dark of the night let your

Em Am B♭ F/G Am
heart come home to me,

Slower, freely
C/G Fmaj7 C/E
to the place in my heart where you're

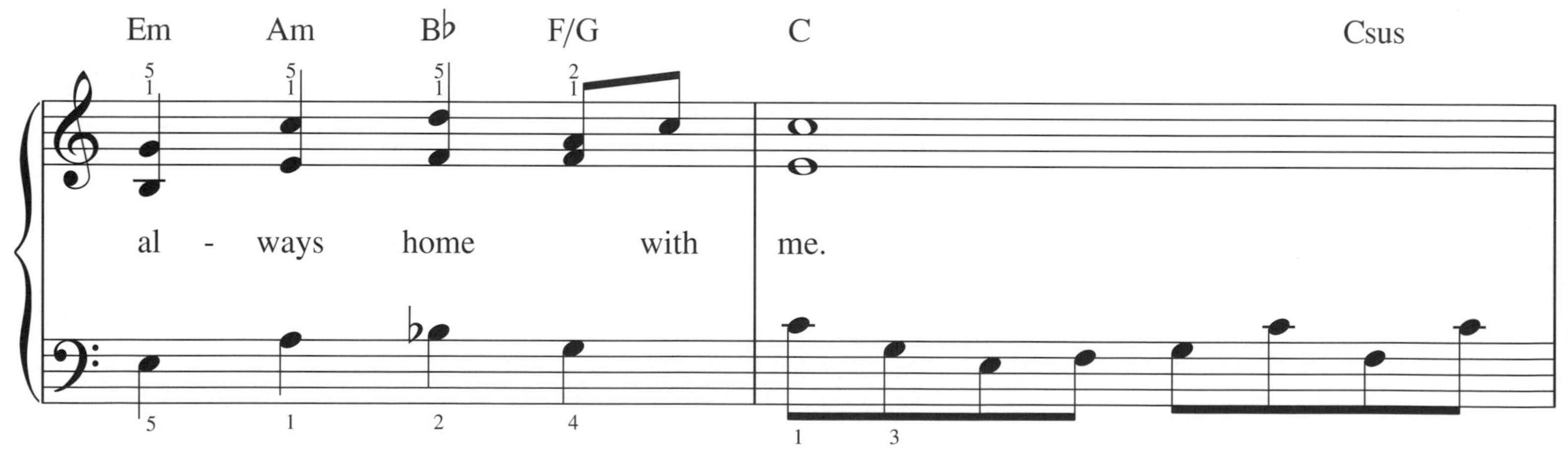
Em Am B♭ F/G C Csus
al - ways home with me.

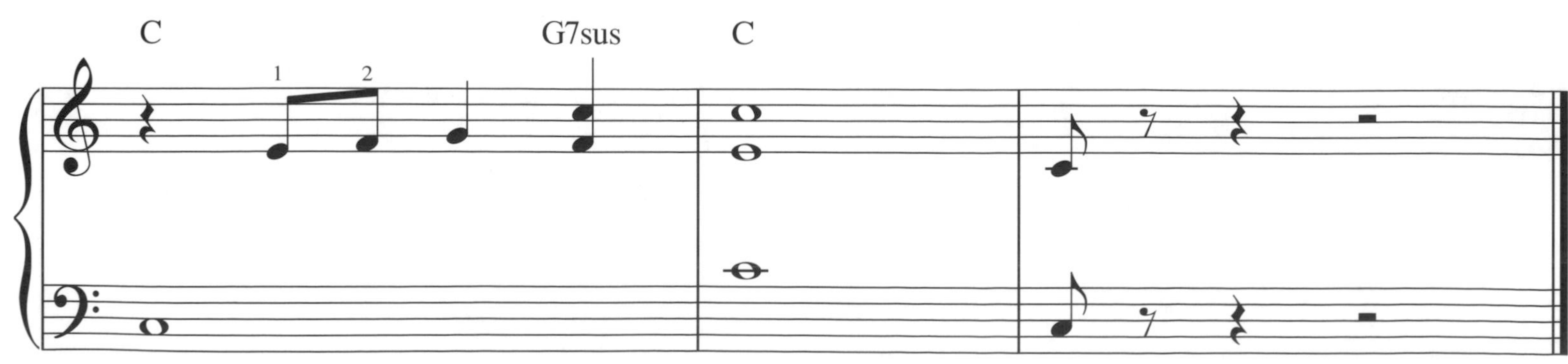
C G7sus C

ROCKIN' AROUND THE CHRISTMAS TREE

Music and Lyrics by
JOHNNY MARKS

G7
Christ - mas tree, let the Christ - mas spir - it ring.

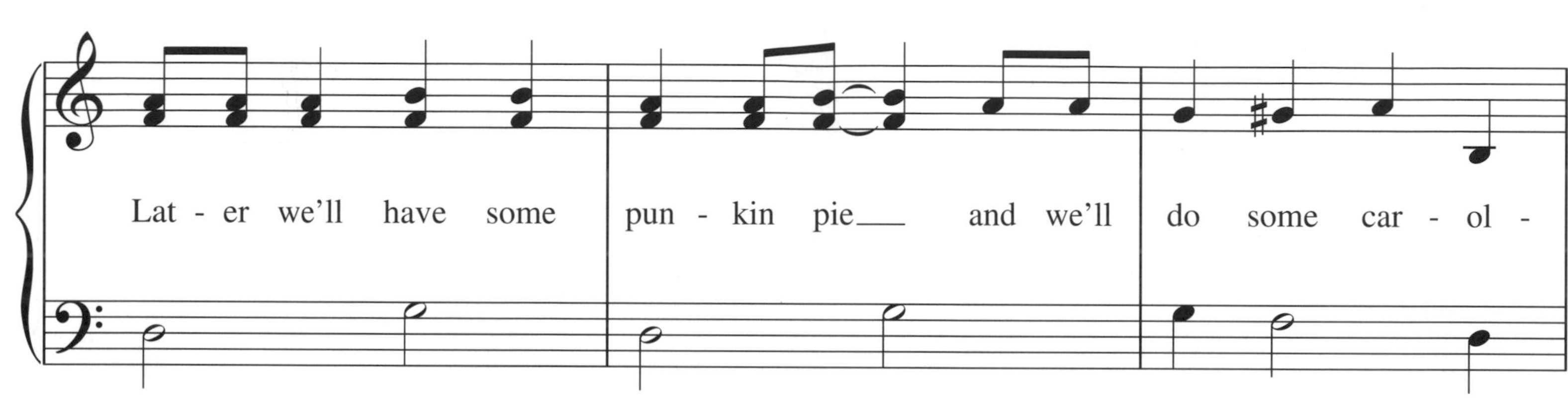
Lat - er we'll have some pun - kin pie and we'll do some car - ol -

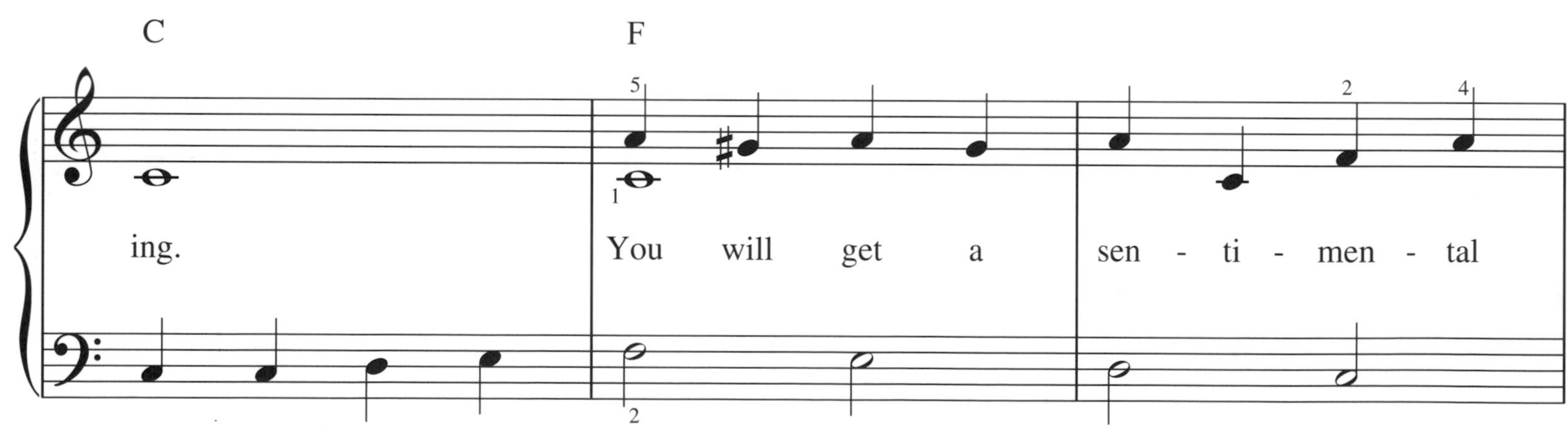
C
F
ing. You will get a sen - ti - men - tal

Em
Am
feel - ing when you hear voic - es sing - ing, "Let's be jol - ly;

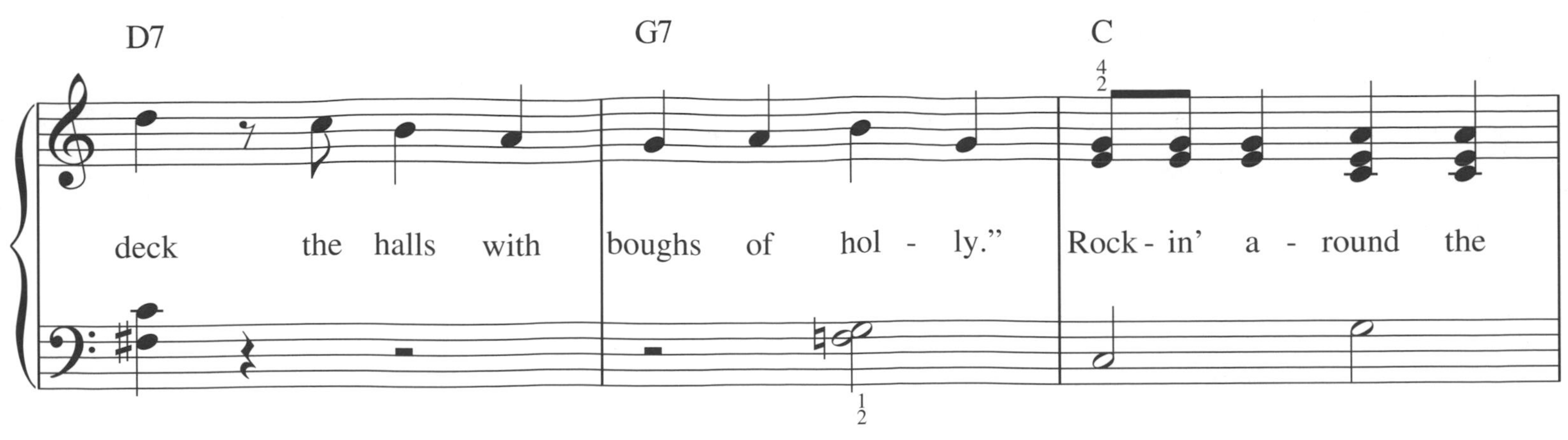
D7
G7
C
deck the halls with boughs of hol - ly." Rock - in' a - round the

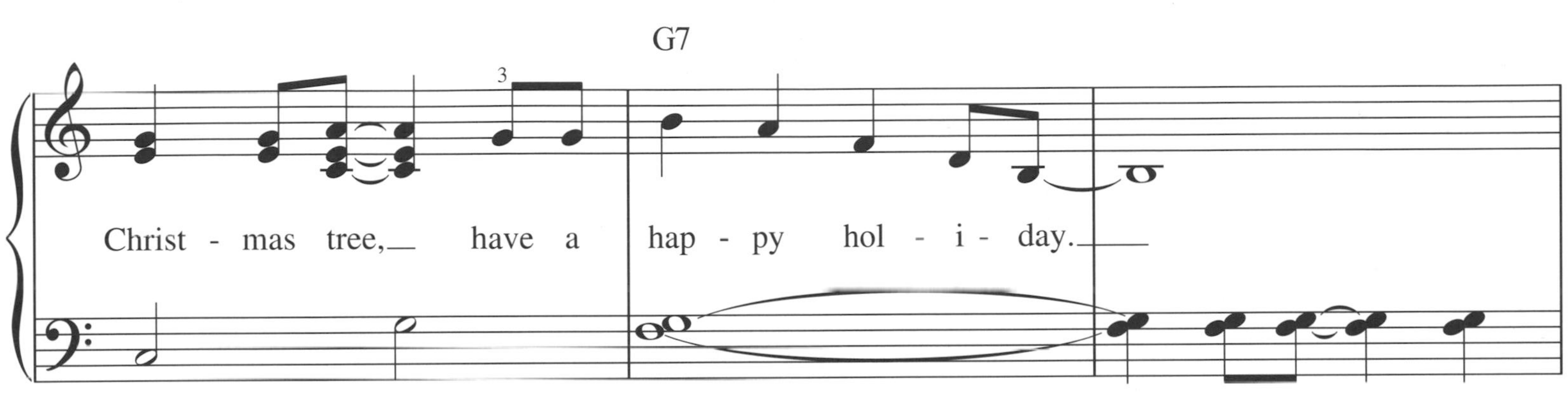
G7
Christ - mas tree, have a hap - py hol - i - day.

Ev - 'ry - one danc - ing mer - ri - ly in the new old fash - ioned

C
Am
F
G7
C
way.

RUDOLPH THE RED-NOSED REINDEER

Music and Lyrics by
JOHNNY MARKS

With motion

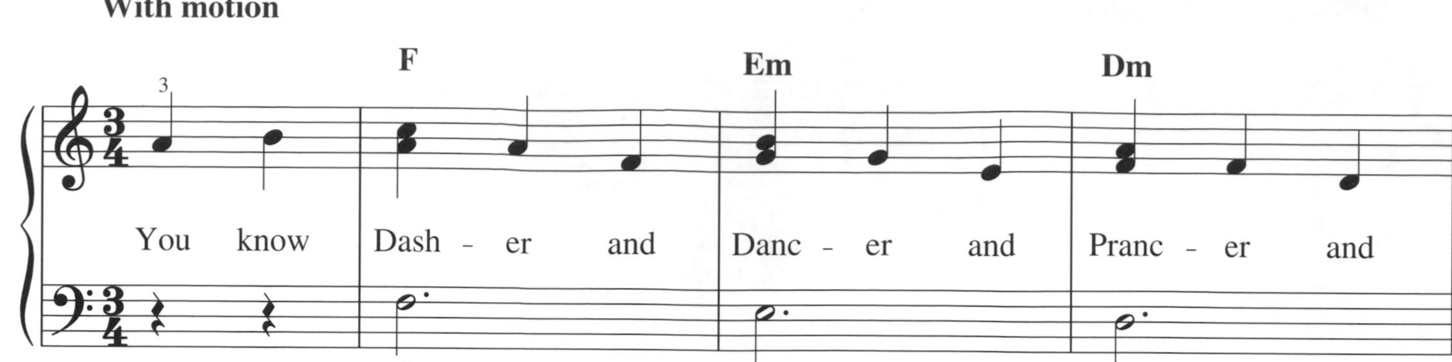

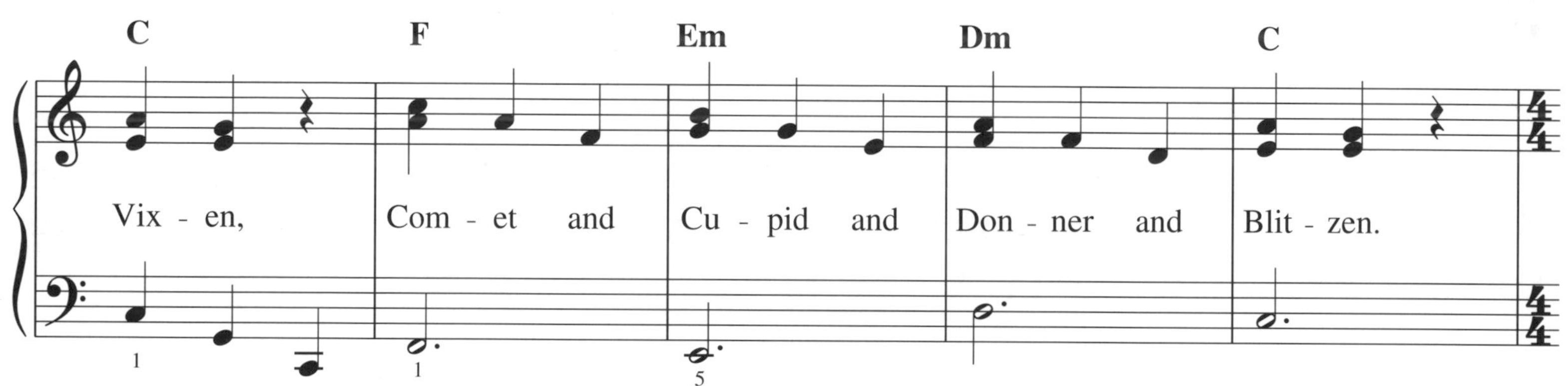

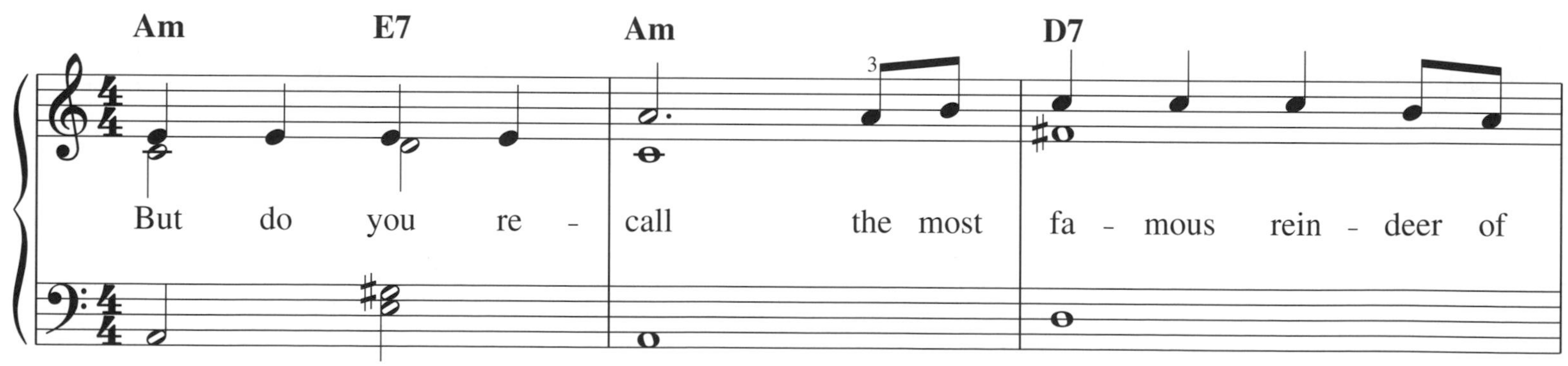

C
Am
3
1
Ru-dolph the Red - Nosed Rein - deer had a ver - y shin - y

G7
Dm7
G7
Dm7
G7
nose, and if you ev - er saw it,

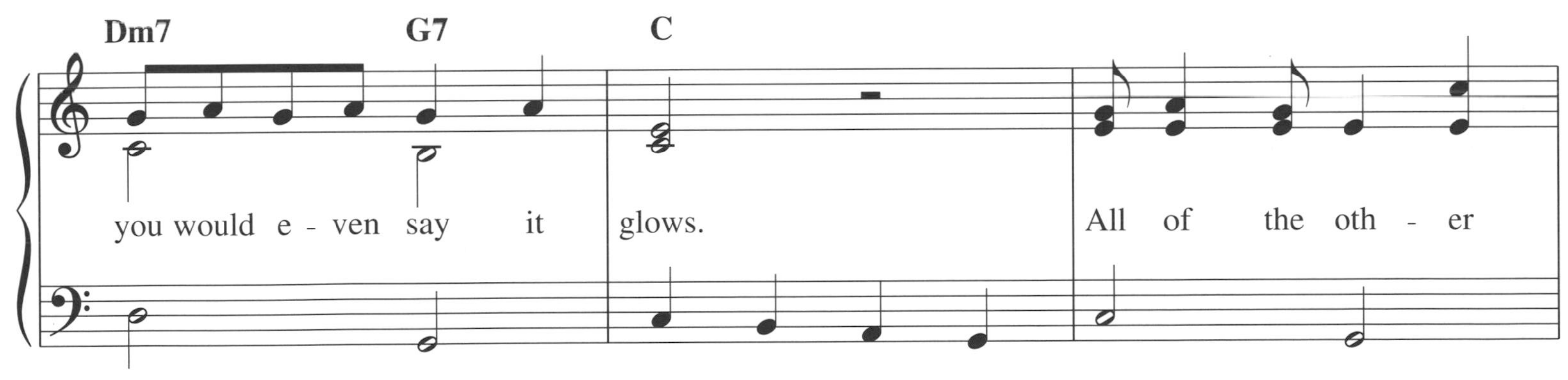
Dm7
G7
C
you would e - ven say it glows. All of the oth - er

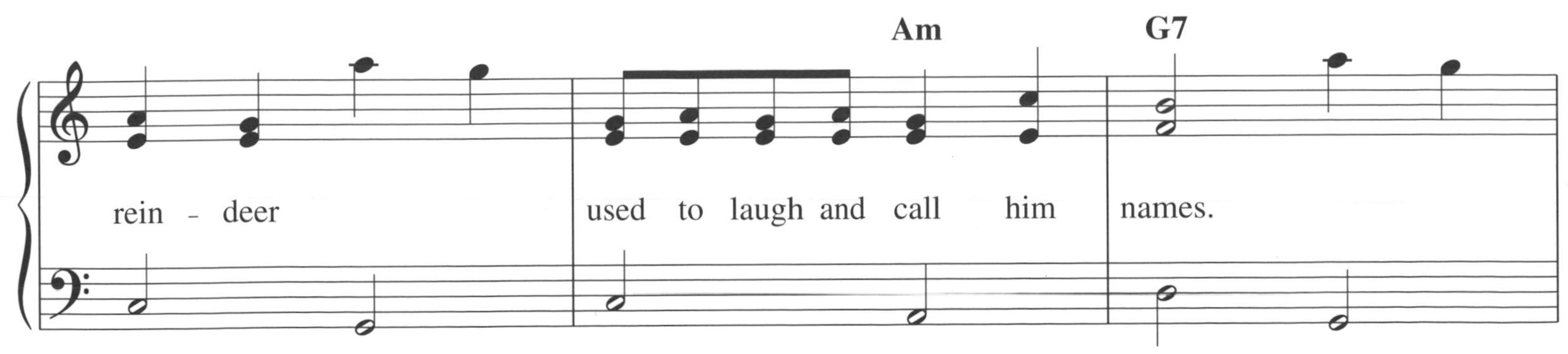
Am
G7
rein - deer used to laugh and call him names.

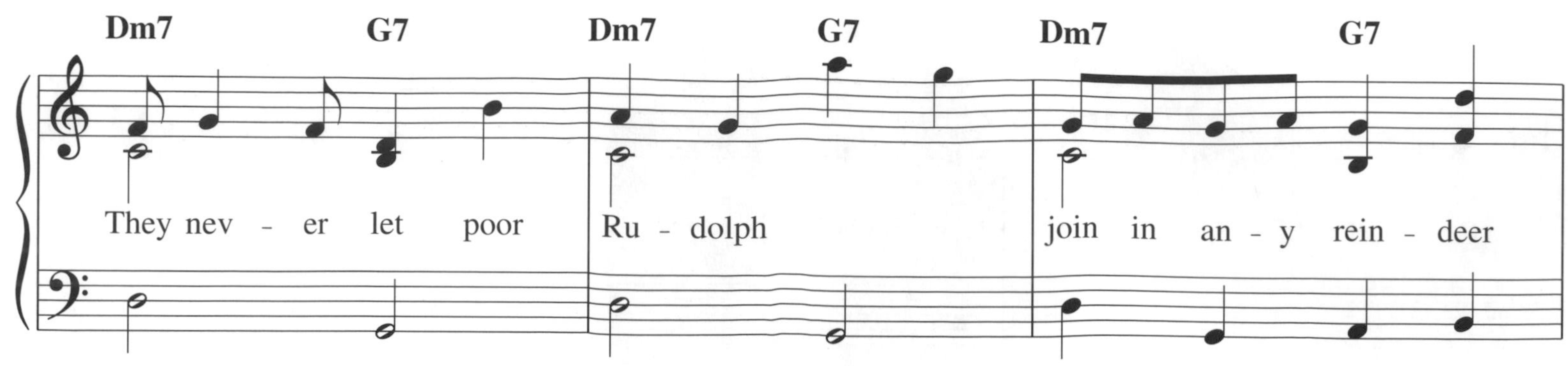
Dm7
G7
Dm7
G7
Dm7
G7
They nev - er let poor
Ru - dolph
join in an - y rein - deer

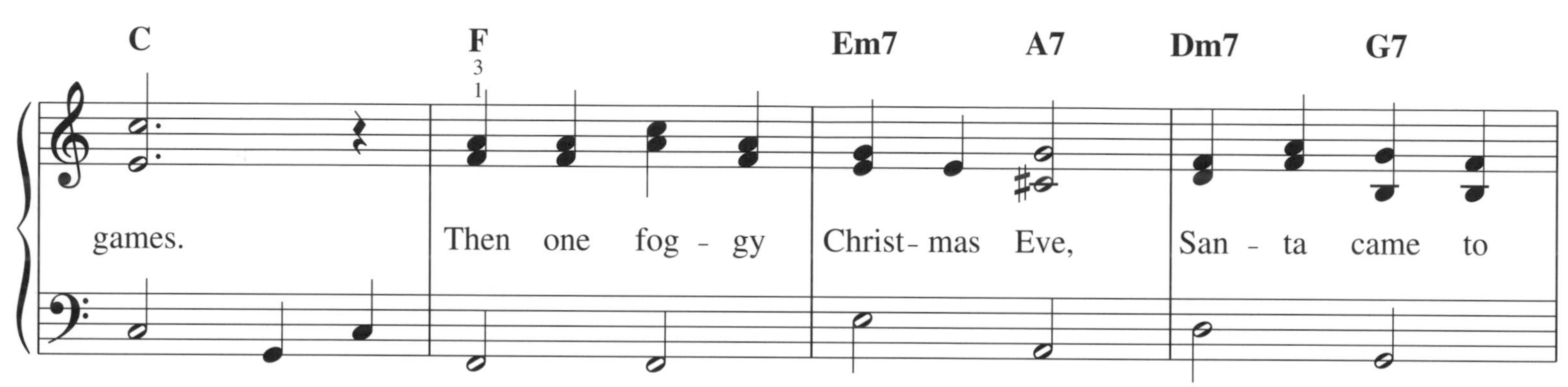
C
F
Em7
A7
Dm7
G7
3
1
games.
Then one fog - gy
Christ - mas Eve,
San - ta came to

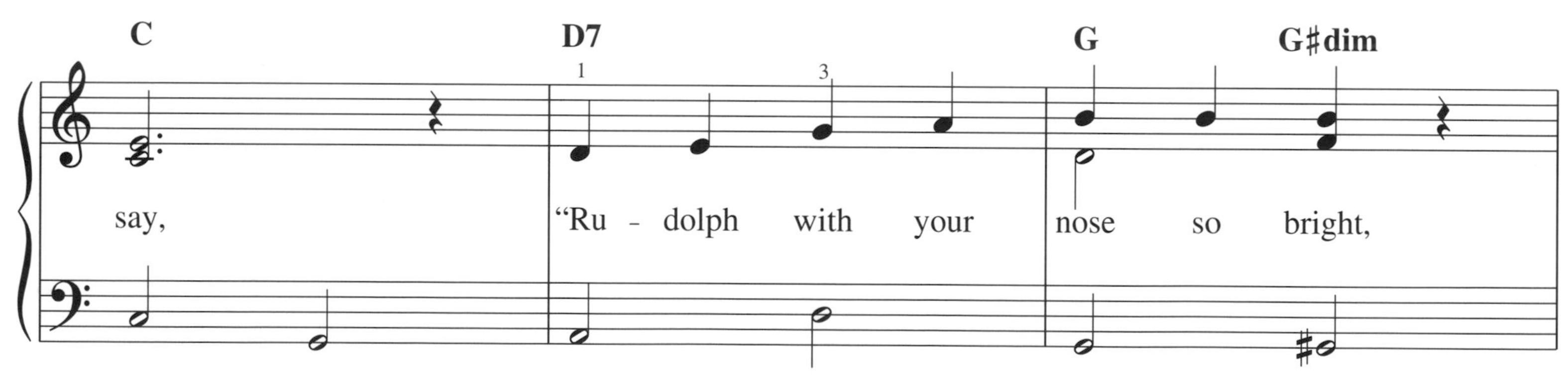
C
D7
G
G♯dim
1
3
say,
"Ru - dolph with your
nose so bright,

Am7
D7
Dm7
G7
C
won't you guide my
sleigh to - night?"
Then how the rein - deer

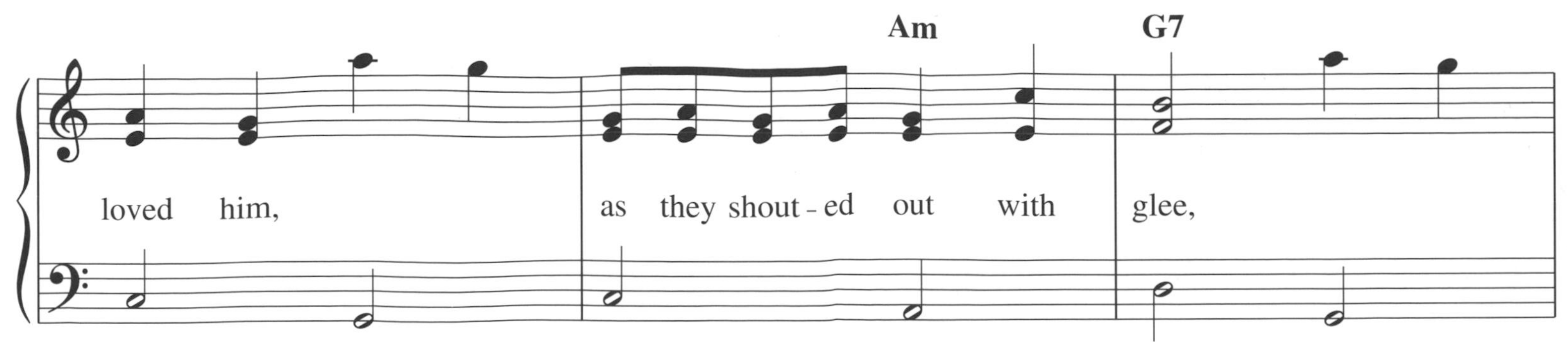
Am
G7
loved him,
as they shout - ed out with
glee,

Dm7
G7
Dm7
G7
Dm7
G7
"Ru-dolph the Red - Nosed
Rein - deer,
you'll go down in his - to -

C
A7
D
ry."

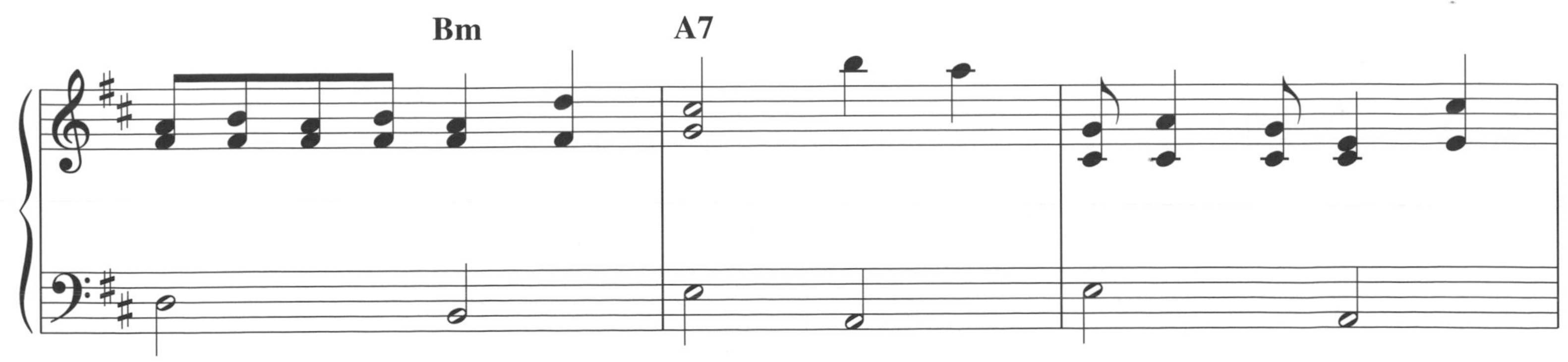
Bm
A7

D

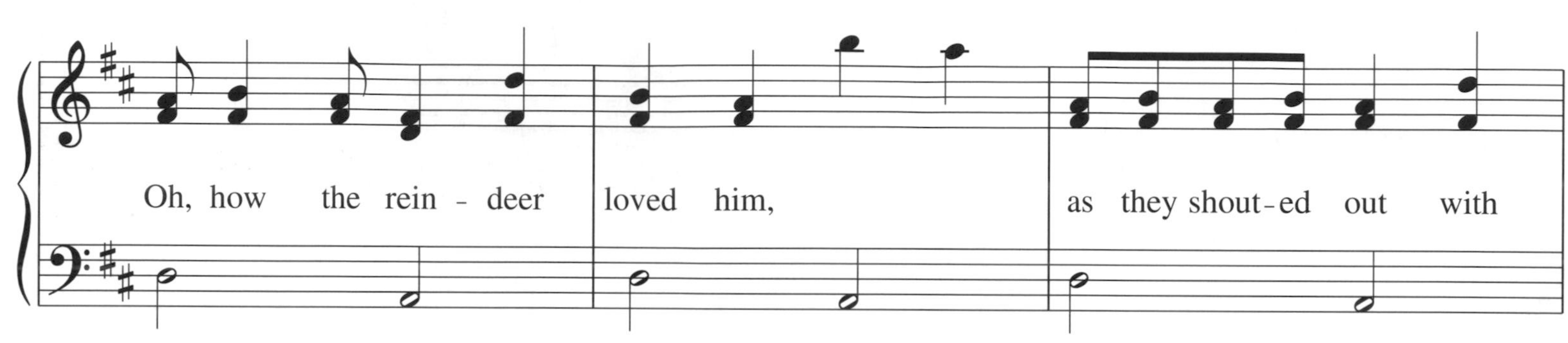
Oh, how the rein - deer loved him,
as they shout-ed out with

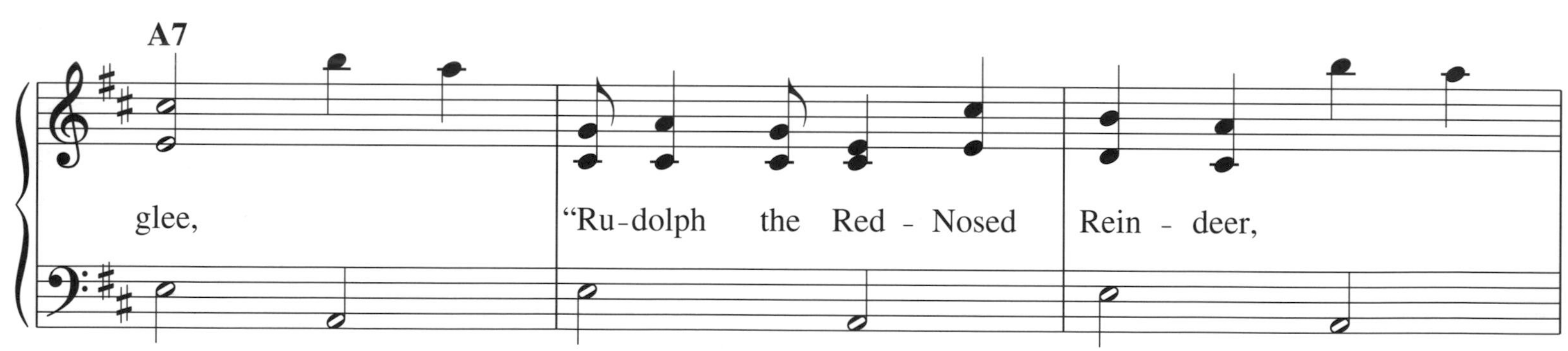
A7
glee,
"Ru-dolph the Red - Nosed Rein - deer,

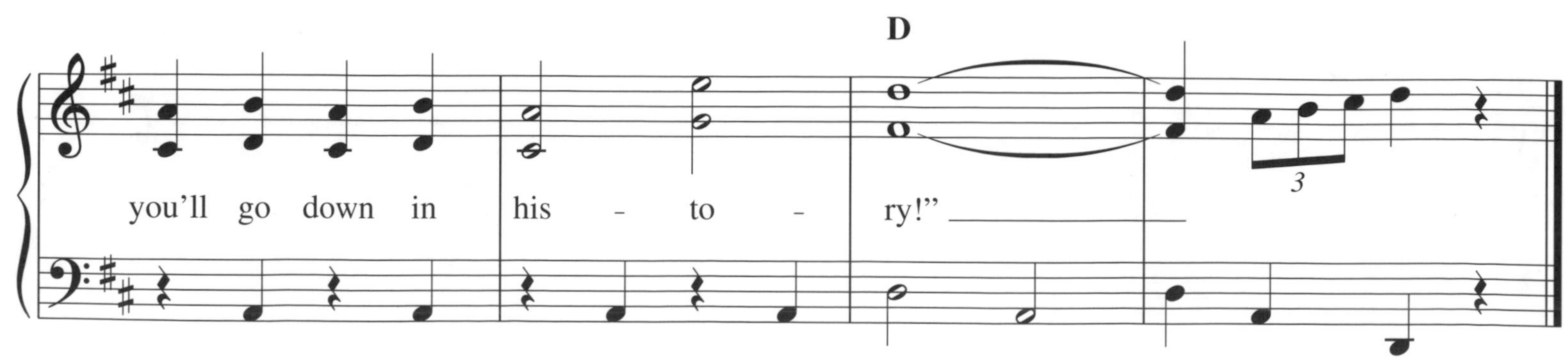
D
you'll go down in his - to - ry!"
3

SANTA CLAUS IS COMIN' TO TOWN

Words by HAVEN GILLESPIE
Music by J. FRED COOTS

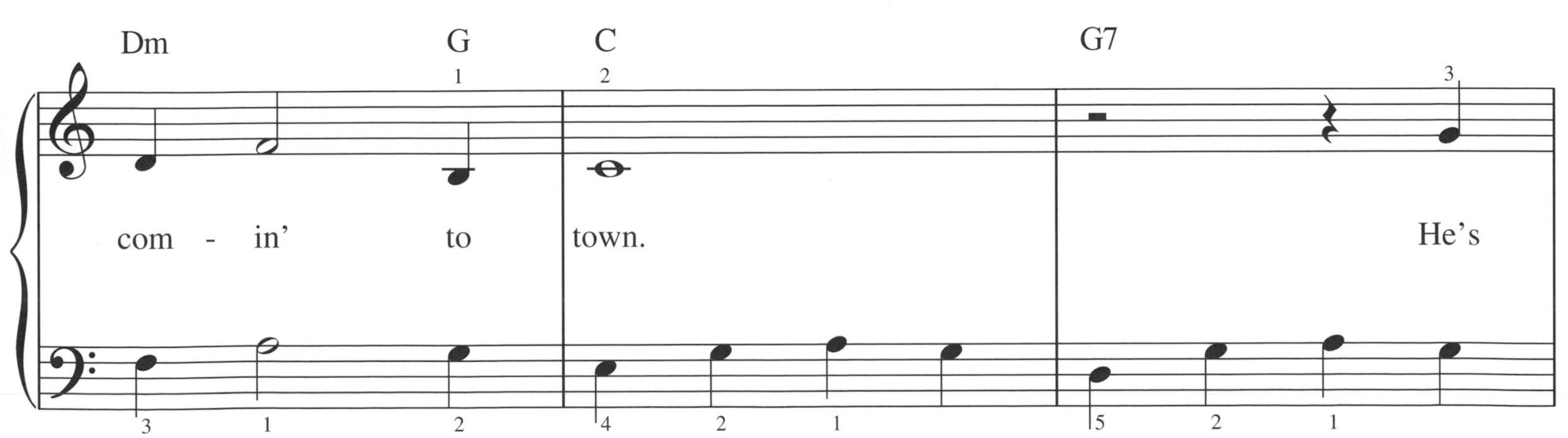

C
F
C
mak - ing a list And check - ing it twice, Gon - na find out who's

F
C
Am
Dm
G
naugh - ty and nice, San - ta Claus is com - in' to

C
C7
town. He sees you when you're

F
C7
F
sleep - in', He knows when you're a - wake, He

D7
G
D7
knows if you've been bad or good, So be good for good - ness

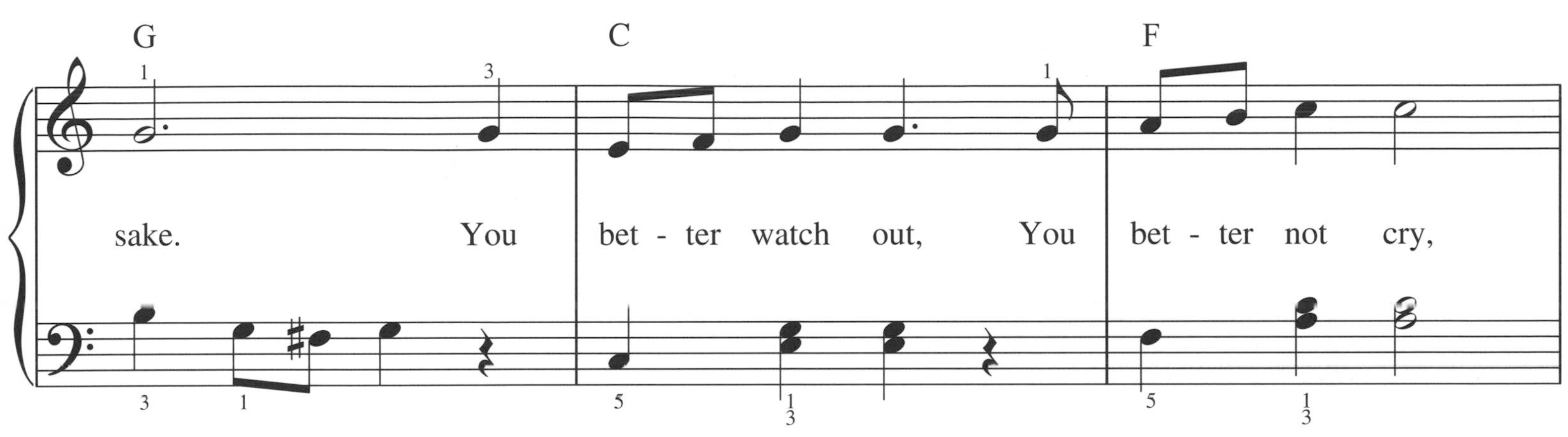
G
C
F
sake. You bet - ter watch out, You bet - ter not cry,

C
F
C
Am
Bet - ter not pout, I'm tell - ing you why: San - ta Claus is

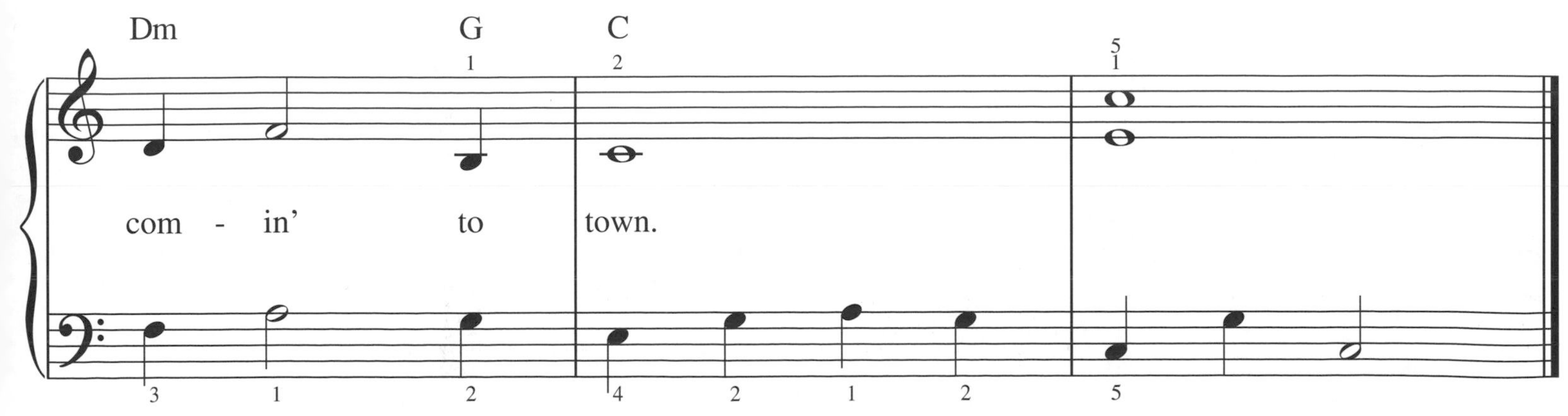
Dm
G
C
com - in' to town.

SILVER BELLS

from the Paramount Picture THE LEMON DROP KID

Words and Music by JAY LIVINGSTON
and RAY EVANS

Moderately
C
F
D7
side - walks, bus - y side - walks dressed in hol - i - day style. In the
street lights, e - ven stop - lights blink a bright red and green As the
G7
C
air there's a feel - ing of Christ - mas. Chil - dren
shop - pers rush home with their treas - ures. Hear the
F
D7
laugh - ing, peo - ple pass - ing, meet - ing smile af - ter smile, And on
snow crunch, see the kids bunch, this is San - ta's big scene, And a -
G7
C
ev - 'ry street cor - ner you hear:
bove all this bus - tle you hear:

C
F
G7
Sil - ver bells,
sil - ver bells,
It's Christ - mas

C
time in the cit - y.
Ring - a - ling,

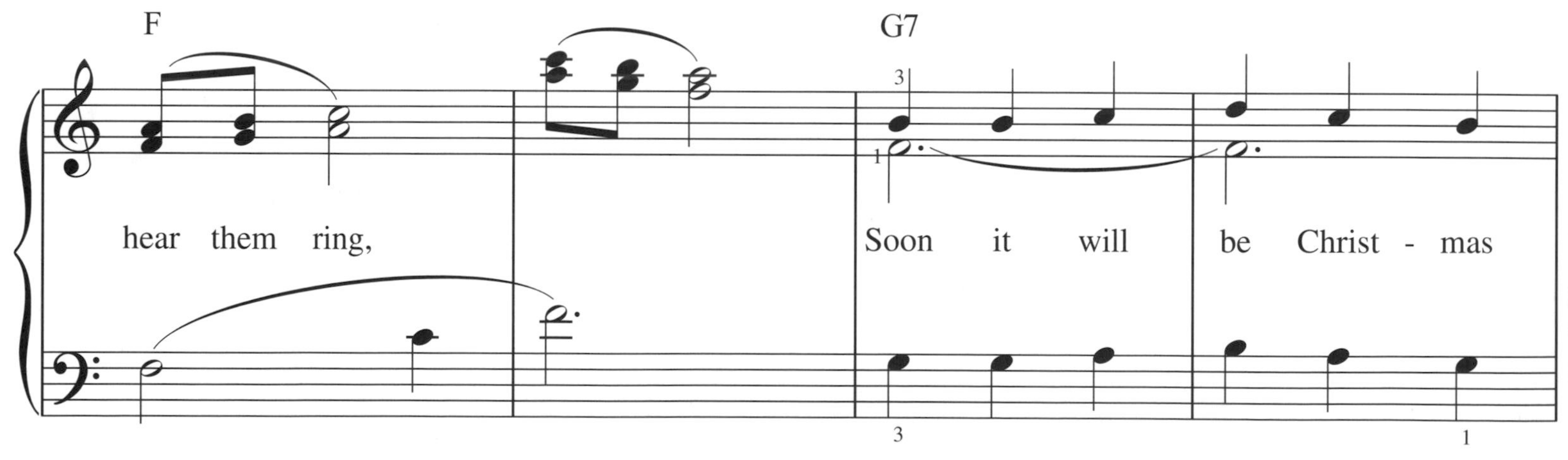
F
G7
hear them ring,
Soon it will be Christ - mas

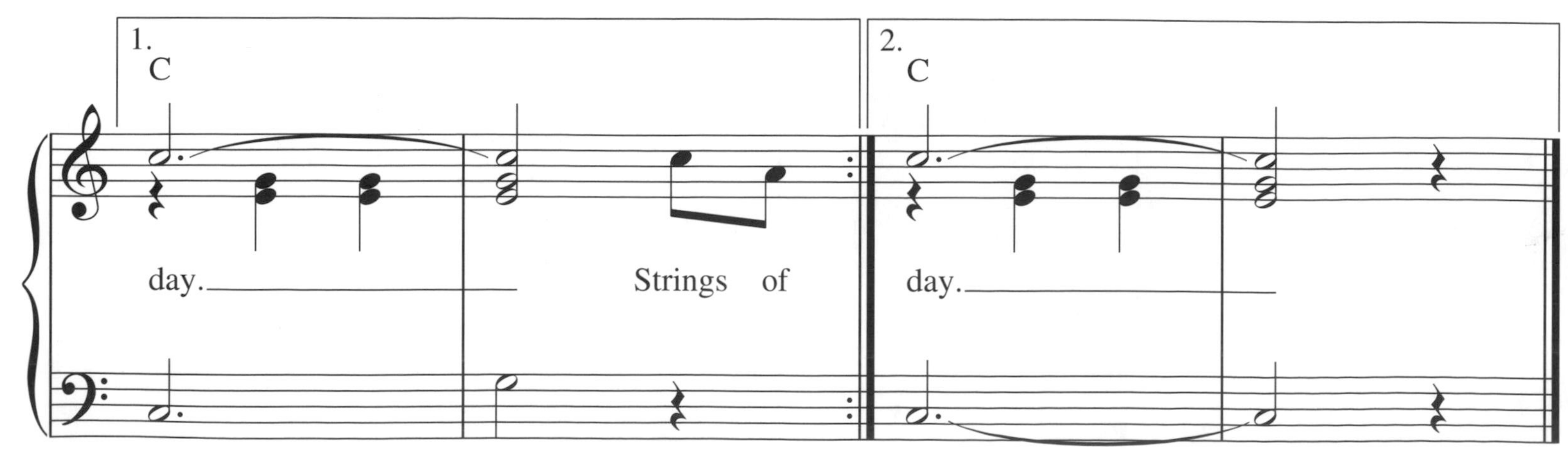
1.
C
2.
C
day.
Strings of
day.

WHAT ARE YOU DOING NEW YEAR'S EVE?

By FRANK LOESSER

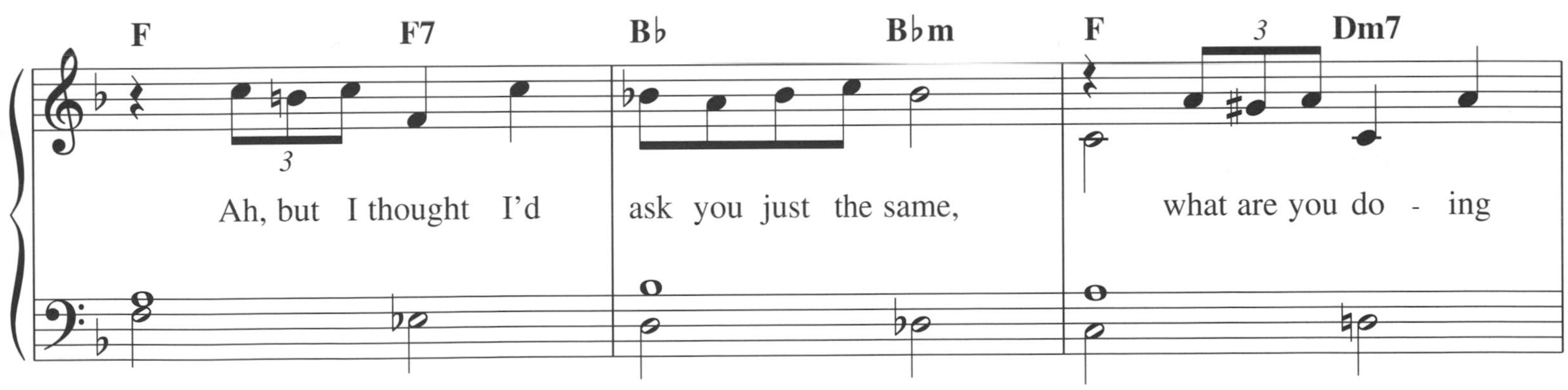

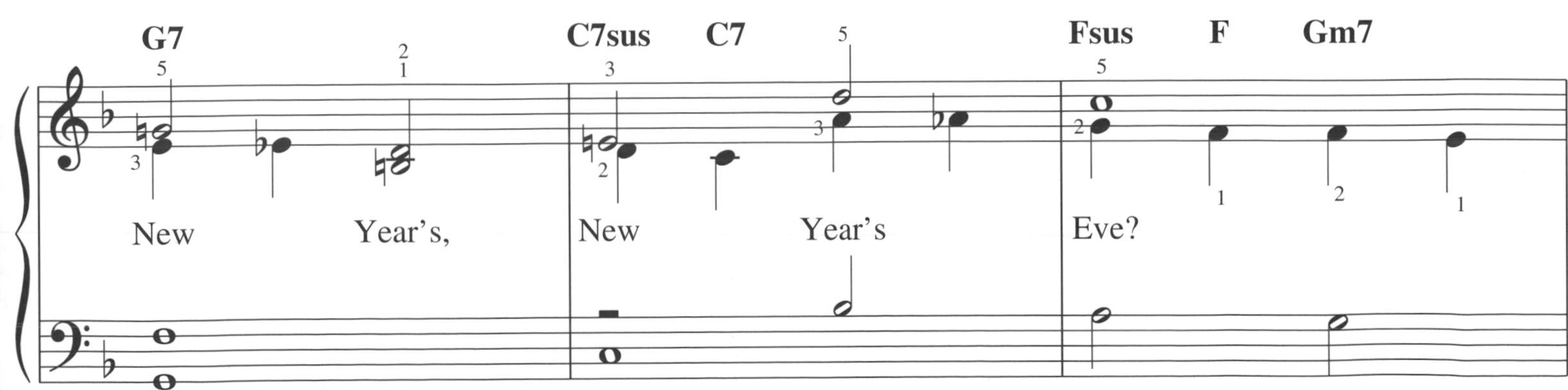

F
Eb7
F
F7
Won - der whose arms will
hold you good and tight,
when it's ex - act - ly

Bb
Bbm
F
Dm7
G7
twelve o - clock that night,
wel - com - ing in the
New Year,

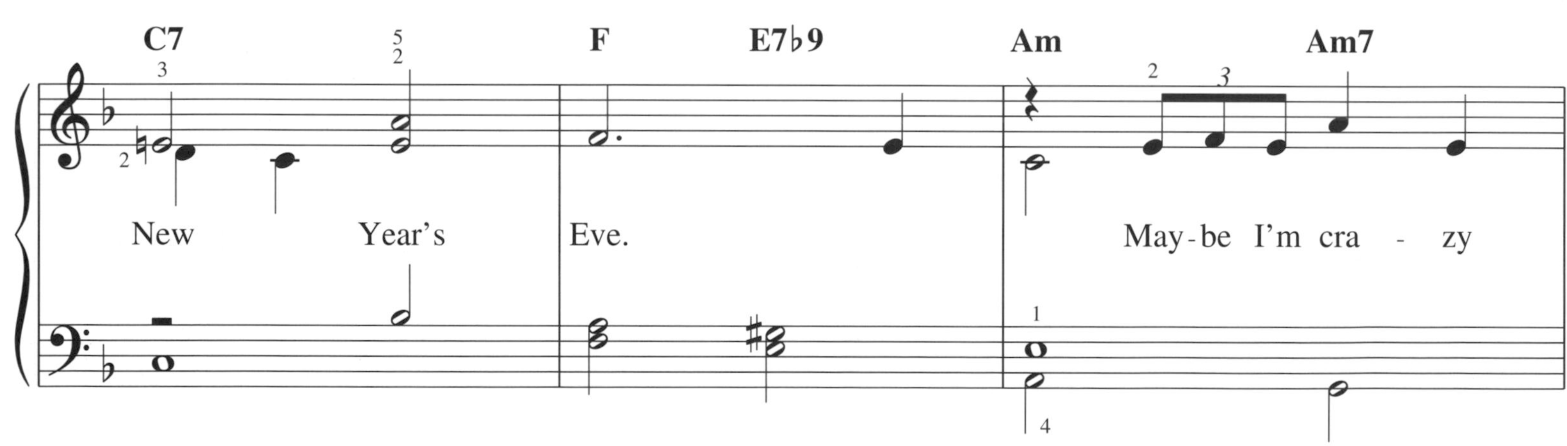
C7
F
E7b9
Am
Am7
New Year's
Eve.
May - be I'm cra - zy

D7/F#
Fm6
Bb9
Am
Bm7b5
Bb9
to sup - pose
I'd ev - er be the
one you chose

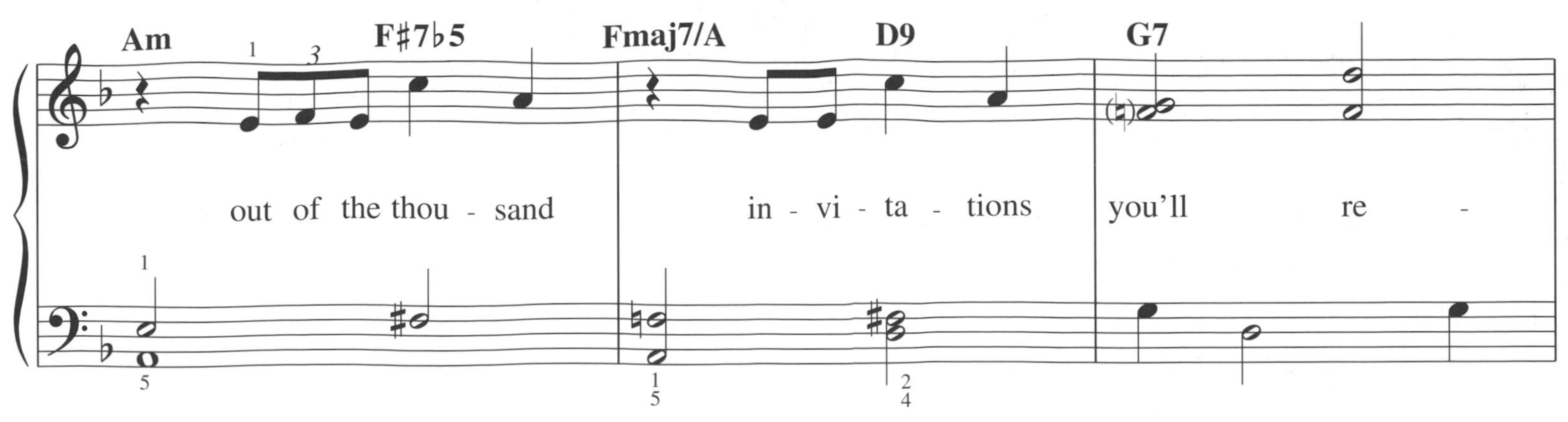
Am
F#7♭5
Fmaj7/A
D9
G7
out of the thou - sand
in - vi - ta - tions
you'll re -

C7
F
E♭7
ceive.
Ah, but in case I
stand one lit - tle chance,

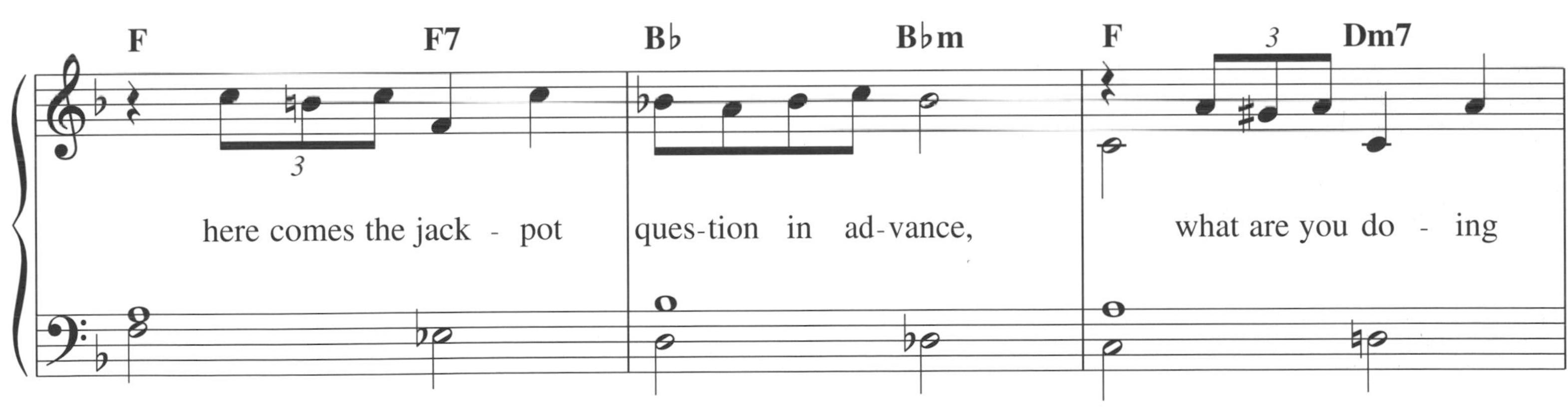
F
F7
B♭
B♭m
F
Dm7
here comes the jack - pot
ques-tion in ad-vance,
what are you do - ing

G7
C7
F
New Year's,
New Year's
Eve?
pp
rit.

THE STAR CAROL

Lyric by WIHLA HUTSON
Music by ALFRED BURT

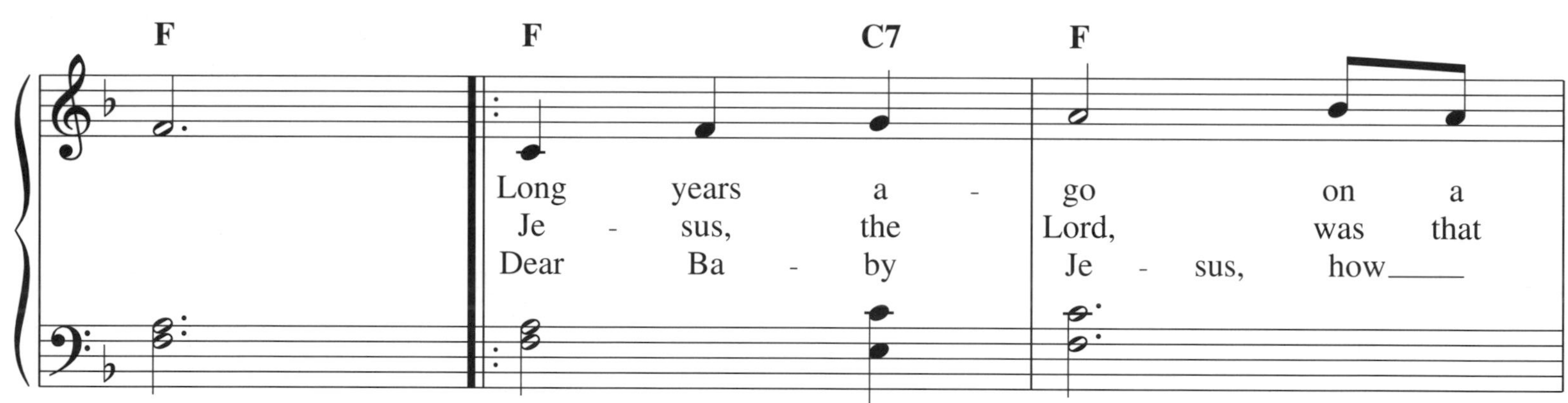

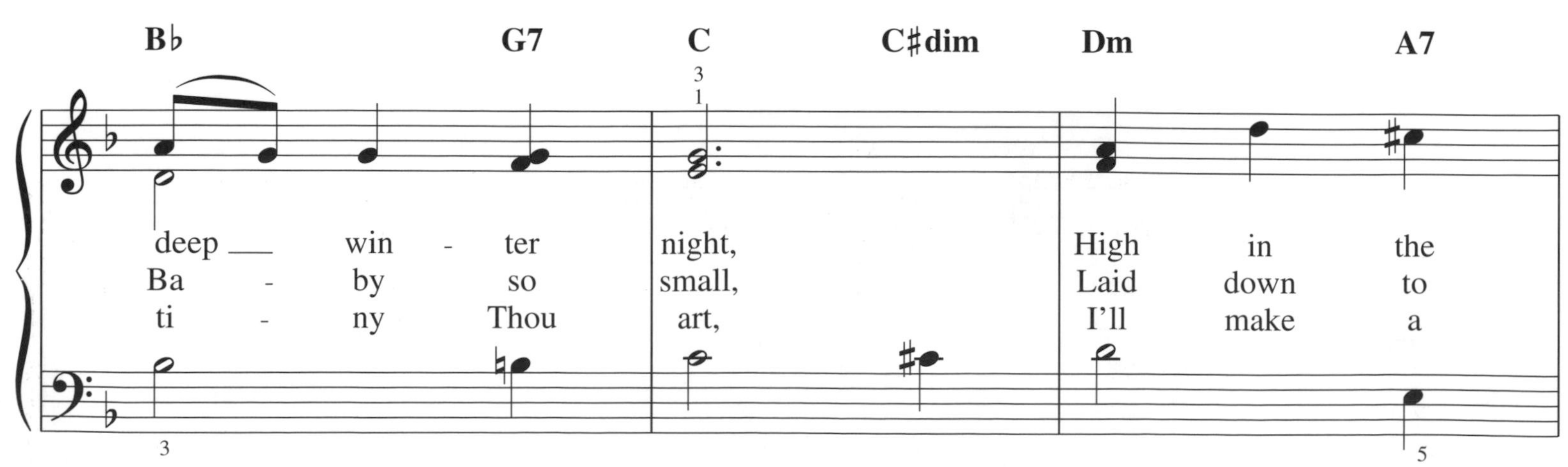

Dm
Gm
heav'ns a star shone
sleep in a hum - ble
place for Thee in my

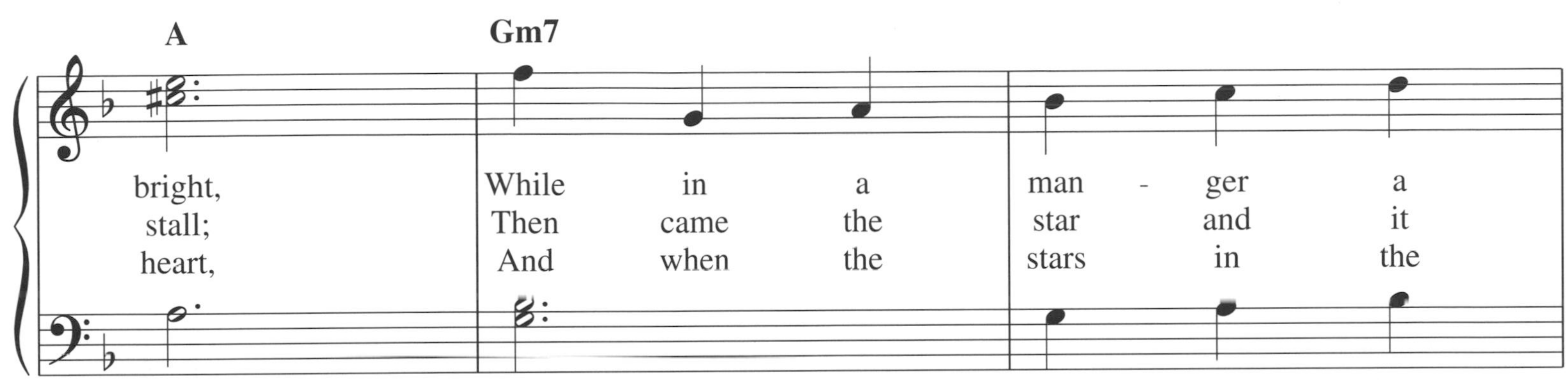
A
Gm7
bright, While in a man - ger a
stall; Then came the star and it
heart, And when the stars in the

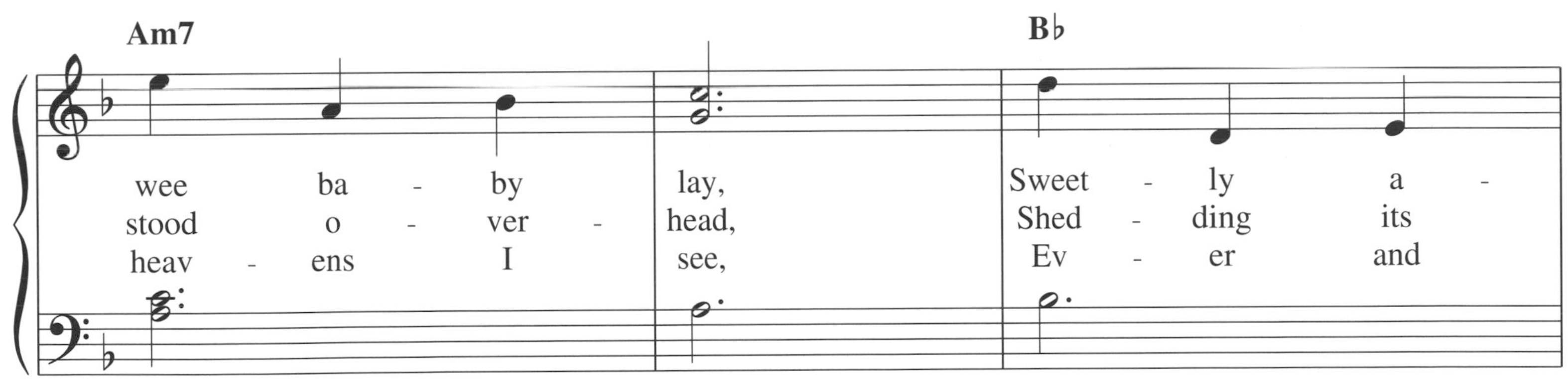
Am7
B♭
wee ba - by lay, Sweet - ly a -
stood o - ver - head, Shed - ding its
heav - ens I see, Ev - er and

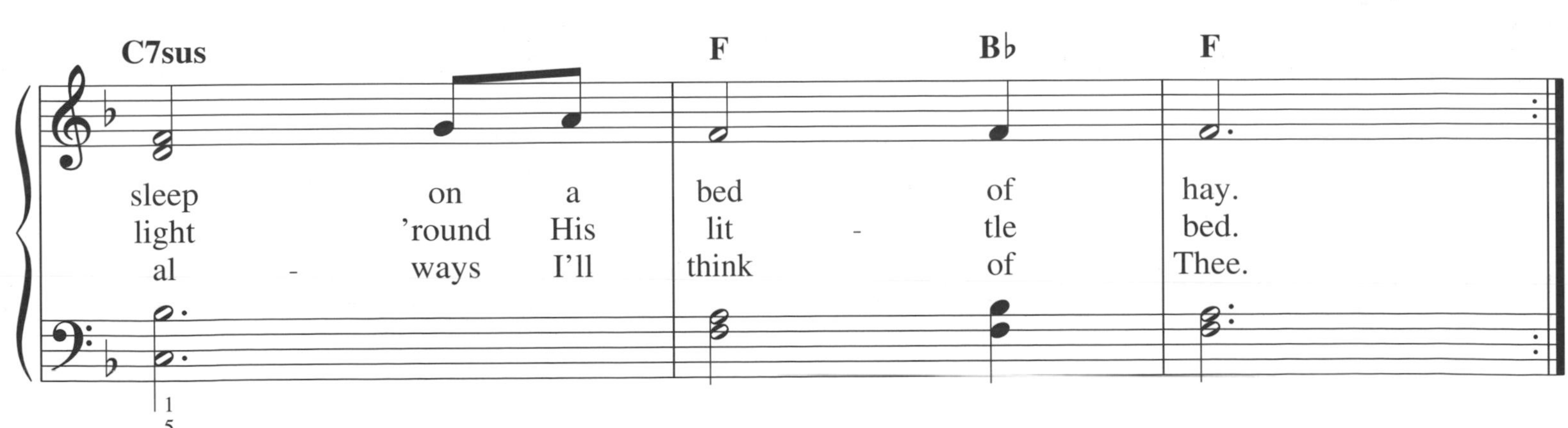
C7sus
F
B♭
F
sleep on a bed of hay.
light 'round His lit - tle bed.
al - ways I'll think of Thee.

THIS CHRISTMAS

Words and Music by DONNY HATHAWAY
and NADINE McKINNOR

Moderately

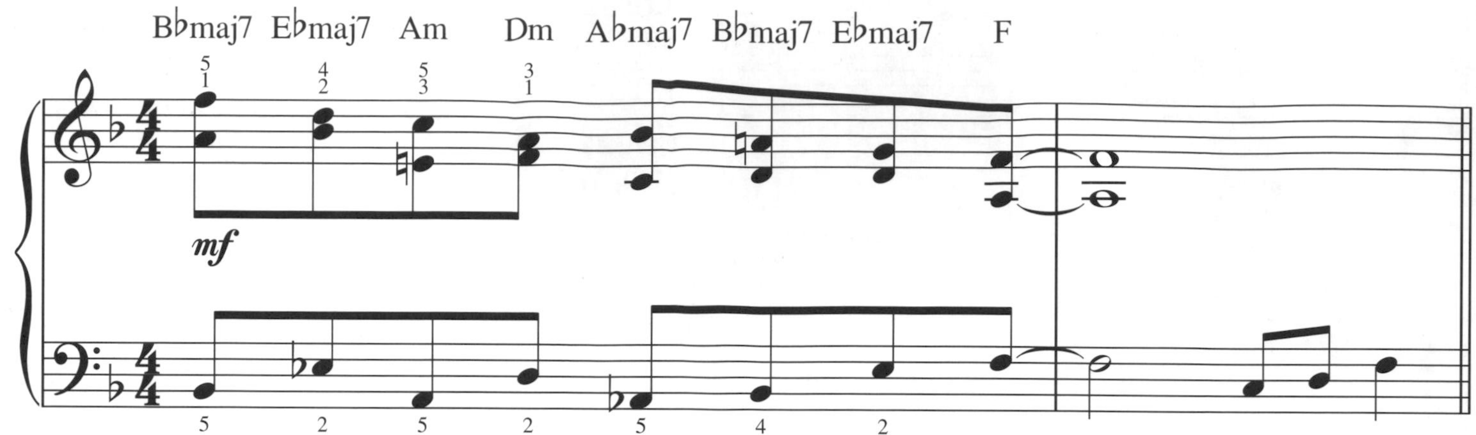

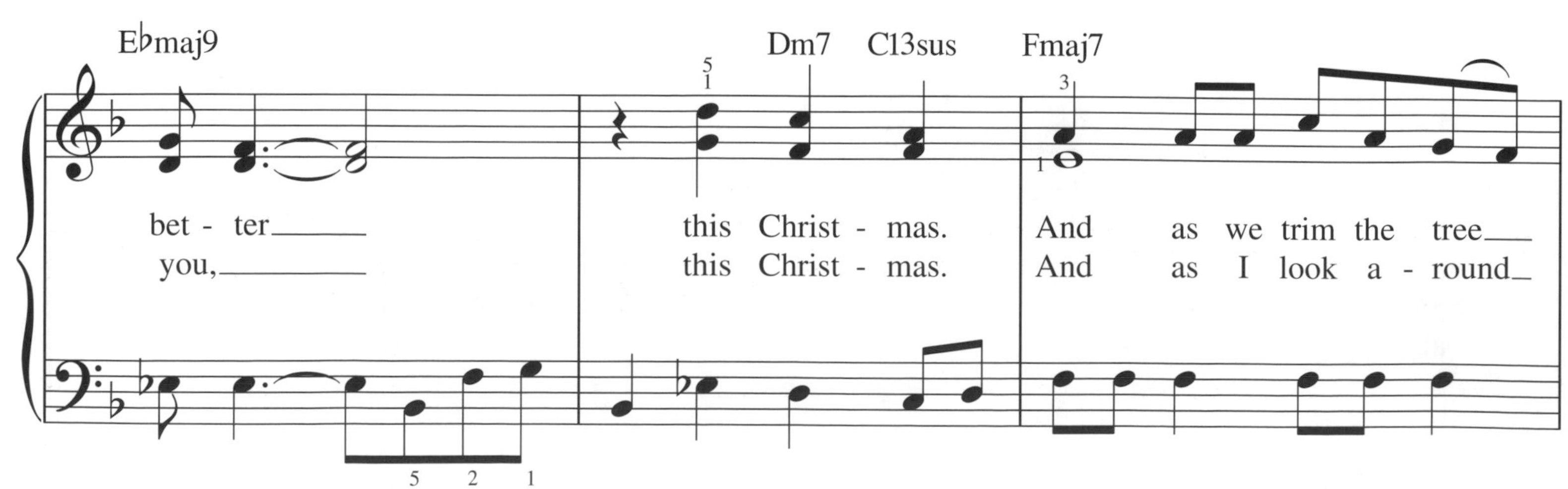

Dm9
E♭maj9
how much fun it's gon - na be to - geth - er
your eyes out - shine the town; they do,
Dm7 C13sus
Am7
D9
this Christ - mas.
this Christ - mas. The fir - re - side is blaz - ing bright. We're
Solo ends
Gm7
C7sus
F
B7♯11
car - ol - in' through the night and this Christ - mas will
B♭maj7
E♭9
Am7
Dm7
Bm7♭5
B7♯11
be a ver - y spe - cial Christ - mas for me.

1.-3.
Bbmaj7 Ebmaj7 Am Dm Abmaj7 Bbmaj7 Ebmaj7 F
Bbmaj7 Ebmaj7 Am Dm Abmaj7 Bbmaj7 Ebmaj7 F
4.
Bbmaj7 Ebmaj7 Am Dm Abmaj7 Bbmaj7 Ebmaj7 F
Mer - ry Christ - mas.
Bbmaj7 Ebmaj7 Am Dm Abmaj7 Bbmaj7 Ebmaj7 F
Shake your hand, shake your hand

B♭maj7 E♭maj7 Am Dm A♭maj7 B♭maj7 E♭maj7 F
now.
Wish your broth-er mer-ry Christ-mas

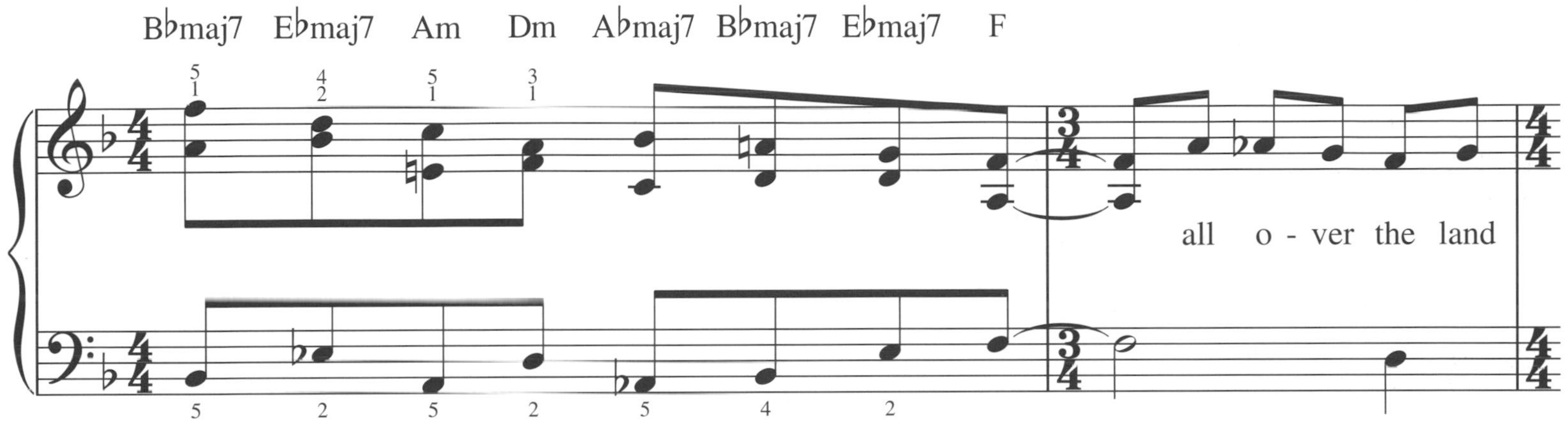
B♭maj7 E♭maj7 Am Dm A♭maj7 B♭maj7 E♭maj7 F
all o - ver the land

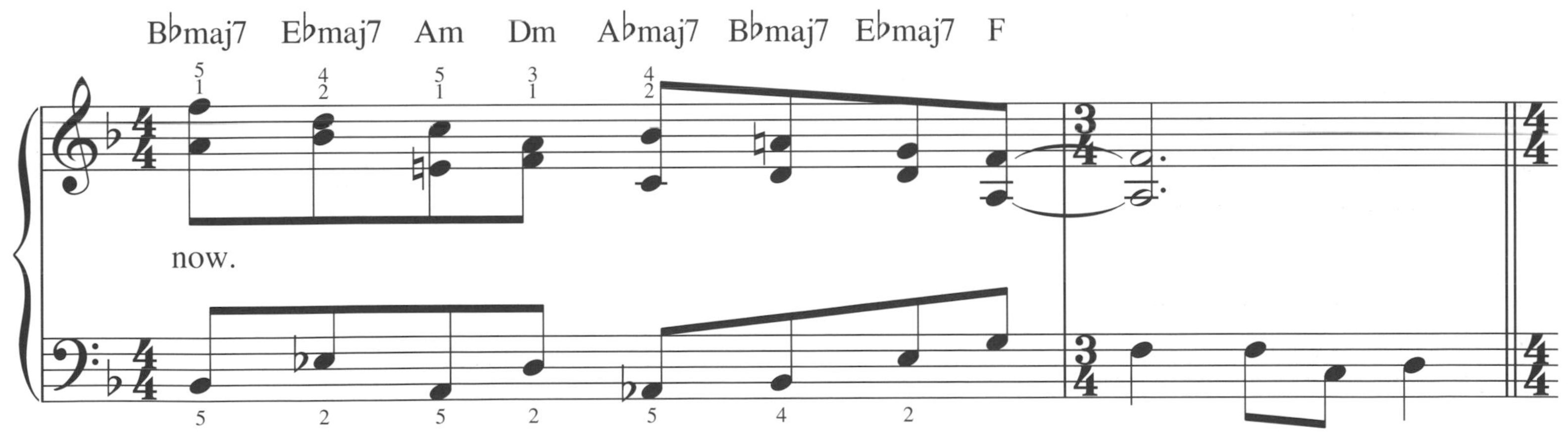
B♭maj7 E♭maj7 Am Dm A♭maj7 B♭maj7 E♭maj7 F
now.

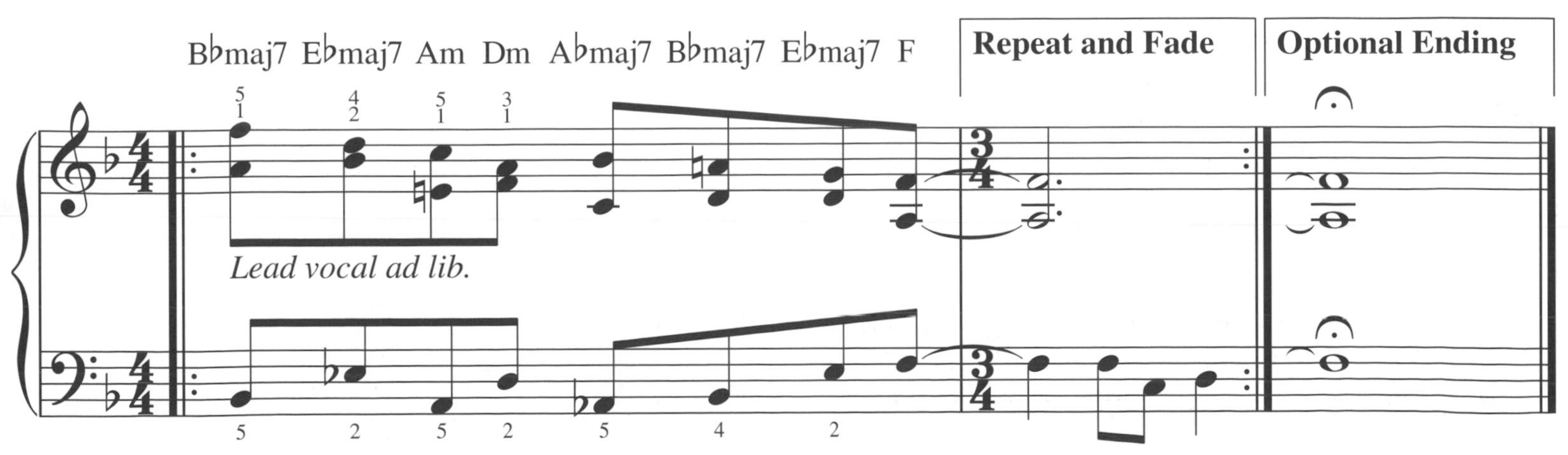
B♭maj7 E♭maj7 Am Dm A♭maj7 B♭maj7 E♭maj7 F
Repeat and Fade
Optional Ending
Lead vocal ad lib.

WHERE ARE YOU CHRISTMAS?

from DR. SEUSS' HOW THE GRINCH STOLE CHRISTMAS

Words and Music by WILL JENNINGS, JAMES HORNER and MARIAH CAREY

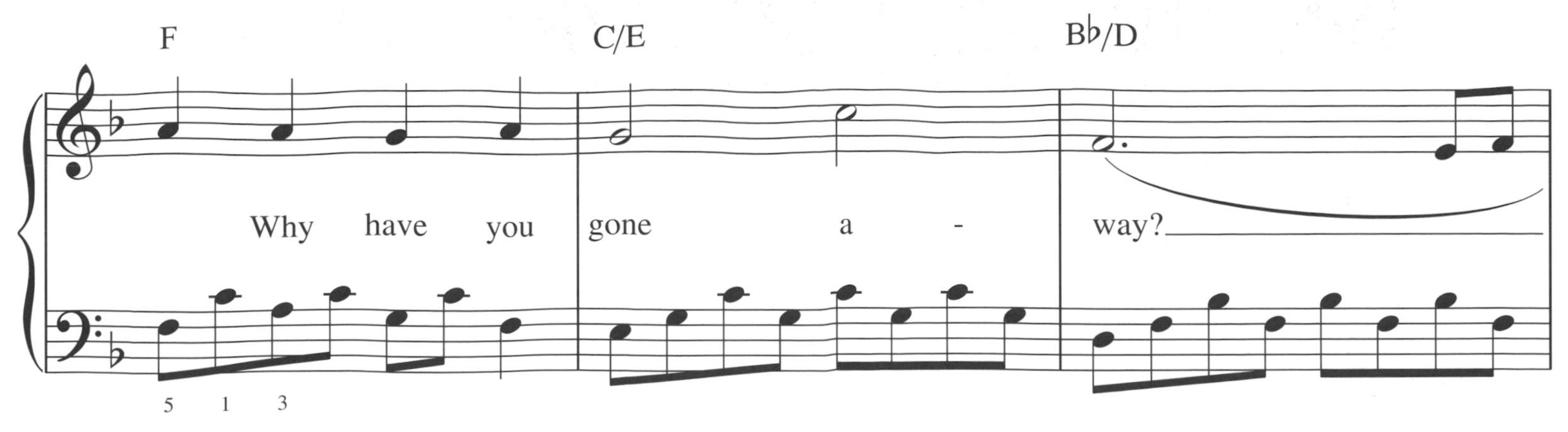
F
C/E
B♭/D
Why have you gone a - way?
5 1 3

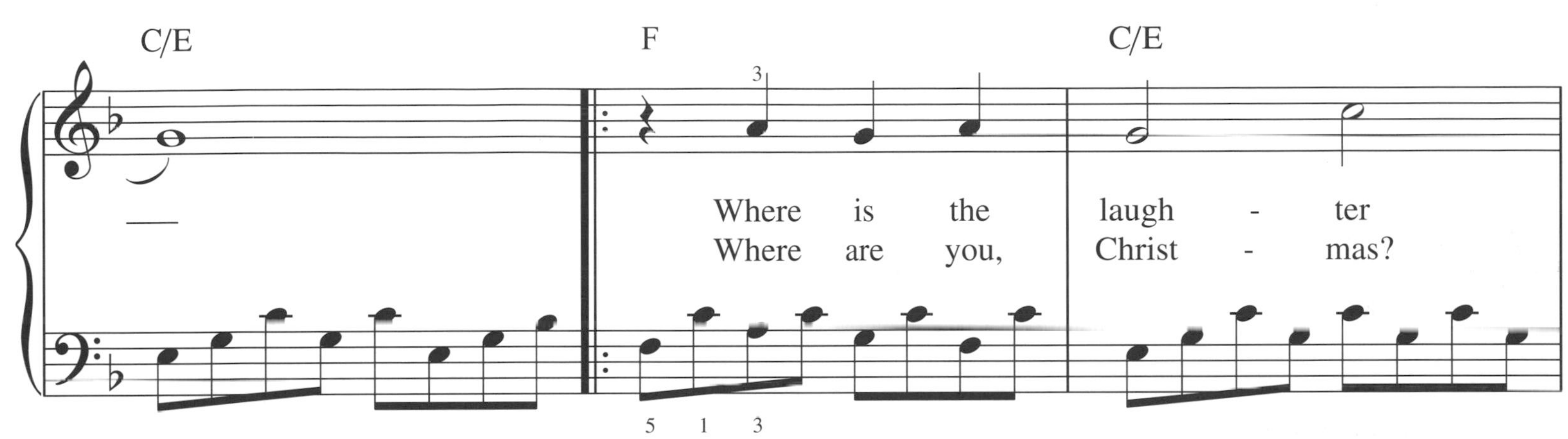
C/E
F
C/E
3
Where is the laugh - ter
Where are you, Christ - mas?
5 1 3

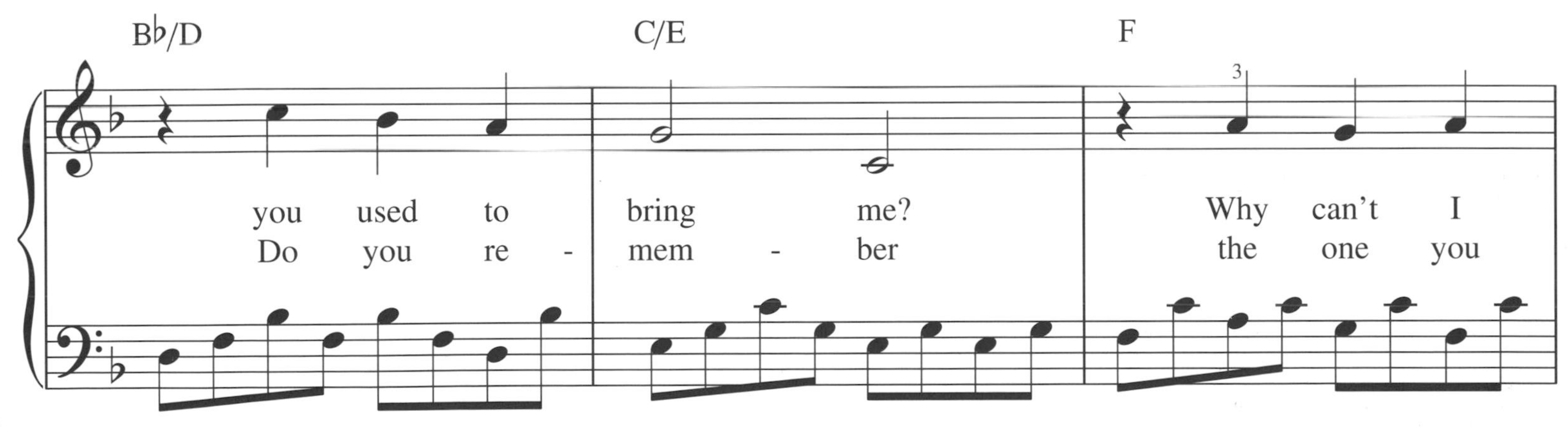
B♭/D
C/E
F
3
you used to bring me?
Do you re - mem - ber
Why can't I
the one you

C/E
B♭/D
C/E
hear mu - sic play?
used to know?

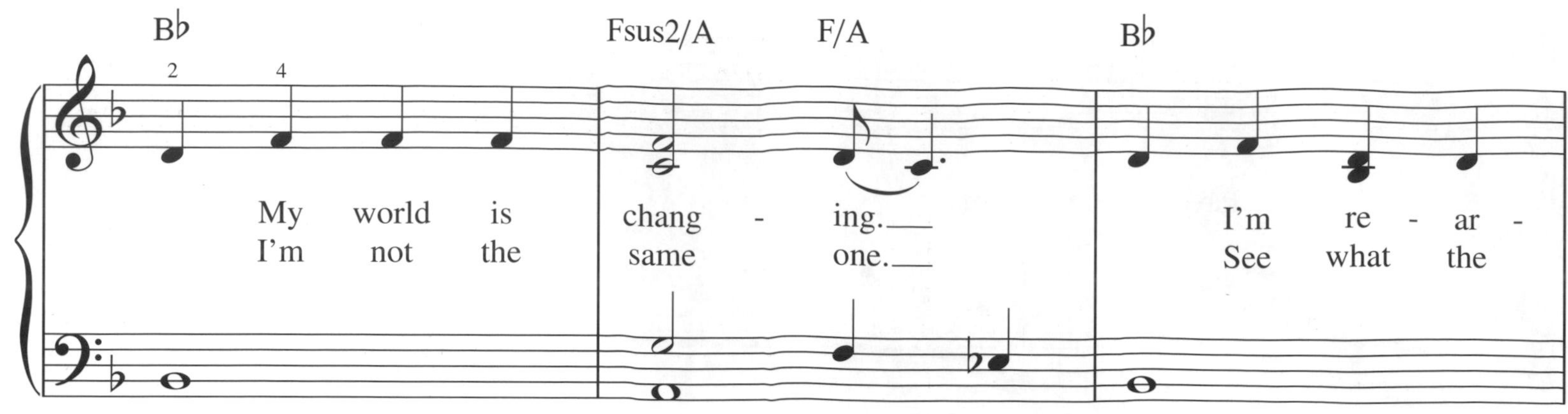
B♭
Fsus2/A
F/A
B♭
2
4
My world is chang - ing.
I'm not the same one.
I'm re - ar -
See what the

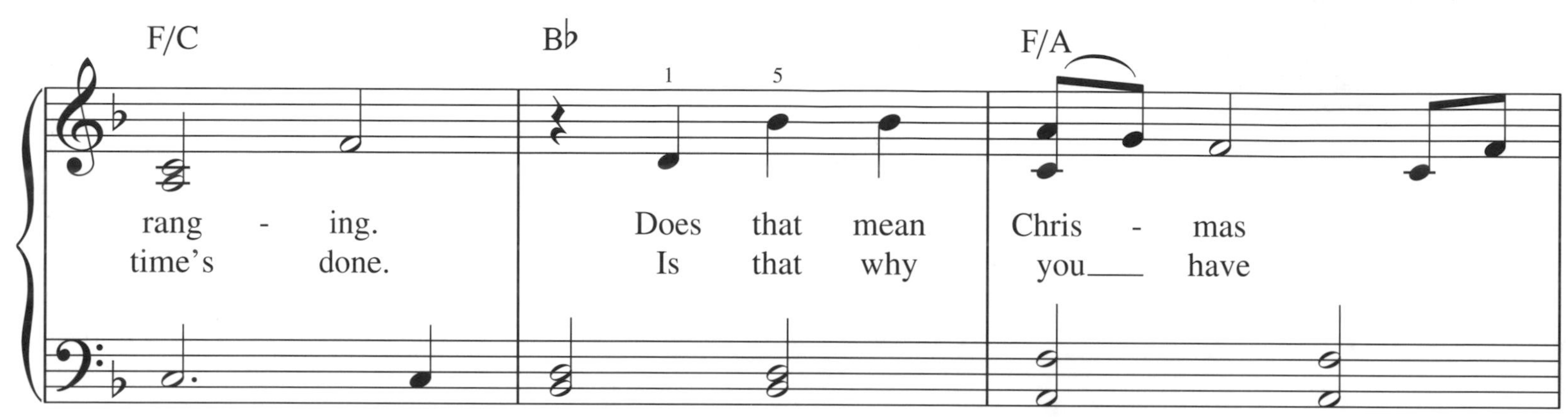
F/C
B♭
F/A
1
5
rang - ing.
time's done.
Does that mean Chris - mas
Is that why you have

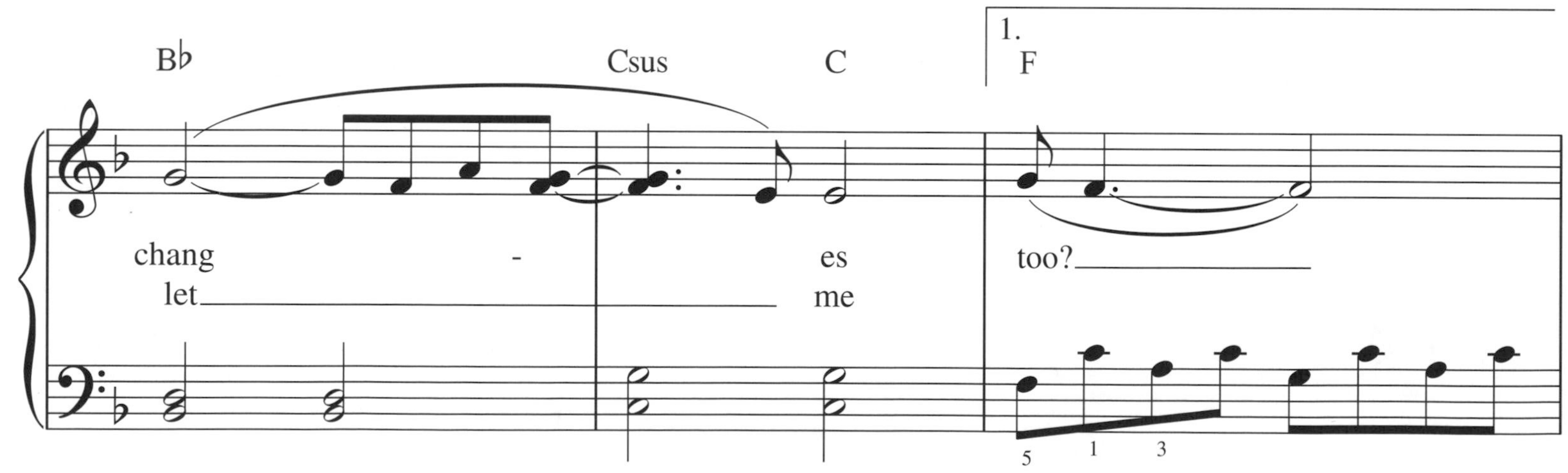
B♭
Csus
C
1.
F
chang - es
let me
too?
5
1
3

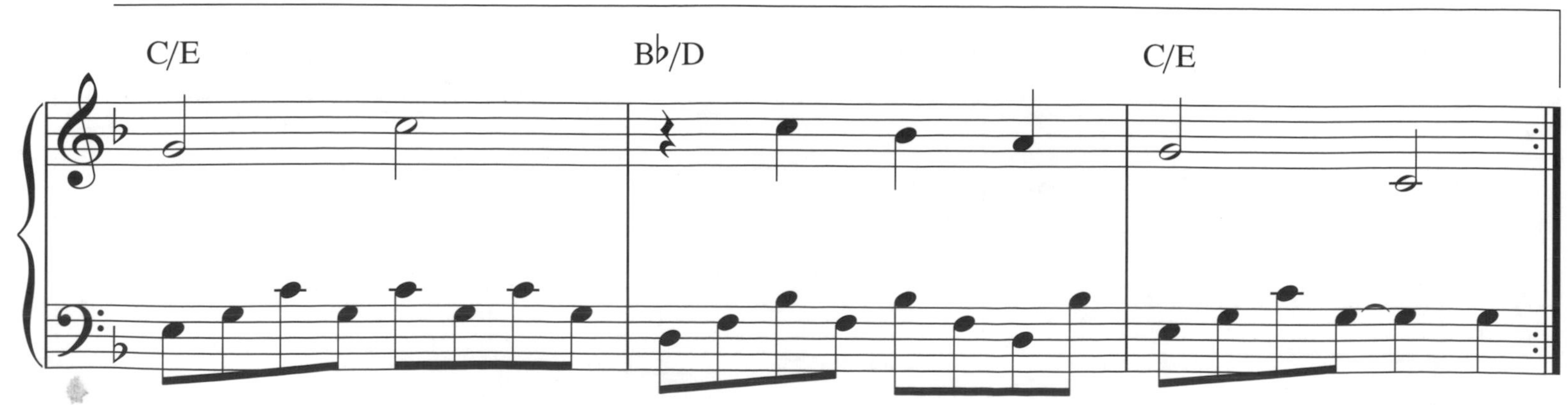
C/E
B♭/D
C/E

2.
F
A7
Dm
go?
Oh,
Christ - mas is
A7/C♯
F/C
A7/C♯
here,
ev - 'ry -
where,
oh.
Dm
A7/C♯
F/C
Christ - mas is
here,
if you
care.
Bm7♭5
B♭
C/B♭
If there is
love
in your

Am7
B♭
F/A
Gm7
heart and your mind,
you will feel like

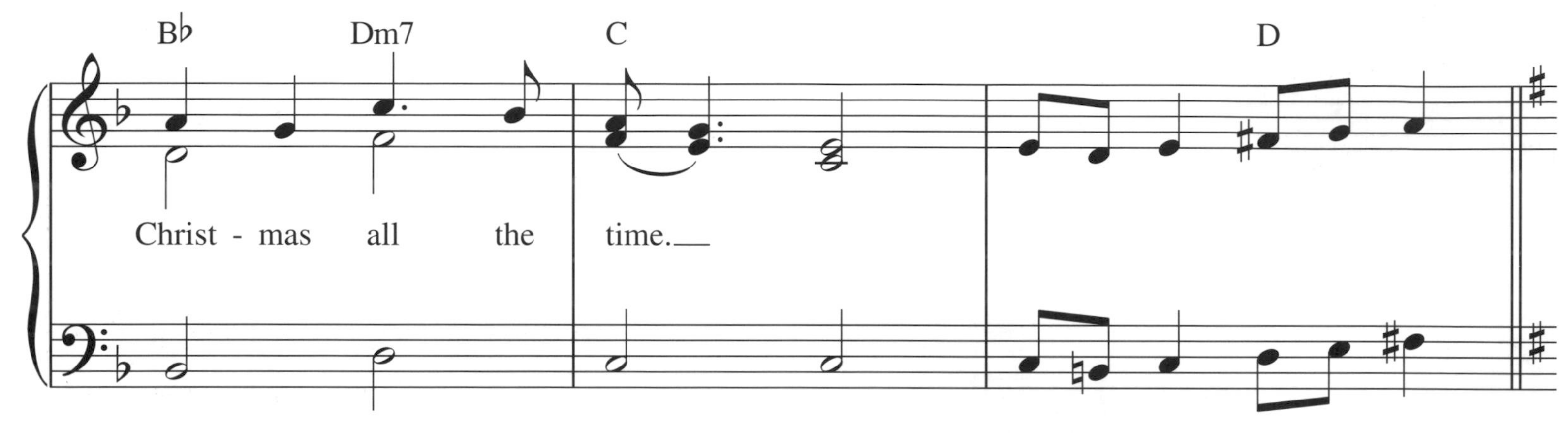
B♭
Dm7
C
D
Christ - mas all the time.

G
D/F♯
C/E
I feel you, Christ - mas, I know I
the joy of Christ - mas stays here in -

D/F♯
G
D/F♯
found you. You nev - er fade a -
side us, fills each and ev - 'ry

1.
C
D
2.
C
way.
Oh,
heart
Dsus
D
G
D/F♯
C/E
with
love.
D/F♯
G
D/F♯
Where are you,
Christ - mas?
Fill your heart with
C/E
D/F♯
D
G(add2)
love.
Mm.

WHO WOULD IMAGINE A KING

from the Touchstone Motion Picture THE PREACHER'S WIFE

Words and Music by MERVYN WARREN
and HALLERIN HILTON HILL

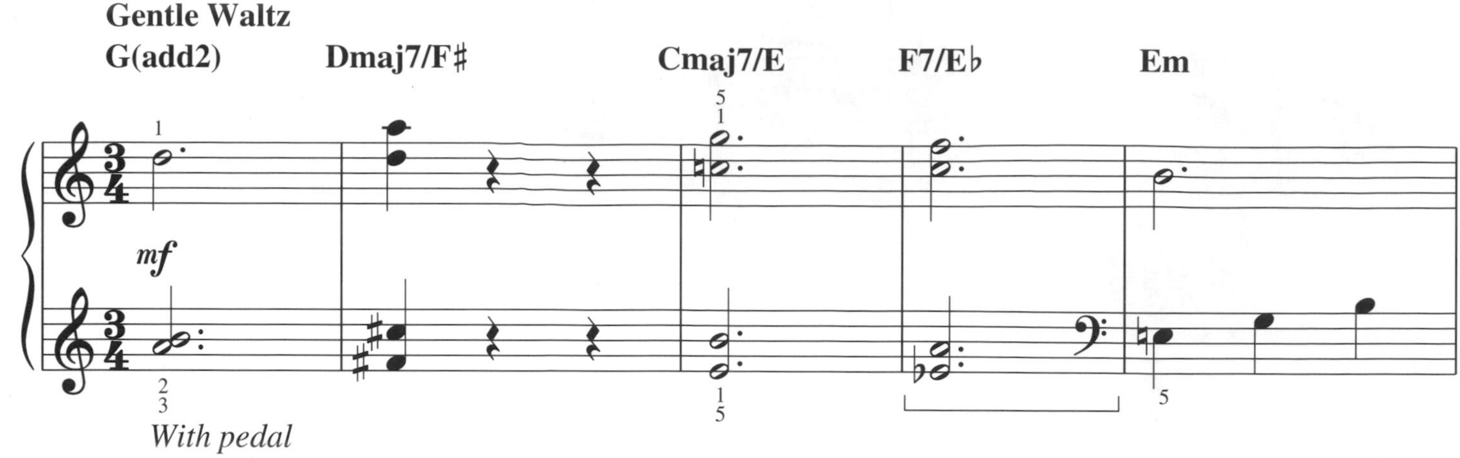

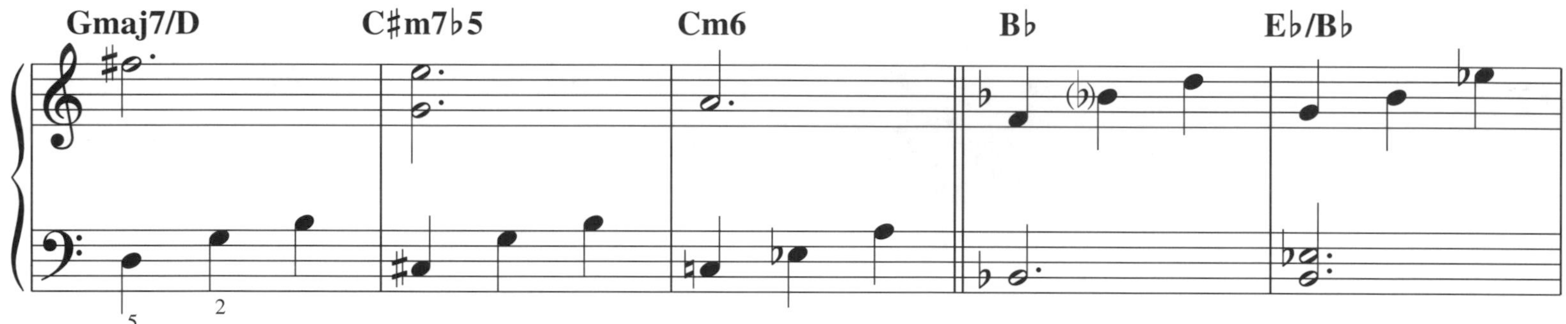

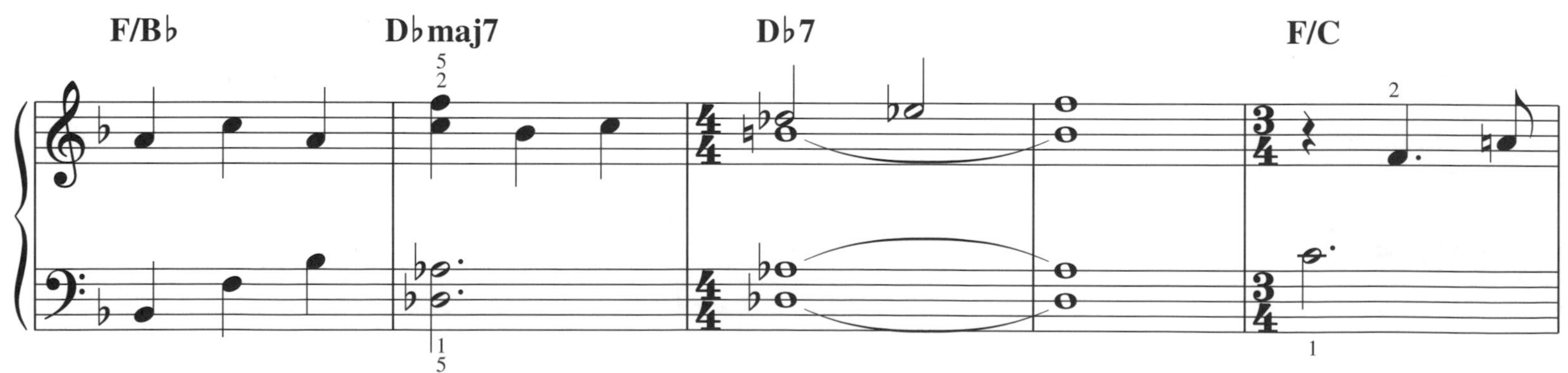

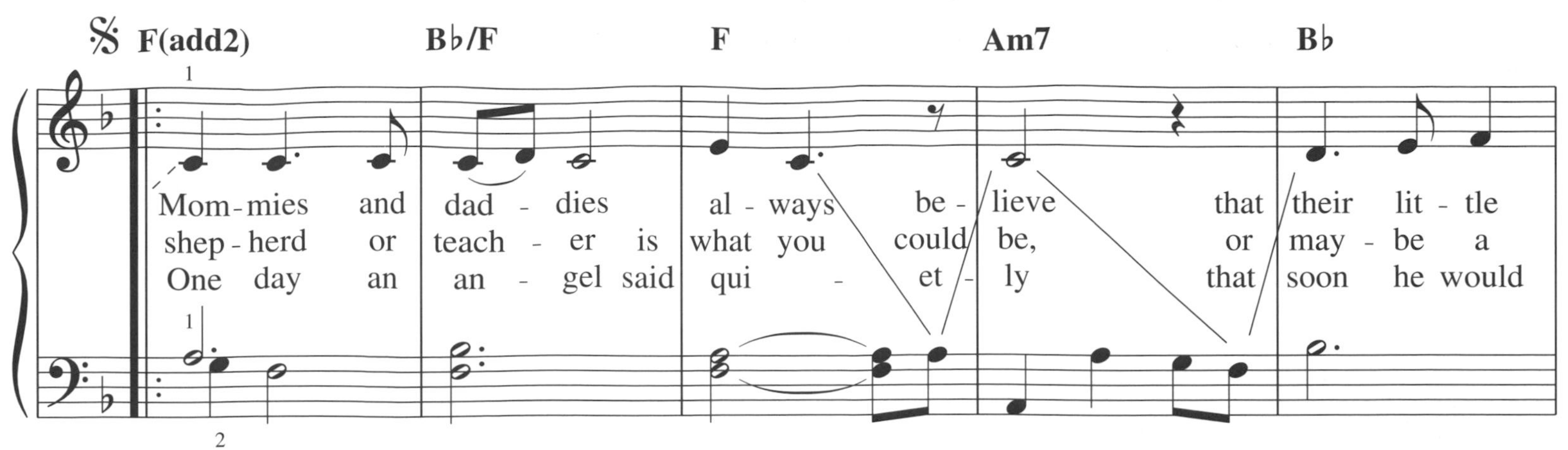
F(add2)
B♭/F
F
Am7
B♭
Mom-mies and dad - dies al - ways be - lieve that their lit - tle
shep-herd or teach - er is what you could be, or may - be a
One day an an - gel said qui - et - ly that soon he would

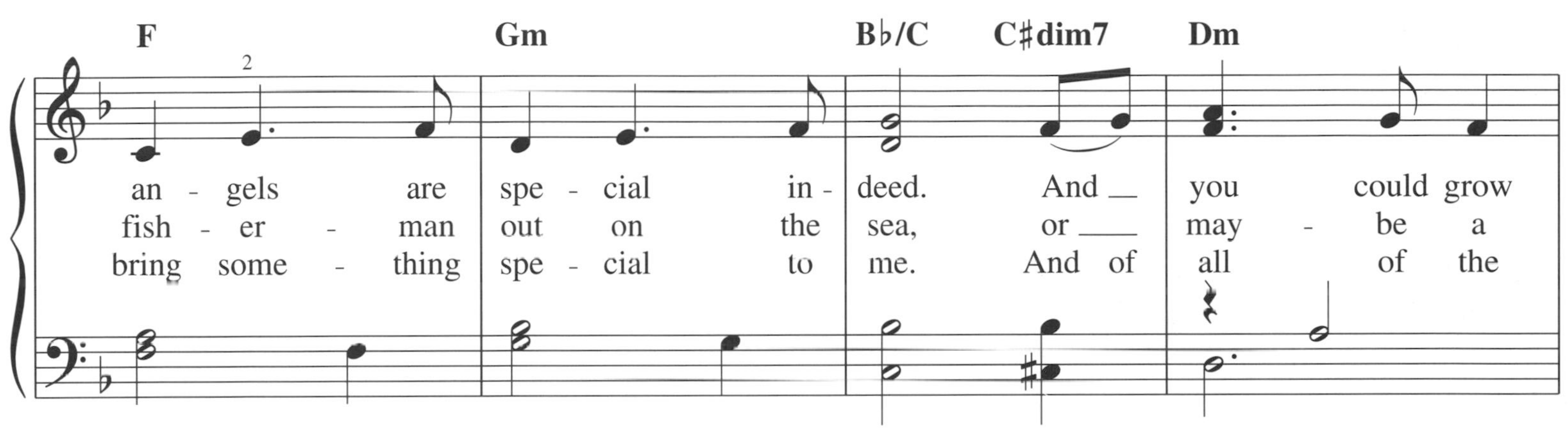
F
Gm
B♭/C
C♯dim7
Dm
an - gels are spe - cial in - deed. And you could grow
fish - er - man out on the sea, or may - be a
bring some - thing spe - cial to me. And of all of the

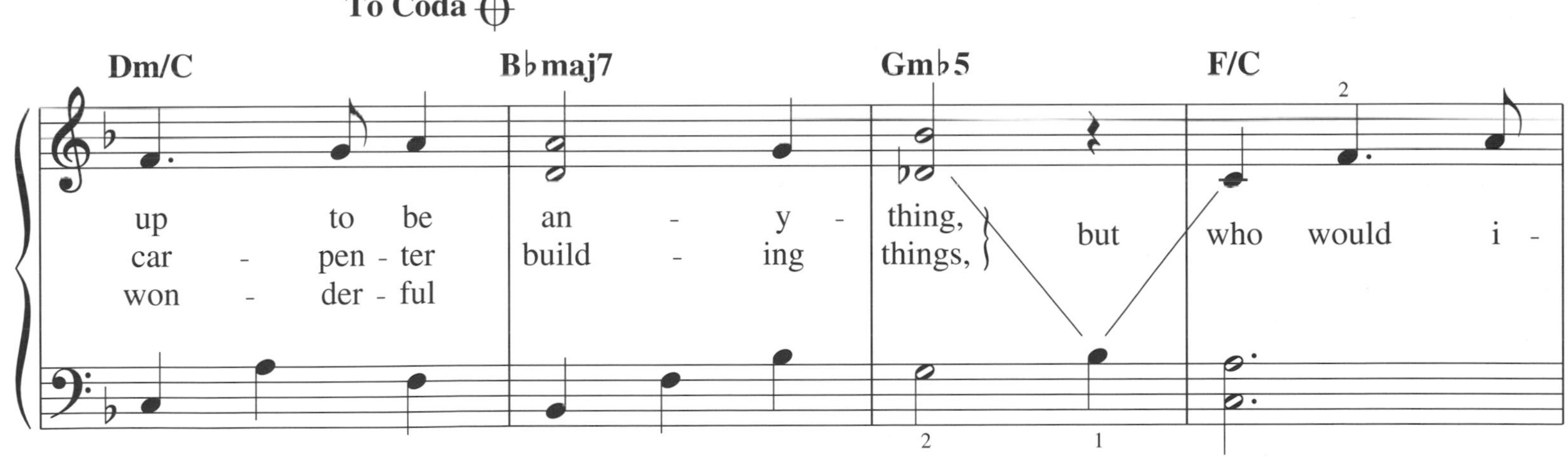
To Coda
Dm/C
B♭maj7
Gm♭5
F/C
up to be an - y - thing, but who would i -
car - pen - ter build - ing things,
won - der - ful

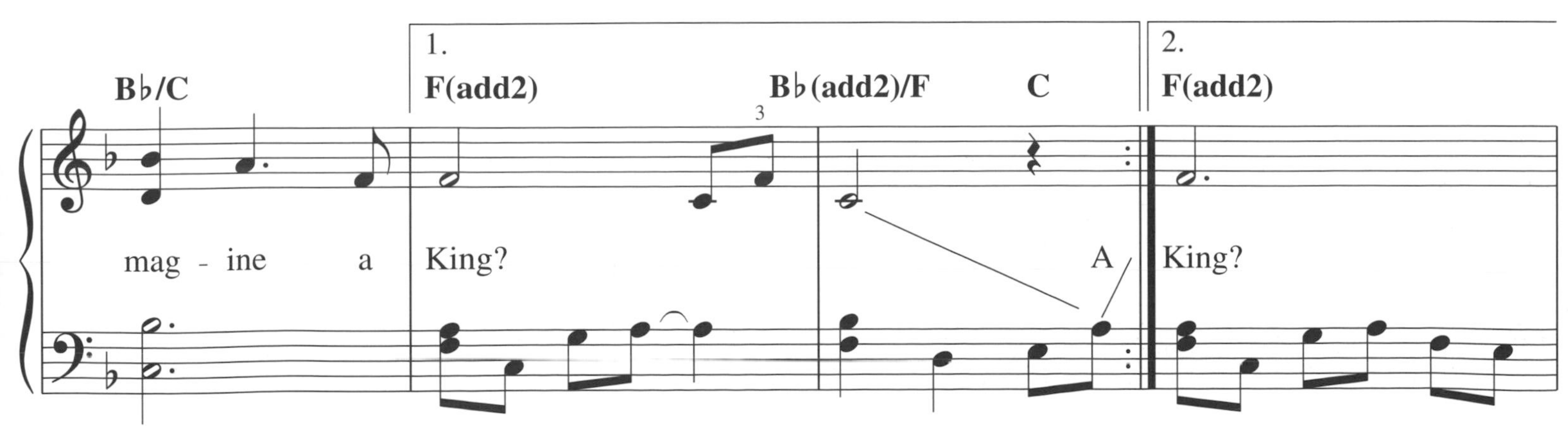
B♭/C
1.
F(add2)
B♭(add2)/F
C
2.
F(add2)
mag - ine a King? A King?

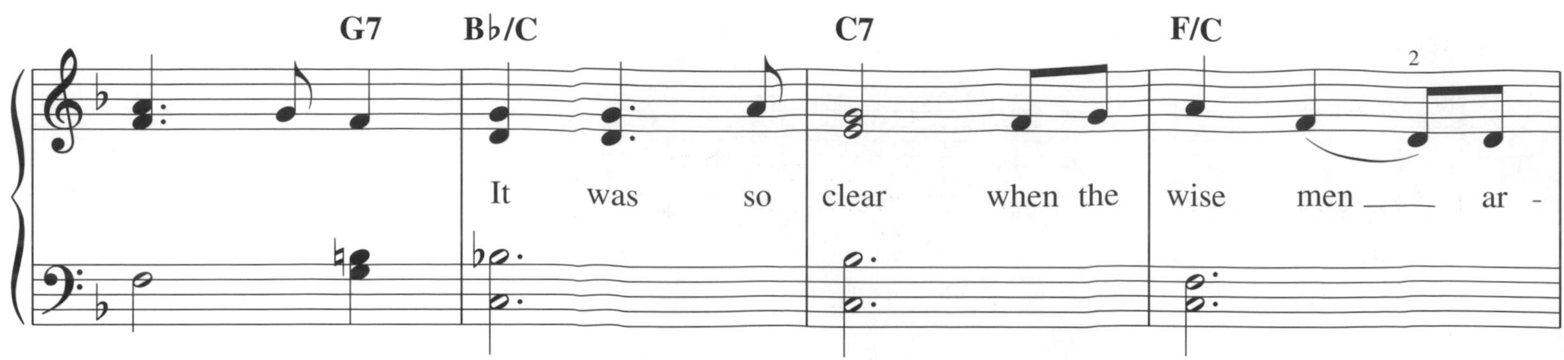
G7
B♭/C
C7
F/C
2
It was so clear when the wise men ar -

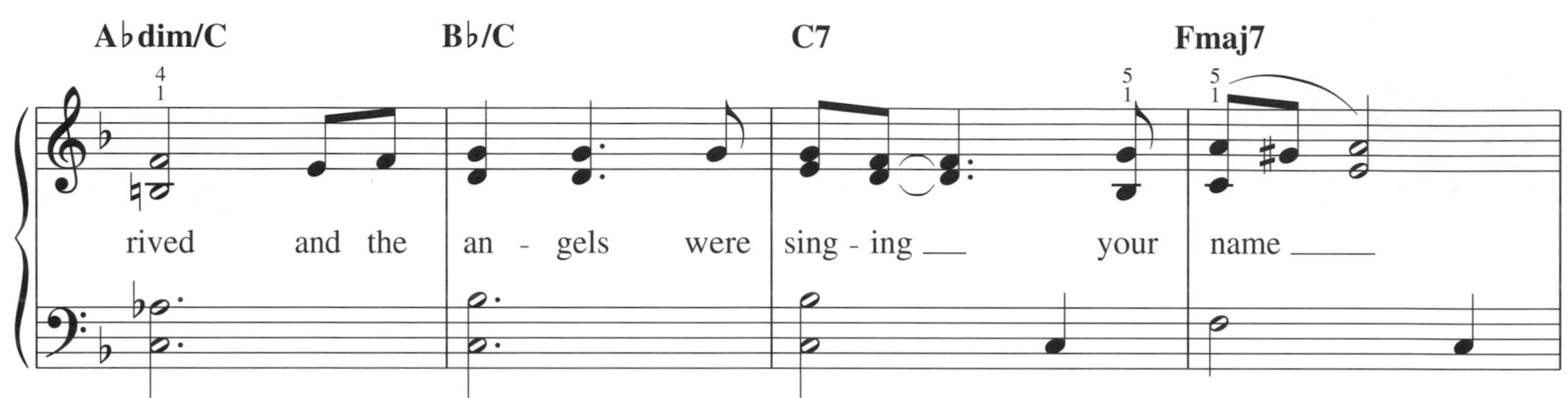
A♭dim/C
B♭/C
C7
Fmaj7
4
1
5
1
5
1
rived and the an - gels were sing - ing your name

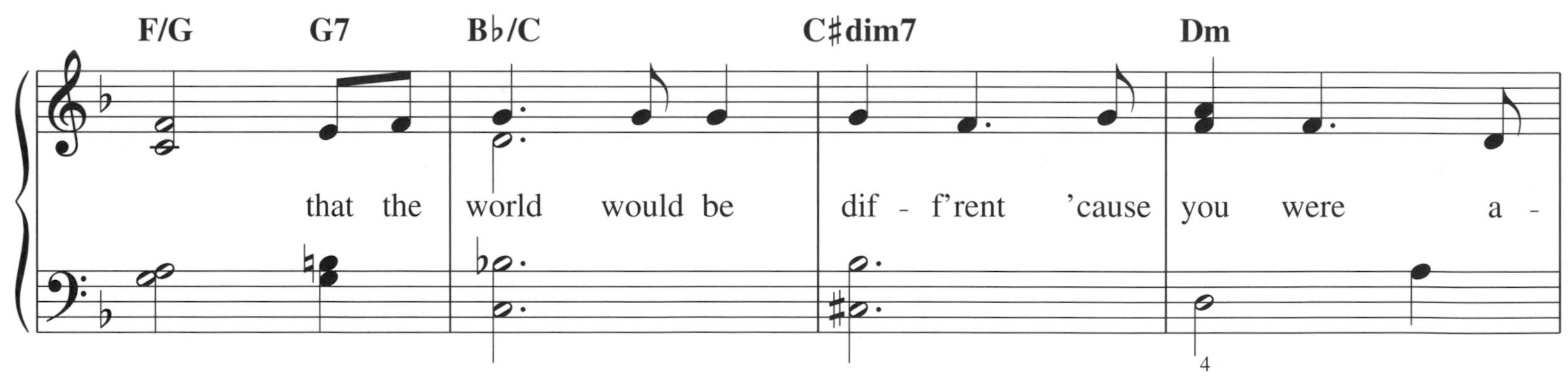
F/G
G7
B♭/C
C♯dim7
Dm
that the world would be dif - f'rent 'cause you were a -
4

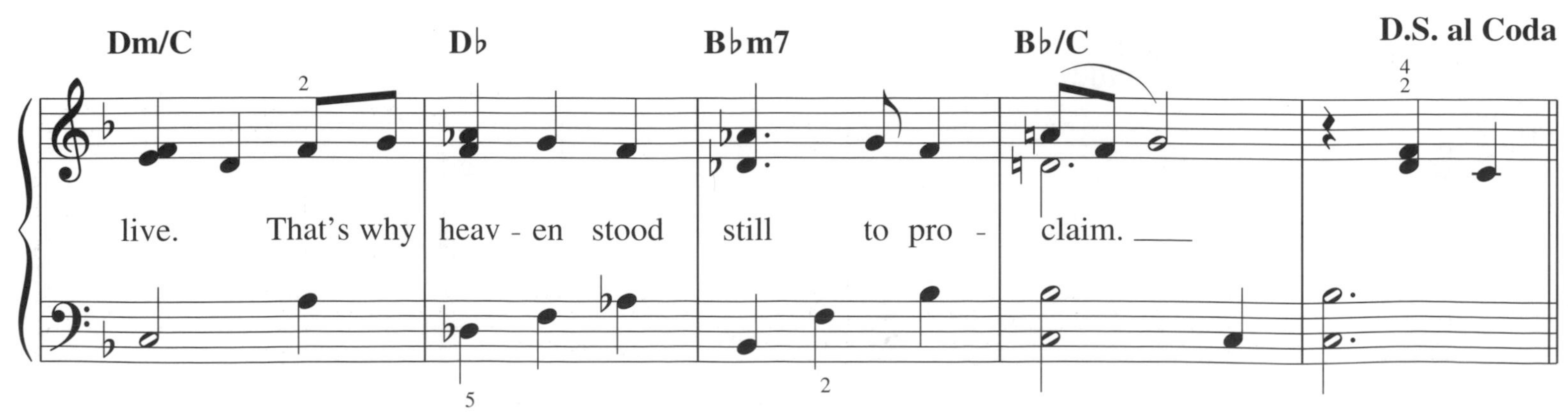
Dm/C
D♭
B♭m7
B♭/C
D.S. al Coda
2
4
2
live. That's why heav - en stood still to pro - claim.
5
2

CODA
Bm7♭5
B♭m6
F/C
gifts he could bring,
who would i -

A7
Dm7
E♭7
F/C
mag - ine,
who could i -
mag - ine,
who would i -

B♭/C
F(add2)
E♭/F
mag - ine a
King?

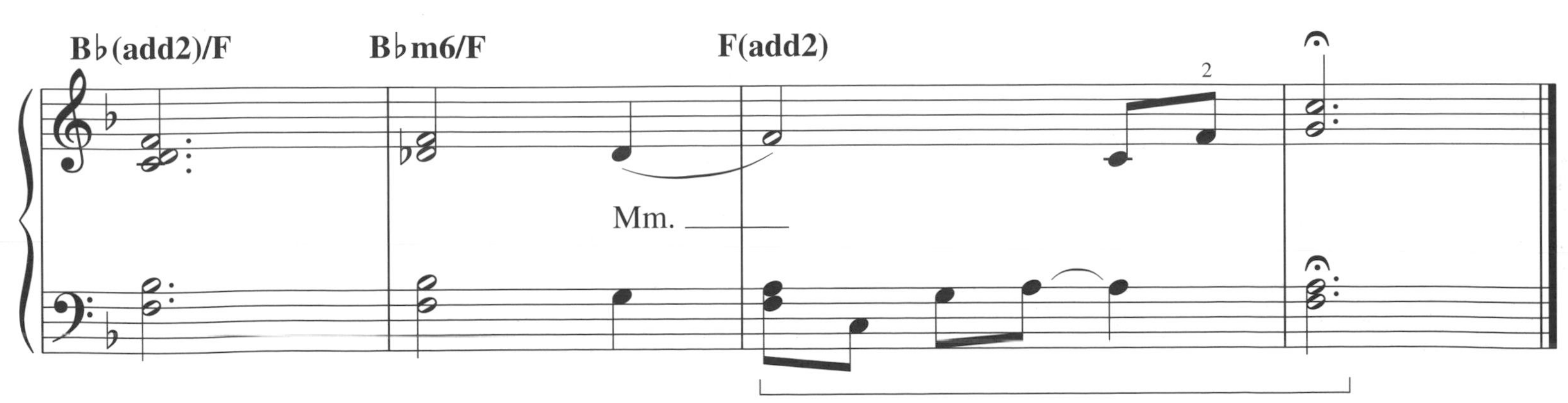
B♭(add2)/F
B♭m6/F
F(add2)
Mm.

WONDERFUL CHRISTMASTIME

Words and Music by
McCARTNEY

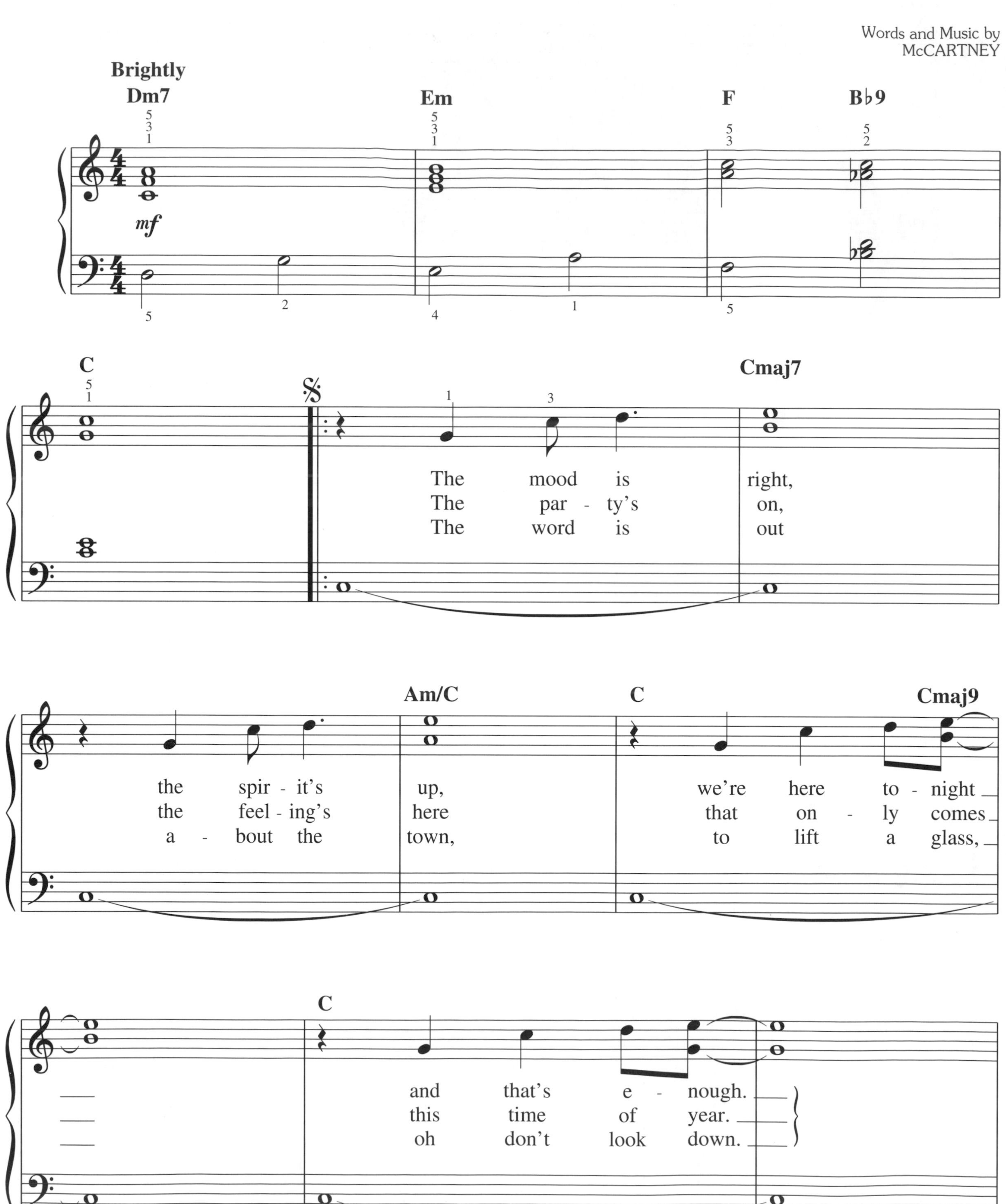

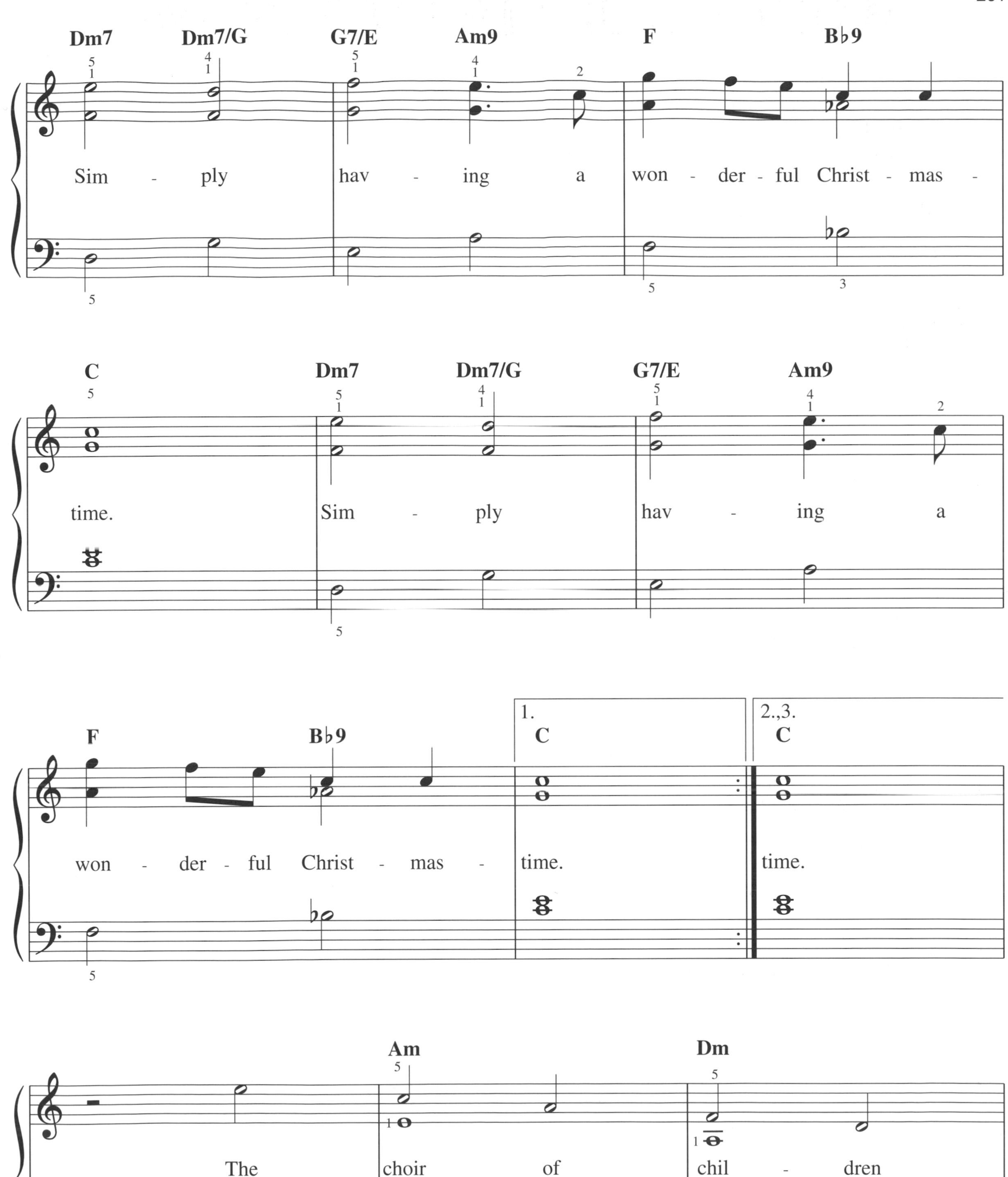
Dm7
Dm7/G
G7/E
Am9
F
B♭9
Sim - ply hav - ing a won - der - ful Christ - mas -
C
Dm7
Dm7/G
G7/E
Am9
time. Sim - ply hav - ing a
F
B♭9
1.
C
2.,3.
C
won - der - ful Christ - mas - time. time.
Am
Dm
The choir of chil - dren
The choir of chil - dren

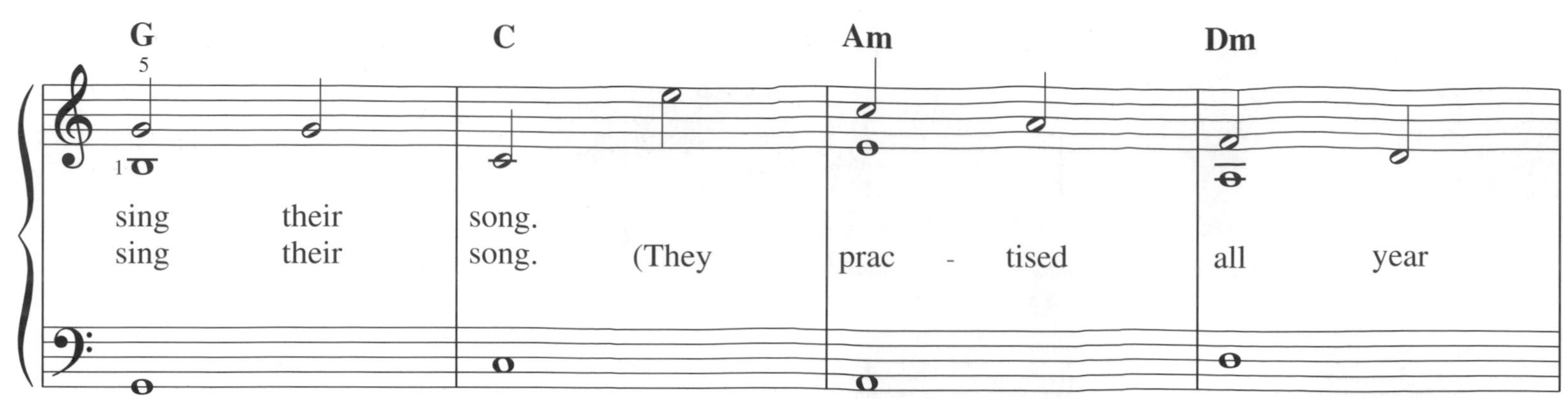
G
C
Am
Dm
5
1
sing their song.
sing their song. (They prac - tised all year

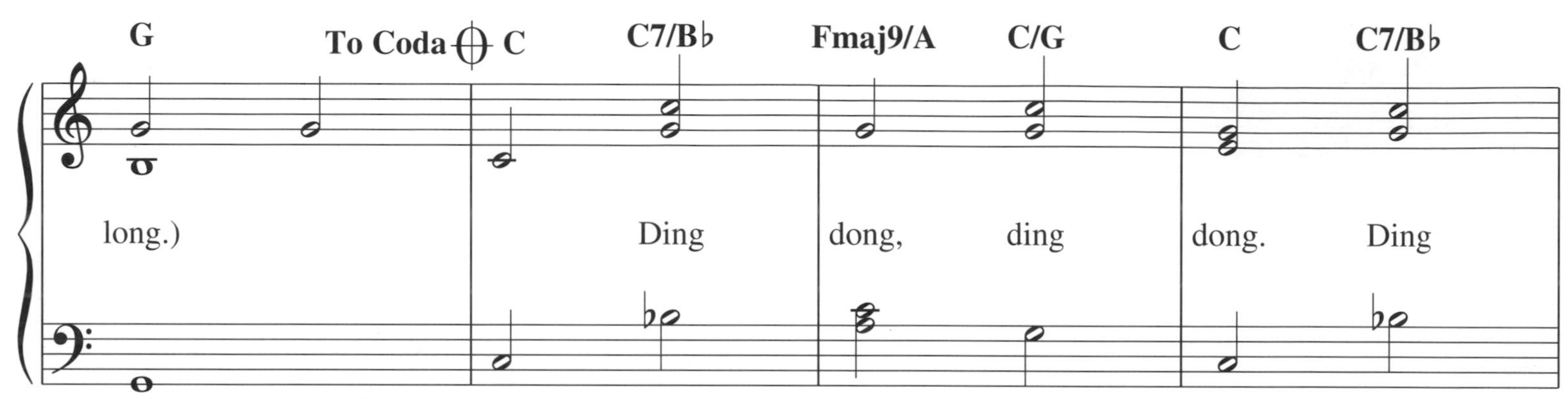
G
To Coda
C
C7/B♭
Fmaj9/A
C/G
C
C7/B♭
long.) Ding dong, ding dong. Ding

Fmaj9/A
C/G
F
Dm7
1
dong, ding. Ooh Ooh.

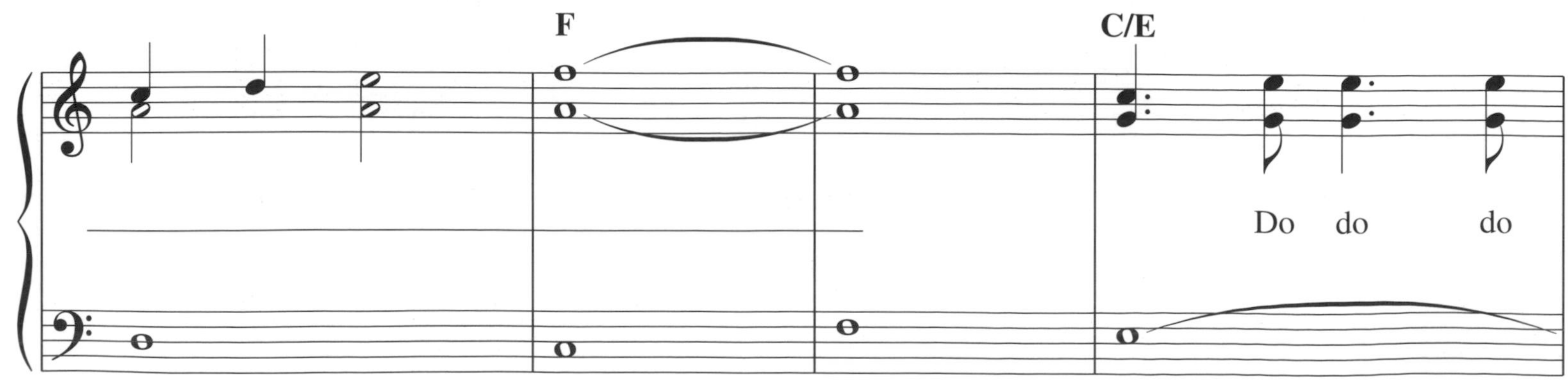
F
C/E
Do do do

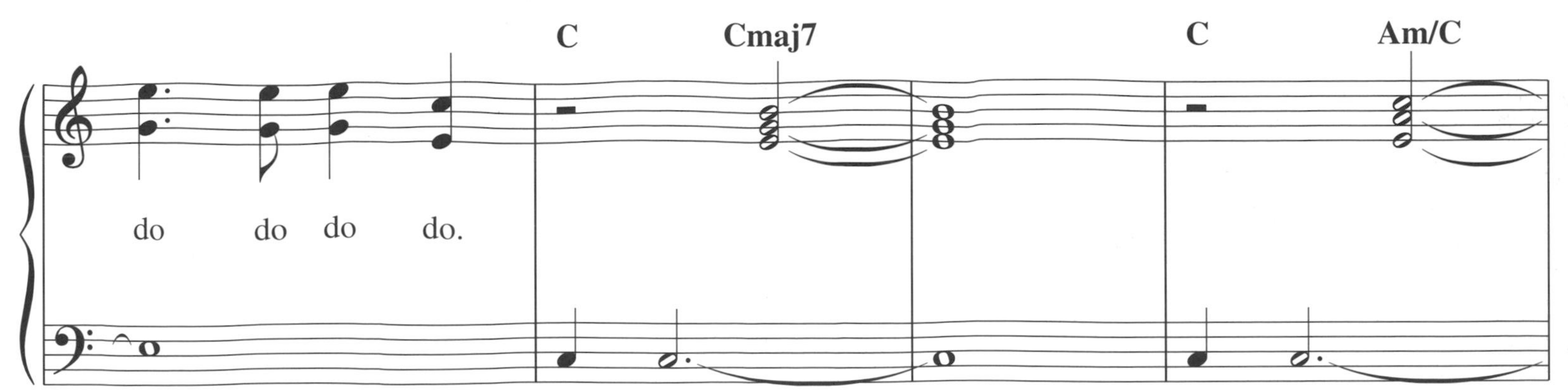
C
Cmaj7
C
Am/C
do do do do.

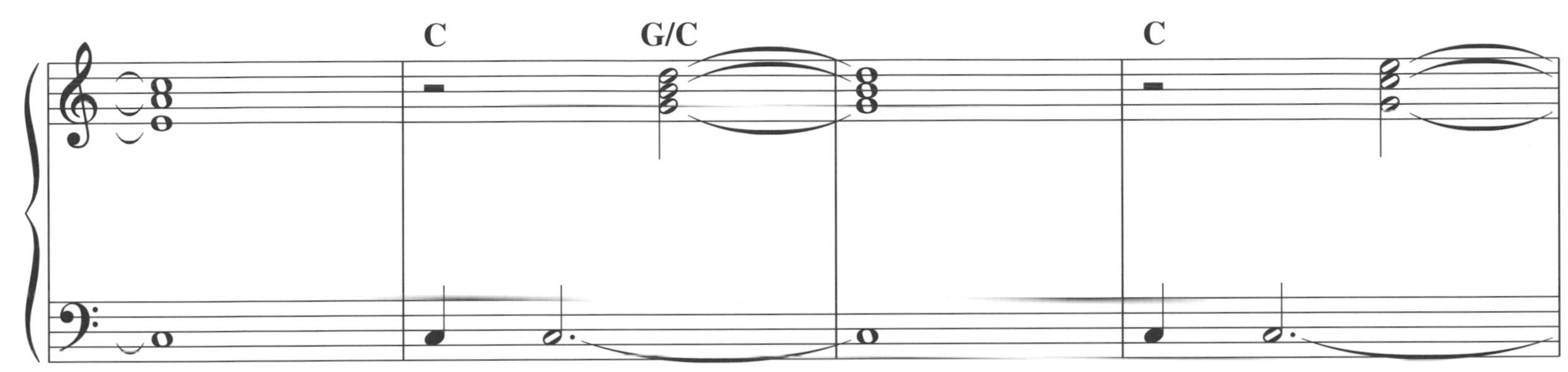
C
G/C
C

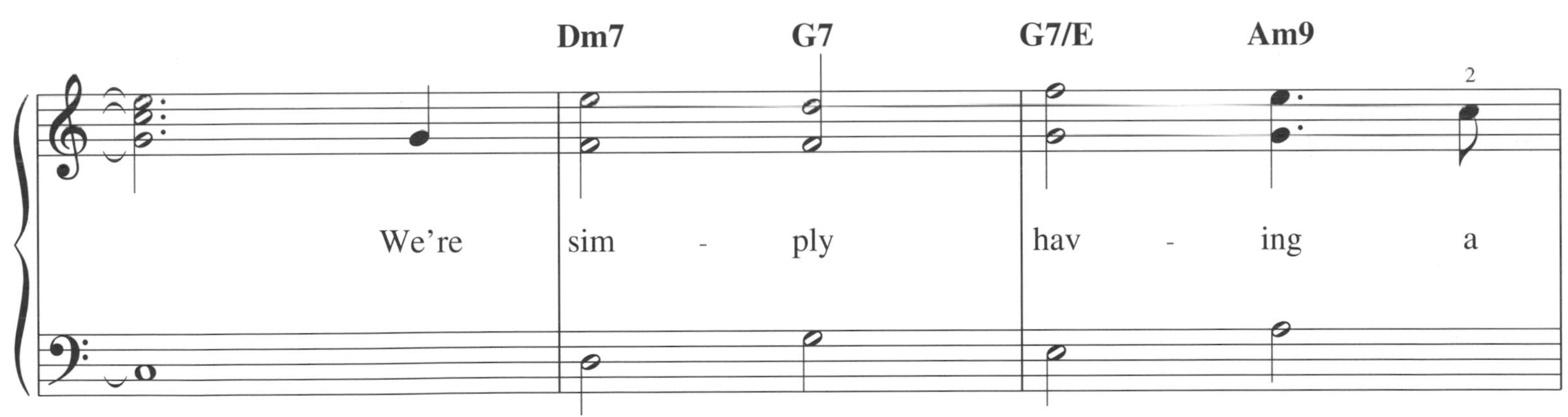
Dm7
G7
G7/E
Am9
2
We're sim - ply hav - ing a

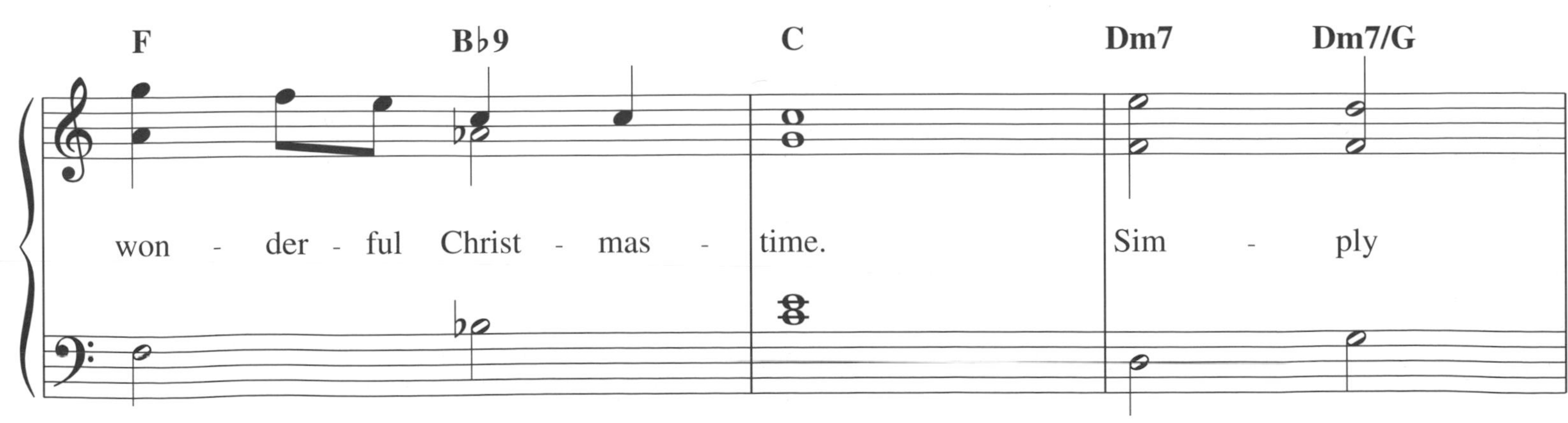
F
B♭9
C
Dm7
Dm7/G
won - der - ful Christ - mas - time. Sim - ply

G7/E
Am9
F
B♭9
C
D.S. al Coda
hav - ing a won - der - ful Christ - mas - time.

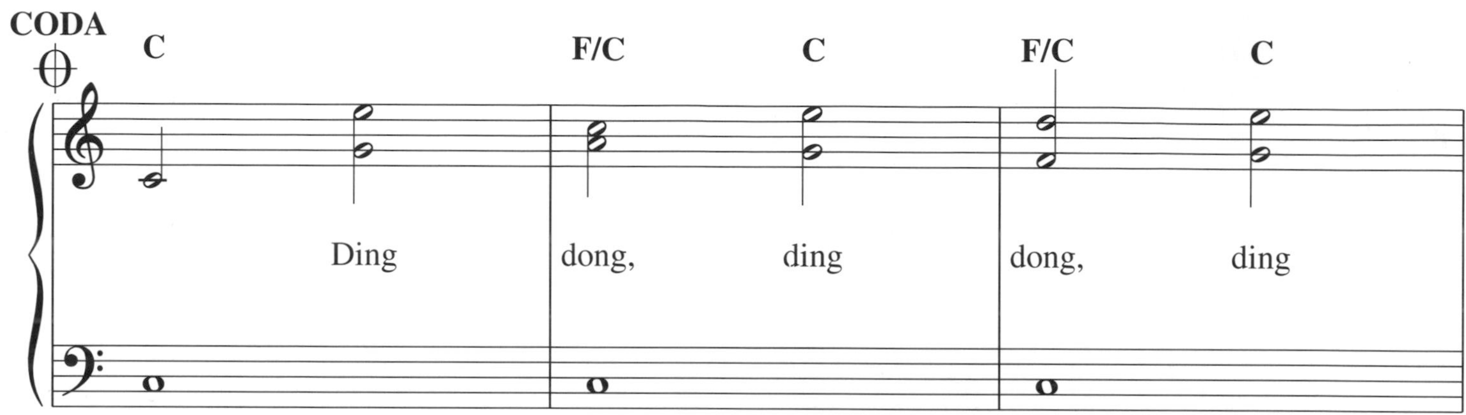
CODA
C
F/C
C
F/C
C
Ding dong, ding dong, ding

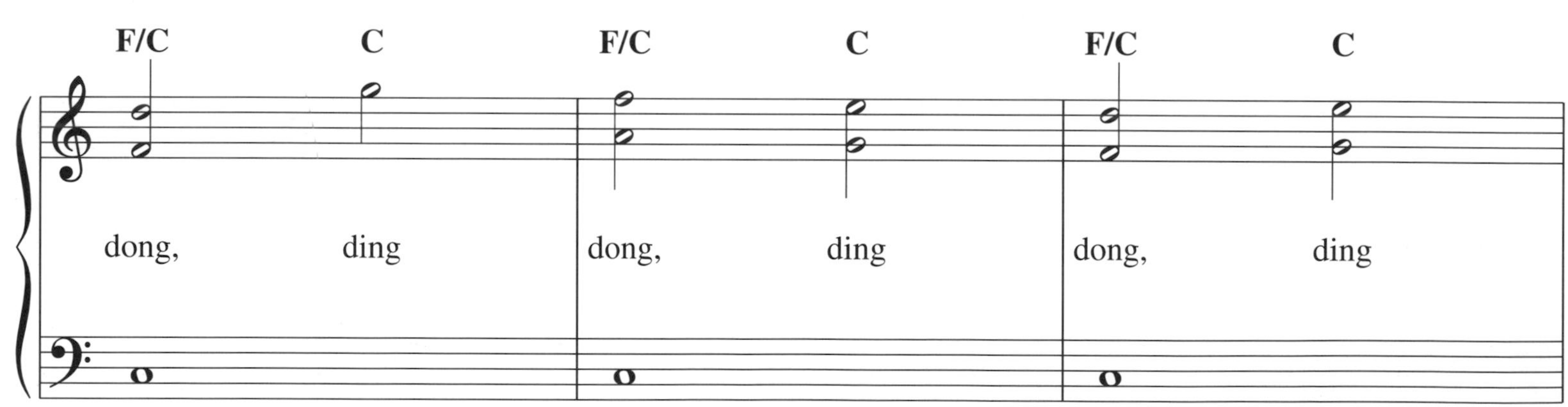
F/C
C
F/C
C
F/C
C
dong, ding dong, ding dong, ding

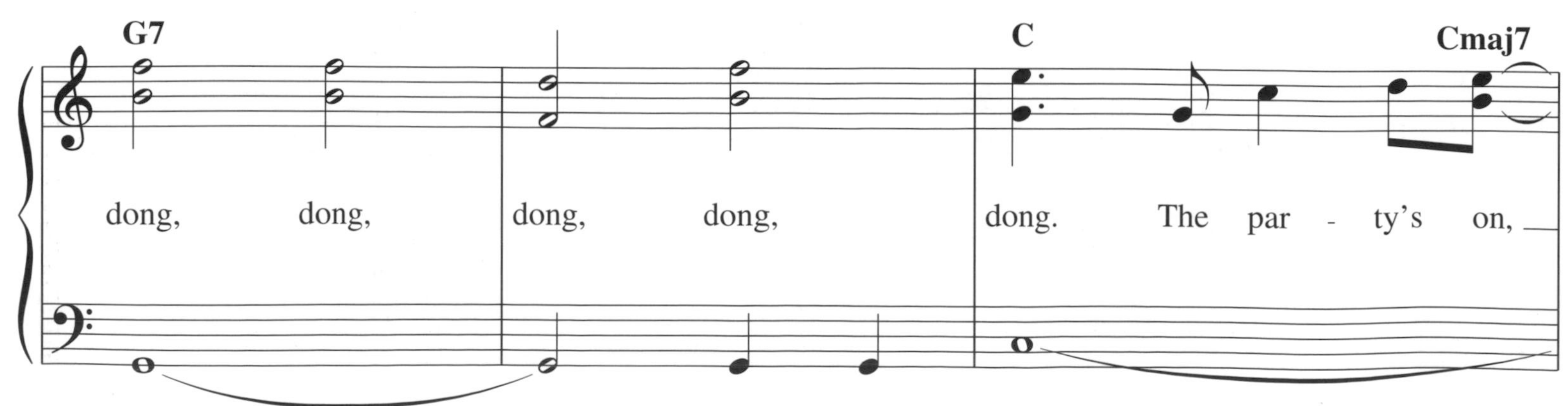
G7
C
Cmaj7
dong, dong, dong, dong, dong. The par - ty's on,

C
Am/C
the spir - it's up,

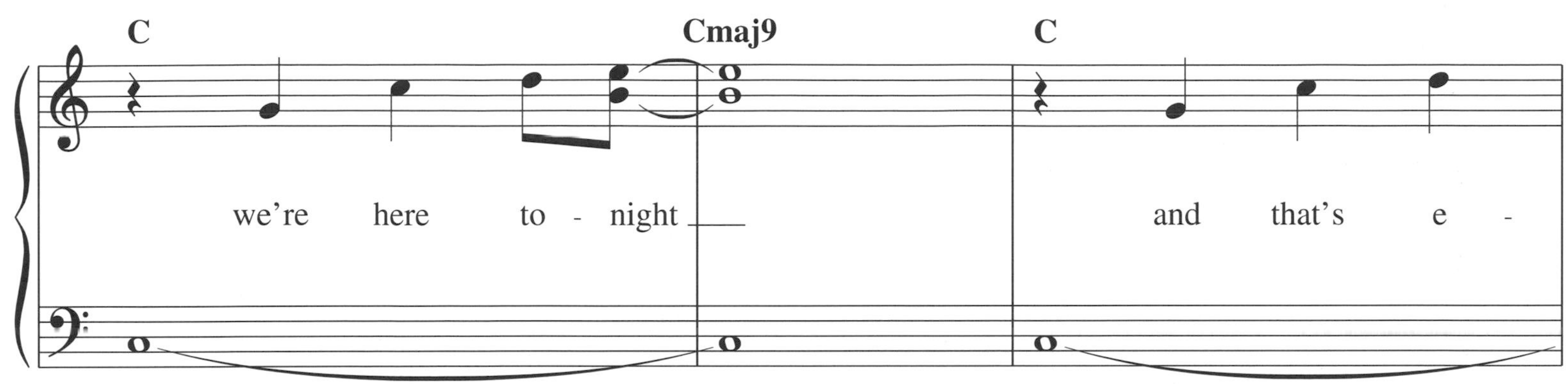
C
Cmaj9
C
we're here to - night
and that's e -

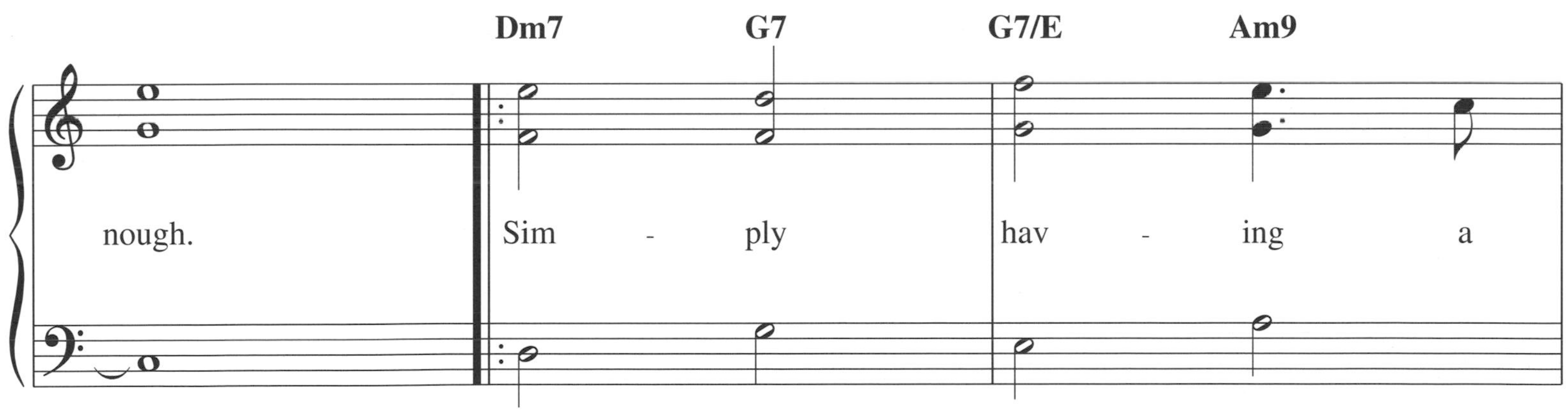
Dm7
G7
G7/E
Am9
nough.
Sim - ply hav - ing a

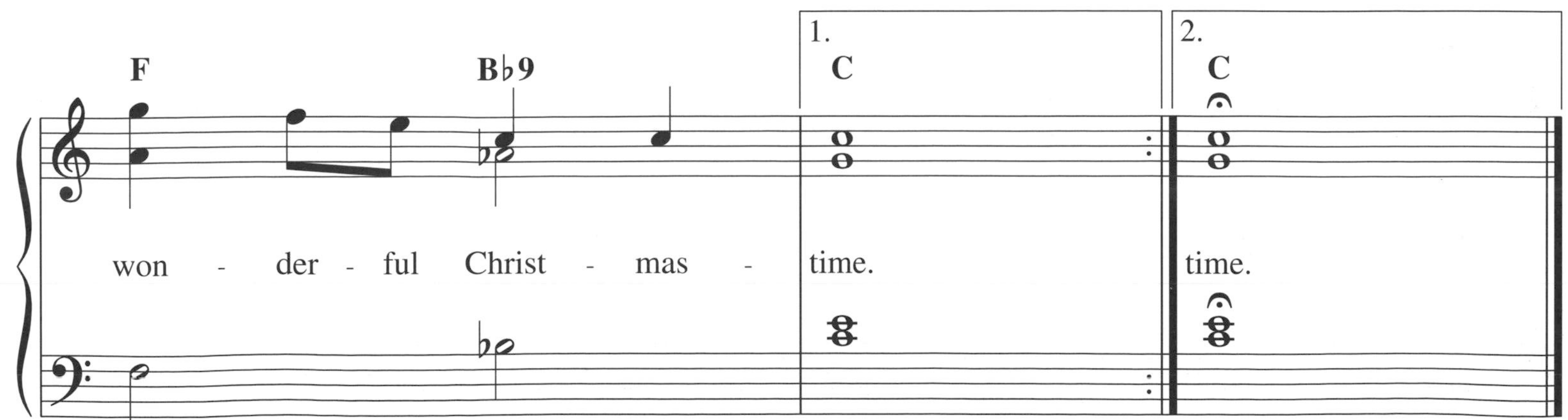
F
B♭9
1.
C
2.
C
won - der - ful Christ - mas - time.
time.

WHEN A CHILD IS BORN

English Lyrics by FRED JAY
Music by ZACAR

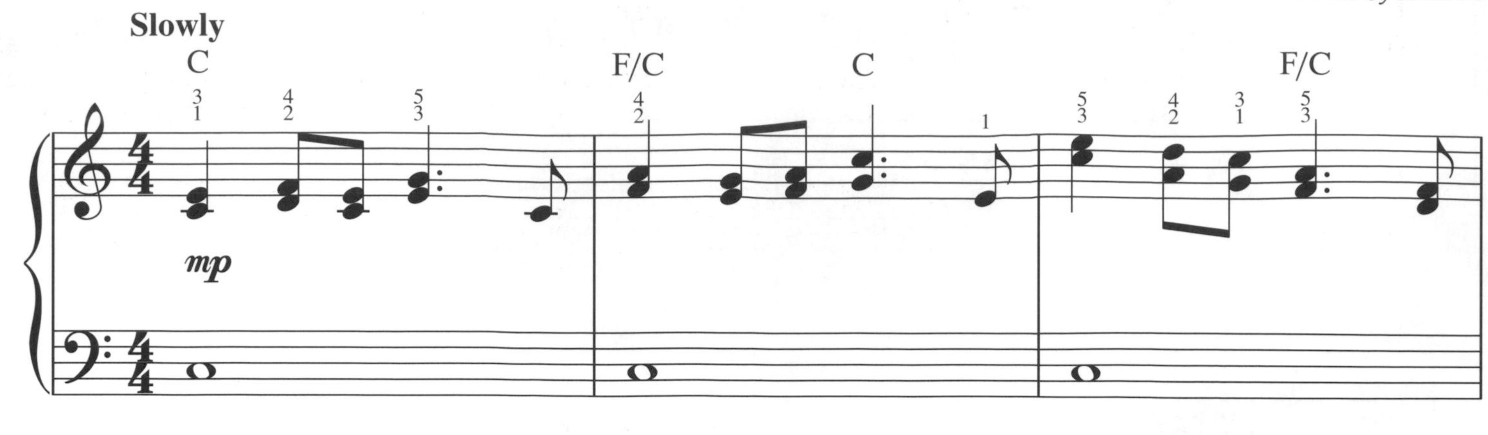

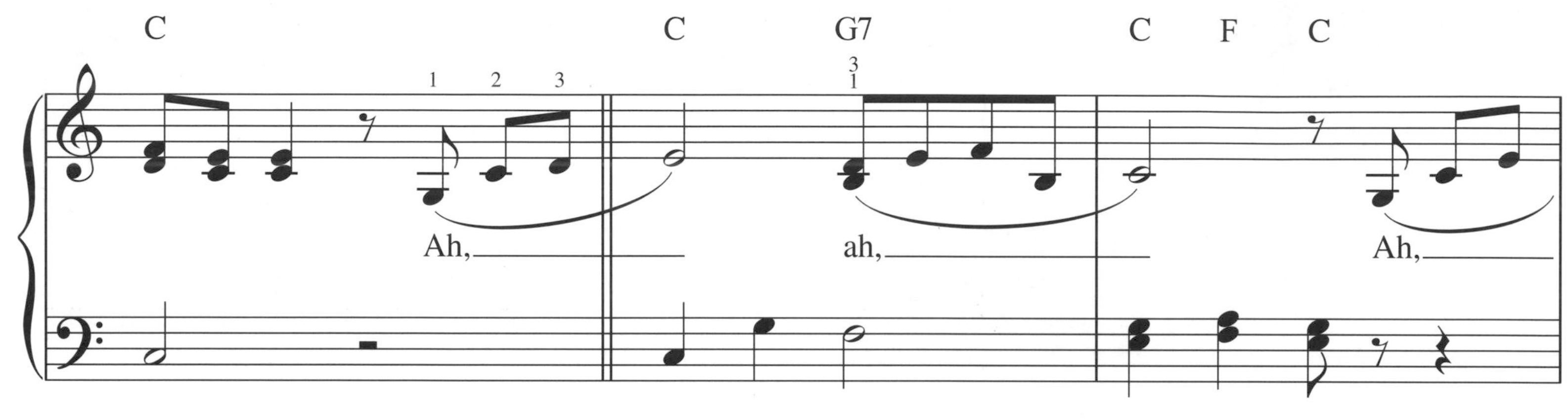

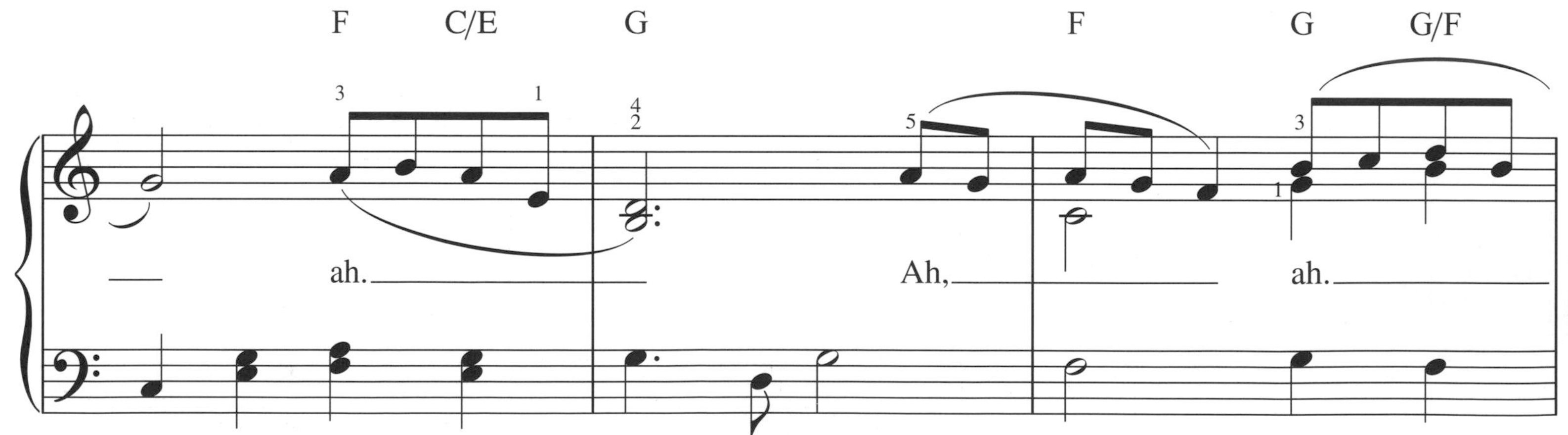

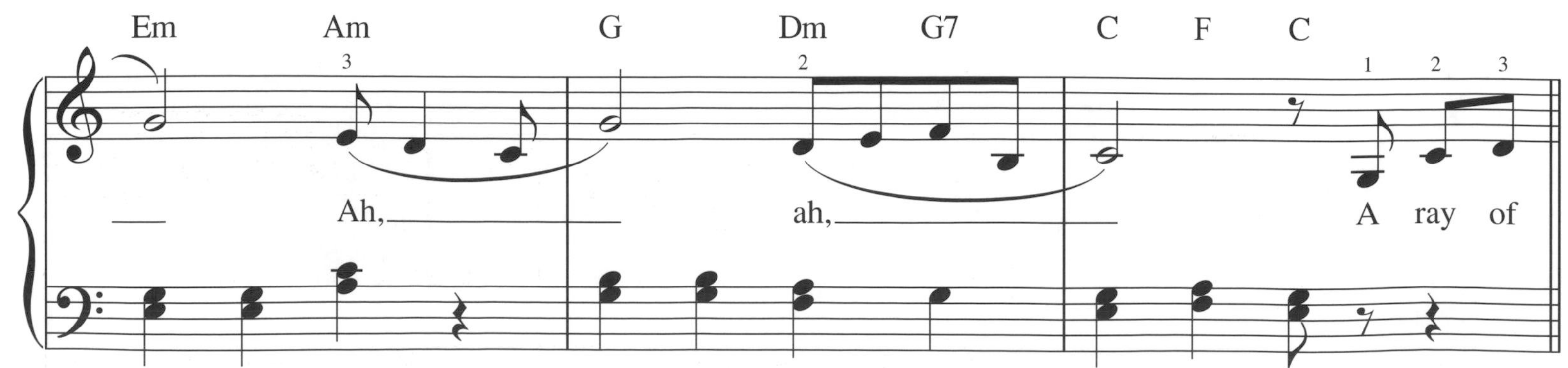

C G7 C F C F C/E
hope flick-ers in the sky. A ti - ny star lights up way up
wish sails the sev - en seas. The winds of change whis-per in the
hue set-tles all a - round. You got the feel you're on sol - id
G F G G/F Em7 Am
high. All a - cross the land dawns a brand-new morn. This comes to pass
trees. And the walls of doubt crum-ble, tossed and torn. This comes to pass
ground. For a spell or two no one seems for - lorn. This comes to pass
G Dm G7 1.,2. C F C 3. C F C
when a Child is born. A si - lent
when a Child is born. A ros - y
when a Child is born.
C G7 C F C F C/E
(Spoken:) And all of this happens because the world is waiting. Waiting for one Child. Black, white, yellow no one knows.

G F G G/F Em Am G Dm G7
But a child that will grow up and turn tears to laughter, hate to love, war to peace, and everyone to everyone's neighbor, and misery and suffering

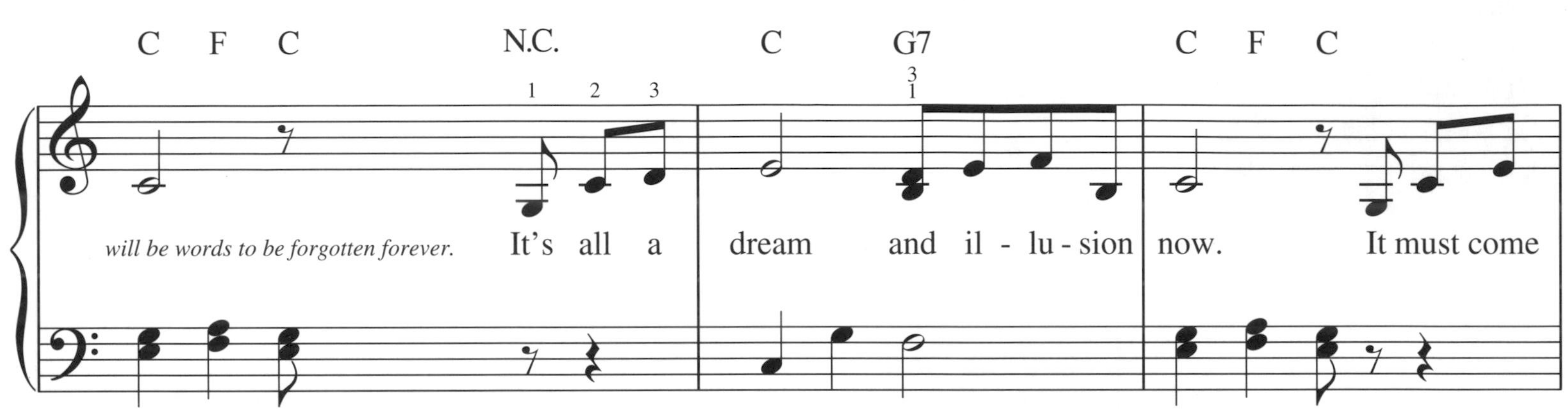
C F C N.C. C G7 C F C
will be words to be forgotten forever. It's all a dream and il - lu - sion now. It must come

F C/E G F G G/F
true some- time soon, some - how. All a - cross the land dawns a brand-new

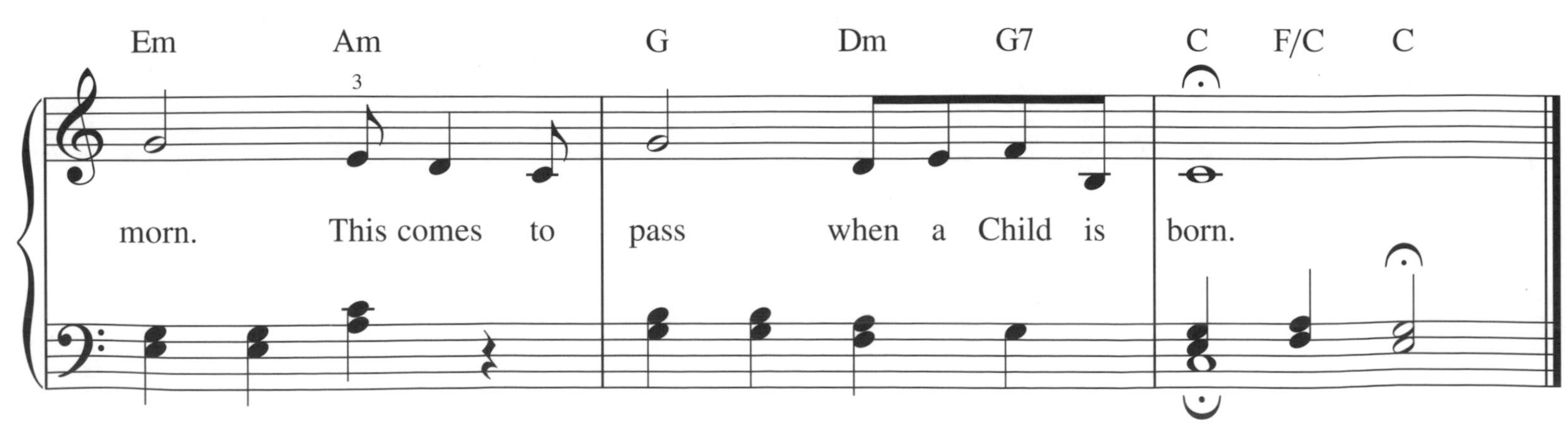
Em Am G Dm G7 C F/C C
morn. This comes to pass when a Child is born.